Generalizing from Laboratory to Field Settings

The Issues in Organization and Management Series

Arthur P. Brief and Benjamin Schneider,
Editors

Generalizing from Laboratory to Field Settings

Research Findings from Industrial-Organizational Psychology, Organizational Behavior, and Human Resource Management

Edited by
Edwin A. Locke
University of Maryland

Lexington Books
D.C. Heath and Company/Lexington, Massachusetts/Toronto

Library of Congress Cataloging in Publication Data
Main entry under title:

Generalizing from laboratory to field settings.

    (Issues in organization and management series)
    Bibliography: p.
    Includes index.
    1. Personnel management—Addresses, essays, lectures. 2. Psychology industrial—Addresses,
essays, lectures. 3. Organizational behavior—Addresses, essays, lectures.
I. Locke, Edwin A. II. Series.
HF5549.G424   1986   658.3   84-48566
ISBN 0-669-09692-X (alk. paper)

Published simultaneously in Canada
Printed in the United States of America
International Standard Book Number: 0-669-09692-X
Library of Congress Catalog Card Number: 84-48566

The paper used in this publication meets the minimum requirements of American National
Standard for Information Sciences—Permanence of Paper for Printed Library Materials,
ANSI Z39.48-1984.
∞ TM

This book is dedicated to the contributing authors, whose enormous efforts and great patience made its publication possible. The editor would also like to thank Ben Schneider and Art Brief for their helpful editorial comments.

Contents

Foreword

Arthur P. Brief
Benjamin Schneider

The Issues in Organization and Management Series is an umbrella for books on theory, research, and practice. Our rather grandiose aims are to facilitate understanding of humans at work and to influence how organizations are managed. The series attempts to accomplish these goals by making available books that draw attention to significant organizational issues of practical and/or conceptual importance.

Well-articulated issues in organization and management that have seemingly been largely resolved or have received extensive treatment elsewhere are not seen as within the scope of the series. Also beyond the domain of the series are textbooks and books based solely on intuition. Rather, the series is committed to publishing books that focus on formulating alternative solutions to underattended problems in systematic ways. By this we mean that the series is concerned with extending the body of empirical knowledge applicable to the understanding and management of organizations. Edwin A. Locke's book *Generalizing from Laboratory to Field Settings* achieves these ends.

Locke's contribution to the series focuses on the consistency of results produced in alternative research settings, laboratory and field. The book goes beyond asking if consistency of results is observed to addressing when it is observed and why. In this way the book aids the reader in assessing the applicability of findings obtained in the laboratory to resolving problems found in the "real world."

The strategy Locke chose for addressing this research question was to have noteworthy scholars review the literature in their areas of expertise to ascertain what conclusions might be drawn from those literatures and if those conclusions were consistent across research settings. Thus, the book also provides analyses of the state-of-the-art in such areas as the use of financial incentives to promote productivity, the impact of feedback on job performance, and the effects of goal setting on goal accomplishment towards organizational effectiveness.

Locke's book, therefore, should appeal to both the producers and consumers of organization and management theory, research, and practice because of its methodological, substantive, and practical insights. We hope that the book will help move some scholars and practitioners away from universalistic and seemingly blind condemnation of the applicability of laboratory findings to problems of real organizations. In addition, we hope that practitioners will note the kinds of interventions that data from two sources indicate can actually be used to facilitate organizational functioning and effectiveness. Finally, it also is our hope that the reviews of the substantive literature provided will demonstrate where closure is safely in hand and where additional attention is needed.

In sum, we are proud to include this book, with its esteemed editor and contributing authors, in the series. It sets a high standard for future inclusions.

I
Introduction

1

Generalizing from Laboratory to Field: Ecological Validity or Abstraction of Essential Elements?

Edwin A. Locke

T he idea for this book came from arguments and discussions I have had over the years with journal editors in my role as an author and with authors in my role as a reviewer. In these discussions one issue came up repeatedly when laboratory experiments were being reviewed. It was expressed typically as follows: "You can't generalize from a simple five-minute task performed by college sophomores in a laboratory to the real world." Initially this position seemed plausible. I had had it used on me and I in turn had used it occasionally on others. It was consistent with the views expressed in leading texts. For example, Runkel and McGrath (1972) state, "The laboratory experiment maximizes rigor of control and precision of measurement at a cost in system realism and in generalizability to behavior in other settings" (p. 108). More recently, however, it occurred to me that the validity of this argument was not as obvious as I (and others) had assumed. I began to wonder: How do we *know* that we can't make such generalizations?

This question pertains to the issue of external validity: generalizability from one experiment or study to other situations. In the behavioral sciences, this issue most frequently arises with respect to the generalizability of laboratory studies to the "real world." Typically the problem has been approached deductively: to generalize you need similarity between laboratory and real life—that is, field settings; laboratory and field settings are very dissimilar; therefore generalization is not justified (or highly dubious).

"Evidence" for the second term of the syllogism is easily provided. Using Runkel and McGrath's (1972) trichotomy of actors, behaviors, and contexts, the subjects in laboratory experiments are college students whereas those in field settings are "real" people. Further, laboratory subjects are typically strangers whereas subjects in field settings are typically coworkers or acquaintances. The tasks in laboratory settings, such as tinker toys and simple addition, are simpler and less

The author is indebted to Dan Ilgen, Rich Kopelman, and Gary Latham for their helpful comments on an earlier draft of this chapter.

meaningful than real life tasks such as repairing a machine, assembling a product, or solving a staffing problem. Laboratory settings are "artificial" rather than "natural" and are plagued by "demand characteristics" which induce ready cooperation and conformity to the expectations of the experimenter whereas in "real life" getting cooperation may be the main problem. Laboratory studies typically last only a few minutes, rarely more than an hour or two, whereas real-life tasks continue for weeks, months, or years.

Other typical differences have been mentioned as well, for example, group size, ambiguity of feedback, the personal significance of performance, and task interdependence, all of which distinguish the typical laboratory experiment from the typical real-life setting (Weick, 1965). In view of these differences, generalizing from laboratory to field settings would seem hopelessly naive.

However, the criticisms of laboratory studies have not gone unanswered. Dipboye and Flanagan (1979) "defend" laboratory studies by damning field studies equally. They show that field studies of the kind typically done by industrial-organizational psychologists are no more representative of the real world than are laboratory studies. While laboratory studies use college students as subjects, field studies use managerial/professional employees to the neglect of other occupational groups. Furthermore, field studies often use "soft" criteria such as self-reports of attitudes or motivation rather than the "hard" measures such as sales or productivity which are of major interest in the real world. In this respect laboratory studies are actually superior to most field studies because they typically use hard performance measures. Both laboratory and field studies are guilty of inadequate sampling in that both more often study males than females. Thus Dipboye and Flanagan conclude that neither labor nor field results can be generalized.

Mook (1983) takes a different tack in answering the criticisms of laboratory studies. He argues that while lab experiments may not be generalizable, such generalizability is not and should not be the purpose or justification of all lab experiments. He argues that lab experiments may be undertaken simply to see if something *can* happen, or to see if a theoretical prediction made about the lab setting is supported, or to test the potency of a manipulated phenomenon under unfavorable or unnatural conditions.

Both of these replies to critics of laboratory studies have plausibility. However, it is important to note that neither defense challenges the basic premise of the critics of laboratory studies: namely, that these studies typically cannot be generalized because they are different in too many respects from real life settings. Dipboye and Flanagan grant the point but reply that field studies cannot be generalized either. Mook agrees but claims that external validity is often irrelevant. Neither challenges the premise that generalization depends on detailed similarity across settings.

It is precisely this major premise of proponents of external validity that I wish to challenge. If one looks at the deductive argument closely, one finds that it is quite equivocal. The argument does not specify *how* similar the two situations have to be to allow generalization nor does it specify *in what respects* there must be similarity, although the implication is that, ideally, you should have total similarity in all respects. For example, since students are different from real employees, the deductive argument would claim or at least imply that to permit generalization you should use real employees in laboratory studies. This argument ignores the possibility that there might be sufficient similarities between the two groups to allow generalization. After all, both students and employees are human beings. Further, many students have worked or are working while in college. And the great majority will become full-time employees after graduation. On the other side of the coin, many employees once were college students. There is no way to determine deductively, from present knowledge, whether there are critical differences between students and employees or, more precisely, what types of differences would affect the generalizability of what types of findings.

Similarly, while laboratory and field tasks may often be different, they may also have characteristics in common, such as skill requirements, repetition, outcomes (success, failure), feedback, and consequences (rewards, punishments). In the same way laboratory and field settings have similarities. For example, both may entail authority relationships and limited time for task completion. Again the significance of the differences versus the similarities cannot be established by deduction.

In sum, the deductive approach attempts to establish standards for generalization from what is already known or at least is thought to be known. But the fact is that almost nothing is known about the actual basis for generalizability of laboratory studies. Our knowledge is not sufficient to make such deductions. Thus the real problem of generalization, at this stage of our knowledge, is more one of induction than of deduction. This is ironic because many of the "authorities" on external validity openly admit as much. Cook and Campbell (1976, p. 236), for example, acknowledge that "assessing external validity is an inductive process." Fromkin and Streufert (1976, p. 457) agree that discussing the issue deductively is "idle speculation." Campbell and Stanley (1963) are less consistent in their discussion. Within the span of a single page (p. 17) they assert that: (1) generalization is never logically justified; (2) it is based on cumulated experience; and (3) determining sources of external validity is guesswork. This is followed by a call for "maximum similarity of experiments to the conditions of application" (p. 18). Thus they seem to advocate both induction (more research) and deduction (based on guesswork).

If we do not know enough to use deduction, then we must use induction. We must look at what has been found in studies thus far. Surprisingly this has never been done in a systematic manner in the behavioral sciences. This book is offered as a first step.

There are several areas of psychology where such an examination of studies might be feasible, for example, social psychology, counseling psychology, clinical psychology, and industrial-organizational (IO) psychology. In business schools the latter field is divided into two subareas: organizational behavior (OB) and human resource management (HRM). I chose to examine the IO psychology/OB/HRM field because it is my own. I selected subareas of IO psychology, OB, and HRM where I thought there might be a substantial number of both laboratory and field studies on the same topic and asked experts in those areas to cumulate the studies and examine the degree to which laboratory findings were replicated in field settings. The areas chosen were: attribution theory, financial incentives, goal setting, job design, objective feedback, participation, performance appraisal, reinforcement schedules, satisfaction-performance relationships, staffing, and training.

I asked the authors to focus primarily on similarity in the *direction* of effects obtained and only secondarily on effect size, which is very variable even within lab and field situations. (Some went along with this request, while others did not!) So long as they included this common core, authors had the option of doing anything they wished, including meta-analysis.

Papers on the above topics, plus John Campbell's commentary, were originally presented as a symposium at the Academy of Management meeting in Boston, in August 1984. (Dan Ilgen's commentary was added later.) All of the papers have undergone at least one, and as many as four, major revisions since then. In some topic areas there were not enough studies to draw any conclusions at all. In other areas a substantial number of studies existed and the findings turned out to be remarkably consistent. In case after case and topic after topic, basically the same results were obtained in the field as in the laboratory. Variation within laboratory and field settings was, where assessed, typically as great as that across the two settings.

The results reported in this book indicate that we must begin to rethink the whole issue of external validity. The evidence indicates that a detailed, point-by-point similarity with respect to subjects, tasks, settings, and so forth is not necessarily required in order to achieve generalizability. Both college students and employees appear to respond similarly to goals, feedback, incentives, participation, and so forth, perhaps because the similarities among these subjects (such as in values) are more crucial than their differences. Task differences do not seem overwhelmingly important. Perhaps all that is needed is that the participants in either setting become involved in what they are doing. The demand characteristics of laboratory settings may not bias the results because equivalent demand characteristics may be present on the job. Employees often try to do what the boss asks because he is the boss. Time span may only be crucial if the phenomenon in question is time dependent (for example, long term learning effects).

Berkowitz and Donnerstein (1982, p. 249) have argued that "the meaning the subjects assign to the situation they are in . . . plays a greater role in determining the generalizability of an experiment's outcome than does the sample's demographic representativeness or the setting's surface realism." Although the studies reviewed in this book did not explicitly measure the meaning subjects assigned to the experiments they were in, the results suggest that generalizability is determined by something other than literal similarity. Thus, although we cannot prove the validity of Berkowitz and Donnerstein's thesis, it would seem to have far more plausibility than the "ecological validity" (that is, representativeness) thesis.

I would, however, go even further than Berkowitz and Donnerstein. I believe that ecological representativeness of the type implied in the external validity thesis is an invalid standard. To achieve similarity between laboratory and field settings on all the dimensions alleged to be involved in external validity (subjects, tasks, settings, and so forth) is impossible. The only way to achieve such similarity would be to run a field study in the laboratory. This, of course, would be a contradiction since laboratory and field studies are by definition different at least with respect to setting. Furthermore, even if one could run such a study, the only generalization that could be made would be from one laboratory study to an identical or very similar field setting. No other generalization could legitimately be made. Thus the very act of making a laboratory study representative of a field setting would preclude generalization to other field settings—ones that were not similar to the initial setting. Since field settings differ from each other at least as much and probably more than lab settings do, there would have to be a different lab study for every field setting. Under these terms, it would be pointless to do laboratory studies at all. It would also be pointless to do field studies.

There is, I believe, a major epistemological error in the ecological representativeness view. *It fails to distinguish between incidental or nonessential similarity and similarity in terms of essentials.* For example, there are numerous attributes of subjects which are incidental to the psychological phenomenon being studied. In a study of the effects of setting performance goals on task performance, for example, subjects' age, gender, work experience, height, weight, and intelligence may be totally irrelevant to the results (Locke, Shaw, Saari, & Latham, 1981). If the goals are assigned rather than self-set, even personality may not be relevant. Thus what is essential, as far as the subject is concerned, may only be the subject's willingness to try for the goal when asked. If this is the essential feature, then generalization to field settings may only require that employees be willing to try for goals at the request of their boss. On the other hand, when comparing the effects of assigned goals to participatively set goals, an added element may enter in: the subjects' personal values regarding participation (Erez, 1984). All other personal characteristics may be irrelevant.

Similarly with respect to task characteristics, it only may be important in goal-setting studies that task performance be measurable and that the subjects have the ability to perform the task and be given feedback regarding progress (Locke et al., 1981).

Thus what is needed when trying to determine the legitimacy of generalization is *the identification of the essential features of field settings that need to be replicated in the lab* (that is, essential subject, task, and setting characteristics). Just what is essential cannot necessarily be known in advance; discovering these essentials is an inductive procedure though plausible hypotheses can be used as guidelines.

The concept of looking for essential features implies a very different generalization strategy than trying to achieve ecological representativeness. Finding essential features would involve not trying to reproduce the total field situation but rather *to abstract out of all conceivable situations those elements which are required as a minimum for the phenomenon to occur.* With respect to "robust" psychological phenomena, these essential features may be very small in number. For example, we might hypothesize (see Locke, 1977) that for a "reinforcer" to change behavior, the minimum criteria are that the individual: (1) must value or want the reinforcer (and as a corollary must believe the value of getting the reinforcer exceeds its cost); (2) must expect that a specific action will bring the reinforcer about (that is, he must know how to get it); and (3) must be able to take the required action at the appropriate time. Given the presence of these features, any differences between lab and field settings (for example, subjects, tasks, and demand characteristics) may be irrelevant as far as reinforcement is concerned. If the hypothesis were supported in the lab, we would then hypothesize that the same results would occur in any field situation which possessed these features.

A key function of lab studies then would be to identify and isolate these essential features so that they could be reproduced in field settings. If generalization succeeded, this would support the validity of the features isolated. If generalization failed, it would imply that one or more essential features had been omitted.

In chapter 7 Richard Kopelman presents an excellent example of the potential usefulness of trying to isolate essential elements of a phenomenon in the laboratory. He found that objective feedback, while it is almost equally consistent in leading to performance improvements in lab and field settings, has considerably larger effects in the field than in the laboratory. His analysis suggests that the allegedly extraneous variables which many laboratory studies controlled (such as competition, anticipation of rewards and punishments, and goal setting) were the very ones which were responsible for the large feedback effects in the field. In other words, feedback by itself does not lead to performance improvement; it only helps when combined with other factors. This has important implications for field application.

The present book is a first step in determining the degree to which laboratory research actually generalizes to field settings. The positive results of most of the chapters give high plausibility to the concept of essential features. In addition many of the chapters make suggestions as to what the essential features accounting for the generalization might be.

Another benefit of this book is that it provides useful and comprehensive summaries of research in many areas of IO psychology, OB, and HRM. The fact that many findings replicate across both laboratory and field settings increases our confidence in their validity and provides a firm base for the building of a meaningful body of scientific knowledge.

References

Berkowitz, L., & Donnerstein, E. (1982) External validity is more than skin deep. *American Psychologist, 37,* 245–257.

Campbell, D.T., & Stanley, J.C. (1963) *Experimental and quasi-experimental designs for research.* Chicago: Rand McNally.

Cook, T.D., & Campbell, D.T. (1976) The design and conduct of quasi-experiments and true experiments in field settings. In M. Dunnette (Ed.) *Handbook of industrial and organizational psychology*. Chicago: Rand McNally.

Dipboye, R.L., & Flanagan, M.F. (1979) Research settings in industrial and organizational psychology: Are findings in the field more generalizable than in the laboratory? *American Psychologist, 34,* 141–150.

Erez, M. (1984) The congruence of goal-setting strategies with sociocultural values and its effect on performance. Unpublished manuscript. Israel Institute of Technology.

Fromkin, H.L., & Streufert, S. (1976) Laboratory experimentation. In M. Dunnette (Ed.), *Handbook of industrial and organizational psychology*. Chicago: Rand McNally, 415–466.

Locke, E.A. (1977) The myths of behavior mod in organizations. *Academy of Management Review, 2*(4), 543–553.

Locke, E.A., Shaw, K.N., Saari, L.M., & Latham, G.P. (1981) Goal setting and task performance: 1969–1980. *Psychological Bulletin, 90,* 125–152.

Mook, D.G. (1983) In defense of external invalidity. *American Psychologist, 38,* 379–387.

Runkel, P.J., & McGrath, J.E. (1972) *Research on human behavior*. New York: Holt, Rinehart and Winston.

Weick, K. (1965) Laboratory experiments with organizations. In J. March (Ed.), *Handbook of organizations*. Chicago: Rand McNally, 194–260.

II
Personnel

I have divided the remaining chapters into four groups: personnel, motivation, attitudes, and overview. The first chapter on personnel is Judy Olian's analysis of staffing research. The topic of staffing includes numerous subtopics. Unfortunately, there were not sufficient numbers of laboratory and field studies on each subtopic to make any firm conclusions possible. However, in areas where there were a reasonable, if small, number of studies, the results do not appear to be very different in lab and field settings. For example, eight out of eight lab studies found that expectancy theory successfully predicted job choice, while nine out of ten field studies did the same. Similarly, the findings for the effects of sex and race on hiring decisions were comparable. Olian suggests that the effect size for expectancy theory predictions of job choice may be overestimated in the lab studies because of certain differences in design. For example, she notes that in lab studies the probability of getting a job offer is typically 1.0, which is not the case in field settings. Further, in field studies there is more time delay between measurement and choice plus more restriction of range in job alternatives than is the case in lab studies. However, it should be noted that all of these features of field studies could easily be built into the lab studies. It remains to be seen how essential these differences are with respect to influencing the results. Again, these are inductive questions.

John Bernardin and Peter Villanova carefully examine the research on performance appraisal and conclude, in line with Dipboye and Flanagan, that both lab and field studies are unrepresentative of real-life appraisal settings. Especially lacking is representativeness with respect to the purpose of the appraisal and the motivation to rate accurately. Nevertheless, the lab and field studies do agree with each other. Fourteen out of nineteen laboratory studies found a significant effect of rater training on accuracy while twelve of fifteen field studies found the same thing. The studies of the effects of the purpose of the ratings on accuracy, though fewer in number, also found the majority of both observing a significant effect for purpose.

An interesting feature of Bernardin and Villanova's study is the attempt to determine what the characteristics of the modal criterion setting (the typical real-life rating situation) are and then to determine what factors would lead to biased ratings in such a setting. Perhaps not surprisingly, supervisors and subordinates do not agree on the answers. Supervisors and administrators believe the major causes of bias are factors which affect one's motivation to rate accurately (thus supporting the authors' contention that the purpose of the ratings may be an important variable). In contrast, subordinates, while recognizing motivational factors, are more likely than supervisors and administrators to believe that inaccurate ratings are caused by lack of job knowledge on the part of the supervisor, including a lack of knowledge about what actions and outcomes are and are not in the employees' control. Bernardin and Villanova nicely tie this issue into attribution theory and support the notion that certain features of the rating situation are more essential than others for attaining accuracy, although which ones can only be determined inductively. Their chapter provides a wealth of ideas and suggestions for future research along these lines.

Christy De Vader, Allan Bateson, and Robert Lord's chapter on attribution theory is one of the more difficult chapters simply because it deals with several different attribution theories and multiple predictions within each. Due to space limitations, all the hypotheses could not be listed. Thus the reader is warned that the chapter will be hard to follow without prior knowledge of the topic. In a very thorough analysis of the attribution literature the authors find either that the results generalize across lab and field settings or, if they do not, the crucial difference was not between lab and field settings but rather within the field settings. Subsequent analyses suggest that the differences within the field settings are caused by differences in the time lag between seeing the stimulus information and making the attribution ratings. Recall that Olian also suggests that time lag could affect the correlations between expectancy theory ratings and subsequent job choice. Thus the time lag dimension seems well worth pursuing in both lab and field settings. This may be an essential characteristic affecting the results of many types of studies.

Irwin Goldstein and Gary Musicante's chapter discusses training. In the absence of a sufficient number of studies on any one training topic, these authors take a more theoretical approach than the others. They treat the lab-field issue as one of transfer of training and try to assess what factors might affect generalization or transfer of training from one setting to another. They immediately attack the notion that physical similarity alone is the key to transfer. They add the notions of psychological similarity including knowledge of principles, learning deficit analysis, training techniques, and the organizational context. To illustrate these points they turn to rater training which, in agreement with Bernardin and Villanova, they conclude has been equally successful in lab and field settings. They identify a number of factors that may affect the success and transfer of rater training in both settings, including the purpose of the appraisal, feedback, length and type of training, and ratee characteristics. This chapter too suggests a wealth of research ideas.

2
Staffing

Judy D. Olian

T he purpose of this chapter is to examine whether the findings from staffing research conducted in lab settings are applicable to real world organizational processes, that is, whether lab results are externally valid. Staffing, as defined here, refers to organizational practices to locate potential applicants from sources external to the firm, to attract them into the firm, and to make choices among the candidates generated.

Contrary to other research streams in industrial–organizational psychology (such as studies of motivation or judgment processes in organizations) which combine both theoretical and applied orientations, the area of staffing has an applied focus. With few theoretical exceptions (for example, Schneider, 1983; Schwab, 1982), most staffing research is motivated by a desire to gain greater insights into how organizations actually recruit and screen applicants in order to improve the efficacy of these activities. Accordingly, a fair yardstick for evaluation of this research is its external validity.

The present review uses both inductive and deductive approaches to evaluate the external validity of staffing research conducted in lab settings. The former strategy is used to compare results of parallel themes of empirical research across lab and field settings. The latter strategy is applied at the conceptual level in asking whether common characteristics of field studies limit the generalizability of results generated in the lab.

Research covered in the review is drawn from materials published between 1970 and 1985 in the following primary sources: *Journal of Applied Psychology, Organizational Behavior and Human Performance, Academy of Management Journal, Personnel Psychology, Journal of Vocational Behavior, Decision Sciences, Industrial and Labor Relations Review, Industrial Relations, Journal of Consulting and Clinical Psychology,* and *American Journal of Sociology.* Studies from other sources are included if they directly pertain to the subject matter.

The author benefited greatly from discussions and written comments from Edwin Locke, Sara Rynes, Donald Schwab, and Susan Taylor.

After differentiating between lab and field investigations, two major categories of staffing research are discussed: (1) the *recruitment process* covering such issues as recruitment sources used by organizations, recruitment activities engaged in by organizational gatekeepers, and applicant reactions to these approaches; and (2) *hiring research* addressing the content of hiring decisions (such as applicant attributes influencing employability) and the decision processes used by organizational representatives.

Lab versus Field Research

An evaluation of the external validity of lab studies presumes an ability to clearly differentiate studies conducted in the lab from those in field settings. For purposes of this review, the crucial discriminator between the two settings is whether decisions were implemented in the actual criterion context. Other features common to lab studies that might introduce demand characteristics are that: (1) the study was conducted in an environment contrived for study purposes, (2) participants were aware that they were part of a research project, and (3) the investigation included experimentally created manipulations.

Thus, studies conducted in classroom settings asking students to make fictitious hiring decisions on the basis of experimentally controlled applicant information (for example, Hakel, Dobmeyer, & Dunnette, 1970; Heneman, 1977) serve as clear examples of lab investigations. Conversely, research into the effects of recruitment procedures on the job search decisions of graduating seniors (for example, Taylor & Bergmann, 1984) are considered field studies because they captured actual job search processes and decisions in a realistic setting for the type of sample studied.

Sometimes, however, when only one or two of these features are present in a study, classification decisions might appear less clear. For example, McIntyre, Moberg, and Posner (1980), McIntyre and Posner (1982), and Newman (1978) sent bogus resumes representing experimentally controlled manipulations to unsuspecting employers. The dependent variable was company responses upon receipt of the resumes. Hence, actual screening decisions were made by company representatives in the criterion environment. Accordingly, such studies are classified as field despite the presence of an experimental manipulation because demand characteristics appeared to have no impact on the results.

Recruitment Research

Research in the area of recruitment is separable into three global themes: (1) sources of recruitment for generating applicants, (2) job seeker reactions to recruitment practices, and (3) candidate evaluations of organization and job features.

Sources of Recruitment

Research covered within this general area concerns the approaches used by organizations to generate recruits (for example, informal referrals, direct applications, and agencies), and their perceived and actual effectiveness (see as examples Miner, 1979; Decker & Cornelius, 1979; Gannon, 1971). Only recently have there been direct attempts to examine the reasons for these apparent differences in source effectiveness (for example, Breaugh, 1981; Ellis & Taylor, 1983; Taylor & Schmidt, 1983). To date, research in this area has been conducted in the field because of difficulties in operationalizing hypotheses of interest in lab settings.

The field research is fairly voluminous, yet there are inconsistencies in the observed effectiveness of alternative recruitment sources. These inconsistencies are possibly a function of differences in the occupational background of desired recruits (see Rosenfeld, 1975) and in the type of criterion (perceptual or objective) used to evaluate source effectiveness. Lab research which controls for confounds such as these would potentially help reduce observed inconsistencies. It is also possible to conduct research in lab settings which builds on findings from the field, in order to clarify some process issues surrounding differential recruitment source.

Reactions to Recruitment Procedures

Applicant responses to alternative aspects of recruitment procedures have been investigated, including studies of the effects of the recruitment message (such as Belt & Paolillo, 1982; Dean & Wanous, 1984; Herriot, Ecob, & Hutchison, 1980; Wanous, 1977), postinterview follow-up procedures (such as Arvey, Gordon, Massengill, & Mussio, 1975; Ivancevich & Donnelly, 1971), and recruiter behaviors and mannerisms (such as Alderfer & McCord, 1970; Rogers & Sincoff, 1978; Rynes & Miller, 1983; Taylor & Bergmann, 1984).

The single largest body of research in this area is on the realistic job preview (RJP) (see Reilly, Brown, Blood, & Malatesta, 1981; Wanous, 1980; Premack & Wanous, 1985, for a meta-analysis). However, there is a predominant methodological setting for the studies. This research, now amounting to over twenty studies, has been conducted in the field with only two exceptions (Parkington & Schneider, 1978; Parmerlee, 1982). The two RJP experiments do not appear to yield results systematically different from those generated in the field along a variety of measured outcomes. This conclusion is probably a reflection of the extreme variability in RJP results across studies rather than testimony to the external validity of lab studies in this area.

In particular, Parmerlee's (1982) lab study found no preview effects on job acceptance rates, which is consistent with Reilly et al.'s (1981) field study. However, two field studies (Macedonia, 1969; Reilly, Tenopyr, & Sperling, 1979) did. Both lab studies found no differences in performance between traditional and RJP groups, a finding consistent with several field investigations (Ilgen & Dugoni, 1977; Wanous, 1973; Youngberg, 1963). However, the RJP group's performance in Macedonia performed worse than the no–preview group, while in Horner (1979), they did better. The latter two studies were conducted in the field. While Reilly et al., (1981) found that RJP interventions, on average, reduced turnover from 25.5 percent to 19.8 percent (a reduction of 28.8 percent in the gross turnover rate), both lab studies observed no effect of previews on voluntary departure from the experiment. However, there were a number of separate field studies that also found no turnover effects (Haccoun, 1978; Ilgen & Dugoni; Krausz & Fox, 1979; Reilly et al., 1981; Wanous, 1973).

Hence, lab studies in this area cannot be dismissed on the grounds that they yield results that diverge systematically from those generated in the field. However, are there sufficient reasons to actually encourage more lab studies in the future? Given the kinds of outcomes typically of interest in RJP research (such as adverse job acceptance rates, performance, job satisfaction, and turnover differences between RJP and control groups), it is important to establish the magnitude of an effect attributable to an RJP intervention and not just the existence of an effect. While lab research can establish the latter point (that an effect is likely to occur), it cannot provide information on the absolute magnitude of the expected change in the field because many moderator variables affecting outcomes of interest in realistic settings are held constant in the lab. Thus, for practical purposes, the predominance of field experiments concerning the consequences of RJP interventions is appropriate. However, because of equivocal findings about the effects of RJPs on job acceptance rates and performance, there has been extensive discussion of possible mediating processes (for example self–selection or "vaccination" effects) that might explain observed differences in RJP results (such as Breaugh, 1983; Miceli, 1983; Reilly et al., 1981). Research on such process issues can be conducted more effectively in the lab, at least at preliminary stages of exploration. Parmerlee (1982) provides an example of a process study conducted in a lab environment.

Five studies have examined the effects of recruitment interview procedures and/or job content information on the probability of applicants' intentions to accept a job offer. Three (Herriot & Rothwell, 1981; Powell, 1984; Taylor & Bergmann, 1984) were conducted in the field, while the other two (Rynes & Miller, 1983; Schmitt & Coyle, 1976) were implemented in lab settings. The studies found that information about attributes of the vacancy tended to significantly influence candidate reactions. With the exception of Herriot and Rothwell, who did not explicitly measure recruiter influences, the studies found that recruiter behaviors were secondary to the job content in influencing applicant propensity to accept a job. Similar to the case of RJP studies, it is not possible to compare the magnitude of recruiter versus job attribute effects across lab and field settings because of confounding influences of contextual features across studies.

*Candidate Evaluations of Organization
and Job Features*

Yet a third issue of interest has been the kinds of organizational and job attributes applicants consider and are attracted to in their job search. A set of related studies has explored process models of attraction to organizations, as a part of which applicants evaluate job/organizational attributes.

In studies of the first type, with few exceptions (for example, Huber, Daneshgar, & Ford, 1971; Sheridan, Richards, & Slocum, 1975), respondent preferences are elicited in the abstract, without relating these rankings or ratings to actual job search or choice decisions. Among the lab studies, differences in results exist between those eliciting direct rankings or ratings of the importance of organizational and job attributes (for example, Feldman & Arnold, 1978; Ullman & Gutteridge, 1974) compared to policy-capturing investigations which generate the same type of information indirectly (such as Einhorn, 1971; Zedeck, 1977). Differences in attribute preferences are even evident within the same study (for example, Strand, Levine, & Montgomery, 1981) when alternative methodologies are used to elicit these preferences. As an example, Zedeck (Study II, 1977) had subjects both rank order and distribute one hundred points across six job attributes based on their relative importance in a job choice decision. He also had respondents provide global evaluations of hypothetical job descriptions which were then regressed on the different attribute levels included in the descriptions. The weights derived from the regression approach provided an indirect estimate of attribute importance. Zedeck found substantial differences in rankings generated by the direct and indirect approaches. Specifically, attributes emerging as most and least important from each of the approaches were security and growth for the point allocation method, advancement and flexibility for the straight ranking approach, and salary and security for the indirect policy-capturing technique.

It is not possible to unequivocally conclude that one approach is more externally valid than the other because of an absence of comparable research conducted in the criterion setting which could serve as a yardstick. However, theoretical and empirical arguments end up favoring the external validity of indirect, policy-capturing methods over methods eliciting direct estimates of attribute importance (see Schwab, Rynes, & Aldag, 1981, for a discussion of this point). First, there is evidence suggesting that direct methods of estimation are prone to social desirability effects. Arnold and Feldman (1981) found that subjects with high needs for social approval (as measured by the Marlowe-Crowne social desirability scale) tended to manifest larger discrepancies between direct and indirect rankings of job attribute importance than did those with lower approval needs. This was particularly true of attributes which one would expect to be sensitive to social desirability reporting tendencies, such as pay, fringe benefits, the need for autonomy, and the use of important skills. In addition, research into information processing capabilities suggests that most individuals do not possess the kind of self-insight required to provide valid estimates of hierarchies of job preferences in abstract contexts (Slovic & Lichtenstein, 1971).

Probably the most persuasive argument in favor of indirect estimates of hierarchies of job attribute preferences is that it most closely resembles the decision process confronted in the criterion setting. The majority of individuals experience information overload in making their job search and choice decisions (Schwab, 1982) and therefore resort to various heuristics to simplify their task. Regardless of the particular process model subscribed to, most theorists portray the job choice process as one in which job seekers concentrate on a small number of job attributes (see Reynolds, 1951; Sheppard & Belitsky, 1966; Simon, 1979; Soelberg, 1967), following which they generate an overall evaluation of the job alternative confronted. Hence, for most job seekers, an attribute by attribute evaluation of a job alternative against some absolute hierarchy of preferences is probably an unrealistic portrayal of their decision processes.

Intuitively, therefore, it seems that indirect methods of eliciting job preferences are probably more descriptive of criterion setting behaviors. Indirect methods, however, are not totally free of potential contaminants relative to the criterion setting. In particular, subjects are required to make numerous (for example, more than 150) concurrent evaluations of brief, hypothetical job descriptions while in reality, they typically examine a few options sequentially. In addition, the intercorrelation across attributes comprising the hypothetical job descriptions is typically constrained by the researcher to zero. This artificial restriction might not be characteristic of organizational conditions, since there is evidence suggesting that job attributes within a given position tend to be correlated (Reynolds, 1951; Rottenberg, 1956). For example, if a job pays well, it also usually provides above average extrinsic and intrinsic benefits, and might also have more open opportunities for advancement. The extent to which these unrealistic operationalizations limit the external validity of policy-capturing approaches is unknown at this point. Until studies compare predictions from policy-capturing approaches generated in the lab with actual job choice behaviors, the superiority of indirect methods over other research approaches, despite their limitations, remains conjecture at this point.

Applicant reactions to job and organizational attributes have also been inferred from studies of process models of the search process. Process models of job search and choice describe and explain how various job and organizational attributes are integrated and change an individual's propensity to apply for and/or accept a particular organizational opening. The most frequently tested among such models has been expectancy theory (Vroom, 1964). Typically, individuals rate the desirability of various job and/or organizational attributes. These valence perceptions are then combined (additively or multiplicatively) with respondent perceptions of the probability of obtaining a job offer (expectancies) and the extent to which holding the job will produce valued outcomes (instrumentalities). The dependent variable is either actual job (or organizational) choice behaviors, or respondent ratings of global attraction to real or hypothetical jobs varying on the attributes previously rated. The validity of the expectancy model is evaluated by correlating estimates of attraction derived from the theoretical model with direct estimates of global attraction to the same job or organizational alternatives, or with actual job choice behaviors.

Table 2–1 summarizes the results and major features of published studies of this kind.[1] Studies were categorized as lab or field, depending on whether the judgment made reflected a behavior implemented in the criterion setting. Of the fourteen pieces of research, ten were implemented in the field and eight in the lab (Greenhaus, Sugalski, & Crispin, 1978; Huber et al.; Stahl & Harrell, 1981, all reported on more than one study). Studies varied along a variety of dimensions in addition to the study context, including design differences (within versus between subject) and slight variations of the expectancy equation (for example, multiplicative versus additive; with or without the expectancy term). Moreover, an overall index of the predictive power of the expectancy model was often not presented. Hence, directly comparable and unconfounded indicators of the predictive power of expectancy theory were not always available for purposes of contrasting findings across lab and field settings.

Bearing these caveats in mind, it appears that with the exception of the third of the Greenhaus et al. (1978) reports, the expectancy model correlates significantly with both hypothetical and actual job (or organizational) choices. This implies only that the expectancy process is an isomorphic but not necessarily paramorphic representation of actual job seeker considerations. There is some indication that the magnitude of support obtained for expectancy theory is stronger in lab relative to field contexts, even when the policy-capturing studies are excluded. The exact reason for differences between settings in the validity of the expectancy model is difficult to pinpoint, because of a confounding of study context with type of criterion variable measured. This point is graphically illustrated in Greenhaus et al., where the magnitude of support for the expectancy model declines successively as it is tested against a fictitious criterion in the lab, a criterion involving weak behavioral indices of choice (job application behaviors) and a hard job choice criterion. The latter two measures were collected in the field. By definition, all field studies included some type of hard criterion while lab studies did not. It is therefore not possible to determine whether differences across settings in the magnitude of support for expectancy theory are attributable to dissimilarities in criterion measures or whether they are a result of other variations across contexts.

While, in general, the lab studies appear to yield higher validity coefficients than those observed in the field, there are several field studies that, at first blush, seem to be exceptions to this generalization. Several authors (for example, Lawler, Kuleck, Rhode, & Sorenson, 1975; Sheridan et al., 1975; Vroom, 1966) have observed that soon after a job is accepted, the perceived attractiveness of the chosen job rises to the detriment of those not accepted. This is a potential explanation for the high correlation found in the Pieters, Hundert, and Beer (1968) study which elicited expectancy theory judgments

Table 2-1
Expectancy Theory Applications to Job and Organizational Choice

Study	Sample	N	Dependent Variable	Results
Lab studies				
Dillard, 1979[a]	Professional accountants	136	Desirability of jobs	$r = .74$
Fischer, 1976	College and graduate students	10	Job preferences	$R^2 = .89^{b,c}$
Greenhaus, Sugalski, and Crispin, 1978	Graduating male college seniors	88	Attractiveness of companies of different sizes	Correct predictions in 60% of cases (chance = 33%)
Hill, 1974	Graduate students	90	Attractiveness of hypothetical jobs	$r = .62$
Huber, Daneshgar and Ford, 1971	Applicants for teaching jobs	30	Hypothetical job ratings[d]	$r = .65^c$
Sheard, 1970	Undergraduate students	382	Organizational preferences	$r = .80$
Stahl and Harrell, 1981	a. High school seniors	30	Effort to obtain job	$R^2 = .85^c$
	b. Male accounting college seniors	59	Effort to obtain job	$R^2 = .75^c$
Field studies				
Connolly and Vines, 1977	High school students	714	Choice of Georgia Tech vs. other college[e]	Correct predictions in 68% of cases (chance = 50%)
Dillard, 1981[f]	Professional accountants	126	Rank of positions chosen/attained	Correct predictions in 58% of cases (chance = 15%)
Greenhaus, Sugalski, and Crispin, 1978	Graduating male college seniors	a. 62	Job application behaviors with different sized companies	Correct predictions in 55% of cases (chance = 33%)
		b. 24	Job choice in big vs. small companies	Correct predictions in 58% of cases, NS (chance = 50%)
Huber, Daneshgar, and Ford, 1971	Applicants for teaching jobs	30	Hypothetical ratings[d]	67% chose job with highest rating (chance = 5%)
Lawler, Kuleck, Rhode, and Sorenson, 1975	Accounting majors (college and graduate students)	197	Job application behaviors	$r = .40$

Table 2–1 continued

Study	Sample	N	Dependent Variable	Results
Oldham, 1976	Female college students	83	Choice of sorority	$r = .41$
Pieters, Hundert, and Beer, 1968	Applicants to Corning Glass	71	Job choice[e]	$r = .67$, chosen organization $r = .34$, unchosen organizations
Sheridan, Richards, and Slocum, 1975	Nursing graduates	49	Job likely to be accepted	Significant dif- differentiation between first and second ranked job
Vroom, 1966	Graduate students	37	Job attractiveness for three most interesting jobs	$r = .67$, chosen or- ganization $r = .24$, unchosen organizations

[a]This study requested desirability ratings of seven alternatives: three jobs internal to the organization and four job categories in different accounting areas outside the firm. Thus, the latter four judgments touched on occupational choices since they were not specific to a particular job. Dillard (1979) is cate- gorized as a lab study because the dependent variable did not reflect actual job choices.

[b]Expected utility additive model under risk is analogous to expectancy theory.

[c]This was an intrasubject, policy-capturing study.

[d]Results are for two-stage weighted model which is analogous to expectancy theory.

[e]Expectancy theory components were evaluated after choice was made.

[f]This study is a four-year follow-up to Dillard (1979) using field data.

after job choices had already been made. Postchoice perceptual distortions might also have influenced results in Dillard (1981), thus artificially raising the validity coef- ficient. Dillard measured valence and instrumentality perceptions toward seven types of job outcomes. Although these perceptions were assessed before individuals' four- year job progression was observed, professionals in his sample had implicitly restricted themselves to one of three internal job choices because consideration of all seven job op- tions was not realistic at that point in their careers. Thus, indices of support for the ex- pectancy model in Dillard's (1981) field study are also probably somewhat inflated.

These field exceptions aside, there are several reasons why we might expect somewhat weaker relationships between subjective measures of attraction to or- ganizations and actual job search or choice behaviors (such as field studies) com- pared to those computed against fictitious criteria in the lab. First, the probability of receiving a job offer is likely to affect the observed validity of the expectancy equa- tion. Expectancy theory does incorporate a subjective probability estimate of the likelihood of attaining a job through the expectancy term. However, the greater the uncertainty about receipt of an offer, the more random error is introduced into the equation, thereby attenuating its validity. In lab studies, the probability of receiving an offer is 1.0, by assumption, while in most cases in the field there is a cer- tain level of uncertainty about being offered a job. For this reason, all things being equal, we would expect lower validity coefficients associated with expectancy predictions in the field relative to the lab.

In addition to noise introduced through uncertain expectancy perceptions in the field, error is potentially increased through an interaction between expectancy and valence perceptions. Rynes and Lawler (1983) and Stahl and Harrell (1981) found evidence that the attractiveness of certain job outcomes (and therefore the job in general) changed as a function of the perceived likelihood of getting a job. For example, the general attractiveness of a vacancy declined when the probability of getting an offer was low (Rynes & Lawler). Such interactions are not accommodated for within the expectancy model and therefore enter the equation as part of the error term. This source of nonsystematic variance is much less likely in the lab because expectancy perceptions in lab studies are usually fixed at 1.0, thus increasing the systematic variance attributable to expectancy models relative to field tests.

A third reason to expect better performance of expectancy theory in the lab is that the validity of the model depends on the extent to which organization and job attributes relevant to the behavior are measured as part of the predictive equation. Since researchers control the attributes along which the fictitious jobs vary, it is quite likely that most job attributes relevant to the decision made in the lab context are at least held constant if not directly measured. In contrast, when researchers survey individuals involved in an actual job choice, they are using standardized measures which may miss idiosyncratic and unmeasured considerations influencing a particular subject's job choice. This, too, would likely lower the predictive ability of expectancy theory in field relative to lab settings.

Two other features of lab studies also probably elevate the support observed for the expectancy model in lab studies relative to its estimated validity in field settings. Measurement of the criterion in lab settings (for example, global ratings of attraction to fictitious jobs) is done immediately before or following assessment of components of the theory. In the field, however, substantial periods (such as three months) often elapse between measurement of theoretical components of the model and collection of the criterion data (that is, the actual job search behaviors). This raises the potential for contaminants such as the effects of forgetting, attitude changes, or intervening events in field relative to lab conditions.

Finally, there is less variability in the jobs confronted by job seekers in the field relative to lab subjects. This occurs because field respondents perform some initial screening before a job is considered and/or because the researcher explicitly instructs them to focus only on a subset of the most preferred alternatives (such as Pieters et al., 1968, Sheridan et al., 1975). Zedeck (1977), for example, showed that estimates of model validity vary as an artifact of attribute variability and, all things being equal, validity is lower where there is less variability among attributes. Thus, both the delayed measurement of expectancy theory components and the restricted variability among attributes act to lower the magnitude of validity estimates observed for expectancy theory in field relative to lab tests.

This discussion provides conceptual and empirical reasons to expect differences between lab and field study attempts to describe job seeker reactions and choice processes. We argue that if the objective is purely descriptive, the field approach which probably yields more accurate (that is, realistic) portrayals of job seeker behaviors is preferable. On the other hand, lab studies are potentially appropriate for exploring normative models of search and choice. In that instance, the issues examined are what search and choice processes result in the best outcomes for the decision-maker. Lab studies can be implemented until the state of knowledge reaches a stage in which one type of normative model is seen as clearly preferable over others. Its utility can then be tested in the field by observing the employment successes of individuals adhering to one strategy compared to those using other approaches, and by training individuals to adopt alternative decision strategies following which their relative successes are observed.

Hiring Research

Research on hiring has examined the impact of various applicant attributes. Two additional subtopics are the effects of recruiter features such as age and sex on hiring behaviors, and models of the information processing strategies of recruiters. (See Schwab and Olian, 1981, for a review of this literature.)

Applicant Attributes

The majority of experimental studies of applicant effects on hiring decisions used a "paper people" approach in which applicant features were manipulated through systematic changes in the content of resumes evaluated by subjects (for example, Hakel et al., 1970; Haefner, 1977). A variety of judgments were requested of subjects, including ratings of applicant suitability (for example, Renwick & Tosi, 1978), rankings of applicants (for example, Simas & McCarrey, 1979), dichotomous (yes/no) hiring decisions (for example, Rosen & Jerdee, 1974), predicted performance and tenure ratings (for example, Rose & Andiappan, 1978), assessments of the probability of hiring the applicant (for example, Imada & Hakel, 1977) and recommended starting salary (for example, Heneman, 1977).

Qualifications. A frequently manipulated applicant characteristic has been the job seeker's level of qualifications (for example, prior experience, grade point average, or highest degree obtained). A meta-analysis (Olian, Schwab, & Haberfeld, 1984) across nineteen lab studies showed a large effect for applicant qualifications. The average effect size (in standard deviation units) was 1.46 (confidence interval of $-0.44 \leq d \leq 3.72$) corresponding to a correlation of .59 between level of qualifications and the hiring decision. Each of the nineteen studies had an effect coefficient >0, indicating that in all cases higher levels of qualifications raised the chances of being hired.

There are no micro field studies on the effects of qualifications. Studies in sociology and economics examining the social and employment consequences of various types of qualifications typically focus on present or lifetime earnings as the dependent variable rather than on success at the time of entry into the firm or labor market. (See Blaug, 1976; Featherman and Hauser, 1976; and Jencks, 1979, for reviews.) Such studies aggregate data across large numbers of organizations and job seekers and sacrifice measurement of and control over potentially important moderator variables. Thus, inferences about the effects of applicant qualifications on the hiring practices of particular firms or categories of organizations are precluded.

There have also been surveys of employers' perceptions of the importance of various applicant criteria such as appearance, experience, job skill, and education. These survey data of managerial beliefs indicate that applicant qualifications might not be of primary importance for certain types of job applicants. For example, a U.S. Department of Labor (1976) survey found that the importance of alternative criteria varied significantly by sample, such that for professional and managerial jobs, prior experience was the highest ranked criterion while for service jobs, attitude was first in importance followed by appearance. Miner's (1979) survey of personnel managers' perceptions revealed that interest in the job and company, followed by work motivation, were seen as the two most important hiring criteria. Thus, survey respondents appear to ascribe less importance to applicant qualifications than do lab subjects. However, survey results cannot be used to invalidate lab findings because the former measure perceptions rather than behaviors and are also not capable of controlling potentially important extraneous factors to the extent possible in lab studies.

Sex. The Olian et al. (1984) meta-analysis also looked at the effect of applicant sex on hiring decisions made by lab study participants. In twenty-six lab studies, the average effect size in standard deviation units was .30 (confidence interval of $-0.38 \leq d \leq 0.98$) corresponding to a correlation of $r = .15$, where positive d and r values reflect an advantage for males over females. Effect sizes for twenty-two of the twenty-six studies were positive, three were negative, and one was zero. Nineteen studies had effect sizes falling within ± 1 standard deviation of 0, where an effect size of 0 implies no sex discrimination.

Results for several field studies of sex effects on hiring decisions are presented in table 2–2. The table differentiates between field experiments and field surveys[2] and also notes the various operationalizations of the dependent variable.

Four of the ten field tests for sex discrimination found evidence of a preference for males over females while the remaining six did not observe any discrimination. However, across studies finding significant effects, there was large variability in the degree of internal validity and in the measure of hiring discrimination. For example, Nieva, Perkins, and Lawler (1980) did not control for potential effects of male-female qualification differences on the hiring decision, while two

Table 2–2
Field Studies of Sex Effects on Selection Decisions

Study	Sample	N	Dependent Variable	Design	Results[a]
Amsden and Moser, 1975	American Economic Association survey respondents	a. 1,284	Employer follow-up after initial interview	Field survey	NS
		b. 1,057	Candidates with ≥ 1 interview		NS
		c. 199	Starting salary		NS
Ferber and Green, 1982	Professors at University of Illinois	450	Initial hiring salary	Field survey	M > F beta = .11 ($p < .01$)
Lyon, Abel, Jones, and Rector-Owen, 1982	First-time job holders in National Longitudinal Survey	2,585	First-year income	Field survey	WM > WF by 40% ($p < .001$) BM > BF by 33–35% ($p < .001$)
McIntyre, Moberg, and Posner, 1980	Companies	152	Responses to mailed resumes	Field experiment	M > F in 66% of cases ($p < .001$)
Moore and Newman, 1977	Ph.D. economists placed between 1960 and 1974	958	Quality of hiring institution	Field survey	NS
Nieva, Perkins, and Lawler, 1980	Job applicants in medical products plant	220	Hiring decision	Field survey[b]	M > F in 72% of cases ($p < .01$)
Parsons and Liden, 1984	Young applicants for jobs in amusement park	a. 213 b. 50	Qualification rating	Field survey	NS NS

[a]W = white; B = black; M = male; F = female.
[b]Study did not control for potential qualification differences among applicants.

others used initial or first-year salary as the dependent variable (Ferber & Green, 1982; Lyon, Abell, Jones, & Rector-Owen, 1982), and the fourth (McIntyre et al., 1980) was a field experiment tabulating responses to mailed resumes ranging from no response to the scheduling of an interview.

Table 2–3 summarizes the frequencies of results of the sex effect research, by study context. The majority of studies did not observe significant sex discrimination. However, this finding was more probable in lab studies, perhaps because of generally smaller samples relative to the field investigations. Where there is a sex effect, it is more likely to be in favor of males regardless of study context, which is consistent with the meta-analysis results across all lab studies producing a positive sign for the average effect.

Thus, both lab and field research fail to support the notion of consistent discrimination against women. The large variability in study results is potentially

Table 2-3
Frequency of Results for Sex Effect Studies

	Pro-male Bias	Pro-female Bias	Not Significant
Lab	5	2	19
Field	4	0	6

attributable to the moderating effect of sex-type of job. Heilman (1983) has hypothesized that discrimination occurs where there is a lack of fit between applicant sex and sex-type of job. Olian et al. (1984) observed some support for this in their meta-analysis, where a finding of sex discrimination against women was more likely on male-type jobs than on those judged to be neuter.[3] Hence, part of the apparent inconsistency across studies reviewed above might be attributable to infrequent control over the sex-type of the vacancy for which applicants were considered. Moreover, the high number of nonsignificant findings might have occurred because some studies combined results across multiple vacancies. If some of those vacancies were male-type jobs and some female-type, a promale bias observed for the former would offset a profemale bias for the latter type of jobs, thereby resulting in an overall nonsignificant effect.

Race. Several lab and field studies have examined the evidence on race discrimination in the hiring context. Table 2-4 presents these results. Some of the same observations made for table 2-2 apply here, including distinctions between field experiments and surveys and the obvious diversity of dependent variable operationalizations. Table 2-5 is a frequency table summarizing these findings by study context.

Among the four lab studies, three showed no evidence of a race effect while a fourth (Mullins, 1982), presenting a videotaped manipulation, found that black applicants were favored over whites. Nine field tests were conducted for race effects, and all but two observed differences. However, the direction of the effect varied across studies. Three studies showed evidence of an advantage for whites over blacks (Abrahams, Atwater, & Alf, 1977; Firth, 1981; Parsons & Liden, 1984). However, Abrahams et al. did not control for possible qualification differences between blacks and whites, and Firth conducted his study in Britain using several national/ethnic manipulations that are not representative of American labor markets. One study (Lyon et al., 1982) observed a race x sex interaction such that among males, whites had a first-year income advantage over blacks, and among females, blacks had an advantage over whites.[4] Two field experiments (McIntyre et al., 1980; Newman, 1978) detected a black advantage in response to resumes mailed to companies.

Results for the race effect are inconsistent, particularly in field settings. The most probable result in the lab is to observe no effect, which is the least frequent

Table 2–4
Race Effects on Selection Decisions

Study	Sample[a]	N	Dependent Variable	Context	Results[a]
Haefner, 1977	Companies	286	Hiring recommendation	Lab	NS
Mullins, 1982	W business undergraduates	176	Overall suit-ability judgment	Lab	B > W; $F = 5.77$ ($p < .05$)
Rand and Wexley, 1975	W under-graduates	160	Overall suit-ability judgment	Lab	NS
Wexley and Nemeroff, 1974	W under-graduates	120	Hiring rating	Lab	NS
Abrahams, Atwater, and Alf, 1977	B and W Navy recruiters	46	Navy placement assignments	Field survey[b]	W > B ($p < .001$)
Firth, 1981	British companies advertising for applicants	282	Responses to mailed resumes	Field experiment[c]	W > non-W; $F = 8.61$ ($p < .001$)
Lyon, Abell, Jones, and Rector-Owen, 1982	First-time job holders in Na-tional Longi-tudinal Survey	2,585	First-year income	Field survey	WM > BM by 2-3% ($p < .01$); BF > WF by 4-6% ($p < .001$)
McIntyre, Moberg, and, Posner, 1980	Companies	458	Responses to mailed resumes	Field experiment	B > W in 63% of cases ($p < .01$)
Newman, 1978	Companies	200	Responses to mailed resumes	Field experiment	B marginally > W ($p < .06$)
Nieva, Perkins, and Lawler, 1980	Job applicants in medical products plants	220	Hiring decision	Field survey[b]	NS
Parsons and Liden, 1984	Young applicants for jobs in amusement park	a. 213 b. 50	Qualifications rating	Field survey	W > B; *beta =* .12 ($p < .01$) NS

[a]W = white; B = black; M = male; F = female.
[b]Study did not control for potential qualifications' differences among applicants.
[c]This study evaluated discrimination against non-British (Australian, French, African, Indian, Pakistani, and West Indian) job applicants. The nationality/race effect reflected significant discrimination against nonwhite relative to white applicants.

finding in the field. Field results are almost equally split between bias in favor of and against whites. While there is substantial macro evidence of black-white dif-ferences in job attainment, it is unclear what portion of those differences is at-tributable to differences in qualifications as opposed to hiring discrimination. For example, Featherman and Hauser (1976) and Jencks (1979) posit that in recent years, only a small portion of the difference between black and white earnings is attributable to discrimination rather than to human capital differences. Ornstein (1976) and Sewell, Hauser, and Wolf (1980) concluded that these attainment dif-

Table 2–5
Frequency of Results for Race Effect Studies

	$B > W$	$W > B$	*Not Significant*
Lab	1	0	3
Field	3[b]	4[b]	2

[a]B = black; W = white.

[b]Lyon et al. (1982) observed a race $\times$ sex interaction such that black females were preferred over white females and white males over black males. Effects for each sex subgroup are entered separately into the frequency table.

ferences are smallest in the first years of employees' careers. Thus, macro survey data are also imprecise about the extent of hiring discrimination in the criterion setting.

Bearing in mind the small number of race studies, probably the strongest statement that can be made about the external validity of lab results is that they are not markedly inconsistent with the highly variable findings observed in more micro field studies.

While the high portion of nonsignificant race findings in the lab might raise suspicions of demand characteristic effects, it is possible that demand effects also operate to a certain extent in field settings. Newman and Krzystofiak (1979) compared race effects from an unobtrusive field experiment to those obtained in a field survey. Stage 1 of the study (Newman, 1978) tabulated responses to resumes mailed to unsuspecting employers. One year later, a subset of these employers was sampled, told they were participating in a study, and asked how they would respond to earlier. Here the authors observed significant differences in the race effect as a function of study methodology, with a marginal race effect ($p < .06$) emerging for the unobtrusive study (Newman, 1978, see table 2–4) and no race effect for the self-report approach (Newman & Krzystofiak, 1979). They concluded that demand characteristics can contaminate field research results, particularly on matters as sensitive as the hiring of minorities.

Other Applicant Attributes. Several other applicant features have been studied in the lab, with a few cases of parallel field studies. Rasmussen (1984) and Wexley, Fugita, and Malone (1975) manipulated verbal and nonverbal behaviors in conjunction with applicant qualification information. Examples of nonverbal behaviors include eye-contact, gestures, body orientation and movement. They found that, while the verbal and nonverbal behaviors had a significant effect on hiring decisions, they were less important than the qualifications' manipulation. Several other studies manipulated nonverbal behaviors alone and observed large effects on hiring decisions (for example, Dipboye & Wiley, 1977; Imada & Hakel, 1977; McGovern & Tinsley, 1978).

Two field studies examined the impact of verbal and nonverbal behaviors on recruiter reactions (Hollandsworth, Kazelskis, Stevens, & Dressel, 1979; Parsons & Liden, 1984). Hollandsworth et al. concluded that applicant verbal content influenced recruiter decisions more than did nonverbal behaviors, even though both had significant effects. However, they did not control for other applicant features such as qualifications that might have covaried with the verbal content. Parsons and Liden did, and also found that applicant verbal cues and, to a somewhat lesser extent, nonverbal cues had a significant effect on the hiring decision. Interestingly, contrary to Rasmussen (1984) and Wexley et al. (1975), Parson and Liden's field study showed relatively small effects of applicant qualifications on the dependent variable, but this discrepancy might have been attributable to the low level of skills needed for the vacant jobs (amusement park positions) in the Parsons and Liden study relative to the skill requirements in the two lab studies (professional managerial jobs).

Thus, the lab data and results of the two field studies agree on the effects of verbal and nonverbal cues on hiring processes. However, it is not possible from these studies to conclude anything about similarities in the magnitude of observed effects since: (1) the content of verbal and nonverbal manipulations varied across studies; and (2) there were differences also in the level of control over other applicant features such as applicant qualifications that might covary with verbal and nonverbal behaviors, thereby contaminating estimated effect parameters.

The influence of the applicant's age on selection decisions has been investigated in two lab studies (Haefner, 1977; Rosen & Jerdee, 1976) showing that younger workers are preferred. This is consistent with field data on placement decisions for professional economists (Moore & Newman, 1977) and with survey results attesting to perceived (McAuley, 1977; Slater, 1972) and actual (Renas, 1971) practices of discrimination against older applicants.

Experimental studies have evaluated the effects of applicant physical attraction (for example, Carlson, 1969; Heilman & Saruwatori, 1979) and handicapped status (for example, Krefting & Brief, 1976; Rose & Brief, 1979). Survey data indirectly address the influence of physical (Felton & Litman, 1965) and mental (Miller & Dawson, 1965) handicaps on employability, and Levitan and Taggart (1977) report a lower probability of full-time work among handicapped relative to nonhandicapped employees. However, except for large scale labor market studies, field studies at the appropriate level of analysis are unavailable on these issues.

Recruiter Effects

Most lab studies examining recruiter effects on hiring decisions have focused on demographic features (for example, sex, race, or age) of the organizational representative. Several lab studies have failed to detect hiring decision differences as a function of sex of the decision-maker (Dipboye, Arvey, & Terpstra, 1977; Gutek & Stevens, 1979; Heneman, 1977; Renwick & Tosi, 1978; Rosen & Mericle, 1979).

However, three other lab studies contrasting the probability of hiring former mental patients versus ordinary applicants found evidence of rater sex effects, with men rejecting a former patient more frequently than women (Farina, Felner, & Boudreau, 1973; Farina & Hagelaur, 1975; Farina, Murray, & Groh, 1978). These latter lab results are consistent with Parsons and Liden (1984), who observed in the field that female interviewers gave significantly higher applicant ratings than did males. In field studies, Abrahams et al. (1977) found no support for an interviewer race effect, and Slater and Kingsley (1976) showed that ratings correlated positively with age of recruiter. No published lab studies to date have examined rater race or age effects. Thus, the one field study showing evidence of an interviewer sex effect is consistent with results observed in three lab studies using nontypical applicants (former mental patients) but inconsistent with five other studies including more traditional job-seeker manipulations.

Process Issues

A final set of lab studies on the hiring decision explores the decision processes adopted by organizational gatekeepers (for example, Einhorn, 1971; Valenzi & Andrews, 1973). Such studies use a policy-capturing methodology to describe the relative impact of various applicant characteristics on the hiring decision and to model the recruiter's method of integrating this information. One field study collected data on interviewers' decisions (Gorman, Clover, & Doherty, 1978), however this research did not address process issues. Field process studies such as protocol approaches are sorely needed to illuminate the content and process of actual recruitment and hiring decisions. To date, no such studies have been conducted.

Discussion and Conclusions

We set out to address the question: Do lab studies of the hiring decision generalize? It appears that we cannot answer this question with a simple yes/no response on the basis of an inductive literature review, even where there are parallel streams of lab and field research. This is not surprising in light of the small number of studies and the large variability in results across studies conducted within the same setting, let alone across contexts.

There were many dimensions along which studies varied within the same context, including the types of individuals providing responses, the nature of vacancies to be filled, and the construct constituting the dependent variable. Each of these sources (sample, vacancy, and dependent variable construct) is likely to contribute systematic variance to the sampling distribution observed for the variable of interest. For example, Olian et al. (1984) observed significant differences in effect size estimates for qualifications and sex as a function of respondent sample (professional versus student) and for sex as a function of the type of job (male-oriented or not). Other studies have observed differences in results for alternative dependent variables even within the same study (for example, Gardner & Berger, 1980; Stone & Sawatzki, 1980). Hence, at least some of the diversity in results within the literature reviewed here is probably attributable to differences among studies in potentially important moderator variables.

While an inductive analysis does not lead to firm conclusions, we can deductively speculate on lab conditions that might limit the external validity of such studies. Said differently, we can attempt to identify research conditions that, if incorporated into the lab, could potentially enhance the realism of lab environments relative to the criterion setting.

An obvious place to start is in the selection of respondents. As previously mentioned, Olian et al.'s 1984 meta-analysis of lab studies detected systematic differences in hiring behaviors as a function of the type of individual making the judgment (professional versus student). This is perhaps attributable to differences in the value students and professionals ascribe to alternative hiring criteria (Vecchiotti & Korn, 1980). In order to bolster the generalizability of lab findings, to the extent possible, experimental studies should use as respondents the same kinds of individuals making actual organizational decisions. Therefore, professional managerial samples are probably preferable to students.

Sample selection alone will not guarantee that managers behave in the lab as they do in the field. Features of the study's design will determine whether they interpret the meaning of the lab task in a manner that triggers their typical hiring decision processes. There are many design features that can be incorporated into experimental environments for that purpose.

The hiring situation itself can be designed to better control for and/or reflect organizational conditions that have a critical impact on the ultimate selection decision. First, applicant information in which the experimental manipulation (for example, sex and race) is embedded is typically very sparse. Actual hiring decisions are invariably made on the basis of more extensive information. Since the decision literature such as Einhorn (1971) and Payne (1976) indicates differences in decision processes as a function of amount of information available, it is likely that the external validity of lab results will be enhanced by presenting subjects with more comprehensive applicant information as the basis for the hiring decision. That will also lower the transparency of the manipulations, to the extent that the problem exists.

Recruiters collect not only more, but also potentially different information when they evaluate actual candidates compared to the type of applicant information conveyed via the paper person manipulation. For example, a major dimension along which hiring decisions are made is the perceived interpersonal compatibility between the candidate and the group (Olian & Rynes, 1984). That type of applicant information is not conveyed to subjects in traditional paper people operationalizations. Thus, the hiring decisions made using paper applicants might not reflect the content or process of actual screening decisions.

It is not just applicant information which is unnecessarily limited in the lab. Lab studies provide subjects with only brief descriptions of the vacancy to be filled, despite the fact that anecdotal descriptions suggest that managers consider broader organizational information before identifying a suitable candidate (for example, Wareham, 1980). For managerial positions in particular, recruiters take into consideration the organizational climate, culture, implicit value system, and so forth as well as the skill requirements of the job in generating an applicant with appropriate attributes. With one exception (Rosen & Mericle, 1979), studies to date have not provided or manipulated organizational contextual information even though it too likely affects hiring decisions.

Another crucial determinant of the hiring decision is the relative costs of selection errors. Such costs can take more than one form. First, what are the organizational costs of false positives (hiring an incompetent) and false negatives (rejecting a star)? In theory (for example, Heneman, Schwab, Fossum, & Dyer, 1983) and probably in practice, hiring standards (and therefore decisions) are affected by these relative costs. Failure to clarify such costs to subjects in lab situations could be an omission of an important determinant of the hiring decision. Future lab studies could explicitly manipulate alternative decision costs and observe how hiring outcomes covary. At a minimum, this type of cost should be controlled for by explicitly building it into the scenario describing the hiring environment.

An alternative type of cost is more personal. What are the consequences to the individual of making a selection error? The extent of personal accountability for a decision may affect the standards used in making the decision. For example, where the personal costs of a selection error are seen as high (such as performance evaluations tied to interviewers' hiring success ratios), individuals might resort to more risk-averse decisions by raising their hiring standards or holding off on a decision until a large number of candidates have been examined. In support of this conjecture, Carlson (1967) observed that selection decisions changed as a function of hiring quota pressures. Since both of these types of costs are probably implicitly considered and therefore systematically affect actual hiring decisions, they should be incorporated into the design of experiments for the enhancement of the generalizability of findings.

Several other design features typical of experimental studies could be altered in the interest of external validity. Requesting subjects to make final hiring ratings or decisions on the basis of resume information is unrealistic. Most organizational hiring processes consist of multiple stages (for example, initial application, one or two interviews, and standardized testing) before a conclusive hiring decision is made. Screening occurs at each stage, thus successively reducing the size of the applicant pool with the final decision reflecting an evaluation of the total information accumulated over all stages of the selection process. Hence, recruiters probably make only first-cut rather than final hiring decisions on the basis of applicant resumes. Decision processes probably vary in tandem, depending on whether one is making a (high cost) final hiring choice in settling on a single candidate versus attempting to make an initial cut (much lower cost) within the applicant pool in order to collect more intensive information about individuals surviving preliminary screening. External validity will be enhanced if operationalizations are more aligned with the sequential nature of the hiring process. If only resume information is provided, subjects should be making initial screening rather than final hiring decisions; alternatively, if the final hiring decision is the focus of interest, subjects should be provided with much richer applicant information that more realistically encompasses the range of information across multiple organizational screening phases.

Recruiters typically examine an applicant pool, and probably reach a hiring decision after going through some comparison process among multiple candidates. Lab studies often present subjects with only one candidate on the basis of which to make a hiring decision. Hence, subjects are forced to make decisions using absolute rather than comparative standards. This design feature might also unnecessarily change the decision outcome relative to the criterion setting and can be easily remedied in the lab.

The generalizability of lab studies also will be greatly enhanced to the extent that some direct interactions occur between subjects acting as organizational recruiters, and confederates in the role of applicants. While this is not an easy recommendation to implement in the lab, its importance is amplified by findings from Gorman et al. (1978) and Imada and Hakel (1977), which showed differences in selection results depending on whether subject-applicant interactions occurred.

A final recommendation for design changes is to encourage researchers to implement longitudinal selection processes in the experimental context. There are some suggestions that recruiters' expectations about applicants guide them in their screening processes. In turn, feedback and experience act to change these expectations in future selection decisions (see Dipboye, 1982; Sackett, 1982). Single-shot experimental tasks are probably an extremely impoverished means of capturing the full range of factors influencing selection judgments. Designs requiring subjects to make multiple hiring decisions separated by provision of feedback on success rates would address interesting research questions in addition to enhancing the external validity of findings.

As mentioned, the particular operationalization chosen for the dependent measure in lab settings affects observed results and is also likely to influence external validity. Organizational gatekeepers ultimately have to make a firm decision, whether the decision is "yes," "no," or "let's wait." Often, however, lab studies request subjects to rate applicants on some kind of desirability or suitability scale without requesting a firm yes/no decision (for example, Dipboye et al., 1977; Renwick & Tosi, 1978). An assumption is made that the candidate with the highest rating will be the one offered the job. It is unclear whether judgments on a scale perceived as continuous elicit the same kind of decision processes that occur when categorical (yes/no) decisions are made. For example, we might hypothesize that dichotomous decisions (or polytomous decisions—if the let's-wait option is feasible) make the finality of the choice (and therefore the decision costs) more salient than in the case of judgments on a continuum. Thus, for external validity purposes, the former type of operationalization of the dependent measure is preferable.

Kahneman and Tversky (1984) and Tversky and Kahneman (1981) present convincing evidence that the framing or description of a decision can exert an important influence on the decision outcome. This suggests, also, that the particular terminology chosen for elicitation of the dependent variable probably affects hiring results. Experimenters ask subjects to identify or hire the best candidate. However, is that the way organizational selection decisions are made? In many instances the primary concern is to hire individuals who are not unsuitable rather than to identify those who are best on some scale. In other words, instead of opting for a pure maximization strategy, recruiters often adopt a satisficing rule (March & Simon, 1958) whereby candidates are hired if they surpass some minimum standard of acceptability. This is probably consistent with typical organizational reward practices which tend to disproportionately weigh negative instances of performance (for example, hiring the unsuitable) at the expense of acknowledging positive performance (hiring the best candidate). Thus, experimental instructions to hire the most suitable candidate are eliciting a maximization strategy on the part of subjects when in reality, a satisficing decision rule might be typical of recruiters' hiring approaches for many jobs and organizations. Attention to this implication of the operationalization of the dependent variable will also likely enhance generalizability of findings.

Several points should be made in closing:

1. The two research areas with the greatest number of lab and field studies on the same issue involved: (a) The application of expectancy theory to job and organizational choice decisions. The studies showed convergence in the overall direction of effect, with some suggestion of stronger effects generated in lab tests. (b) Sex discrimination. Regardless of study setting, the most probable outcome of studies of sex discrimination in the hiring context was not to observe an effect. If an effect was observed, it was likely to be in favor of males in both lab and field settings.

2. In other staffing areas, firm conclusions, either way, about the generalizability of lab studies were not warranted because of a diversity of findings within lab and field contexts and/or a dearth of parallel studies across settings. Before any conclusive statements can be made about the generalizability of lab research, variables explaining and reducing the inconsistency in findings within a given setting need to be explored. Once a more homogeneous body of findings emerges within both lab and field settings, clearer comparisons of results across settings can be performed.

3. As Dipboye and Flanagan (1979) note, there is nothing inherently generalizable about field studies. Lab studies incorporating realistic design and measurement procedures along the lines suggested above, in theory, can have strong external validity.

4. In some situations, the external validity of results from a lab study are not of primary importance because the research addresses theoretical questions (Mook, 1983). Research on the underlying processes explaining RJP effects might fall into this category. There is fairly consistent evidence of the practical effectiveness of RJPs in reducing turnover. However, a researcher might want to know why the procedure works (for example, because of a "vaccination" effect) where individuals strengthen themselves psychologically in advance of any negative job experiences, or alternatively, because of the commitment an applicant generates toward an organization because of its openness. Practically, it does not really matter whether the lab study realistically reflects the criterion setting since the primary issue of interest is whether, in any setting, being shown a RJP increases commitment or vaccinates the subject. For such purposes, lab studies do not need to be judged against an external validity standard.

5. However, if—as we stated at the outset—the primary objective of staffing research is to illuminate organizational recruitment and hiring procedures in the interest of increasing their utility, the most efficient research strategy is probably to implement a multi-method approach. For example, research on the reasons underlying the differential efficacy of alternative recruitment sources could begin in the field. Protocol analyses will reveal whether there are differences in the type of information exchanged between employers and applicants as a consequence of using alternative sources. Lab studies could then build on these data and explore whether having different applicant or employer information (as a function of differential source usage) affects subsequent job choice and hiring decisions.

Notes

1. Applications of expectancy theory to occupational choice decisions are excluded from this review since they normally precede choice of a particular job or organization (Wanous, 1977). In that sense, occupational choice decisions are not directly influenced by organizational recruitment activities.

2. Field experiments manipulated gender (for example, through the construction of bogus resumes mailed to actual employers) while field surveys measured or estimated various applicant features including sex and related them to some indicator of the screening decision. All else being equal, the latter type of studies did not achieve the level of control over extraneous factors reached in field experiments.

3. Olian et al. (1984) could not compute effect sizes for female-type jobs because of the absence of appropriate studies.

4. Results of this study are entered into table 2–5 separately for each sex subgroup: once for females where B > W, and once for males where W > B.

References

Abrahams, N.M., Atwater, D.C., & Alf, E.F. (1977) Unobstrusive measurement of racial bias in job-placement decisions. *Journal of Applied Psychology, 62,* 116–119.

Alderfer, C.P., & McCord, C.G. (1970) Personal and situational factors in the recruitment interview. *Journal of Applied Psychology, 54,* 377–385.

Amsden, A.H., & Moser, C. (1975) Supply and mobility of women economists: Job search and affirmative action. *The American Economic Review, 65,* 83–91.

Arnold, H.J., & Feldman, D.C. (1981) Social desirability response bias in self-report choice situations. *Academy of Management Journal, 24,* 249–259.

Arvey, R.D., Gordon, M., Massengill, O., & Mussio, S. (1975) Differential drop-out rates of minority and majority job candidates due to "time lags" between selection procedures. *Personnel Psychology, 38,* 175–180.

Belt, J.A., & Paolillo, J.G.P. (1982) *An empirical assessment of two factors influencing response to recruitment advertisements.* Unpublished manuscript, Wichita State University.

Blaug, M. (1976) The empirical status of human capital theory: A slightly jaundiced survey. *Journal of Economic Literature, 3,* 827–855.

Breaugh, J.A. (1981) Relationships between recruiting sources and employee performance, absenteeism, and work attitudes. *Academy of Management Journal, 24,* 142–147.

Breaugh, J.A. (1983) Realistic job previews: A critical appraisal and future research directions. *Academy of Management Review, 8,* 612–619.

Carlson, R.E. (1967) Selection interview decisions: The effect of interviewer experience, relative quota situation, and applicant sample on interviewer decisions. *Personnel Psychology, 20,* 259–280.

Carlson, R.E. (1969) Relative influence of a photograph vs. factual written information on an interviewer's employment decision. *Personnel Psychology, 22,* 45–56.

Connolly, T., & Vines, C.V. (1977) Some instrumentality-valence models of undergraduate college choice. *Decision Sciences, 8,* 311–317.

Dean, R.A., & Wanous, J.P. (1984) Effects of realistic job previews on hiring bank tellers. *Journal of Applied Psychology, 69,* 61–68.

Decker, P.J., & Cornelius, E.T. (1979) A note on recruiting sources and job survival rates. *Journal of Applied Psychology, 64,* 463–464.

Dillard, J.F. (1979) Applicability of an occupational goal-expectancy model in professional accounting organizations. *Decision Sciences, 10,* 161–176.

Dillard, J.F. (1981) An update on the applicability of an occupational goal-expectancy model in professional accounting organizations. *Decision Sciences, 12,* 32–38.

Dipboye, R.L. (1982) Self-fulfilling prophecies in the selection-recruitment interview. *Academy of Management Review, 7,* 579–586.

Dipboye, R.L., Arvey, R.D., & Terpstra, D.E. (1977) Sex and physical attractiveness of raters and applicants as determinants of resume evaluations. *Journal of Applied Psychology, 3,* 288–294.

Dipboye, R.L., & Flanagan, M.F. (1979) Research settings in industrial and organizational psychology: Are findings in the field more generalizable than in the laboratory? *American Psychologist, 34,* 141–150.

Dipboye, R.L., & Wiley, J.W. (1977) Reactions of college recruiters to interviewee sex and self-presentation style. *Journal of Vocational Behavior, 10,* 1–12.

Einhorn, H.J. (1971) Use of nonlinear, noncompensatory models as a function of task and amount of information. *Organizational Behavior and Human Performance, 6,* 1–27.

Ellis, R.A., & Taylor, M.S. (1983) Role of self-esteem within the job search process. *Journal of Applied Psychology, 68,* 632–640.

Farina, A., Felner, R.D., & Boudreau, L.A. (1973) Reactions of workers to male and female mental patient job applicants. *Journal of Consulting and Clinical Psychology, 41,* 363–372.

Farina, A., & Hagelaur, H.D. (1975) Sex and mental illness: The generosity of females. *Journal of Consulting and Clinical Psychology, 43,* 122.

Farina, A., Murray, P.J., & Groh, T. (1978) Sex and worker acceptance of a former mental patient. *Journal of Consulting and Clinical Psychology, 46,* 887–891.

Featherman, D.L., & Hauser, R. (1976) Sexual inequalities and socioeconomic achievement in the U.S., 1962-1973. *American Journal of Sociology, 41,* 462–483.

Feldman, D.C., & Arnold, H.J. (1978) Position choice: Comparing the importance of organizational and job factors. *Journal of Applied Psychology, 63,* 706–710.

Felton, J.S., & Litman, M. (1965) Study of employment of 222 men with spinal cord injury. *Archives of Physical Medicine and Rehabilitation, 46,* 809–814.

Ferber, M.A., & Green, C.A. (1982) Traditional or reverse sex discrimination? A case study of a large public university. *Industrial and Labor Relations, 35,* 550–564.

Firth, M. (1981) Racial discrimination in the British labor market. *Industrial and Labor Relations Review, 34,* 265–272.

Fischer, G.W. (1976) Multidimensional utility models for risky and riskless choice. *Organizational Behavior and Human Performance, 17,* 127–146.

Gannon, M.J. (1971) Sources of referral and employee turnover. *Journal of Applied Psychology, 55,* 226–228.

Gardner, D.G., & Berger, C.J. (1980) *The effects of sex stereotypes, amount of relevant information, and awareness of organizational selection practices on sex discrimination for a managerial position.* Unpublished manuscript, Purdue University.

Gorman, C.D., Clover, W.H., & Doherty, M.E. (1978) Can we learn anything about interviewing real people from "interviews" of paper people? Two studies of the external validity of a paradigm. *Organizational Behavior and Human Performance, 22,* 165–192.

Greenhaus, J.H., Sugalski, T., & Crispin, G. (1978) Relationships between perceptions of organizational size and the organizational choice process. *Journal of Vocational Behavior, 13,* 113–125.

Gutek, B.G., & Stevens, D.A. (1979) Effects of sex of subjects, sex of stimulus cue, and androgyny level on evaluations in work situations which evoke sex role stereotypes. *Journal of Vocational Behavior, 14,* 23–32.

Haccoun, R.R. (1978) *The effects of realistic job previews and their position within the selection sequence on telephone operator behavior and attitudes.* Unpublished manuscript, University of Montreal.

Haefner, J.E. (1977) Race, age, sex, and competence as factors in employer selection of the disadvantaged. *Journal of Applied Psychology, 62,* 199–202.

Hakel, M.D., Dobmeyer, T.W., & Dunnette, M.D. (1970) Relative importance of three content dimensions in overall suitability ratings of job applicant resumes. *Journal of Applied Psychology, 54,* 65–71.

Heilman, M.E. (1983) Sex bias in work settings: The lack of fit model. In L.L. Cummings & B. Staw (Eds.), *Research in organizational behavior* (Vol. 5, pp. 269–298). Greenwich, CT.: JAI Press.

Heilman, M.E., & Saruwatori, L.R. (1979) When beauty is beastly: The effects of appearance and sex on evaluations of job applicants for managerial and nonmanagerial jobs. *Organizational Behavior and Human Performance, 23,* 360–372.

Heneman, H.G., III. (1977) Impact of test information and applicant sex on applicant evaluations in a selection simulation. *Journal of Applied Psychology, 62,* 524–526.

Heneman, H.G., III, Schwab, D.P., Fossum, J.A., & Dyer, L. (1983) *Personnel-human resources management* (2nd ed.). Homewood, IL: Richard D. Irwin.

Herriot, P., Ecob, R., & Hutchinson, M. (1980) Decision theory and occupational choice: Some longitudinal data. *Journal of Occupational Psychology, 53,* 223–236.

Herriot, P., & Rothwell, C. (1981) Organizational choice and decision theory: Effects of employers' literature on the selection interview. *Journal of Occupational Psychology, 54,* 17–31.

Hill, R.E. (1974) An empirical comparison of two models for predicting preferences for standard employment offers. *Decision Sciences, 5,* 243–254.

Hollandsworth, J.G., Jr., Kazelskis, R.D., Stevens, J., & Dressel, M.E. (1979) Relative contributions of verbal, articulative, and nonverbal communication to employment decisions in the job interview setting. *Personnel Psychology, 32,* 359–367.

Horner, S.O. (1979) *The effects of expectations through realistic job previews (RJPs) on Marine Corps attrition.* Paper presented at the meeting of the American Psychological Association.

Huber, G.P., Daneshgar, R., & Ford, D.L. (1971) An empirical comparison of five utility models for predicting job preferences. *Organizational Behavior and Human Performance, 6,* 267–282.

Ilgen, D.R., & Dugoni, B.L. (1977) *Initial orientation to the organization.* Paper presented at the meeting of the Academy of Management Association, Orlando, FL.

Imada, A.S., & Hakel, M.D. (1977) Influence of nonverbal communication and rater proximity on impressions and decisions in simulated employment interviews. *Journal of Applied Psychology, 62,* 295–300.

Ivancevich, J.M., & Donnelly, J.H. (1971) Job offer acceptance behavior and reinforcement. *Journal of Applied Psychology, 55,* 119–122.

Jencks, C. (1979) *Who gets ahead?* New York: Basic Books.

Kahneman, D., & Tversky, A. (1984) Choices, values, and frames. *American Psychologist, 39,* 341–350.

Krausz, M., & Fox, S. (1979) *The impact of different types of realistic previews upon initial expectations, expectation fulfillment, satisfaction, and withdrawal rates.* Unpublished manuscript, Tel Aviv University, Department of Labour Studies.

Krefting, L.A., & Brief, A.P. (1976) The impact of applicant disability on evaluative judgments in the selection process. *Academy of Management Journal, 19,* 675–680.

Lawler, E.E., Kuleck, W.J., Rhode, J.G., & Sorensen, J.E. (1975) Job choice and post decision dissonance. *Organizational Behavior and Human Performance, 13,* 133–145.

Levitan, S.A., & Taggart, R. (1977) Employment problems of disabled persons. *Monthly Labor Review, 100,* 3–13.

Lyon, L., Abell, T., Jones, E., & Rector-Owen, H. (1982) The national longitudinal survey data for labor market entry: Evaluating the small effects of racial discrimination and the large effects of sexual discrimination. *Social Problems, 29,* 524–539.

Macedonia, R.M. (1969) *Expectations, stress and survival.* Unpublished doctoral dissertation, New York University, New York.

March, J.G., & Simon, H.A. (1958) *Organizations.* New York: Wiley.

McAuley, W.J. (1977) Perceived age discrimination in hiring. *Industrial Gerontology, 24,* 21–28.

McGovern, T.V., & Tinsley, H.E. (1978) Interviewer evaluations of interviewee nonverbal behavior. *Journal of Vocational Behavior, 13,* 163–171.

McIntyre, S.H., Moberg, D.J., & Posner, B.Z. (1980) Preferential treatment in preselection decisions according to sex and race. *Academy of Management Journal, 23,* 738–749.

McIntyre, S.H., & Posner, B.Z. (1982) *Sex-discrimination in response to mailed resumes: How companies respond and how job candidates react.* Paper presented at the meeting of the American Institute for Decision Sciences, San Francisco.

Miceli, M.P., (1983) Why realistic job previews cannot meet our unrealistically high expectations. *Proceedings of the 43rd Annual Meeting of the Academy of Management,* 282–286.

Miller, D., & Dawson, W.H. (1965) Effects of stigma on re-employment of ex-mental patients. *Mental Hygiene, 49,* 281–287.

Miner, M.G. (1979) *Recruiting policies and practices* (PPF-BNA Survey No. 126). Washington, D.C.

Mook, D.G. (1983) In defense of external invalidity. *American Psychologist,* 1983, 379–387.

Moore, W.J., & Newman, R.J. (1977) An analysis of the quality differentials in male-female academic placements. *Economic Inquiry, 15,* 413–433.

Mullins, T.W. (1982) Interviewer decisions as a function of applicant race, applicant quality and interviewer prejudice. *Personnel Psychology, 35,* 163–174.

Newman, J.M. (1978) Discrimination in recruitment: An empirical analysis. *Industrial and Labor Relations Review, 32,* 15–23.

Newman, J.M., & Krzystofiak, F. (1979) Self-reports versus unobtrusive measures: Balancing method variance and ethical concerns in employment discrimination research. *Journal of Applied Psychology, 64,* 82–85.

Nieva, V.F., Perkins, D.T., & Lawler, E.E. (1980) Improving the quality of life at work: Assessment of a collaborative selection process. *Journal of Occupational Behaviour, 1,* 43–52.

Oldham, G.R. (1976) Organizational choice and some correlates of individuals' expectancies. *Decision Sciences, 7,* 873–884.

Olian, J.D., & Rynes, S.L. (1984) Organizational staffing: Integrating practice with strategy. *Industrial Relations, 23,* 170–183.

Olian, J.D., Schwab, D.P., & Haberfeld, Y. (1984) *The impacts of applicant sex and qualifications on hiring decisions: Preliminary results of a meta-analysis.* Unpublished manuscript, University of Maryland, College Park.

Ornstein, M.D. (1976) *Entry into the American labor force.* New York: Academic Press.

Parkington, J.J., & Schneider, B. (1978) *A laboratory study of some effects of a realistic task preview* (Research Report No. 17), College Park: University of Maryland, Department of Psychology.

Parmerlee, M. (1982) *A laboratory investigation of realistic job previews.* Paper presented at the meeting of the Academy of Management Association, San Diego.

Parsons, C.K., & Liden, R.C. (1984) Interviewer perceptions of applicant qualifications: A multivariate field study of demographic characteristics and nonverbal cues. *Journal of Applied Psychology, 69,* 557–568.

Payne, J.W. (1976) Task complexity and contingent processing in decision making: An information search and protocol analysis. *Organizational Behavior and Human Performance, 16,* 366–387.

Pieters, G.R., Hundert, A.T., & Beer, M. (1968) Predicting organizational choice: A post hoc analysis. *Proceedings of the 76th Annual American Psychological Association Convention,* 573–574.

Powell, G.N. (1984) Effects of job attributes and recruiting practices on applicant decisions: A comparison. *Personnel Psychology, 37,* 721–732.

Premack, S., & Wanous, J.P. (1985) *A meta-analysis of realistic job preview experiments.* Unpublished manuscript, Ohio State University, College of Administrative Science.

Rand, T.M., & Wexley, K.N. (1975) Demonstration of the effect, "similar to me," in simulated employment interviews. *Psychological Reports, 36,* 535–544.

Rasmussen, K.B. (1984) Nonverbal behavior, verbal behavior, resume credentials, and selection interview outcomes. *Journal of Applied Psychology, 69,* 551–556.

Reilly, R., Brown, B., Blood, M.R., & Malatesta, C.Z. (1981) The effects of realistic previews: A study and discussion of the literature. *Personnel Psychology, 34,* 823–834.

Reilly, R., Tenopyr, M., & Sperling, S. (1979) Effects of job previews on job acceptance and survival of telephone operator candidates. *Journal of Applied Psychology, 64,* 218–220.

Renas, S.R. (1971) The impact of Public Law 90-202 upon selected firms in greater Augusta, Georgia. *Dissertation Abstracts International, 31,* 4335A.

Renwick, P.A., & Tosi, H. (1978) The effects of sex, marital status, and educational background on selection decisions. *Academy of Management Review, 21,* 93–103.

Reynolds, L.G. (1951) *The structure of labor markets.* New York: Harper Brothers.

Rogers, D.P., & Sincoff, M.Z. (1978) Favorable impression characteristics of the recruitment interviewer. *Personnel Psychology, 31,* 495–504.

Rose, G.L., & Andiappan, P. (1978) Sex effects on managerial hiring decisions. *Academy of Management Journal, 21,* 104–112.

Rose, G.L., & Brief, A.P. (1979) Effects of handicap and job characteristics on selection evaluations. *Personnel Psychology, 32,* 385–392.

Rosen, B., & Jerdee, T.H. (1974) Effects of applicant's sex and difficulty of job on evaluations of candidates for managerial positions. *Journal of Applied Psychology, 59,* 511–512.

Rosen, B., & Jerdee, T.H. (1976) The influence of age stereotypes on managerial decisions. *Journal of Applied Psychology, 61,* 428–432.

Rosen, B., & Mericle, M.F. (1979) Influence of strong versus weak fair employment policies and applicant's sex on selection decisions and salary recommendations in a management simulation. *Journal of Applied Psychology, 64,* 435–439.

Rosenfeld, C. (1975) Job seeking methods used by American workers. *Monthly Labor Review,* August, pp. 39–42.

Rottenberg, S. (1956) On choice in labor markets. *Industrial and Labor Relations Review, 9,* 183–199.

Rynes, S.L., & Lawler, J. (1983) A policy-capturing investigation of the role of expectancies in decisions to pursue job alternatives. *Journal of Applied Psychology, 68,* 620–631.

Rynes, S.L., & Miller, H.E. (1983) Recruiter and job influences on candidates for employment. *Journal of Applied Psychology, 68,* 147–154.

Sackett, P.R. (1982) The interviewer as hypothesis tester: The effects of impressions of an applicant on the interviewer questioning strategy. *Personnel Psychology, 35,* 789–804.

Schmitt, N., & Coyle, B.W. (1976) Applicant decisions in the employment interview. *Journal of Applied Psychology, 61,* 184–192.

Schneider, B. (1983) An interactionist perspective on organizational effectiveness. In D. Whetton & K.S. Cameron (Eds.), *Organizational effectiveness: A comparison of multiple models* (pp. 27–54). New York: Academic Press.

Schwab, D.P. (1982) Organizational recruiting and the decision to participate. In K. Rowland & G. Ferris (Eds.), *Personnel Management* (pp. 103–155). Boston: Allyn and Bacon.

Schwab, D.P., & Olian, J.D. (1981) *From applicant to employee: Gatekeeping in organizations.* Unpublished manuscript, University of Wisconsin-Madison.

Schwab, D.P., Rynes, S.L., & Aldag, R.J. (1981) *Theories of research on job search and choice.* Unpublished manuscript, University of Wisconsin-Madison.

Sewell, W.H., Hauser, R., & Wolf, W. (1980) Sex, schooling, and occupational status. *American Journal of Sociology, 86,* 551–583.

Sheard, J.L. (1970). Intrasubject prediction of preferences for organization types. *Journal of Applied Psychology, 54,* 248–252.

Sheppard, H.L., & Belitsky, A.H. (1966) *The job hunt.* Baltimore: Johns Hopkins University Press.

Sheridan, J.E., Richards, M.D., & Slocum, J.W. (1975) Comparative analysis of expectancy and heuristic models of decision behavior. *Journal of Applied Psychology, 60,* 361–368.

Simas, K., & McCarrey, M. (1979) Impact of recruiter authoritarianism and applicant sex on evaluation and selection decisions in a recruitment interview analogue study. *Journal of Applied Psychology, 64,* 483–491.

Simon, H.A. (1979) Rational decision making in business organizations. *American Economic Review, 69,* 493–513.

Slater, R. (1972) Age discrimination in Great Britain. *Industrial Gerontology, 19,* 12–19.

Slater, R., & Kingsley, S. (1976) Predicting age-prejudiced employers. *Industrial Gerontology, 23,* 121–128.

Slovic, P., & Lichtenstein, S. (1971) Comparison of Bayesian and regression approaches to the study of information processing in judgment. *Organizational Behavior and Human Performance, 6,* 649–744.

Soelberg, P.O. (1967) Unprogrammed decision making. *Industrial Mangement Review, 8,* 19–29.

Stahl, M.J. & Harrell, A.M. (1981) Modeling effort decisions with behavioral decision theory: Toward an individual differences model expectation theory. *Organizational Behavior and Human Performance, 27,* 303–325.

Stone, C.I., & Sawatzki, B. (1980) Hiring bias and the disabled interviewee: Effects of manipulating work history and disability information of the disabled job applicant. *Journal of Vocational Behavior, 16,* 96–104.

Strand, R., Levine, R., & Montgomery, D. (1981) Organizational entry preferences based upon social and personnel policies: An information integration perspective. *Organizational Behavior and Human Performance, 27,* 50–68.

Taylor, M.S., & Bergmann, T. (1984) *The impact of organizational recruitment practices upon applicants' reactions: A field investigation.* Unpublished manuscript, University of Maryland, College Park.

Taylor, M.S., & Schmidt, D.W. (1983) A process-oriented investigation of recruitment source effectiveness. *Personnel Psychology, 36,* 343–354.

Tversky, A., & Kahneman, D. (1981) The framing of decisions and the psychology of choice. *Science, 211,* 453–458.

Ullman, J.C., & Gutteridge, T.G. (1974) Job search in the labor market for college graduates: A case study of MBAs. *Academy of Management Journal, 17,* 381–386.

U.S. Department of Labor. (1976) *Recruitment, job search, and the United States Employment Service.* Washington, D.C.: U.S. Government Printing Office.

Valenzi, E., & Andrews, I.R. (1973) Individual differences in the decision process of employment interviewers. *Journal of Applied Psychology, 58,* 49–53.

Vecchiotti, D.I., & Korn, J.H. (1980) Comparison of student and recruiter values. *Journal of Vocational Behavior, 16,* 43–50.

Vroom, V.H. (1964) *Work and motivation.* New York: Wiley.

Vroom, V.H. (1966) Organizational choice: A study of pre- and postdecision processes. *Organizational Behavior and Human Performance, 1,* 212–225.

Wanous, J.P. (1973) Effects of a realistic job preview on job acceptance, job attitudes, and job survival. *Journal of Applied Psychology, 58,* 327–332.

Wanous, J.P. (1977) Organizational entry: Newcomers moving from outside to inside. *Psychological Bulletin, 84,* 602–618.

Wanous, J.P. (1980) *Organizational entry: Recruitment, selection, and socialization of new-comers.* Reading, MA: Addison-Wesley.

Wareham, J. (1980) *Secrets of a corporate headhunter.* New York: Playboy Paperbacks.

Wexley, K.N., Fugita, S.S., & Malone, M.P. (1975) An applicant's nonverbal behavior and student-evaluators' judgments in a structured interview setting. *Psychological Reports, 36,* 391–394.

Wexley, K.N., & Nemeroff, W.F. (1974) The effects of racial prejudice, race of applicant, and biographical similarity on interviewer evaluations of job applicants. *Journal of Social and Behavioral Sciences, 20,* 66–78.

Youngberg, C.F. (1963) *An experimental study of job satisfaction and turnover in relation to job expectations and self-expectations.* Unpublished doctoral dissertation, New York University, New York.

Zedeck, S. (1977) An information processing model and approach to the study of motivation. *Organizational Behavior and Human Performance, 18,* 47–77.

3
Performance Appraisal

H. John Bernardin
Peter Villanova

The purpose of this chapter is twofold. First, we have assessed the congruence between laboratory and field studies in three areas of research in performance appraisal (namely, rating formats, rater training, and rating purpose). Second, we have critiqued both types of research and suggested research needs and methodologies for enhancing the generalizability of results. Based on a survey of people directly involved with appraisal systems as raters, ratees, or administrators, critical areas for research are identified and a modal criterion model is proposed. It is our thesis that most laboratory and field studies on performance appraisal ignore critical boundary variables (Fromkin & Streufert, 1976), lack psychological realism, and ignore major issues related to generalizability. These strong statements assume that applied researchers are concerned about the appraisal of *actual* job performance or what Naylor, Pritchard, and Ilgen (1980) refer to as organizational behavior. Generalizability to other appraisal situations involving performance in assessment centers, interviews, and work samples is beyond the scope of this chapter.

Fromkin and Streufert (1976) have discussed the importance of identifying boundary variables which can limit the external validity of research findings. Boundary variables are critical differences between the research setting and criterion setting which could alter the existence or magnitude of the relationship between two or more variables. For example, several studies have found a positive/negative relationship between some type of rater training program and some measure of effectiveness (for example, accuracy, halo, leniency, discriminability). Virtually every study on the effects of rater training, however, has ignored the purpose for which the data are to serve (for example, merit pay, promotion, reductions in force, feedback). Data in rater training studies are almost always collected for experimental purposes only. Thus, it may be that the significant results obtained for training in the experimental context have no generalizability to most criterion settings where the appraisal data serve some critical purpose, that is, rater motivation in these situations is unaffected by the training procedures under study.

Purpose of appraisal could also be a critical boundary variable in rating format studies. Purpose of appraisal is rarely considered in this context despite the fact that two rating formats (forced choice and mixed standard) were specifically developed to inhibit deliberate rating distortion. Of course, the extent to which deliberate rating distortion is a problem is related to the purpose for which the data are to serve. It is no surprise that format has had little effect in rating situations where data serve no administrative purpose and the extent of rating distortion is probably minimal (Bernardin & Beatty, 1984).

Personal contact between rater and ratee (that is, life goes on after the performance appraisal) could be another boundary variable. For example, a training program found to inhibit leniency in a research setting may have no effect in a criterion setting where trained raters are also supervisors of the persons who are rated. Related to this issue is the confidentiality of ratings. Perhaps confidentiality is a boundary variable for several relationships.

In this chapter we present evidence from three sources: (1) a review of the contemporary empirical literature on performance appraisal, (2) a survey completed by personnel practitioners, and (3) another survey completed by practitioners, supervisors, and subordinates. We first conducted a review of the literature on performance appraisal (PA) research, coding studies with regard to characteristics that are pivotal in assessing their generalizability. We also conducted a survey of practitioners for purposes of developing a modal appraisal situation. Finally, we took the information from these two sources (literature and survey) and compared the characteristics of each to assess the extent of congruence between them. In so doing, we made the assumption that research with characteristics more proximal to the modal appraisal setting is more immediately generalizable to it (Cook & Campbell, 1979). For our purposes, the characteristics of the setting include any component of the appraisal process. The second survey was used to generate critical research needs from the perspective of those directly involved with ongoing appraisal systems.

Literature Review

Research in appraisal was content analyzed for the years 1980–1984 from the *Journal of Applied Psychology, Public Personnel Management, Personnel Psychology, Proceedings of the Academy of Management, Academy of Management Journal,* and *Organizational Behavior and Human Performance.* In addition, certain volumes were reviewed from *Personnel Journal* (1980–1982), *Personnel Administrator* (1980–1982), the *Journal of Occupational Behavior* (1980–1982), *Administrative Science Quarterly* (1982–1984), and the *Journal of Occupational Psychology* (1982–1984).

Each study was coded for the following characteristics: (1) the nature of the study (lab, field, or student ratings of professor), (2) subject characteristics, (3) type of organization, (4) independent variables under study, (5) dependent variables, (6) purpose of appraisal, (7) confidentiality of ratings, (8) ratee characteristics, and (9) rating format(s) under study. Due to the number of studies involving student ratings of instructors and the unique nature of this rating situation, we have distinguished these results from results of other field settings.

A total of ninety-four studies were independently coded by two researchers, with complete agreement on all codings. The percentage of studies falling into the laboratory, field, and student rating categories were 53.2, 34, and 12.8 percent, respectively.

With regard to the independent variables under study, rating format studies were the most popular (23 percent of the research reviewed). Other frequent research topics were rater training (23 percent), rater ability factors (16 percent), and purposes of appraisal (8.5 percent).

The most frequently studied dependent variables were severity/leniency (30 percent), halo (35 percent), accuracy (19 percent), ratee discriminability (21 percent), interrater reliability (15 percent), and validity (convergent, discriminant, 11 percent).

Because of the greater frequency of research directed at the effects of rating formats and rater training, we decided to concentrate our discussion on these areas and, in addition, to review the studies on appraisal purpose. After narrowing the focus of the chapter to these three topics, we expanded our literature review in order to identify as many studies in these areas as possible.

Rating Format Comparisons

There have been numerous reviews and discussions of the results of rating format comparisons (for example, Bernardin & Beatty, 1984; Borman, in press; Green, Bernardin & Abbott, in press; Jacobs, in press). We were able to locate forty-two empirical comparisons between two or more rating formats. Twelve were lab studies using either videotaped ratees or paper-people vignettes; thirteen involved student ratings of professors; and seventeen were field studies involving police officers, computer programmers, technical engineers, department store managers, military personnel, state troopers, residence hall counselors, and several other occupations.

There were over twenty-five different dependent variables used in these studies (Bernardin & Beatty, 1984, p. 190). Regardless of the research setting or the dependent variable under study (for example, halo, leniency, discriminability, accuracy), rating format had little effect. Schmidt (1977) has argued that the most useful criterion of effectiveness across all data purposes is the disattenuated correlation between sets of ratee ratings from two formats. Most of the studies did not report the information necessary to calculate this corrected correlation. However, for the ten studies which allowed a correction for unreliability in each rating format, only one study (Cotton & Stoltz, 1960) resulted in a correlation between pairs of scores on the same ratees below .70 (namely, .63). Four of the ten correlations exceeded 1.00 after correction for attenuation (Bendig, 1954; Campbell, Dunnette, Arvey & Hellervik, 1973; Shapira & Shirom, 1980; Bernardin, Elliott & Carlyle, 1980). All of these are field studies. Pulakos (1984b) reported an attenuated correlation of .94 between BARS and BOS in a laboratory study. Only the laboratory studies could provide an accuracy measure and, again, there were generally no differences between formats.

Before we derive the same conclusion regarding formats that is found in almost every review on the subject, let's return to our discussion of possible boundary variables and their effects on research outcomes. We proposed that rating purpose may be an important boundary variable with regard to certain rating formats. In fact, of the forty-two studies that we reviewed involving format comparisons, all but three (Bernardin & Orban, 1984; Sharon & Bartlett, 1969; Taylor & Wherry, 1951) collected performance ratings for research purposes only. As stated earlier, forced choice scales and mixed standard scales were specifically developed to control or eliminate deliberate rating distortion. We located five field studies involving a comparison of the mixed standard format with one or more other formats (Arvey & Hoyle, 1974; Saal & Landy, 1977; Bernardin & Orban, 1984; Dickinson & Zellinger, 1980; Edwards, 1982). Only one of these studies collected ratings in the context of an important purpose (that is, the ratings were used as a source of information for promotions). This single study (Bernardin & Orban) found support for the mixed standard approach.

Our review of the empirical comparisons involving forced choice scales revealed the same methodological consistency across seven field studies. Although it is well known that forced choice scales were developed to control deliberate rating distortion, data collection for all but three of the seven comparisons involving this format was made for research purposes only. The three studies which manipulated the purpose for the appraisal found support for the forced choice method (Sharon & Bartlett, 1969; Sisson, 1948; Taylor & Wherry, 1951). Researchers seem to have lost sight of the fact that forced choice scales are specifically designed to reduce leniency. King, Hunter, and Schmidt (1980), for example, only discuss the method in the context of reducing halo, a variable more closely linked to rater ability rather than to rater motivation (Bernardin & Cardy, 1982).

In addition to generally ignoring the purpose for which appraisal data will or has served, format comparisons face another problem in both the lab and the field. This is the problem of format labeling. Across both lab and field studies, researchers have used more than one format even when claiming to be using only one. For example, Bernardin and Smith (1981) discussed this issue with regard to behaviorally anchored rating scales. The argument applies to other formats as well. A format (for example, BARS, mixed standard) used in one study is often substantially different from the "same" format used in another study. Thus, lab versus field comparisons are confounded by format differences across different research strategies. This confounding applies to all dependent variables under study (Bernardin & Beatty, 1984). For this reason, it is useless to discuss effect sizes, number of significant findings, etcetera as functions of the two research strategies.

Our review of the lab and field research on rating formats reaches a different conclusion than that which is commonly accepted today. Indeed, rating format, specifically mixed standard scales and forced choice scales, may inhibit or prevent rating inflation which is common in situations where ratings have important administrative significance. Unfortunately, most field research and all laboratory research on rating formats has yet to include this significant boundary variable which could augment or change effects commonly observed in the literature.

Rater Training

Despite the fact that performance appraisal systems of one form or another can be found in 90 percent of American organizations, of the thirty-four rater training studies we located, twenty-six involved student raters in an experimental context (see table 3–1). The majority of both laboratory and field studies found significant effects for rater training. Only three studies were found which involved ratings relevant to actual administrative decisions (Bernardin, 1984; Ivancevich, 1979; Warmke & Billings, 1979). Nineteen of the thirty-four studies, or 56 percent, are laboratory studies involving ratings of hypothetical ratees. From the lab research, we know that we can provide rater training which replaces one response set with another (spread out your ratings across dimensions, for example; Bernardin & Pence, 1980). With the advent of the so-called true scores through the Borman (1978) and Murphy, Kellam, Balzer, and Armstrong videotapes (1982) and the myriad of "paper people," our new dependent variable is accuracy and we are on a research path which will predictably end up with the "training" comprised of the subjects memorizing each and every performance specimen or, at the least, doing precisely what Borman (1978) had his experts do when deriving "true scores." It would not be surprising that subjects so trained would rate more like the "experts" than those who were not so trained. The potential generalizability of such training to typical appraisal situations is negligible.

Campbell, Daft, and Hulin (1982) have recommended that we as researchers should avoid asking questions to which we already know the answers and should avoid research tailored for particular research methodologies. It seems we are doing both of these things in our laboratory research methodologies. It is a sad commentary on our discipline that an obvious applied area like rater training should

Table 3–1
Training Studies

	Laboratory	Field	
		Students/Professors	Others
Significant effects	11, 16, 18, 31, 42, 48, 51, 52, 57, 58, 64, 69, 73, 74	8, 13, 20, 27, 38, 70	9, 10, 26, 49, 71, 77
Nonsignificant effects	21, 23, 62, 79, 82	37	43, 78

be studied almost exclusively with student raters in an experimental context. It is equally sad that our concentration on dependent variables has focused almost exclusively on psychometric characteristics such as halo, leniency, and accuracy, disregarding other more useful *applied* variables (for example, ratee agreement with the rating, perceived fairness in the process, rater evaluations of the training).

Also worth noting is the absence of concern over motivational variables. Virtually every rater training study has concentrated on the rater's *ability* to rate accurately (for example, if we make raters aware of halo error, they commit less; if we have them practice and become familiar with a difficult rating form, they ultimately rate more accurately). It takes no great insight to realize that, even if the content of the training program is superb, it will not necessarily result in better raters if it fails to motivate them to either acquire the necessary skills or use them. That ability and effort combine to produce behavior has been recognized for years in the performance literature (Campbell, Dunnette, Lawler, & Weick, 1970). We need to pay closer attention to the implications of this relationship for rating accuracy. (See Bernardin & Beatty, 1984, pp. 267–276 for a discussion of possible research avenues.)

As we noted earlier in the chapter, purpose could act as a boundary variable in an appraisal situation. With regard to training, purpose may be a significant moderator of relationships initially derived in controlled laboratory settings. Of the thirty-four studies that dealt with the effects of training, only three of these involved real data, severely limiting any conclusions at this time. Only one study (Bernardin, 1984) found effects of the training in an administrative context. This implies that the motivational effect of rating purpose may be of greater magnitude than the ability-directed and motivationally deficient characteristics of virtually all training interventions currently under study. Such training appears to have great applicability for assessment centers, work samples, and interviewing where presumably rater motivation to rate accurately would be high and relatively stable across ratees. However, if the interest of researchers in rater training is with generalizability to appraisals of actual organizational behavior, it is time to reassess the laboratory paradigms which are currently dominating this area of research. Such approaches should also incorporate other potential boundary variables such as realistic time manipulations and rater/ratee personal contact.

Appraisal Purpose

Our review of the empirical literature on purpose of appraisal identified some features of this work that make it an outstanding example of contemporary research on performance appraisal. For example, we found that research on this topic has used the more sophisticated data collection and analytic strategies at our disposal (for example, Williams, DeNisi, Blencoe & Cafferty, 1985; Zedeck & Cascio, 1982). Also, the fact that recent investigations have been conducted is laudable in light of the apparent neglect of this topic just a few years ago. On the other hand, we also found that manipulations of the purpose of appraisal have been simple one-liners providing abbreviated information to the subject as to the purpose of the appraisal (for example, Bernardin, 1978; Murphy et al., 1982; McIntyre, Smith, & Hassett, 1984; Zedeck & Cascio, 1982). We found no attempts to more realistically engage the subject through the purpose manipulations. Table 3–2 presents a summary of the sixteen studies we identified involving the purpose of appraisal data. Despite the simplistic manipulations, the majority of both lab and field studies found significant effects for the purpose of appraisal data. The laboratory studies indicate that raters weight performance data differently as a function of appraisal purpose (for example, Bazerman & Atkin, 1982; Williams et al., in press). The field studies indicate consistently greater leniency for appraisal data when the data are used for more important personnel decisions such as promotions and retention (for example, Bernardin & Orban, 1984; Taylor & Wherry, 1951). The laboratory studies using leniency as the dependent variable have not supported this finding, however (Bernardin, Abbott & Cooper, 1984; McIntyre et al., 1982; Murphy et al., 1982). This is not at all surprising given the manipulations made in the laboratory studies. We support the views of Berkowitz and Donnerstein who argued that "the meaning the subjects assign to the situation they are in . . . plays a greater role in determining the generalizability of an experimenter's outcome than does the sample's demographic representatives or the setting's realism" (1982, p. 249). With regard to purpose manipulations, we believe the meaning student subjects assign to such a situation does not even approach that which is attached to actual appraisal situations where, for example, a coworker's, subordinate's, and/or acquaintance's promotion, merit increase, or retention may be on the line. Laboratory research should now be directed at interactive variables in the context of more psychologically realistic purpose manipulations. For example, individual difference variables have great potential in this line of research (Bernardin & Beatty, 1984). Cummings (1983) has argued that if trust and commitment characterize the sentiments of employees toward the organization, performance evaluation systems will place greater emphasis on employee performance and career development than on employee control. As noted by Cummings, the extent to which performance evaluation is used as a control device in organizations

Table 3–2
Studies of the Purpose of Appraisal

		Field	
	Laboratory	*Students/Professors*	*Others*
Significant effects	5, 60, 81, 82	7, 8, 40, 66, 76	17, 72
Nonsignificant effects	11[a], 51[a], 55[a]	3, 25	

[a]Nonsignificant effects with leniency or accuracy as the dependent variable.

depends on the level of trust between the employed and employer as well as the commitment of the employee to organizational effectiveness and the commitment of the employer to employee career development.

This aspect of trust has also been implicated in the work of Bernardin and his associates in which they have administered "Trust in the Appraisal Process Survey" to raters (for example, Bernardin & Orban, 1984). This research found preliminary support for the role of trust in rating distortion. Raters who report less trust in the accuracy of the appraisal process also rate more leniently. This behavior on the part of raters may be an attempt to exercise some control over what they perceive to be an arbitrary and capricious system of evaluation. More creative laboratory paradigms would certainly allow for investigations of these potentially interactive variables.

A Proposed Modal Criterion Setting

Cook and Campbell (1976) and Tunnel (1977) have discussed techniques for increasing external validity. One model recommended has been termed "generalization to modal instances" (Cook & Campbell, 1976, p. 286). This practical model requires a specification of respondents, work settings, and conditions of testing which are modal for a given research area. Let's say we're trying to develop a model of the performance appraisal process. External validity for our model would be quite low if student ratings of either professors or hypothetical vignette ratees were used as the method of study. Other than generalizing to somewhat different situations involving student ratings of professors, one would have to seriously question the generalizability of such research. However, a model or theory of the appraisal process which has been tested under conditions most common for appraisal should be more generalizable. Emphasis in this approach should, of course, be placed on common psychological variables with the importance of "mundane realism" dependent on the psychological compatibility of the testing and criterion settings, that is, to the extent that mundane realism augments psychological realism, it is important. A number of practitioners were surveyed for purposes of developing a modal appraisal situation. If one then chooses to adopt this practical model for enhancing external validity, the modal appraisal characteristics will be available.

A questionnaire was prepared in order to derive a modal criterion setting. Questions were written for each of the fifteen relevant parameters of a performance appraisal system identified by Bernardin and Beatty (1984). In addition, practitioners were asked to indicate for which purposes the appraisal data serve (Bernardin & Beatty, 1984, p. 8). A total of 125 personnel administrators who were members of either American Society of Personnel Administrators or the International Personnel Management Association completed the survey. The public and private sectors were equally represented. Respondents were asked to indicate the most common characteristics of performance appraisal systems within their organization. The survey was mailed to a random sample of 150 members of each association. Time precluded a larger scale study. Given the small sample used, the proposed modal criterion setting presented should be interpreted with caution. The results of the survey are summarized in table 3–3. Despite all the hoopla over behavioral rating scales, trait ratings are apparently still the most common format across both public and private sector organizations. Ratings are used for important personnel decisions, although public sector respondents indicated that step increases were for the most part automatic regardless of the type of rating form used.

This modal criterion setting is proposed as a frame of reference for assessing the generalizability and potential generalizability of appraisal research. The model is not by any means a recommended system of appraisal. In fact, there are several modal characteristics which are anathema to current academic recommendations. However, we can predict that the greater the compatibility of the research setting with the modal criterion setting, the greater the probability that a finding in the research setting will generalize to a greater number of real appraisal situations. Certainly some of the modal characteristics can be considered more essential than others. Thus, in the construction of laboratory paradigms or the selection of field settings, researchers concerned about generalizability should attempt to hold constant or manipulate such characteristics in their research. For example, a laboratory finding that BARS ratings were less lenient than trait ratings would have very

Table 3–3
Proposed Modal Criterion Setting

1. A supervisor evaluates the performance of six subordinates on an individual basis.
2. Ratees sign off on the rating form and indicate whether they agree or disagree with the rating.
3. A supervisor's ratings are signed off at the next highest level. A supervisor's boss rarely disagrees.
4. Ratees are aware of how fellow workers are evaluated.
5. Ratings are done on an annual basis.
6. Ratings are used as a basis for important personnel decisions (such as step increases and merit pay).
7. Raters feel they don't have adequate time in order to do good performance appraisals.
8. Supervisors are responsible for subordinate work products, that is, supervisory evaluations are affected by subordinate performance.
9. Supervisors have performed the major tasks of the subordinates' jobs.
10. Important countable results are unavailable.
11. Raters feel they themselves rate more accurately than other raters.
12. Raters feel uncomfortable doing appraisals.
13. Supervisors do not feel that formal performance appraisals play a major role in performance feedback for subordinates.
14. Raters evaluate ratee traits (such as dependability, attitude, and initiative).
15. Ratings are formally made relative to scale content, not persons.

little potential for generalizability when modal characteristics 2, 4, 6, 7, 8, and 11 are not a part of the laboratory conditions. To the extent that these characteristics are either manipulated or held constant in the laboratory setting, there is a greater probability that the finding will generalize. Of course, the key here is the psychological fidelity of the research setting and the criterion setting rather than the literal similarity. It is thus not essential that ratees sign off on a rating form (modal characteristic #2). It is probably essential, however, that raters believe that ratees will see the resultant ratings. Results from the survey to be discussed in the next section should help identify the essential psychological variables of interest.

Factors Affecting Appraisal Accuracy

Our survey work also revealed the extent to which practitioners believe rating accuracy is affected by various appraisal factors. We content analyzed narratives describing the various factors affecting rating accuracy and found twenty relatively independent factors. We then asked another group of supervisors, subordinates, and administrators to indicate the extent to which they felt each of the factors was affecting rating accuracy. We then compared this result to our content analysis of the research in terms of these factors, that is, whether a factor was manipulated, held constant, or even considered.

The narratives were written by forty-two supervisors representing twenty-seven private and eight public organizations, seventy personnel administrators representing thirty-one private and twenty-four public organizations, and ninety-six subordinates representing twelve private and eight public organizations. Unfortunately, this sample can in no way be considered random. It represents participants from several seminars, responses to a questionnaire mailed to members of the American Society of Personnel Administrators, and future raters in projects related to performance appraisal. Supervisors and personnel administrators also wrote narratives regarding their experiences as ratees. A total of 155 useful narratives were written in response to the following question:

> Based on your own personal experience, what factors contribute the most to inaccuracy (accuracy) in performance appraisal? Write a description of a first hand experience you have had as a performance rater, an administrator of an appraisal system, or as the object of a performance appraisal which illustrates what you view as the major reasons for the inaccuracy (accuracy) in appraisal.

The 155 narratives were then clustered into categories by two graduate students and a separate Likert-type item was written for each cluster (see table 3–4). A survey was then conducted to measure the extent to which administrators, raters, and ratees felt each of the factors contributed to appraisal inaccuracy in their organization. Table 3–4 also presents the mean ratings for each of the factors. The surveys were completed by a nonrandom sample of supervisors, personnel administrators, and subordinates who had participated in one or more seminars in personnel management or who were students in an MBA program. A total of fifty,

Table 3–4
Major Factors Affecting Appraisal Inaccuracy

To what extent is each statement related to appraisal inaccuracy in your organization?
5   To a great extent
4   To a significant extent
3   To some extent
2   To a limited extent
1   Not at all

	Supervisors N = 85	Administrators N = 38	Subordinates N = 134
1. Raters have personal prejudices against certain employees.	2.5	2.7	3.5
2. Raters don't have enough time to devote to performance appraisal.	3.8	2.9	2.5
3. Raters do not consider performance appraisal to be important relative to other duties.	3.2	3.9	2.7
4. Raters are unaware of or do not consider performance factors beyond the control of the employee.	2.4	2.8	4.0
5. Raters do not sample a sufficient amount of ratee behavior.	2.2	3.0	3.2
6. Raters do not understand the employee's job.	2.3	2.5	3.6
7. Raters rate higher than deserved to please certain employees.	3.4	3.6	4.4
8. Raters rate higher than deserved to promote a troublesome employee.	2.4	2.1	1.5
9. Raters rate higher than deserved because they prefer to avoid confrontations.	3.9	3.8	2.2
10. Raters rate higher than deserved because there is no one telling them to rate lower.	2.5	3.9	2.7
11. Raters rate higher than deserved because of friendship.	3.0	3.3	3.4
12. Raters rate lower than deserved in order to get rid of a troublesome employee.	2.1	2.5	2.5
13. Raters feel uncomfortable evaluating other people.	3.7	3.6	2.4
14. Raters have ambiguous criteria on which to rate (for example, personality traits).	3.2	4.2	3.6
15. Raters do not consider all important aspects of an employee's job.	2.4	2.9	3.2
16. Raters are not rewarded for accurate appraisals.	3.4	4.0	3.3
17. Raters avoid the whole responsibility if they possibly can.	2.6	2.9	2.2
18. Raters forget how employees performed early in the appraisal period.	2.3	3.1	2.8
19. Raters weight how the employee performed late in the appraisal period more heavily than early performance.	2.4	3.1	2.9
20. Raters attach too much weight to relatively unimportant performance factors.	2.5	3.0	3.7

twenty-nine, and sixty-eight different private and public sector organizations were represented in responses by the supervisors, administrators, and subordinates, respectively.

We have drawn several implications from these results with regard to essential research needs in performance appraisal. As we see them, the major implications are:

1. Supervisors and administrators feel factors related to a deliberate motivation to distort ratings have more to do with inaccuracy than the ability to rate. Subordinates felt that factors related to the rater's knowledge about the rated job were relatively more important. The importance attached to rater motivational factors by raters and administrators suggests a need to study this general source of rating variance and to investigate methods to control deliberate distortion, including rater training. Our review found very few studies which addressed the issue of deliberate rating distortion. One recent study which investigated deliberate rating distortion by raters found strong effects (Bernardin & Orban, 1984). The survey results also suggest we should look more carefully at rating formats designed to control rating distortion, such as forced choice.

   One boundary variable identified as critical in terms of leniency is the extent of positive consequences for the rater who inflates ratings. An inflated rating can be predicted, for example, if the consequence of such a rating is to promote an obnoxious subordinate into a new division. Under those conditions, a training program aimed at enhancing observational skills will probably not inhibit leniency error or increase accuracy. Kane and Lawler (1979) discussed the issue of rater motivation in the context of the "tendency to dissemble." They viewed this tendency as a function of the probability of being detected in making invalid ratings, the expected value to the rater of making invalid ratings, and the expected disincentive value to the rater if invalid ratings are exposed. Kane (1980) has developed these relationships into their expectancy components. This suggests a study in which leniency is regressed on the expectancy components. We were unable to identify any studies which investigated this relationship. Our survey results indicate practitioners would be most interested in such a study and, of course, realistic interventions which could reduce the tendency to dissemble.

2. The greatest difference in responses between supervisors and subordinates concerned the extent to which raters adequately consider factors affecting employees which are beyond the employees' control (item 4 in table 3–4). Subordinates thought this was a source of inaccuracy to a "significant extent" while supervisors thought it was a problem only to a "limited extent." This finding is of course in line with applied predictions in attribution theory (see chapter 4 of this book) and suggests a rater training program which focuses on identifying potential constraints on individual performance and defining and

agreeing with the subordinate on the boundaries of causality as much as possible prior to the appraisal period. Subordinate agreement with the supervisor's appraisal would be a useful dependent variable. It would not be difficult to conceptualize a laboratory setting which could be used to unambiguously test such an approach to training. The boundary variable that should be manipulated in the laboratory is the ambiguity in attributions regarding individual performance and the alleged constraints. In a field study, Bernardin (1984) successfully reduced disagreements in self versus supervisory appraisals as a function of this training.

3. Subordinates also felt that supervisors did not really understand the subordinates' jobs (see items 5, 6, 14, 15, and 20 in table 3–4). For example, supervisors do not weight the various job factors appropriately in making their ratings. More specifically, a rater may attribute more importance to the successful completion of some aspects of the job while discounting the importance of others. That is, the job and its various components may be redefined in a personal manner by the incumbent. Some aspects of the job are viewed as more important, perhaps due to the ability of the incumbent to perform them, while other aspects of the job are discounted because the incumbent does not perform them as well. It is likely that such redefinitions and attributions of job criticality may lead to different rater strategies with some raters giving more weight to the successful performance of some aspects of the job, and other raters viewing other tasks as more crucial. These redefinitions and attributions of criticality, as noted above, may stem from the rater's own ability or previous success at performing the tasks required.

No research has yet been conducted to investigate this phenomenon. Attempts have been made, however, that suggest this may be a worthwhile area of study. For example, Mitchell and Kalb (1982) showed that supervisors who have had experience with a subordinate's job tend to attribute poor performance to external factors. However, supervisors with little experience on the job may attribute the performance of a poorly performing subordinate to internal factors in accordance with the actor-observer bias commonly found in attribution studies. For supervisors who make more attributions to external causes for poor performance, the performance appraisals may be more lenient; likewise, supervisors with no experience may be more severe raters. Also, in the former condition, there would probably be greater agreement between rater and ratee on the rater's appraisal.

Little research has been directed at discovering the role of attributions for the performance of others on performance appraisal. What is commonly assumed is that a ratee is evaluated on a continuum of success or proficiency on the job. Process variables such as attributions for this level of performance are often neglected, leading to confusion as to whether the rater is rating performance per se, or other attributes of the ratee such as effort or ability.

Now that we have recognized this omission in performance appraisal research, how might we study it? One possible way is to use a paradigm similar to that of

Mitchell and Kalb (1982), in which raters are first provided with experience on the job on which they will be rating subordinates' performance. Some supervisors may be "held out," that is, not given any experience with the job. There will have to be some inducement in the form of a monetary incentive to realistically involve the raters. Further, unlike the Mitchell and Kalb paradigm, several levels of performance outcomes may be desired, as well as several levels of supervisory experience with the subordinates' job.

More important, and certainly more difficult to achieve in the lab, is the definition of task criticality mentioned above. Such a redefinition of task criticality will require an extended period of incumbency on the part of the rater. This may preclude a direct test of the effects of rater experience in the lab. Perhaps one means would be to explore this in a field setting. A rater's past performance record on the job that he now supervises may be used as an independent variable in the ratings of subordinates. Also, different levels of performance on the various dimensions may prove to be useful covariates that can be used to obtain an unbiased appraisal of subordinate performance, one free of rater idiosyncrasies with regard to differential weighting of performance. Since many U.S. companies use internal promotions as a standard practice and many also use task-based appraisal systems, a field test of the above would be very useful providing sufficient variance is available.

Discussion

Our literature review and two surveys lead to several suggestions for future research. As stated earlier, forced choice scales and mixed standard scales were specifically developed to control or eliminate deliberate rating distortion, a condition indicated in our survey to be most evident when appraisal data were used for important decisions (a modal characteristic). Is it possible to study the effects of these formats in the laboratory with students in such a way that the results may be generalizable to the modal criterion setting? With regard to the purpose boundary variable, the typical method for manipulating purpose of the appraisal is unacceptable. In general, this method has amounted to a single line in the directions provided to raters (for example, these ratings will be used as feedback to the instructor; they will be used to decide whether this instructor receives a merit increase). Our survey data indicated that raters typically rate with the knowledge that they will interact with the ratee subsequent to the rating process. All of these factors should affect the tendency to dissemble and thus should be either manipulated or held constant in a format comparison involving a method specifically designed to control that tendency.

It is possible to control these aspects of performance which are to be rated (for example, by videotape) while still providing an experimental context involving some or all of the modal characteristics discussed above. Thus, one or more instructors' lectures could be videotaped and the same person could interact before and after the viewing of the videotape in such a way that all of the critical modal variables could either be manipulated or held constant. Ratings from forced choice scales should then be more accurate (using "true scores") and less lenient than more transparent scales. Such a design would provide either a between- or within-subjects comparison of the two supposedly nontransparent formats as well.

What external validity might this have? We believe a great deal. Florida and Tennessee have passed legislation mandating state-administered performance-based merit pay systems for their teachers. Given cost considerations, the only realistic rating source for such appraisals is probably in the individual schools (for example, principals, assistant principals), where the tendency to dissemble would be great. A rating format which can control this inevitable problem would undoubtedly be welcomed by state administrators concerned about rating inflation, where numbers are to be linked to monetary allocations.

Regarding rater training, our literature review indicated that training efforts typically focused on providing raters with an opportunity to acquire better rating skills while disregarding the raters' motivation to acquire and/or use the skills. Again, a motivational component that could act as a critical boundary variable seems to have been omitted in our research. What form might research take in investigating this critical variable? One suggestion we make is to vary the amount of disincentive to dissemble. This could be done by using a policy-capturing approach to understand raters' weighting of performance information and consequent biases. For example, raters could participate in an organizationally sponsored program designed to uncover rater inconsistency and inaccuracy. Via videotape raters would be presented with orthogonally varied performance outcomes on various dimensions. The profile of each rater's performance-rating policy could be reviewed in a separate meeting between the rater and his immediate supervisor. Implementing such a program allows the identification of rater idiosyncrasies and the communication to the rater that the organization has the capability to discover rating bias. Bernardin and Beatty (1984) have suggested other potentially useful areas which are amenable to both laboratory and field methods.

Summary

We find that the fit between the research literature and the modal criterion setting of our survey can be likened to that of fitting square pegs into round holes. There appears to be an increasing emphasis on methodologically unconfounded, internally valid laboratory and field research, the results of which have added little to our understanding of performance appraisal. In the immortal words of Robert Wherry, "We don't know what we are doing, but we are doing it very carefully and hope you are pleased with our unintelligent diligence" (1957, p. 1). We should add that we are also doing it very quickly since such research is so easy to conduct. The research paradigms currently in vogue establish an appraisal situation which is far more like assessment in assessment centers, or work samples, or ratings of employment interviewees. There is also considerable overlap between this type of performance appraisal research and laboratory research on leadership (Bernardin & Beatty, 1984). Yet there is little attempt to merge the research literature.

A modal criterion setting has been proposed as a framework for future research methodologies on the general type of performance appraisal conducted in over 90 percent of U.S. organizations. Certainly a more systematic and detailed delineation of the modal setting is in order. Another survey has identified several critical issues related to appraisal which have been largely ignored in both laboratory and field studies. The results of this and similar surveys should direct applied researchers to areas most in need of "application" and help in the development of more psychologically realistic research settings.

References

1. Aleamoni, L.M., & Hexner, P.Z. (1980) A review of the research on student evaluation and a report on the effect of different sets of instructions on student course and instructor evaluations. *Instructional Science, 9,* 67–84.

2. Arvey, R.D., & Hoyle, J.C. (1974) A Guttman approach to the development of behaviorally based rating scales for systems analysts and programmer/analysts. *Journal of Applied Psychology, 59,* 61–68.

3. Bayroff, A., Haggerty, H., & Rundquist, E. (1954) Validity of ratings as related to rating techniques and conditions. *Personnel Psychology, 7,* 93–114.

4. Bendig, A.W. (1954) Reliability and number of rating scale categories. *Journal of Applied Psychology, 38,* 38–40.

5. Bazerman, M., & Atkin, R. (1982) *Performance appraisal: A model of the rater and an empirical test.* Unpublished manuscript, Boston University, School of Management.

6. Berkowitz, L., & Donnerstein, E. (1982) External validity is more than skin deep. *American Psychologist, 37,* 245–257.

7. Berkshire, J.R., & Highland, R.W. (1953) Forced-choice performance rating: A methodological study. *Personnel Psychology, 6,* 355–378.

8. Bernardin, H.J. (1978) Effects of rater training on leniency and halo errors in student ratings of instructors. *Journal of Applied Psychology, 63,* 301–308.

9. Bernardin, H.J. (1980) *Frame of reference training to increase interrater agreement in field training officer ratings.* Technical Report to the Law Enforcement Assistance Administration, U.S. Department of Justice.

10. Bernardin, H.J. (1984) *Attributional training to increase self versus supervisory performance appraisals.* Unpublished manuscript, Florida Atlantic University, College of Business, Boca Raton.

11. Bernardin, H.J., Abbott, J.R., & Cooper, D. (1984) The effects of appraisal purpose and training on rating characteristics. *Proceedings of the Southern Management Association,* 217–224.

12. Bernardin, H.J., & Beatty, R.W. (1984) *Performance appraisal: Assessing human behavior at work.* Boston: Kent-Wadsworth.

13. Bernardin, H.J., & Boetcher, L.R. (1978) *The effects of rater training and cognitive complexity on psychometric error in ratings.* Paper presented at the American Psychological Association.

14. Bernardin, H.J. & Cardy, R.L. (1982) Appraisal accuracy: The ability and motivation to remember the past. *Public Personnel Management Journal, 11,* 352-357.

15. Bernardin, H.J., Elliott, L., & Carlyle, J.J. (1980) A critical assessment of mixed standard rating scales. *Proceedings of the Academy of Management,* 308-312.

16. Bernardin, H.J., Erickson, J.B., Orban, J.A., Buckley, M.R., & Goretsky, C.H. (1981) *Frame of reference training with moderate and high performance, feedback, and diary-keeping: The effect on rater accuracy.* Paper presented at the Academy of Management.

17. Bernardin, H.J., & Orban, J. (1984) *Leniency effect as a function of rating format, purpose for appraisal and rater individual differences.* Paper presented at the annual meeting of the Academy of Management.

18. Bernardin, H.J., & Pence, E.C. (1980) Rater training: Creating new response sets and decreasing accuracy. *Journal of Applied Psychology, 65,* 60-66.

19. Bernardin, H.J., & Smith, P.C. (1981) A clarification of some issues regarding the development and use of behaviorally anchored rating scales. *Journal of Applied Psychology, 66,* 458-463.

20. Bernardin, H.J., & Walter, C.S. (1977) The effects of rater training and diary keeping on psychometric error in ratings. *Journal of Applied Psychology, 62,* 64-69.

21. Borman, W.C. (1975) Effects of instructions to avoid halo error on reliability and validity of performance evaluation ratings. *Journal of Applied Psychology, 60,* 556-560.

22. Borman, W.C. (1978) Exploring upper limits of reliability and validity in performance ratings. *Journal of Applied Psychology, 63,* 135-144.

23. Borman, W.C. (1979) Format and training effects of rating accuracy and rater errors. *Journal of Applied Psychology, 64,* 410-421.

24. Borman, W.C. (1986) Behavioral approaches to evaluating individuals' work performance. In R. Berk (Ed.), *Performance assessment: The state of the art.* Baltimore: Johns Hopkins University Press.

25. Borreson, H.A. (1967) The effects of instructions and item content on three types of ratings. *Educational and Psychological Measurement, 27,* 855-862.

26. Brown, E.M. (1968) Influence of training, method, and relationship on the halo effect. *Journal of Applied Psychology, 52,* 195-199.

27. Buckley, M.R., & Bernardin, H.J. (1980) *An assessment of the components of an observer training program.* Paper presented at the Southeastern Psychological Association.

28. Campbell, J.P., Daft, R.L., & Hulin, C.L. (1982) *What to study: Generating and developing research questions.* Beverly Hills: Sage.

29. Campbell, J.P., Dunnette, M.D., Arvey, R.D., & Hellervik, L.V. (1973) The development and evaluation of behaviorally based rating scales. *Journal of Applied Psychology, 57,* 15-22.

30. Campbell, J.P., Dunnette, M.D., Lawler, E.E., & Weick, K.E. (1970) *Managerial behavior, performance, and effectiveness.* New York: McGraw-Hill.

31. Cardy, R.L., Dobbins, G.H., & Keefe, T.J. (1984) *Rater training and appraisal accuracy: An examination of the frame of reference approach.* Unpublished manuscript, State University of New York at Buffalo.

32. Cook, T.D., & Campbell, D.T. (1976) The design and conduct of quasi-experiments and true experiments in field settings. In M.D. Dunnette (Ed.), *Handbook of industrial and organizational psychology.* Chicago: Rand McNally.

33. Cotton, J., & Stolz, R.E. (1960) The general applicability of a scale for rating research productivity. *Journal of Applied Psychology, 44,* 276–277.

34. Cummings, L.L. (1983) Performance-evaluation systems in the context of individual trust and commitment. In F. Landy, S. Zedeck, & J. Cleveland (Eds.), *Performance measurement and theory.* Hillsdale, NJ: Lawrence Erlbaum.

35. Dickinson, T.L. & Zellinger, P.M. (1980) A comparison of the behaviorally anchored rating and mixed standard scale formats. *Journal of Applied Psychology, 65,* 147–154.

36. Driscoll, L.A., & Goodwin, W.L. (1979) The effects of varying information about use and disposition of results on university students' evaluations of faculty and courses. *American Educational Research Journal, 16,* 25–37.

37. Edwards, J.E. (1982) *Format and training effects in the control of halo and leniency.* Paper presented at the Academy of Management.

38. Fay, C.H., & Latham, G.P. (1982) Effects of training and rating scales on rating errors. *Personnel Psychology, 35,* 104–116.

39. Fromkin, H.L. & Streufert, S. (1976) Laboratory experimentation. In M.D. Dunnette (Ed.), *Handbook of industrial and organizational psychology.* Chicago: Rand McNally, 415–466.

40. Fusilier, M.R. (1980) The effects of anonymity and outcome contingencies on rater beliefs and behavior in a performance appraisal situation. *Proceedings of the Academy of Management,* 273–277.

41. Green, L., Bernardin, H.J., & Abbott, J.R. (in press) A comparison of rating formats after correction for attenuation. *Educational and Psychological Measurement.*

42. Hedge, J.W. (1984) *Rater training.* Unpublished manuscript, Brook Air Force Base, San Antonio, Tex.

43. Ivancevich, J.M. (1979) Longitudinal study of the effects of rater training on psychometric error in ratings. *Journal of Applied Psychology, 64,* 502–508.

44. Jacobs, R. (in press) Variations for rating scales: Much ado about nothing. In R. Berk (Ed.), *Performance assessment: The state of the art.* Baltimore: Johns Hopkins University Press.

45. Kane, J.S. (1980) *Performance distribution assessment: A new framework for conceiving and appraising job performance.* Unpublished manuscript, University of Massachusetts, Amherst, Department of Management.

46. Kane, J.S. & Lawler, E.E. (1979) Performance appraisal effectiveness: Its assessment and determinants. In B. Staw (Ed.), *Research in organizational behavior (Vol 1).* Greenwich, Conn.: JAI Press.

47. King, L.M., Hunter, J.E., & Schmidt, F.L. (1980) Halo in multidimensional forced-choice performance evaluation scale. *Journal of Applied Psychology, 65,* 507–516.

48. Latham, G.P., Wexley, K.N., & Pursell, E.D. (1975) Training managers to minimize rating errors in the observation of behavior. *Journal of Applied Psychology, 60,* 550–555.

49. Levine, J., & Butler, J. (1952) Lecture versus group discussion in changing behavior. *Journal of Applied Psychology, 36,* 29–33.

50. Maher, H. (1959) Studies of transparency in forced-choice scales: I. Evidence of transparency. *Journal of Applied Psychology, 43,* 275–278.

51. McIntyre, R.M., & Bentson, C.A. (1984) *A comparison of methods for training behavioral observations: Modeling works.* Paper presented at the American Psychological Association.

52. McIntyre, R.M., Smith, D.E., & Hassett, C.E. (1984) Accuracy of performance ratings as affected by rater training and perceived purpose of rating. *Journal of Applied Psychology, 69,* 147–156.

53. Mitchell, T.R, & Kalb, L.S. (1982) Effects of job experience on supervisor attributions for a subordinate's poor performance. *Journal of Applied Psychology, 67,* 181–188.

54. Murphy, K.R., Balzer, W., Kellam, K, & Armstrong, J. (1983) *Purpose of rating and accuracy in observing behavior and evaluating performance.* Paper presented at the annual meeting of the American Psychological Association, Anaheim, Calif.

55. Murphy, K.R., Kellam, K.L., Balzer, W.K., & Armstrong, J.G. (1982) *Effects of the purpose of rating on accuracy in observing and evaluating performance.* Unpublished manuscript, New York University, New York.

56. Naylor, J.C., Pritchard, R.D., & Ilgen, D.R. (1980) *A theory of behavior in organizations.* New York: Academic Press.

57. Pulakos, E.D. (1984a) A comparison of rater training programs: Error training and accuracy training. *Journal of Applied Psychology, 69,* 581–588.

58. Pulakos, E.D. (1984b) *The development of training programs to increase accuracy with different rating tasks.* Unpublished manuscript, Personnel Decisions Research Institute, Minneapolis, Minn.

59. Ross, L. (1977) The intuitive psychologist and his shortcomings: Distortions in the attribution process. In L. Berkowitz (Ed.), *Advances in experimental social psychology* (vol. 10). New York: Academic Press.

60. Rozelle, R.M., & Baxter, J.C. (1981) Influence of role pressures on the perceiver: Judgments of videotaped interviews varying judge accountability and responsibility. *Journal of Applied Psychology, 66,* 437–441.

61. Saal, F.E., & Landy, F.J. (1977) The mixed standard rating scale: An evaluation. *Organizational Behavior and Human Performance, 18,* 19–35.

62. Sauser, W.I., & Pond, S.B. (1981) Effects of rater training and participation on cognitive complexity: An exploration of Schneier's cognitive reinterpretation. *Personnel Psychology, 34,* 609–626.

63. Schmidt, F.L. (1977) *The measurement of job performance.* Unpublished manuscript, U.S. Office of Personnel Management.

64. Senderak, M.P. (1984) Improving rating accuracy through rater schematic training and rating task simplification. Unpublished doctoral dissertation, Virginia Polytechnic Institute and State University, Blacksburg.

65. Shapira, Z., & Shirom, A. (1980) New issues in the use of behaviorally anchored rating scales: Level of analysis, the effects of incident frequency, and external validation. *Journal of Applied Psychology, 65,* 517–523.

66. Sharon, A.T., & Bartlett, C.J. (1969) Effect of instructional conditions in producing leniency on two types of rating scales. *Personnel Psychology, 22,* 251–263.

67. Sisson, E.D. (1948) Forced choices: The new army rating. *Personnel Psychology, 1,* 365–381.

68. Smith, D.E., Hassett, C.E., & McIntyre, R.M. (1982) *Using student ratings for administrative decisions: Are ratings contaminated by perceived uses of the information?* Paper presented at the meeting of the Western Academy of Management, Colorado Springs, Colo.

69. Smith, D.E., & Thornton, G.C. (1984) *Rater training programs based on Borman's performance appraisal model: Increasing rating accuracy.* Unpublished manuscript, Colorado State University, Ft. Campbell.

70. Spool, M.D. (1979) *Rater training to increase inter-rater agreement.* Unpublished manuscript, Marathon Oil, Findley, Ohio.

71. Stockford, L., & Bissell, H.W. (1949) Factors involved in establishing a merit rating scale. *Personnel, 26,* 94–116.

72. Taylor, E.K., & Wherry, R.J. (1951) A study of leniency in two rating systems. *Personnel Psychology, 4,* 39–47.

73. Taylor, K., Bernardin, H.J., & Riegelhaupt, B.J. (1984) Halo error: An assessment of priming as a reduction technique. *Perceptual and Motor Skills, 59,* 447–457.

74. Thornton, G.C., & Zorich, S. (1980) Training to improve observer accuracy. *Journal of Applied Psychology, 65,* 351–354.

75. Tunnell, G.B. (1977) Three dimensions of naturalness: An expanded definition of field research. *Psychological Bulletin, 84,* 426–437.

76. Veres, J.C., Field, H.S., & Bayles, W.R. (1983) Administrative vs. research performance ratings: An empirical test of rating data quality. *Public Personnel Management, 12,* 290–298.

77. Wakeley, J.H. (1961) *The effects of specific training on accuracy in judging others.* Unpublished doctoral dissertation, Michigan State University, East Lansing.

78. Warmke, D.L., & Billings, R.S. (1979) Comparison of training methods for improving the psychometric quality of experimental and administrative performance ratings. *Journal of Applied Psychology, 64,* 124–131.

79. Wetzel, C.G., Wilson, T.D., & Kort, J. (1981) The halo effect revisited: Forewarned is not forearmed. *Journal of Experimental Social Psychology, 17,* 427–439.

80. Wherry, R.J. (1957) The past and future of criterion evaluation. *Personnel Psychology, 10,* 1–5.

81. Williams, K.J., DeNisi, A.S., Blencoe, A.G., & Cafferty, T.P. (1985) The role of appraisal purpose in information acquisition and utilization. *Organizational Behavior and Human Decision Processes, 35,* 314–339.

82. Zedeck, S., & Cascio, W. (1982). Performance appraisal decisions as a function of rater training and purpose of the appraisal. *Journal of Applied Psychology, 67,* 752–758.

4

Attribution Theory: A Meta-Analysis of Attributional Hypotheses

Christy L. De Vader
Allan G. Bateson
Robert G. Lord

Attributional principles have become increasingly important for understanding perceptions in a number of applied areas such as performance appraisal, leadership, and motivation (Calder, 1977; Green & Mitchell, 1979; Mitchell, Green, & Wood, 1981; Phillips & Lord, 1981; Wood & Mitchell, 1981). Yet the fundamental question of whether attributional results generalize from laboratory to field settings has not been empirically addressed. This issue is important because performance appraisal, leadership, and motivation are areas which are particularly conducive to research in field settings. In addition, there exists a substantial data base developed in the laboratory on related social psychological topics such as interpersonal and group processes on which to formulate hypotheses that may explain events that occur in real world settings. We will address the issue of generalizing results from laboratory to field settings by using a quantitative form of meta-analysis labeled *validity generalization* to integrate the ambiguous or contradictory findings of separate studies on the same topic.

Validity Generalization

Validity generalization, one type of meta-analysis, was developed within the context of industrial-organizational psychology by Schmidt and Hunter, and their colleagues (Schmidt & Hunter, 1977; Schmidt, Gast-Rosenberg, & Hunter, 1980). Validity generalization has several advantages over other meta-analytic techniques. First, it corrects for some sources of artifactual variance across studies. Second, it provides an estimate of the population effect size, whereas many meta-analyses focus only on cumulating significance indices. Third, it provides a test of homogeneity of variance, which gauges whether the results of the studies come from a single population or whether situational variables moderate the effect size distribution (Hunter, Schmidt, & Jackson, 1982).

Validity generalization postulates seven sources of artifactual variance which may act to reduce or attenuate individual study results: sampling error, differences across studies in criterion and predictor reliability, differences across studies in range restriction, clerical errors, criterion contamination, and mistakes in data analysis. The three sources of error which it is practical to estimate when cumulating studies are those sources due to sampling, predictor unreliability, and range restriction.

It is interesting to note that sampling error has accounted for the majority of explained variance in validity generalization studies. Since sampling error is simply a function of the N-size of the different studies, it is always possible to precisely estimate for sampling error since all studies will report sample size. Reliability and range restriction in predictors, however, are often left unreported so that assumed distributions must be used to estimate these additional sources of artifactual variance (Alexander, Carson, Alliger, & Cronshaw, 1984; Pearlman, Schmidt, & Hunter, 1980).

Applying the Schmidt-Hunter validity generalization technique requires the calculation of an N-size weighted mean r as the best estimate of the population correlation. Next, the N-size weighted total variance of the sample correlations around the mean is calculated. This is usually called the observed variance. It is this observed variance which is inflated to a certain extent by sampling error and other artifacts. The variance due to these artifacts is then estimated (see Hunter et al., 1982, for this and other formulas), and this estimate is subtracted from the observed variance. The issue then becomes whether the remaining residual variance is small enough to warrant the conclusion that all the observed correlations came from a single population. If 75 percent or more of the variance can be explained by methodological artifacts, then the assumption of homogeneity is warranted (Pearlman et al., 1980; Schmidt & Hunter, 1981). By grouping together both lab and field studies that test a similar set of hypotheses it is possible to determine whether the correlations came from a single population. When homogeneity exists, a search for moderator variables is not necessary and generalization from laboratory to field settings is warranted. If less than 75 percent of the variance is accounted for, it is not possible to generalize from the lab to the field. When heterogeneity exists, this procedure can be repeated separately for the lab and field data. Homogeneity within settings and heterogeneity when aggregating across settings would provide the clearest indications that laboratory results do not generalize to field settings.

In addition to the corrections to the observed variance, the frequency-weighted mean r is corrected for attenuation caused by criterion unreliability and range restriction. This corrected mean r is a final estimate of the unattenuated population r which is the best estimate of the population correlation for each of the relationships under consideration.

Attribution Hypotheses Tested

The hypotheses tested were selected on the basis of two criteria. First, the hypothesis had to be central to attribution theory. Second, there had to be enough data for each principle to use the validity generalization procedure. Consequently, the following principles were selected to be of primary interest: Weiner's ability, luck, task difficulty, and effort dimensions; actor-observer differences; Kelley's covariation principles of consistency, consensus, and distinctiveness; egocentric or self-serving biases; attributions of responsibility; and causality attributions.

Attributions served mainly as dependent variables. Insufficient numbers of studies were located to perform the analyses for all hypotheses in each of the three topical areas. The studies included in the analyses and the topical domain(s) for which they were relevant are indicated in table 4–1.

Lord and Smith (1983) discuss attribution theory and, more specifically, the types of attributions made under three different categories: causality for a specific event, responsibility for a specific outcome, and the personal qualities of those persons involved in the specific event of interest. This chapter focuses on causal and responsibility attributions for the topical areas of leadership, motivation, and performance appraisal.

Assessments of causality require the attributor to produce an explanation for the event of interest. More specifically, the attributor must determine whether the event would have occurred without the presence of a specific factor (Hamilton, 1980). In general, for performance appraisal, supervisors were required to assess whether an individual's performance level was due to any of a number of causal factors such as effort, ability, and external characteristics.

In the topical domain of leadership, causal explanations were provided for the leader's own performance or for the performance of subordinates. Causal assessments for an individual's motivation were made in a similar manner.

Responsibility attributions typically involve asking the question of whether an individual's actions or behavior were responsible for the outcome of interest. If so, the next issue involves a determination of the sanctions for the successful/unsuccessful outcomes on the basis of whether the individual could have done otherwise (Hamilton, 1980).

For performance appraisal, the supervisor judges the degree of responsibility of a subordinate for performance and subsequent outcomes of a particular task.

Table 4–1
Studies Included in the Analyses by Topical Area

Topical Area	References
Performance appraisal	1, 5, 9, 10, 13, 17, 18, 20, 22, 23, 24, 27, 28, 29, 30, 31, 33, 34, 36, 37, 39, 40, 41, 42, 43, 44, 47, 48, 50, 56, 57, 58, 59, 60
Leadership	2, 7, 15, 16, 17, 25, 26, 29, 30, 35, 40, 53, 54, 55
Motivation	2, 3, 4, 6, 8, 11, 12, 14, 19, 21, 32, 38, 45, 46, 51, 52, 57

Attributions of leader responsibility are made for organizational, group, or leader performance. Measurement of the motivation involved in responsibility attributions consists of the determination of a significant interaction of motivation and performance. To elaborate, high motivation and high performance result in an internal attribution while high motivation and low performance result in an external attribution.

Performance Appraisal

In the performance appraisal area, four major attributional hypotheses were tested (see table 4–2). The first concerned attributions of causality (Weiner, Frieze, Kukla, Reed, Rest, & Rosenbaum, 1971). The hypothesis tested was that differential performance would affect attributions to each of the four causal dimensions. Laboratory studies manipulated level of performance, while field studies usually selected participants based on prior performance evaluations. Typically, supervisors, superiors, or peers evaluated the performance of one or more workers. Workers were selected who varied with respect to performance level (high-low) and outcomes (successful-unsuccessful). In this way, studies tested the hypothesis that both performance level and outcome affect whether performance is attributed to effort, luck, ability, or task difficulty in a working situation.

Variability existed in how the four causal factors were organized or measured. With respect to performance appraisal the measures formed three different groupings. Those grouped according to locus of causality (internal/external) predicted that good (successful) performance would be attributed to high ability and greater effort than poor (unsuccessful) performance, which should be attributed to low ability and low effort. The second set of studies, grouped according to stability, hypothesized that unexpected performance is attributed to luck and effort while expected performance is attributed to ability and task difficulty. The final group of studies reported results separately for each causal dimension. Recorded for each study was the specific hypothesis tested, a measure of effect size, and descriptive information about the study.

The second hypothesis examined under performance appraisal involved the existence of actor-observer differences, that is, whether actors and observers made different attributions for a person's performance such that actors (workers) attributed their own performance to the situation whereas observers (supervisors and coworkers) attributed the performance of the individual being rated to internal, dispositional characteristics. Generally, the actor/observer difference was implemented having two separate individuals make attributional ratings. A few studies modified this approach and required each individual to provide attributions for their own and another's performance.

Kelley's covariation hypotheses were also examined within the context of performance appraisal. Kelley (1967, 1971, 1973) postulated that causal attributions can be affected by various combinations of each of three variables: consensus (high

Table 4–2
Attribution Principles Tested for Performance Appraisal

Attribution Principle	Independent Variable	Dependent Variable	Design
Weiner's principles: ability, luck, effort, task difficulty	Level of performance	Attributions to the four causal dimensions	Experimental
Actor-observer differences	Level of performance and rater	Attributional rating to situational or dispositional characteristics of ratee	Predominantly experimental
Kelley's covariation principles	Combinations of consistency, consensus, and distinctiveness	Attributions to internal or external causes	Experimental
Responsibility	Ratee's (subordinate's) performance and task outcome	Supervisor's attributions of ratee's responsibility for specific outcomes	Experimental

or low), distinctiveness (high or low), and consistency (high or low). Thus, the Kelley model focuses on the circumstances under which attributions are either internal or external. Some studies have extended the basic hypothesis to include the proposition that by manipulating consistency, consensus, and distinctiveness, the attributions made by the rater will influence the feedback to the ratee. Our analyses included studies of both types. (The actual hypotheses for Kelley's theory are too complex to describe here. See his articles listed in the references at the end of this chapter for details on the theory.)

The fourth and final hypothesis investigated within this area focused on responsibility attributions. The typical study required that the rater (usually the supervisor) provide responsibility attributions for specific outcomes resulting from the ratee's (subordinate's) own behavior or performance.

Leadership

In the leadership area, four sets of attributional hypotheses were examined: Weiner's dimensions, self-serving biases, Kelley's covariation hypotheses, and responsibility attributions (see table 4–3). Unlike the preceding hypotheses that focused on the causes of attributions, this group of studies involving Weiner's dimensions centered upon the consequences of attributions for leaders' reactions to subordinate performance. The most frequent independent variable was subordinate performance, which influenced the attributions a leader made about subordinate performance, which, in turn, influenced the leader's response. For instance, if a leader attributes a subordinate's poor performance to a lack of effort,

Table 4–3
Attribution Principles Tested for Leadership

Attribution Principle	Independent Variable	Dependent Variable	Design
Weiner's principles: ability, luck, effort, task difficulty	Subordinate performance	The leader's subsequent behavior as a function of intervening attributions	Correlational
Self-serving biases	Successful or unsuccessful performance	Attributions of performance to internal and external factors	Correlational
Kelley's covariation principles	Combinations of consistency, consensus, and distinctiveness	Others' perceptions of target's leadership ability	Experimental
Responsibility	Organizational (group) performance or leader behavior	Ratings of leader responsibility for performance (behavior)	Correlational, experimental

the leader or manager will probably respond with some form of punishment or reprimand. Conversely, if poor performance is attributed to task difficulty, a leader would be predicted to respond less punitively. Provided the manipulation of performance affected the causal attributions to effort, ability, luck, and task difficulty as predicted, the relationship between each of the attributions and a leader's subsequent behavior was examined.

Self-serving bias is indicated if a leader or manager attributes successful behavior or peformance to internal factors yet makes external attributions for poor or unsuccessful performance. Thus, managers supervising a workgroup performing below quota may attribute performance to faulty supplies or outdated equipment rather than to a lack of supervisory capability on their part.

The few studies that focused on leadership and Kelley's covariation hypotheses were highly similar in design to the analogous performance appraisal studies. These studies examined the extent that the consistency, consensus, and distinctiveness of a leader's behavior influenced others' perceptions of leadership ability.

In the reviewed studies responsibility attributions with respect to leadership have been assessed predominantly by hypothesizing that raters will ascribe higher levels of responsibility for organizational and group performance to the leader rather than to group or organizational members.

Motivation

The studies investigating the relationship between motivation and Weiner's four causal dimensions hypothesized that level of motivation (high versus low) interacts

Table 4–4
Attribution Principles Tested for Motivation

Attribution Principle	Independent Variable	Dependent Variable	Design
Weiner's principles: ability, luck, effort, task difficulty	Self-ratings of motivation or success/failure experience	Attributions to the four causal dimensions	Correlational, experimental
Self-serving biases	Success/failure experience relative to prior expectancies	Attributions to internal or external factors	Correlational, experimental
Responsibility	Success/failure experience or level of motivation	Responsibility attributions	Correlational

with performance level (good versus poor) to affect an individual's attributions of ability, luck, effort, and task difficulty (see table 4–4). Studies testing this hypothesis were of varied design. The experimental studies generally manipulated success/failure and measured both individual motivation and subsequent ascribed attributions. The correlational studies typically measured actual performance while measuring attributions. In the majority of these studies both the attributional and motivational ratings were provided by the same individual.

Studies testing hypotheses about egocentric biases and responsibility attributions frequently manipulated as the independent variable whether an individual experienced success or failure on task performance. Weiner et al. (1971) described the tendency of individuals to assume credit for successful outcomes and to dissociate themselves from unsuccessful outcomes. Studies testing this egocentric or self-serving bias hypothesis predict that internal responsibility attributions will be made for success outcomes and external attributions will be made for failure outcomes.

The analysis of responsibility attributions tested the hypothesis that motivation and performance level interacted to affect subsequent responsibility attributions. It was expected that high motivation and good performance would result in high responsibility attributions but that high motivation and poor performance would result in low responsibility attributions. The corresponding hypothesis for low motivation was that good performance would lead to low ascribed responsibility but poor performance would lead to high responsibility attributions.

Methodology

An extensive literature review was performed to locate studies for inclusion in the validity generalization analyses. The process involved a search through the psy-

Table 4-5
Summary of Direction of Findings for Each Topical Domain

	Positive Correlation				Negative Correlation			
	Weiner's Dimensions	*Actor-Observer*	*Covariation*	*Responsibility*	*Weiner's Dimensions*	*Actor-Observer*	*Covariation*	*Responsibility*
Laboratory studies[a]	20, 23, 24, 27, 29, 30, 33, 37	41	28, 40, 47, 50, 56, 57	10, 13, 24, 31, 41				43
Field studies[a]	5, 9, 17, 18, 24, 36, 39	18, 34, 48, 49, 58	42, 44, 49, 60	24, 36, 39, 42, 59	1, 18, 36		44	1, 59
Laboratory studies[b]	2, 26, 29, 30, 35, 53		2	30				
Field studies[b]	17	7, 16, 25, 54, 55		15, 40				

Laboratory studies[c]	2 6 8	38 57 51	51	21	
Field studies[c]	11 12 14 45 46 57	3 4	46	45 46	3 4	19

Note: Each number in the body of the table corresponds to the reference number assigned to each study included in the analyses.

[a] Results for performance appraisal.

[b] Results for leadership.

[c] Results for motivation.

chological abstracts from 1958–1985, the acquisition of major review articles, and a check through the reference lists of all relevant attribution articles. This procedure resulted in the examination and coding of over 250 articles. All of these articles, however, were not used for the final analyses due to the inability to transform the statistics into correlations, because the tested hypotheses were irrelevant to the areas under investigation, or because the samples involved children, teenagers, or nonnormal as opposed to normal adults.

Studies were grouped according to whether they examined any one or more of the three topical areas of interest. The hypotheses for each included study were recorded and classified into one of the attributional categories of interest. Only studies which clearly stated a priori hypotheses were included in the analysis. This was done in response to recent criticism (Fiedler, 1982) that attribution theory has often been used to search for possible explanations only after the original hypotheses have failed to yield significant results. For each of the topical areas, first the validity generalization was performed for each of the hypotheses, aggregating both the lab and the field studies. For results indicating nonhomogeneity, the analyses were performed again but separately for the lab and field studies. Due to the nature of the reported data in the areas of leadership and motivation, it was not possible to perform the validity generalization procedure for some of the hypotheses.

Results

Table 4–5 displays the direction of findings for the three topical areas of interest. Clearly, most of the obtained correlations are positive. However, it is difficult to get a clear understanding of the results because a result may be listed as positive or negative and yet be relatively small. It is for this reason that the measure of effect size, as used in the validity generalization procedure, is the best estimate of the strength of a result.

The Pearson correlation was the measure of effect size used for the analyses. Where the studies were correlational, we directly obtained the zero-order correlation for the hypothesis of interest. For experimental studies, it was straightforward to convert F and t statistics to correlations. It was thus possible to use the same effect size measure for all studies and to compute tests of significance for the mean and true r's subsequent to the validity generalization analyses.

Tables 4–6 and 4–7 present the results of the validity generalization analyses for each of the major hypotheses tested in each topical domain. For each hypothesis, the tables display the total number of subjects, number of results (independent samples), followed by the percentage of variance accounted for as well as the difference between the observed and predicted variance or residual variance. The last two columns contain the frequency weighted mean r and the true r, corrected for sampling error, range restriction, and criterion unreliability.

Table 4–6
Results of the Validity Generalization Analysis for Performance Appraisal

Attribution Principle	Total N	N of Results	Percent Variance Accounted For	Residual Variance	Mean R	True R
Weiner's principles	1,879	20	35.4	.030	.348[a]	.477[a]
Lab	750	7	100.0	− .030	.450[a]	.600[a]
Field	1,129	13	27.5	.039	.279	.389
Actor-observer	666	11	100.0	− .015	.401[a]	.543[a]
Lab	375	5	100.0	− .032	.413[a]	.558[a]
Field	291	6	100.0	− .015	.385[a]	.524[a]
Kelley's covariation	467	7	100.0	− .005	.317[a]	.438[a]
Field	245	6	100.0	− .015	.386[a]	.525[a]
Responsibility	411	7	36.5	.037	.281[a]	.391[a]
Lab	256	3	100.0	− .020	.286[a]	.398[a]
Field	155	4	17.7	.027	.273	.380[a]

Note: Homogeneity cannot be accepted if percent variance accounted for is less than 75 percent.
[a] $p \leq .01$.

Performance Appraisal

The analysis providing the tests of the hypotheses for Weiner's dimensions shows that a significant amount of variance remains unexplained after correcting for artifacts, indicating that differences exist in the underlying subpopulation correlations. Further analysis of the hypotheses, using experimental setting as a moderator, indicates that the field studies are still not homogeneous. Substantial within-setting differences exist for field studies. The opposite was found for laboratory settings where the variances were shown to be homogeneous. This indicates that generalization of field results is not warranted, but it also indicates that the lab/field distinction is *not* the critical moderator. Therefore, a further search for additional moderating variables appears necessary.

One logical possibility for the first hypothesis is that each of Weiner's four dimensions could serve as moderator variables. The inability to generalize across research settings may have resulted because the four hypotheses representing Weiner's dimensions were grouped together and an average correlation used in the analyses (see table 4–6). The hypotheses were therefore reanalyzed to determine whether the results could be generalized across settings within each causal factor. The procedure involved four analyses, one for each factor, utilizing the correlation coefficient reported for each factor. The results of this analysis, although not reported here, indicated that the results could not be generalized across settings within each causal factor (luck, effort, ability, and task difficulty). Furthermore, when each dimension was separated into lab and field, the results paralleled those found in the initial analysis. The laboratory studies were homogeneous but the

Table 4-7
Results of the Validity Generalization Analysis for Leadership and Motivation

Attribution Principle	Total N	N of Results	Percent Variance Accounted For	Residual Variance	Mean R	True R
			Leadership			
Weiner's principles	756	7	100.0	− .054	.621	.784[a]
Lab	651	6	100.0	− .053	.603[a]	.767[a]
Self-serving biases						
Field	282	3	78.5	.004	.228[a]	.320[a]
Kelley's covariation						
Lab	258	2	93.1	.0007	.232[a]	.326[a]
Responsibility	278	3	43.7	.018	.206	.290[a]
Field	56	2	54.0	.033	.466	.620[a]
			Motivation			
Weiner's principles	989	6	100.0	.040	.500[a]	.660[a]
Lab	184	2	100.0	− .027	.473[a]	.627[a]
Field	805	4	100.0	− .012	.280[a]	.390[a]
Self-serving biases						
Field	870	5	100.0	− .005	.292[a]	.406[a]
Responsibility						
Field	541	6	100.0	− .005	.289[a]	.402[a]

Note: Homogeneity cannot be accepted if percent variance accounted for is less than 75 percent.
[a] $p \leq .01$.

field settings were not. In addition, the effect size of the true r for the field studies testing Weiner's principles indicates that the effect (.39) is not significantly different from zero. This discrepancy suggests that the significant factors are within the field studies rather than the research setting (lab versus field). Variables which could account for this difference will be discussed later.

For actor-observer differences, all of the variance among findings could be explained by methodological artifacts, indicating that the results could be generalized across settings. This is shown in column three of table 4-6. For both actor-observer differences and Kelley's covariation principles, homogeneity was supported and the corrected and uncorrected mean correlations were significant at the .01 level. Values for the true r were .54 for actor-observer differences and .44 for Kelley's covariation principles. The true r for actor-observer differences represents the strength of the relationship between whether an actor or observer provides the ratings and the type of attributions they make regarding performance, thus strengthening our basis for believing that actor-observer differences exist when appraising performance.

The results of the analyses for responsibility attributions produced results indicating the existence of different underlying subpopulation correlations. Analyses using experimental setting as a moderator show that laboratory settings are homogeneous but field settings are not. Thus, the conclusion is that the lab/field distinction is not the critical moderator.

Leadership

The results for leadership are not as numerous as those for performance appraisal (see table 4–7). Consequently, it was not possible to perform the validity generalization procedure on the combined effects for lab and field studies for any of the attribution principles tested. Nevertheless, for some hypotheses we can report within-setting validity generalization results. In reference to Weiner's dimensions, the results suggest that the laboratory studies are homogeneous, and the mean frequency weighted (.60) and the true correlations (.77) are highly significant. In the leadership domain it was only possible to locate field studies for self-serving biases. The results show that homogeneity can be accepted within field settings. The mean (.228) and true (.320) correlations are significant. There was no significant within-setting variation in results for laboratory studies testing hypotheses for Kelley's covariation principles, as indicated by the significant amount of explained variance (93 percent). The mean (.23) and true (.33) correlations, although smaller than the others, are significant. Results for responsibility attributions indicate nonhomogeneity within the field settings. Moreover, the mean correlation (.46) is not significant, but the true correlation (.62) is significant.

Motivation

As shown in table 4–7, a thorough test of Weiner's dimensions was possible. Results show that generalization from laboratory to field settings is warranted, and that both the mean (.50) and the true (.66) correlations are significant.

The results for studies of self-serving biases, which could only be analyzed in field settings, indicate that the variances are homogeneous and the mean (.29) and true (.41) correlations are significant. The results for responsibility attributions are less conclusive considering results can only be reported for studies in field settings. However, there is no significant within-group variance for field settings, and the mean (.28) and true (.40) correlations for this particular subgroup are significant.

Discussion

The results of our validity generalization analysis create an encouraging impression. An examination of each of the mean correlations and the corrected true correlations (that is, effect size) indicates that the correlations are predominantly quite large and significant. The true r's range from .29 to .78. These correlations are even more impressive when it is noted that, of the studies used in the analyses, 76 percent were experimental studies and only 24 percent were correlational studies.

Furthermore, it was found that with only two exceptions, when it was possible to cumulate enough lab and field studies, the results generalized between the two settings and the resulting correlations were significant. Where generalization was not warranted, the lab/field distinction was not the relevant moderator. In all cases where nonhomogeneity existed and the research setting was used as a moderator variable, the analyses showed that the results could be generalized across laboratory settings but not across field settings. This suggests that the key differences were within the field settings.

In field studies, attributional ratings were made in settings involving complex, interpersonal, social interaction sequences. The complexity of the social situation contributes to a difference concerning the object of the attributional rating. In laboratory settings, 80 percent of the ratings were provided by one individual for a group's performance. Conversely, for attributions in the field settings, 50 percent were provided by a single individual for the performance of several individuals, such as a coach providing attributional ratings of the team or a supervisor making attributional ratings of the work group.

Another difference between lab and field studies was the time lag between when behavior was observed and when attributions were measured. Fully 100 percent of the laboratory studies investigating Weiner's dimensions did so with immediate ratings of attributions. For the field studies, 62 percent involved delayed attributions while only 38 percent involved immediate attributions. Some studies took a delayed measure twenty-four hours after presentation of the stimulus whereas other studies obtained the attributional rating two weeks, one month, or six months later. The results of applying validity generalization to investigate the delayed/immediate factor as a moderator indicates that homogeneity for field studies exists for the immediate attributions but not for the delayed attributional studies. The most plausible explanation for this result is that the variability of the time lag is the source of the unexplained variance. This is consistent with the findings of Ross and Sicoly (1979), who noted that delayed attributions may be determined by the ease with which attributors recall information.

Of increasing importance to the study of attribution theory and the lab/field distinction is the recent consideration given to the question of whether attributions occur spontaneously as part of normal (typical) social perception (Pyszczynski & Greenberg, 1981; Wong & Weiner, 1981; Hastie, 1984; Winter & Uleman, 1984). Currently, the available evidence indicates that people frequently make attributions spontaneously. However, using a sentence completion task, Hastie found that one-fourth of the responses provided by subjects were causal explanations.

Hastie's finding regarding the frequency with which spontaneous attributions are made has implications for generalizability of attributions in a broader sense than the lab/field distinction. It is possible that validity generalization occurs because most studies explicitly asked subjects to make attributions as part of the research process. Validity generalization, from lab to field settings, does not imply that normal interpretive processes mirror those uncovered through research explicitly requiring attributions of subjects. That is, though findings generalize from lab to field settings, they do not necessarily describe typical attributional processes. More research on this issue is certainly needed.

One beneficial aspect of a validity generalization analysis is that it indicates those areas where further research is desirable and even necessary in order to achieve reasonably conclusive results. The application of attributional principles to the domain of leadership is necessary, especially with respect to responsibility attributions, Kelley's covariation principles, and self-serving biases. The paucity of studies on attribution theory in the leadership domain is due to its recent development as an area of active research interest (Mitchell & Wood, 1980).

References

Alexander, R.A., Carson, K.P., Alliger, G.M., & Cronshaw, S. (1984) Empirical distributions of range-restricted SDX. Unpublished manuscript, University of Akron.

Calder, B.J. (1977) An attribution theory of leadership. In B.M. Staw & G.R. Salancik (Eds.), *New directions in organizational behavior*. Chicago: St. Clair Press, pp. 179–204.

Fiedler, K. (1982) Causal schemata—Review and criticism of research on a popular construct. *Journal of Personality and Social Psychology, 42*, 1001–1013.

Green, S.G., & Mitchell, T.R. (1979) Attributional processes of leaders in leader-member interactions. *Organizational Behavior and Human Performance, 23*, 429–458.

Hamilton, V.L. (1980) Intuitive psychologist or intuitive lawyer? Alternate models of the attribution process. *Journal of Personality and Social Psychology, 39*, 767–772.

Hastie, R. (1984) Causes and effects of causal attribution. *Journal of Personality and Social Psychology, 46*, 44–56.

Hunter, J.E., Schmidt, F.L., & Jackson, G.B. (1982) *Meta-analysis: Cumulating research findings across studies*. Beverly Hills: Sage.

Kelley, H.H. (1967) Attribution theory in social psychology. In D. Levine (Ed.), *Nebraska symposium on motivation* (Vol. 15). Lincoln: University of Nebraska Press.

Kelley, H.H. (1971) Causal schemata and the attribution process. In E.E. Jones et al., (Eds.), *Attribution-perceiving the causes of behavior*, Morristown, N.J.: General Learning Press.

Kelley, H.H. (1973) The process of causal attribution. *American Psychologist, 28*, 107–128.

Lord, R.G., & Smith, J.E. (1983) Theoretical, information processing, and situational factors affecting attribution theory models of organizational behavior. *Academy of Management Review, 8*, 50–60.

Mitchell, T.R., & Wood, R.E. (1980) Supervisor's responses to subordinate poor performance: A test of an attributional model. *Organizational Behavior and Human Performance, 25*, 123–128.

Mitchell, T.R., Green, S.G., & Wood, R.E. (1981) An attributional model of leadership and the poor performing subordinate: Development and validation. In B.M. Staw

& L.L. Cummings (Eds.) *Research in organizational behavior* (Vol. 3). Greenwich, Conn.: JAI Press, pp. 197–234.

Pearlman, K., Schmidt, F.L., & Hunter, J.E. (1980) Validity generalization results for tests used to predict job proficiency and training success in clerical occupations. *Journal of Applied Psychology, 65,* 373–406.

Phillips, J.S., & Lord, R.G. (1981) Causal attributions and perceptions of leadership. *Organizational Behavior and Human Performance, 28,* 143–163.

Pyszczynski, T.A., & Greenberg, J. (1981) Role of disconfirmed expectancies in the instigation of attributional processing. *Journal of Personality and Social Psychology, 40,* 31–38.

Ross, M., & Sicoly, F. (1979) Egocentric biases in availability and attribution. *Journal of Personality and Social Psychology, 37,* 322–336.

Schmidt, F.L., and Hunter, J.E. (1977) Development of a generalized solution to the problem of validity generalization. *Journal of Applied Psychology, 62,* 529–540.

Schmidt, F.L., Gast-Rosenberg, I., & Hunter, J.E. (1980) Validity generalization: Results for computer programmers. *Journal of Applied Psychology, 65,* 643–661.

Schmidt, F.L., and Hunter, J.E. (1981) Employment testing. *American Psychologist, 36,* 1128–1137.

Weiner, B., Frieze, I., Kukla, A., Reed, L., Rest, S., & Rosenbaum, R. (1971) Perceiving the causes of success and failure. In E. Jones, D. Kanouse, H. Kelley, R. Nisbett, S. Valins, & B. Weiner (Eds.), *Attribution: Perceiving the causes of behavior.* Morristown, N.J.: General Learning Press, pp. 95–120.

Winter, L., & Uleman, J.S. (1984) When are social judgments made? Evidence for the spontaneousness of trait inferences. *Journal of Personality and Social Psychology, 47,* 237–252.

Wong, P.T.P., & Weiner, B. (1981) When people ask "why" questions, and the heuristics of attributional search. *Journal of Personality and Social Psychology, 40,* 650–663.

Wood, R.E., & Mitchell, T.R. (1981) Manager behavior in social context: The impact of impression management on attributions and disciplinary actions. *Organizational Behavior and Human Performance, 28,* 356–378.

References Included in the Validity Generalization

1. Ames, R. (1975) Teachers' attributions of responsibility: Some unexpected nondefensive effects. *Journal of Educational Psychology, 67,* 668–676.

2. Ayers-Nachamkin, B., Cann, C.H., Reed, R., & Horne, A. (1982) Sex and ethnic differences in the use of power. *Journal of Applied Psychology, 67,* 464–471.

3. Beckman, L. (1970) Effects of students' performance on teachers' and observers' attributions of causality. *Journal of Educational Psychology, 61,* 76–82.

4. Beckman, L. (1973) Teachers' and observers' perceptions of causality for a child's performance. *Journal of Educational Psychology, 65,* 198–204.

5. Bernstein, W.M., Stephan, W.G., & Davis, M.H. (1979) Explaining attributions for achievement: A path-analytic approach. *Journal of Personality and Social Psychology, 37,* 1810–1821.

6. Berscheid, E., Giraziano, W., Monson, T., & Dermer, M. (1976) Outcome dependency: Attention, attribution, and attraction. *Journal of Personality and Social Psychology, 34,* 978–989.

7. Bettman, J.R., & Weitz, A. (1983) Attributions in the board room: Causal reasoning in corporate annual reports. *Administrative Science Quarterly, 28,* 165–183.

8. Boski, P. (1983) A study of person perception in Nigeria: Ethnicity and self versus other attributions for achievement-related outcomes. *Journal of Cross-Cultural Psychology, 14,* 85–108.

9. Carver, C.S., De Gregorio, E., & Gillis, R. (1980) Field-study evidence of an ego-defensive bias in attribution among two categories of observers. *Personality and Social Psychology Bulletin, 6,* 44–50.

10. Carver, C.S., & Scheier, M.F. (1982) Outcome expectancy, locus of attribution for expectancy, and self-directed attention as determinants of evaluations and performance. *Journal of Experimental Social Psychology, 18,* 184–200.

11. Covington, M.V., & Omelich, C.L. (1979) Are causal attributions causal? A path analysis of the cognitive model of achievement motivation. *Journal of Personality and Social Psychology, 37,* 1487–1504.

12. Deaux, K. (1979) Self-evaluations of male and female managers. *Sex Roles, 5,* 571–580.

13. Dossett, D.L., & Greenberg, C.I. (1981) Goal setting and performance evaluation: An attributional analysis. *Academy of Management Journal, 24,* 767–779.

14. Downey, H.K., Chacko, T.I., & McElroy, J.C. (1979) Attribution of the "causes" of performance: A constructive, quasi-longitudinal replication of the Staw (1975) study. *Organizational Behavior and Human Performance, 24,* 287–299.

15. Drory, A., & Ben-Porat, A. (1980) Leadership style and leniency bias in evaluation of employees' performance. *Psychological Reports, 46,* 735–739.

16. DuBrin, A.J. (1964) Trait and interpersonal self-descriptions of leaders and non-leaders in an industrial setting. *Journal of Industrial Psychology, 2,* 51–55.

17. Eden, D., & Shani, A.B. (1982) Pygmalion goes to boot camp: Expectancy, leadership, and trainee performance. *Journal of Applied Psychology, 67,* 194–199.

18. Felson, R. (1981) The attributions of actors and observers concerning performance in a football game. *The Journal of Sport Psychology, 115,* 15–23.

19. Fletcher, G. (1983) The analysis of verbal explanations for marital separation: Implications for attribution theory. *Journal of Applied Social Psychology, 13,* 245–258.

20. Foesterling, F., & Engelken, R. (1981) Expectancies in relation to success and failure, causal attributions, and perceived task similarity. *Personality and Social Psychology Bulletin, 7,* 578–582.

21. Frieze, I., & Weiner, B. (1971) Cue utilization and attributional judgments for success and failure. *Journal of Personality, 39,* 591–605.

22. Garcia, L., Erskine, N., Hawn, K., & Casay, S. (1981) The effect of affirmative action on attributions about minority group members. *Journal of Personality, 49,* 427–437.

23. Gilbert, S.J. (1983) Variant-effect schema predictions of discounting and augmentation effects. *The Journal of Social Psychology, 119,* 289–290.

24. Gill, D.L., Ruder, K., & Gross, J.B. (1982) Open-ended attributions in team competition. *Journal of Sport Psychology, 4,* 159–169.

25. Gottheil, E., & Vielhaber, D. (1966) Interaction of leader and squad attributes related to performance of military squads. *The Journal of Social Psychology, 68,* 113–127.

26. Green, S.G., & Liden, R.C., (1980) Contextual and attributional influences on control decisions. *Journal of Applied Psychology, 65,* 453–458.

27. Greenberg, J., Pyszczynski, T., & Solomon, S. (1982) The self-serving attributional bias: Beyond self-presentation. *Journal of Experimental Social Psychology, 18,* 56–67.

28. Hamner, W.C., Kim, J.S., Baird, L., & Bigoness, W.J. (1974) Race and Sex as determinants of ratings by potential employers in a simulated work-sampling task. *Journal of Applied Psychology, 59,* 705–711.

29. Hargrett, N.T. (1981) Potential behavioral consequences of attributions of locus of control. *Journal of Applied Psychology, 66,* 62–68.

30. Ilgen, D.R., & Knowlton, W.A. (1980) Performance attributional effects on feedback from superiors. *Organizational Behavior and Human Performance, 25,* 441–456.

31. Johnson, T.J., Feigenbaum, R., & Wetby, M. (1964) Some determinants and consequences of the teacher's perception of causation. *Journal of Educational Psychology, 55,* 237–246.

32. Kerr, N.L., & Sullaway, M.E. (1983) Group sex composition and member task motivation. *Sex Roles, 9,* 403–417.

33. Knowlton, W.A., & Mitchell, T.R. (1980) Effects of causal attributions on a supervisor's evaluation of subordinate performance. *Journal of Applied Psychology, 65,* 459–466.

34. Lau, R.R., & Russell, D. (1980) Attributions in the sports pages. *Journal of Personality and Social Psychology, 39,* 29–38.

35. Lord, R.G., Binning, J.F., Rush, M.C., & Thomas, J.C. (1978) The effect of performance cues and leader behavior on questionnaire ratings of leadership behavior. *Organizational Behavior and Human Performance, 21,* 27–39.

36. Martin, R.P., & Curtis, M. (1981) Consultants' perceptions of causality for success and failure of consultation. *Professional Psychology, 12,* 670–676.

37. Meyer, J.P., & Koelbl, S.L.M. (1982) Students' test performances: Dimensionality of causal attributions. *Personality and Social Psychology Bulletin, 8,* 31–36.

38. Mitchell, M., Hyde, M., & Friedman, D. (1983) The effect of frequency information on actor entity attributions. *Personality and Social Psychology Bulletin, 9,* 359–363.

39. Mitchell, T.R., & Kalb, L.S. (1981) Effects of outcome knowledge and outcome valence on supervisors' evaluations. *Journal of Applied Psychology, 66,* 604–612.

40. Mitchell, T.R., & Kalb, L.S. (1982) Effects of job experience on supervisor attributions for a subordinate's poor performance. *Journal of Applied Psychology, 67,* 181–188.

41. Mitchell, T.R., Larson, J.R., & Green, S.G. (1977) Leader behavior, situational moderators, and group performance: An attributional analysis. *Organizational Behavior and Human Performance, 18,* 254–268.

42. Mitchell, T.R., & Wood, R.E. (1980) Supervisor's responses to subordinate poor performance: A test of an attributional model. *Organizational Behavior and Human Performance, 25,* 123–128.

43. Muzdybaev, K. (1982) Attribution of responsibility and organizational behavior. *Personality and Social Psychology Bulletin, 8,* 43–48.

44. Peterson, C. (1980) Attribution in the sports pages: An archival investigation of the covariation hypothesis. *Social Psychology Quarterly, 43,* 136–141.

45. Porac, J., Ferris, G.R., & Fedor, D.B. (1983) Causal attributions, affect, and expectations for a day's work performance. *Academy of Management Journal, 26,* 285–296.

46. Porac, J.F., Nottenburg, G., & Egert, J. (1981) On extending Weiner's attributional model to organizational contexts. *Journal of Applied Psychology, 66,* 124–126.

47. Pruitt, D.J., & Insko, C.A. (1980) Extension of the Kelley attribution model: The role of comparison-object consensus, target-object consensus, distinctiveness, and consistency. *Journal of Personality and Social Psychology, 39,* 39–58.

48. Rejeski, W.J., & McCook, W. (1980) Individual differences in professional teachers' attributions for children's performance outcomes. *Psychological Reports, 46,* 1159–1163.

49. Ross, P.F. (1966) Reference groups in man-to-man job performance ratings. *Personnel Psychology, 19,* 115–142.

50. Rusbult, C.E., & Medlin, S.M. (1982) Information availability, goodness of outcome and attributions of causality. *Journal of Experimental Social Psychology, 18,* 292–305.

51. Schlenker, B.R., Miller, R.S., Leary, M.R., & McCown, N.E. (1979) Group performance and interpersonal evaluations as determinants of egotistical attributions in groups. *Journal of Personality, 47,* 575–594.

52. Shrout, P.E., & Fiske, D.W. (1981) Nonverbal behaviors and social evaluation. *Journal of Personality, 49,* 115–128.

53. Smith, T.W., & Brehm, S.S. (1981) Person perception and the type A coronory-prone behavior pattern. *Journal of Personality and Social Psychology, 40,* 1137–1149.

54. Sonnenfeld, J. (1981) Executive apologies for price fixing: Role biased perceptions of causality. *Academy of Management Journal, 24,* 191–198.

55. Staw, B.M., McKechnie, R.I., & Puffer, S.M. (1983) The justification of organizational performance. *Administrative Science Quarterly, 28,* 582–600.

56. Staw, B.M., & Ross, J. (1980) Commitment in an experimenting society: A study of the attribution of leadership from administrative scenarios. *Journal of Applied Psychology, 65,* 249–260.

57. Stephan, W.G., & Gollwitzer, P.M. (1981) Affect as a mediator of attributional egotism. *Journal of Experimental Social Psychology, 176,* 443–458.

58. Taylor, D.M., & Doria, J.R. (1981) Self-serving and group-serving bias in attribution. *The Journal of Social Psychology, 113,* 201–211.

59. Thompson, S.C., & Kelley, H.H. (1981) Judgments of responsibility for activities in close relationships. *Journal of Personality and Social Psychology, 41,* 469–477.

60. Wilson, T.D., & Linville, P.W. (1982) Improving the academic performance of college freshman: Attribution theory revisited. *Journal of Personality and Social Psychology, 42,* 367–376.

61. Yarkin, K.L., Town, J.P., & Wallston, B.S. (1982) Blacks and women must try harder: Stimulus persons' race and sex attributions of causality. *Personality and Social Psychology Bulletin, 8,* 21–24.

5

The Applicability of a Training Transfer Model to Issues Concerning Rater Training

Irwin L. Goldstein
Gary R. Musicante

T he key focus for researchers concerned with learning and training is the transfer issue. That is, researchers are interested in determining how what is learned in one setting transfers to another setting. The question of generalizability of results from one setting, a laboratory environment for example, to another setting such as a work environment involves the same principles which determine whether there is transfer of learning from one setting to another. As a result, it appears worthwhile to examine the history of that literature to examine what clues it offers about the variables underlying transfer from lab to field settings. In summary, the premise is that the variables that provide information about generalizability are the same variables that help explain transfer of learned behavior from one environment to the other. After examining that issue, this chapter will focus on some of these variables and techniques which provide information about the potency of variables in lab and field settings as applied to a particular training problem—that is, rater training.

The first thought concerning transfer from one environment to the other came early in the history of psychology. It is known as the theory of identical elements. This theory was proposed by E.L. Thorndike and R.S. Woodworth (1901). They predicted that transfer would occur as long as there were identical elements in the two situations. These identical elements could include aims, methods, and approaches, and were later defined in terms of stimuli and responses. Holding (1965) summarized the work on transfer by detailing the type of transfer expected based on the similarity of the stimuli and responses (see table 5–1).

In the first case, as presented in table 5–1, the stimuli and responses are identical. If the tasks are identical in training and transfer, trainees are simply practicing the final task during the training program, and high positive transfer is predicted. The second case assumes that the task characteristics, both stimuli and responses, are so different that practice on one task has no relationship to performance on the transfer task. The third case is common to many training programs. The stimuli are somewhat different in training and transfer settings, but the

Table 5-1
Type of Transfer Based on Stimulus and
Response Similarity[a]

Task Stimuli	Response Required	Transfer
Same	Same	High positive
Different	Different	None
Different	Same	Positive
Same	Different	Negative

[a]Adapted from D.H. Holding, *Principles of Training.* London: Pergamon Press Ltd., 1965.

responses are the same. It is assumed that the learner can generalize training from one environment to another. The fourth case presents the basic paradigm for negative transfer. A response to training stimuli is practiced so that the same response is given each time those stimuli appear. If the response becomes inappropriate, negative transfer results.

Critics of this theory have argued that the analysis of transfer need not be limited to mechanistic situations in which there are identical stimulus and response elements. Actually, Thorndike and Woodworth did not originally intend for the identical-elements view to be specific to stimulus and response components (Ellis, 1965). Their original elements consisted of factors such as general principles and attitudes, as well as the more specific components. A theory based upon principles suggests that training should focus on the general principles necessary to gain proficiency on a task so that the learner may apply them to solve problems in the transfer task. An interesting experiment by Hendrickson and Schroeder (1941) demonstrated the transfer of principles related to the refraction of light. Two groups were given practice shooting at an underwater target until each was able to hit the target consistently. The depth of the target was then changed. One group was taught the principles of refraction of light through water. In the next session of target shooting, this group performed significantly better than the group which had not been taught the principles.

The principles model appears to be close to what Berkowitz and Donnerstein (1982) were referring to when they noted that generalizability is based upon the degree to which subjects attach similar meaning to the situation. Indeed, this entire concept provides the foundation for the next set of constructs, constructs commonly referred to as psychological and physical fidelity.

Simulators which are used for training purposes are based upon a conceptual model that states that a training environment must be designed which permits transfer or generalizability of performance from the lab or training environment to the work environment. Presumably, then, this literature provides information about what parameters determine generalizability or, in training terms, what variables underlie transfer.

Training simulators are designed to replicate the essential characteristics of the real world that are necessary to produce learning and transfer. These efforts can vary from flight simulators, which have a substantial degree of physical fidelity (that is, representation of the real world of operational equipment), to role-playing methods, in which the degree of physical simulation is minimal. Theorists believe that the most important aspect of a simulator may be psychological fidelity—the reproduction of those behavioral and cognitive processes that are necessary to perform the job. This point parallels Berkowitz and Donnerstein's idea that generalizability does not depend upon similarity in physical conditions but rather to the degree that subjects attach similar meaning to the situation.

Unfortunately, as those persons who are familiar with simulation efforts know, the actual relationship between physical and psychological fidelity and its relevance to performance is not completely known. This shall be explored further when some research findings are examined. However, it is clear that trainers at least would agree that two variables underlying generalizability would be:

1. Representation of the relevant physical characteristics (including stimulus and response parameters) from the work environment to the lab environment.
2. Representation of the relevant behavioral or psychological processes from the work environment to the lab environment.

Researchers in this field have been extremely concerned with these issues. Most of this concern stems from the world of flight simulators where errors in design of lab or training environments can result in disasters. On the other hand, adding unnecessary physical fidelity to a flight simulator (for example, motion simulation) can waste millions of dollars. This has led some investigators to ask further questions about generalizability or transfer.

Two studies (Wheaton et al., 1976; Swezey, 1982–83) specified and tested a model to determine the transfer potential of a training device. This model provided further cues concerning variables that might affect generalizability. It included the following parameters:

1. *Task commonality*—whether the device permitted the trainee to practice skills required for the actual performance on the real task.
2. *Equipment similarity*—whether the device involved physically similar equipment and the same information requirements.
3. *Learning deficit analysis*—an examination of the tasks to determine their relationship to the input repertoire of trainees and the difficulty level of learning the necessary skills and knowledge.
4. *Training technique analysis*—an estimate of the instructional effectiveness of the device based upon the degree to which relevant principles of learning were utilized.

Characteristics 1 and 2 (task commonality and equipment similarity) have a distinct resemblance to factors involving psychological and physical fidelity. However, factors 3 and 4 introduced other variables. Factor 3 (learning deficit analysis) considered the individual characteristics of the trainee. The assumption was that the training program must be matched to the characteristics of the trainee and what was required on the job. Factor 4 related to the support variables used in the learning situation, that is, did the environment provide instructional systems which are most effective for that type of learning, for example, providing feedback when it was appropriate to do so?

Interestingly, questions concerning this last factor, instructional support systems, have stimulated considerable research. For example, Gagné (1962) examined the utility of laboratory learning principles in the performance of a series of tasks. His review found that the best-known principles, including feedback, distribution of practice, and meaningfulness, were "strikingly inadequate to handle the job of designing effective training situations" (p. 85). He reached this conclusion after examining data from a variety of different tasks, including tracking and problem solving. Gagné suggested that it is necessary to organize the total task into a set of distinct components that mediate final task performance. When these component tasks are present in the instructional program, there should be an effective transfer of learning from the instructional setting to the job setting. Thus, the principles of training design would consist of identifying the task components that make up the final performance, placing these parts into the instructional program, and arranging the learning and integration of these components in an optimal sequence. This original article eventually formed the foundation for an instructional theory which specifies different types of learning behaviors and the learning conditions necessary to support that behavior (Gagné & Briggs, 1979).

This leaves us with the suggestion that there might be four factors (see table 5–2) which relate to transfer or generalizability. The first two (physical and psychological fidelity) were presented earlier. In addition, from the work of Wheaton et al. (1976) and Swezey (1982–83), we would add points 3 and 4 (learning deficit

Table 5–2
Factors Underlying Transfer

1. Some degree of physical similarity between the training or lab setting and the work world environment. This includes relationships between the stimulus and response environment.

2. Some degree of representation of the relevant behavioral or psychological processes from the work environment to the lab environment.

3. An analysis of the characteristics of the trainee that includes whether the program fits those characteristics.

4. An analysis of the instructional variables used to support the learning in the lab that includes whether the variables used are likely to support transfer to the work environment.

5. A positive transfer climate that provides support for trained behavior in the work environment.

analysis and training technique analysis). An analysis of these four factors would probably reveal that there is at least one major factor missing. That is, behavior can be learned in one environment, the stimulus and response situation can be compatible, but it is still possible that the organizational environment is not supportive. In other words, there are organizational context or boundary conditions which can limit generalizability.

A growing literature indicates that transfer of training from the lab or training environment requires a positive transfer climate in the work organization. It is becoming increasingly obvious that situations which should result in positive transfer have at best resulted in zero transfer because of a failure to consider issues related to the work organization. A number of empirical studies have begun to identify some of the factors that determine the extent of transfer support in the organization.

Baumgartel and Jeanpierre (1972) found that persons who were in favorable organizational climates (for example, those with freedom to set personal performance goals, encouragement of risk-taking, growth orientation, and willingness of top management to spend money for training) were most likely to be able to apply new knowledge gained in training programs. This effect was even more pronounced when the person was in a lower-level position in the organization where the trainee did not have the influence to affect change unless there was a favorable climate. Other authors (Leifer & Newstrom, 1980; Michalak, 1981) make the following points:

1. We must have a system which unites the trainer, trainee, and manager in the tranfer process.

2. Before training, the expectations for the trainee and manager must be clear.

3. We must identify obstacles to transfer and provide strategies to overcome these problems.

4. We must work with managers to provide opportunities for the maintenance of trainees' learned behavior in the work organization.

Thus, positive transfer climate is presented as a fifth factor, as shown in table 5–2.

Before examining the research evidence on a particular training program to see if any of these variables appear, it is necessary to ask an additional question. That is, this chapter has addressed the point of transfer of training from a training situation to a work environment, and variables have been identified that appear to be related to the transfer process. An additional question is whether it is possible to ask about the relationship between training lab studies and training in work organizations using the factors identified in transfer studies. Our point is that the answer to this question is yes.

The generalizability question is whether data concerning a learning variable (such as knowledge of results) or a training method variable (such as rater training programs) can be generalized from lab results to field studies. The proposition advanced here is that it is necessary to ask questions very similar to those posed in the five points listed in table 5–2. For example, is the psychological fidelity or the behavioral process the same in the laboratory and organizational environment or are they changed by demand characteristics? Are the subjects the same in terms of learning deficits or other relevant subject characteristics? It is even possible to ask if the learning variable support was the same for the lab as for the organizational environment, for example, is the technique to be learned with feedback in the lab but without feedback in the organization?

In order to explore these issues, it is necessary to choose a particular type of training program and examine whether the five points described in table 5–2 provide a helpful schema to understand the question of generalizability. The particular technique chosen for this analysis is rater training. The reason rater training was chosen is that there were a sufficient number of empirical field and laboratory studies. Thus, by using the available literature on rater training, it is possible to initially explore the applicability of the transfer model.

The objective here is to examine the research evidence in rater training to determine what variables influence the generalizability of laboratory and field studies. Our thesis is that the variables that explain transfer of learned behavior from one environment to another also help determine the generalizability of laboratory and field rater training studies. An examination of these variables may enhance understanding of when and why rater training programs work.

Rater training programs are frequently cited as a strategy to improve performance appraisal ratings (Goldstein, 1980; Wexley, 1984). Goldstein concluded from his review of the literature that rater training may be successful in reducing certain rating errors, particularly when using a workshop format (for example, Latham, Wexley, & Pursell, 1975); however, the reason why rater training programs produce these effects remains unclear. Several studies have demonstrated that the effects of rater training diminish over time (Bernardin, 1978; Ivancevich, 1979), fueling criticism regarding the effectiveness of this technique.

Recently, investigators have studied the possibility that the effects of rater training may be moderated by organizational contextual variables such as purpose of appraisal (McIntyre, Smith, & Hassett, 1984; Warmke & Billings, 1979; Zedeck & Cascio, 1982). Although initial findings are mixed, the general conclusion that organizational contextual variables influence the performance appraisal process (DeCotiis & Petit, 1978; Kane & Lawler, 1979; Landy & Farr, 1983) implies that the generalizability of strategies used to improve performance appraisal ratings such as rater training may also be affected (Wexley, 1984).

Generalizability may be enhanced by the identification of those conditions that make more or less likely both the occurrence and transfer of desired outcomes (such as decreased leniency error and halo effect), increased accuracy, and interrater reliability. Our thesis is that the generalizability of a rater training program may be more a function of the presence or absence of a given set of factors than of whether or not the training program is conducted in a laboratory or a field setting.

Sixteen empirically based studies were reviewed to investigate what conditions facilitate the generalizability of rater training programs. For the purposes of this inductive survey, rater training was defined as any formal or informal program with the expressed goal of improving performance ratings. Rater training techniques included workshops, videotapes, diaries, group discussions, lectures, and/or rater participation in scale construction. Studies selected were those that incorporated one or more of the above forms of rater training into the research design and investigated at least one of the three categories of criteria for assessing rater training programs described by Borman (1979), namely, accuracy; leniency error and halo effect; convergent and discriminant validity, and interrater reliability.

Rater training field studies were operationalized as those in which raters, regardless of setting, evaluated individuals with whom they actually interacted. As a result, studies in which students rated actual instructors rather than hypothetical ratees met the field criteria while studies where corporate managers rated simulated performers did not. Given this operationalization, seven field and nine laboratory studies were reviewed. (See table 5–3 and also chapter 3.)

The first step taken in the survey was a content analysis of the studies. This analysis revealed several differences between laboratory and field rater training studies. These included the nature of the sample, dependent variables, and research method and design.

Table 5–3
Empirical Rater Training Research[a]

Laboratory Studies:

Bernardin and Pence (1980)
Borman (1975)
Borman (1979)
Fay and Latham (1982)
Latham, Wexley, and Pursell (1975)
McIntyre, Smith, and Hassett (1984)
Thornton and Zorich (1980)
Wexley, Sanders, and Yukl (1973)
Zedeck and Cascio (1982)

Field Studies:

Bernardin (1978)
Bernardin and Walter (1977)
Brown (1968)
Friedman and Cornelius (1976)
Ivancevich (1979)
Pursell, Dossett, and Latham (1980)
Warmke and Billings (1979)

[a]Refer to text for criteria used to operationalize laboratory and field studies. In general, rater training field studies involved training raters (regardless of setting) to rate individuals with whom they interacted.

Nature of the Sample. Rater training laboratory research primarily utilizes undergraduate students. Two exceptions (Borman, 1975; Latham et al., 1975) involve managers who evaluated either hypothetical employees or job candidates. Field studies, on the other hand, use college students in the context of evaluating their instructors (Bernardin, 1978; Bernardin & Walter, 1977; Friedman & Cornelius, 1976), as well as relevant samples from other settings such as nurses, electricians, and engineers (Brown, 1968; Ivancevich, 1979; Pursell, Dossett, & Latham, 1980; Warmke & Billings, 1979).

Dependent Variables. Halo, accuracy, and interrater reliability have all been investigated in laboratory studies of rater training. While these studies support the general conclusion that rater training serves to reduce common rating errors such as halo and leniency, the findings regarding accuracy and interrater reliability remain less clear (Bernardin & Pence, 1980; Borman, 1975, 1979; McIntyre et al., 1984; Thornton & Zorich, 1980; Zedeck & Cascio, 1982). Results from field research concerning halo and leniency corroborate laboratory study findings. Accuracy has not been studied in field settings, presumably due to the fact that "true" criterion scores are hard to find in such settings (Bernardin & Buckley, 1981).

Research Method and Design. Both laboratory and field rater training studies have utilized a variety of training formats, ranging from a five-to-six minute lecture (Borman, 1975) to an intense fourteen-hour training program (Ivancevich, 1979), and from control groups to rater participation in scale construction (Friedman & Cornelius, 1976; Warmke & Billings, 1979). Two longitudinal field studies have investigated the effects of rater training over time (Bernardin, 1978; Ivancevich, 1979). Both suggest that the positive effects associated with rater training may be unstable. Although an alternative explanation exists for the findings of a third field study (Warmke & Billings, 1979), this study may also provide evidence of decay over time.

In contrast, only one laboratory study has considered whether the positive effects of rater training are retained over time (Latham et al., 1975), and this particular study, while not operationalized here as field research, has many of its qualities such as corporate setting with manager raters.

Although several differences between laboratory and field rater training studies have been cited, the fact remains that *results* from the two settings are rather similar. Workshop training to reduce halo and leniency, for example, has been fairly effective in both laboratory and field. Other training formats such as discussion groups have not been as successful in either of the two settings. At least in the context of rater training research, these potentially powerful variables (sample, dependent variables, and research method and design) have neither greatly affected the outcomes studied nor served to distinguish in any meaningful way between laboratory and field studies.

An alternative possibility, one that emerges from a review of recent performance appraisal models, is that the effects of rater training may be mediated by process variables. Some of the variables that may inhibit or facilitate the generalizability of rater training programs are identified in table 5–4. Not surprisingly, table 5–4 includes two process characteristics already addressed in the literature—purpose of rating and stability of effect. The cognitive and contextual variables identified in table 5–4, along with others, may represent real upper limits to the generalizability of rater training programs. By and large, they reflect the current emphasis on cognitive and contextual variables in psychology. Our position is that process variables, such as purpose of rating, can be derived from the transfer model and serve to either inhibit or facilitate the generalizability of rater training programs conducted in both laboratory and field. Specifically:

1. Requirements of physical and psychological fidelity demonstrate the importance of providing some degree of physical similarity and representation of behavioral processes in both laboratory and field settings. Physical fidelity is reflected in rater training studies that offer real life or videotaped ratees, plus rating scales commonly used to evaluate performance in the work world. Psychological fidelity is found in studies where, for example, participation in scale construction or diary-keeping is encouraged.

2. An analysis of individual trainer/trainee characteristics, another factor underlying transfer, can help determine the extent to which crucial rater characteristics, such as motivation to use the appraisal system accurately, are present.

Table 5–4
Some Potential Inhibitors/Facilitators of Generalizability of Rater Training Programs

Purpose(s) of rating

Stability of effect

Feedback and reinforcement

Type of training

Length/amount of training

Nature of contact between trainer and trainee, rater and ratee

Trainer effectiveness

Trainer-trainee/rater-ratee characteristics (for example, motivation to use appraisal system accurately, acceptance and perceived relevance of the system, and ability to use the system)

3. Instructional variables, such as feedback, imply that training programs are dynamic and that the positive effects of rater training may diminish over time unless reinforced.

4. The consideration of organizational context or boundary conditions demonstrates the importance of such factors as purpose of rating. An analysis of boundary conditions may reveal that rater training cannot be effective unless such variables are mastered.

Table 5–5 summarizes the proposed correspondence between variables from table 5–4 (in addition to others discussed earlier, such as nature of the sample and research method and design) and factors underlying transfer cited in table 5–2.

What follows is a tentative overview of what the effect of some of the variables noted in tables 5–4 and 5–5 might be in the context of rater training. We will also consider whether the proposed correspondence between factors underlying transfer and these study attributes (table 5–5) improves our understanding of generalizability. Unfortunately, this analysis is limited, given the nominal information in journal articles regarding most cognitive and contextual variables.

Table 5–5
Rater Training Study Characteristics Classified by Factors Underlying Transfer

Factor	*Characteristics*
Physical fidelity	Length and amount of training Training format/research method Stability of effect Type of rating scale(s) Ratee presentation format
Psychological fidelity	Nature of contact between trainer and trainee/rater and ratee Rater involvement in training/appraisal process Criteria
Trainee characteristics	Nature of sample Trainer-trainee/rater-ratee characteristics (for example, motivation to use appraisal system accurately)
Instructional variables	Trainer effectiveness Feedback and reinforcement
Transfer climate	Purpose(s) of rating Organizational climate (for example, performance-pay contingencies, time pressures on raters)

Note: The proposed correspondence between factors underlying transfer (table 5–2) and rater training study characteristics (table 5–4 and others derived from the literature) was independently developed and agreed upon by the coauthors.

Purpose of Rating. Zedeck & Cascio's (1982) laboratory study suggests that training for some purposes may lead to more accurate evaluations than training for others. Warmke & Billings (1979) conclude from their field investigation that training affects experimental but not administrative ratings. This research reflects a fairly recent shift in emphasis to consideration of contextual variables and suggests that the design of a rater training program should be contingent upon the purpose of appraisal (Wexley, 1984). Given the general finding that administrative ratings tend to be more lenient than experimental ratings (Aleamoni & Hexner, 1973; Borreson, 1967; Centra, 1974; Heron, 1956; Musicante, 1983; Ory & Braskamp, 1980; Sharon, 1970; Sharon & Bartlett, 1969; Taylor & Wherry, 1951), it may be desirable to use a rater training program that is particularly resistant to leniency errors.

Stability of Effect; Feedback and Reinforcement. Rater training research, particularly in field settings, has witnessed the dissipation of the positive effects of training over time (Bernardin, 1978; Ivancevich, 1979). The implication of this finding is that it may be necessary to provide follow-up rater training to keep rating errors from reoccurring. In fact, this has been recommended by researchers such as Fay and Latham (1982).

Type of Training. Training that focuses on particular criteria (for example accuracy and halo) in a workshop format has been considerably more successful in reducing those errors than simple instructions or lectures which urge raters to not make rating errors. Similarly, training programs such as Bernardin and Walter's (1977) diary technique and Friedman and Cornelius's (1976) rater participation in scale construction approach appear to facilitate the occurrence of desired criteria such as decreased halo and leniency errors.

Length and Amount of Training. Rater training programs that are more comprehensive tend to be longer (Bernardin, 1978). In general, it appears that comprehensive rater training programs are more effective in reducing common rating errors than abbreviated training programs.

Nature of Contact. This factor refers not only to trainer-trainee interactions but to rater-ratee relationships as well. Performance appraisal research appears to indicate that meaningful, direct contact results in more accurate appraisals and, by extension, more successful rater training programs. As relevant contact increases, common rating errors such as halo and leniency may be less likely to occur.

Trainer Effectiveness. It should be obvious that effective trainers may help to maximize both the occurrence and transfer of desired outcomes such as decreased halo and leniency and increased rating accuracy and interrater reliability.

Rater/Ratee Characteristics. If participants' motivation to use the appraisal system accurately is low, the rater training program may be ineffective. One set of goals for the training program may be to improve rater acceptance of the appraisal system and increase its perceived relevance.

Any determination of generalizability requires the assessment of whether rater training study characteristics, as derived from the transfer model, correspond to those characteristics typically found in the work environment. To the extent that empirical studies have high physical and psychological fidelity, include subjects with similar qualities to those found in the work world, and so forth, generalizability should be enhanced. In most cases, unfortunately, it is difficult to accurately make such an assessment.

Journal articles rarely indicate the degree of correspondence of the study characteristics cited above (such as length/amount of training) to the work environment. This is attributable, in part, to the unique way many of these characteristics are considered in a particular study and, also, to the fact that most studies either do not provide the detailed information necessary to make such an appraisal or do not consider these variables at all. In addition, it is frequently unclear what set of conditions exist or should exist in the real world training environment. For example, how long must a rater training program be for maximum transfer to occur?

To clarify these problems, it may be useful to review the available evidence for a few of the study variables listed in tables 5–4 and 5–5. One relatively straightforward study characteristic is length/amount of training. All of the journal articles cited in table 5–3 provide information on this variable. As noted earlier, length of training varies from a five-to-six minute lecture to an intense fourteen-hour training program. With only two exceptions, laboratory studies have training programs less than or equal to one hour in length. Conversely, all of the field rater training studies identified in table 5–3 include training sessions at least one hour in duration.

On the basis of this one variable, it would appear that field rater training programs should have greater generalizability than laboratory rater training programs. It is unclear, though, whether the length/amount of training found in either laboratory or field investigations is sufficient to ensure generalizability. In part, this is attributable to the fact that there is no generally agreed upon length or amount of training necessary to ensure maximum transfer to the work environment. Based on examination of a number of rater training programs in the work world, the length/amount of both laboratory and field rater training programs would seem to be low.

Another study characteristic, criteria, demonstrates similar difficulties in assessing the generalizability of rater training programs. As previously noted, laboratory studies of rater training have considered halo, accuracy, and interrater reliability. While these studies tend to support the conclusion that rater training reduces halo and leniency, findings regarding accuracy are less clear. Field research has also utilized halo and leniency measures but accuracy has not been studied, presumably due to the fact that true criterion scores are hard to find (Bernardin & Buckley, 1981). Accuracy, however, is precisely the criterion of interest in the work environment. Consequently, it is unclear whether either laboratory or field studies are generalizable with respect to this study variable.

Purpose of appraisal, a third variable of interest, further complicates any attempt to determine whether field or laboratory studies are more generalizable. Work organizations are concerned almost exclusively with training for administrative purposes such as tenure and promotion decisions. However, nearly all laboratory and field rater training studies focus on experimental and research uses. It is unclear to what extent findings from this nonadministrative appraisal context generalize to work environments.

Conclusions

Rater training research suggests that the variables that explain transfer of learned behavior from one environment to another also help determine the generalizability of laboratory and field rater training studies. Rater training field studies appear to be no more successful in dealing with these variables than corresponding laboratory studies. Results from field research have no greater claim to generalizability than laboratory study findings (Dipboye & Flanagan, 1979). Both sets of studies typically lack the sophistication required for generalizability. Ultimately, the generalizability of rater training programs and their outcomes may be facilitated by the careful delineation of cognitive and contextual variables that can be derived from the transfer model. An emphasis on these variables and a match to needs identified in the workplace is more important than whether research is done in a laboratory or a field setting.

Training raters how to conduct proper performance appraisals is crucial. Rater training from the perspective taken above involves identifying the context in which the appraisal is embedded and training raters accordingly. If the art of rater training can be developed to both identify process variables and prescribe strategies to deal with them, rater training programs may prove more successful in achieving their stated goals of reduced rating errors and increased accuracy.

The proposed transfer model may provide a useful key to examining the issues involving generalizability. Further delineation of the model may result in rater training diagnostic applications. Ideally, elaboration of the transfer model will have positive consequences not only for rater training but for the development and evaluation of training programs in general. In order to further explore these possibilities, it will be necessary to apply the transfer model to other training techniques.

References

Aleamoni, L.M., & Hexner, P.Z. (1973) *The effect of different sets of instructions on student course and instructor evaluation* (Research Report No. 339). Urbana, IL: University of Illinois, Measurement and Research Division, Office of Instructional Resources.

Baumgartel, H., & Jeanpierre, F. (1972) Applying new knowledge in the back-home setting: A study of Indian managers' adoptive efforts. *Journal of Applied Behavioral Science, 8*, 674–694.

Berkowitz, L., & Donnerstein, E. (1982) External validity is more than skin deep: Some answers to criticisms of laboratory experiments. *American Psychologist, 37*, 245–257.

Bernardin, H.J. (1978) Effects of rater training on leniency and halo errors in student ratings of instructors. *Journal of Applied Psychology, 63*, 301–308.

Bernardin, H.J., & Buckley, M.R. (1981) Strategies in rater training. *Academy of Management Review, 6*, 205–212.

Bernardin, H.J., & Pence, E.C. (1980) Effects of rater training: Creating new response sets and decreasing accuracy. *Journal of Applied Psychology, 65*, 60–66.

Bernardin, H.J., & Walter, C.S. (1977) Effects of rater training and diary-keeping on psychometric error in ratings. *Journal of Applied Psychology, 62*, 64–69.

Borman, W.C. (1975) Effects of instructions to avoid halo error on reliability and validity of performance evaluation ratings. *Journal of Applied Psychology, 60*, 556–560.

Borman, W.C. (1979) Format and training effects on rating accuracy and rater errors. *Journal of Applied Psychology, 64*, 410–421.

Borreson, H.A. (1967) The effects of instructions and item content on three types of ratings. *Educational and Psychological Measurement, 27*, 855–862.

Brown, E.M. (1968) Influence of training, method, and relationship on the halo effect. *Journal of Applied Psychology, 52*, 195–199.

Centra, J.A. (1974) The relationship between student and alumni ratings of teachers. *Educational and Psychological Measurement, 34*, 321–326.

DeCotiis, T., & Petit, A. (1978) The performance appraisal process: A model and some testable propositions. *Academy of Management Review, 3*, 635–646.

Dipboye, R.L., & Flanagan, M.F. (1979) Research settings in industrial and organizational psychology. *American Psychologist, 34*, 141–150.

Ellis, H.C. (1965) *The transfer of learning.* New York: Macmillan.

Fay, C.H., & Latham, G.P. (1982) Effects of training and rating scales on rating errors. *Personnel Psychology, 35*, 105–116.

Friedman, B.A., & Cornelius, E.T. (1976) Effect of rater participation in scale construction on the psychometric characteristics of two rating scale formats. *Journal of Applied Psychology, 61*, 210–216.

Gagné, R.M. (1962) Military training and principles of learning. *American Psychologist, 17*, 83–91.

Gagné, R.M., & Briggs, L.J. (1979) *Principles of instructional design.* New York: Holt, Rinehart & Winston.

Goldstein, I.L. (1980) Training in work organizations. *Annual Review of Psychology, 31*, 229–272.

Hendrickson, G., & Schroeder, W. (1941) Transfer of training in learning to hit a submerged target. *Journal of Educational Psychology, 32*, 206–213.

Heron, A. (1956) The effects of real-life motivation on questionnaire response. *Journal of Applied Psychology, 40,* 65–68.

Holding, D.H. (1965) *Principles of training.* London: Pergamon.

Ivancevich, J.M. (1979) Longitudinal study of the effects of rater training on psychometric error in ratings. *Journal of Applied Psychology, 64,* 502–508.

Kane, J.S., & Lawler, E.E., III. (1979) Performance appraisal effectiveness: Its assessment and determinants. In B. Staw (Ed.), *Research in organizational behavior* (pp. 425–478). Greenwich, Conn.: JAI Press.

Landy, F.J., & Farr, J.L. (1983) *The measurement of work performance: Methods, theory, and applications.* New York: Academic Press.

Latham, G.P., Wexley, K.N., & Pursell, E.D. (1975) Training managers to minimize rating errors in the observation of behavior. *Journal of Applied Psychology, 60,* 550–555.

Leifer, M.S., & Newstrom, J.W. (1980) Solving the transfer of training problem. *Training & Development Journal, 34,* 42–46.

McIntyre, R.M., Smith, D.E., & Hassett, C.E. (1984) Accuracy of performance ratings as affected by rater training and perceived purpose of rating. *Journal of Applied Psychology, 69,* 147–156.

Michalak, D.F. (1981) The neglected half of training. *Training & Development Journal, 35,* 22–28.

Musicante, G.R. (1983) *Predicting student ratings and instructor rater attitudes toward a teaching appraisal system.* Unpublished master's thesis, University of Maryland, College Park.

Ory, J.C., & Braskamp, L.A. (1980) *Faculty perceptions on the quality and usefulness of three types of evaluative information* (ERIC Document Reproduction Service No. ED 189 296).

Pursell, E.D., Dossett, D.L., & Latham, G.P. (1980) Obtaining valid predictors by minimizing rating errors in the criterion. *Personnel Psychology, 33,* 91–96.

Sharon, A.T. (1970) Eliminating bias from student ratings of college instructors. *Journal of Applied Psychology, 54,* 278–281.

Sharon, A.T., & Bartlett, C.J. (1969) Effect of instructional conditions in producing leniency on two types of rating scales. *Personnel Psychology, 22,* 251–263.

Swezey, R.W. (1982–83). Application of a transfer training model to training device assessment. *Journal of Educational Technology System, 11,* 225–238.

Taylor, E.K., & Wherry, R.J. (1951) A study of leniency in two rating systems. *Personnel Psychology, 4,* 39–47.

Thorndike, E.L., & Woodworth, R.S. (1901) (I) The influence of improvement in one mental function upon the efficiency of other functions. (II) The estimation of magnitudes. (III) Functions involving attention, observation and discrimination. *Psychological Review, 8,* 247–261, 384–395, 553–564.

Thornton, G.C., III, & Zorich, S. (1980) Training to improve observer accuracy. *Journal of Applied Psychology, 65,* 351–354.

Warmke, D.L., & Billings, R.S. (1979) Comparison of training methods for improving the psychometric quality of experimental and administrative performance ratings. *Journal of Applied Psychology, 64,* 124–131.

Wexley, K.N. (1984) Personnel training. *Annual Review of Psychology, 35,* 519–551.

Wexley, K.N., Sanders, R.E., & Yukl, G.A. (1973) Training interviewers to eliminate contrast effects in employment interviews. *Journal of Applied Psychology, 57,* 233–236.

Wheaton, G.R., Fingerman, R.W., Rose, A.M., & Leonard, R.L. (976) *Evaluation and application of the predictive model* (Research Memorandum 76–16). Alexandria, Va.: U.S. Army Research Institute.

Zedeck, S., & Cascio, W.F. (1982) Performance appraisal decisions as a function of rater training and purpose of the appraisal. *Journal of Applied Psychology, 67,* 752–758.

III
Motivation

This part reports the results of studies of four of the best-known motivation or performance improvement techniques: goal setting, feedback, participation, and money. For each of these there are a reasonable number of laboratory and field experiments, thus making meaningful conclusions about generalization possible.

Gary Latham and Thomas Lee review the goal setting studies. They report that over 90 percent of both lab and field studies found specific, challenging goals to lead to higher performance than do-your-best or no goals. This finding is in full agreement with earlier reviews. Latham and Lee go on, however, to document the consistency of goal setting effects across hard versus soft criteria, quantity versus quality of performance, and individual versus group goals. Since the base rate of success for goal setting studies is so high, it is not surprising that the technique seems to work no matter how the studies are subdivided. Clearly goal setting is one of the most robust findings in the psychological literature.

Richard Kopelman reviews the studies on feedback. Those familiar with the goal setting and feedback literature know that the studies show quite consistently that goal setting and feedback together lead to higher performance than either one alone. Feedback is necessary to track progress against goals. Goals are one way of giving meaning to feedback (of evaluating whether the feedback indicates good or poor performance). Furthermore it is hard if not impossible (at least in a laboratory or work setting) to provide people with feedback and not have them *do something* with it, for example, decide whether or not they should work harder. Thus, in reviewing feedback studies, it is difficult to know the degree to which other factors such as implicit goal setting are adequately controlled. Usually they are not. Everyone but behavior mod advocates (who persist in believing that feedback by itself has some sort of magical reinforcing power) seems to recognize this.

Thus studies purporting to assess the effects of feedback are almost always assessing the effects of feedback in combination with other unmeasured factors. Kopelman reports that laboratory and field studies are almost equally consistent in finding positive effects of feedback (plus . . . ?) on performance. However, the effect size in field settings appears to be considerably larger than in laboratory settings. The probable reason, as noted in chapter 1, is that more of the confounding factors are present in field settings than in laboratory settings. Locke and Bryan some years ago found that if feedback is *truly* divorced from all other factors (by giving it in a form that *cannot* be used to set goals), then it has no motivational effect on performance at all.

Kopelman provides a very interesting discussion of the various factors that make feedback work. Recent research and theorizing in control theory and self-efficacy theory is beginning to identify these factors and the means by which they affect subsequent performance. In addition to goal setting, some of these factors are improvement in ability, increased meaningfulness, anticipated rewards, and competition.

David Schweiger and Carrie Leana review the most ideologically loaded topic in this book: participation in decision making. Participation is one of those techniques that is supposed to work because it's "good." Unfortunately the data are not as accommodating as they should be. Consistent with Locke and Schweiger's earlier review, the updated review finds that employee participation in decision making is no more likely to lead to better performance than authoritative decision making by the leader. This finding is equally true of laboratory and field studies. Latham and Lee as well as Schweiger and Leana analyzed the effects of participation in goal setting separately from their other studies and both concluded that participation goal setting is no more effective than authoritative goal setting in either locus. This is not to say that participation does not work; rather it is not as robust a phenomenon as other motivational techniques. The conditions under which it is most effective are not yet known. One important contingency factor may be degree of subordinate knowledge, although this pertains more to the cognitive than to the motivational benefits of participation.

The results for the effects of participation on subordinate satisfaction are more positive, with generally beneficial effects being found in both laboratory and field settings.

Douglas Jenkins reviews the studies on experimentally manipulated monetary incentives. He finds, consistent with the previous three chapters, that the findings are highly similar in lab and field settings, although the number of studies in each case is relatively small. In this case the effect sizes are also comparable (about 30 percent) and they are consistent with estimates from previous reviews of this literature.

Thomas Mawhinney's chapter is relatively brief since there are relatively few studies of reinforcement schedule effects with normal, adult humans.

Overall, this group of chapters provides impressive evidence for the generalizability of the results of laboratory studies to field settings. The findings are especially striking because the base rates of success for three of the techniques (goal setting, feedback, and money) are high whereas the base rate for one (participation versus performance) is low. Thus the generalizability is not simply a function of the technique being so powerful that it works everywhere.

6
Goal Setting

Gary P. Latham
Thomas W. Lee

I n 1968 Locke published a seminal review of the goal setting literature. The empirical data showed clearly that a specific, challenging goal results in higher performance than does a generalized goal such as "do your best"; that a specific, challenging goal, if accepted, leads to higher performance than an easy goal; and that variables such as participation in decision making affect performance only to the extent that they lead to the setting and/or acceptance of a specific, hard goal.

Locke's review focused primarily on well-controlled laboratory experiments, many of which he himself had conducted. This prompted Heneman and Schwab (1972) to compare these laboratory studies unfavorably with work being done on expectancy theory:

> A noteworthy aspect of research on expectancy theory is the emphasis on investigating employees in their natural work environments, thus providing a high degree of external validity. In the case of motivation, this is in direct contrast to research on . . . goal setting theory (Locke, 1968), which has usually entailed student subjects working on laboratory tasks in experimental situations. The "cost" of external validity has been, of course, a general inability to make causal inferences. (p. 8)

Similarly, Campbell, Dunnette, Lawler, and Weick (1970) stated that the difference between college students setting specific goals with regard to addition problems and the behavior of employees in industrial settings must be considered.

And considered it was. Ironically, a myriad of methodological problems has led to a subsequent decline in research on expectancy theory (see Locke, 1975; Pinder, 1984) while work on goal setting in both laboratory and field studies continues to proliferate in the scientific literature. For example, in a review of the literature from 1969 to 1980, Locke, Shaw, Saari, and Latham (1981) found that 99 out of 110 studies showed that specific, hard goals produced better performance than

---

We thank E.A. Locke, C.C. Pinder, and J.R. Terborg for their helpful suggestions in preparing this chapter.

medium, easy, do-your-best, or no goals. The laboratory tasks included figure selection (Bavelas, 1978), chess (Campbell & Ilgen, 1976), simple addition (Locke & Bryan, 1969), and perceptual speed tasks (Mento, Cartledge, & Locke, 1980). The field studies involved logging (Latham & Kinne, 1974; Latham & Locke, 1975), driving trucks (Latham & Baldes, 1975; Latham & Saari, 1982), dieting (Bandura & Simon, 1977), maintenance work (Ivancevich, 1977), training (Wexley & Nemeroff, 1975), die casting (Adam, 1975), and returning survey questionnaires (Dossett, Latham, & Saari, 1980), to name just a few.

Pinder (1977) has argued that in many instances it is premature to apply motivation theories to work settings. An exception is goal setting. In 1984 he stated that:

> Goal Setting Theory has been exposed to more research in field settings than have most other theories of work motivation . . . Goal Setting Theory has demonstrated more scientific validity to date than any other theory or approach to work motivation presented in this book. (p. 169)

Chidester and Grigsby's (1984) research supports Pinder's conclusion. They performed a meta-analysis on twenty-two studies that had tested the goal specificity hypothesis and on twenty-one studies that had tested the goal difficulty hypothesis.

> Overall, the meta-analysis results indicate strong support for Locke's original two hypotheses. Although individual disconfirming studies can be found, the overall mean correlations and effect sizes suggest that disconfirming results are due to sampling error or experimental artifacts. Unequivocally, setting either difficult or specific goals reliably results in increased productivity. (p. 205)

The meta-analysis also revealed that one can expect a median 16 percent increase above base line performance using goal difficulty and goal specificity. This finding is in agreement with research reported by Locke and Latham (1984).

With regard to the effects of participation and goal setting, Latham and his colleagues have conducted eleven studies since 1975. Of these, four were conducted in the laboratory and seven were conducted in the field. The samples included loggers, word processors, engineers and scientists, government employees, and college students. The tasks included falling trees, typing, test performance in a selection battery, R&D work, brainstorming, basic arithmetic, and performance in a business game. Yet the conclusions were the same. If assigned goals are higher than those that are set participatively, then performance is higher with the assigned goals (Latham, Steele, & Saari, 1982). If goal difficulty is held constant, there is no significant difference in performance between those with assigned rather than participatively set goals (Dossett, Latham, & Mitchell, 1979; Latham & Saari, 1979a; Latham & Marshall, 1982; Latham et al., 1982). When participation occurs in the absence of goal setting, there is no main effect on performance (Latham & Steele, 1983). Thus it would appear that participation by itself has no direct effect on motivation as defined by working harder or faster. Participation is important in our culture from a motivational standpoint only to the extent that it leads to the setting of higher goals than is the case when the goal is assigned unilaterally (Latham, Mitchell, & Dossett, 1978). Participation in goal setting, however, can have cognitive effects to the extent that it increases understanding of task requirements or promotes the development of strategies for goal attainment (Latham & Baldes, 1975; Latham & Saari, 1979a; Locke & Latham, 1984).

These findings are in partial conflict with the meta-analysis performed by Chidester and Grigsby (1984). They found, as did Latham, that participation in field settings can lead to the setting of higher goals than is the case when the goals are assigned (Latham et al., 1978). In laboratory studies, they found, as did Latham, that this was not always the case. In a laboratory setting, the experimenter is not reluctant to set extremely hard goals (for example, Latham et al., 1982).

The Latham et al. studies are in conflict with that of Chidester and Grigsby in that the meta-analysis showed that the motivational effects of specific hard goals are strongly moderated by participation. The reason for this conflict in findings is that Chidester and Grigsby unexplainably confounded the variable of goal acceptance with that of participation: "Participation in goal setting (which also includes studies demonstrating acceptance of goals) had a clear and consistent moderator effect across all studies" (p. 205).

Acceptance of a goal can and does occur in the absence of participation in setting it (Locke & Latham, 1984). Thus there is no theoretical justification for lumping together these two independent variables.

These contradictory findings underscore a fundamental difficulty in the application of meta-analysis. One needs to understand the theory as well as the empirical data one is investigating before this technique can be used properly.

A second problem in using meta-analysis is that the researcher must either know or provide compelling estimates of (1) the reliabilities of independent and dependent variables, (2) sample sizes, and (3) population and sample variances for all variables of interest. Without each of these types of information, specific sources of error variance cannot be corrected. Thus the likelihood of clarifying conflicting research decreases and the usefulness of meta-analysis is minimized.

A limitation of most goal setting studies is that the information necessary for a thorough meta-analysis is missing. A problem with many meta-analyses reported in the literature is that researchers tend to correct only a single source of error (usually sampling error because sample sizes are routinely reported) and ignore the remaining sources. This is what was done by Chidester and Grigsby (1984).

The purpose of this chapter is to show the extent to which laboratory-obtained findings regarding goal setting generalize to field settings. Specifically, five questions are addressed:

1. Do specific, hard (challenging) goals lead to higher performance than nonspecific goals (such as do-your-best or no goals) in both laboratory and field experiments?

2. If the answer is yes, is this true for both quantity and quality of performance?

3. If the answer is yes, is this true for both soft criteria such as ratings and hard criteria such as outcome measures?

4. If the answer to question 1 is yes, are goals effective for groups as well as for individuals in both laboratory and field settings?

5. Does participation in goal setting result in higher performance than assigned goals in either laboratory or field situations?

The issue of generalizability is an important one. The attack on the laboratory experiment is well underway in developmental and social psychology despite its defense by Henshel (1980) as well as Berkowitz and Donnerstein (1982). Incredibly, the attack is underway in industrial-organizational psychology despite the seminal article by Weick (1965) and the review of the literature by Dipboye and Flanagan (1979). Nevertheless, both Guion and Landy, the editor and associate editor respectively of the *Journal of Applied Psychology*, have questioned the meaningfulness of the dependent variable in a laboratory study on goal setting (*Personal Communication*). Their concern with the laboratory experiment is by no means limited to research on goal setting. In an editorial, Guion (1983) stated that the limits of the usefulness of studies involving college sophomores can be reached very quickly. Landy and Bates (1973) have expressed the same concern.

Method

The goal setting literature published from 1968 to 1984 was reviewed. As noted, Locke et al. (1981) reported that the vast preponderance of the evidence shows the superiority of specific, hard goals over medium, easy, do-your-best, or no goals on job performance. Rather than replicate all of their work, we chose to concentrate our review on specific hard goals versus nonspecific goals. Parenthetically, our review of the literature confirmed the superiority of specific, hard goals over specific, medium or easy goals.

Because the information necessary for a complete meta-analysis was missing from the published literature, a frequency analysis was performed instead. A debate on the appropriateness of meta-analysis is beyond the scope of this chapter. Suffice it to say that an adequate meta-analysis requires parameters or compelling estimates of the reliabilities for all measured variables, sample sizes, and parameters or compelling estimates of the variance for all variables. This information is not available in the majority of published goal setting studies. To correct for only one or two of the seven sources of variance is an abuse of the meta-analysis procedure. Moreover, there is no empirical data showing that a frequency count and a meta-analysis yield different conclusions when the data from the vast majority of reviewed studies obtained significant results. A meta-analysis can be useful when there are an abundance of significant and nonsignificant findings regarding the effect of a given independent variable. Lack of significance, however, is not an issue in goal setting studies. Thus a simple frequency count allowed us to look at the consistency of the findings without having to discard studies that omitted information necessary for performing a complete meta-analysis.

Results

The tables list different total numbers of studies. This difference is because certain studies could not be classified into a given table. Table 6–1 lists those studies that explicitly compared the effects of specific, hard goals with do-your-best or no goals. The results are overwhelming in both laboratory and field settings. In the laboratory, thirty-seven out of thirty-eight experiments showed that a specific, challenging goal had a positive effect on performance. This finding was supported by twenty-seven out of twenty-eight studies conducted in the field.

Table 6–2 lists those studies (regardless of whether laboratory or field) that investigated the quality (for example, the judgment or rating of "goodness" of the work) and/or quantity (for example, the amount of the work) of performance. The results are again clear. Specific, hard goals affect both the quality and quantity of performance positively in both laboratory and field settings. Of the sixty-two studies identified, sixty-one studies supported goal setting across the various cells.

Table 6–3 lists those studies that used hard criteria (for example, dollar amount or countable outcomes) and soft criteria (for example, performance ratings). Again, the results show the positive benefit of goal setting, regardless of whether the research was conducted in the laboratory or the field. Surprisingly, there are few studies which used subjective performance measures.

Table 6–1
Specific, Challenging versus Nonspecific Goals

	Lab	*Field*
Specific, challenging goals were superior to no goals or do-your-best goals	2, 8, 10, 12, 18, 19, 20, 21, 22, 24, 25, 32, 37, 42, 43, 45, 46, 50, 51, 55, 56, 57, 60, 65, 67, 68, 71, 72, 73, 75, 77, 78, 79, 82, 84, 85, 86 ($n = 37$)	1, 3, 5[a], 6[a], 7[a], 14, 15, 16, 26, 27, 28, 34, 35, 36, 38, 39, 41, 47, 48, 64, 69, 70[a], 76, 81[a], 83[a], 87, 88 ($n = 27$)
No goals or do-your-best goals were equal or superior to specific, challenging goals	78 ($n = 1$)	47 ($n = 1$)

Note: The numbers in each quadrant identify the studies either supporting or not supporting goal setting theory.

[a]Correlational-survey studies.

Table 6–2
Quality and Quantity Criteria

	Lab	Field	Total
Quality	3/3	1/1	4/4
	10[a], 42, 43	4	
Quantity	28[b]/29	7/7	35/36
	2, 8, 15, 17, 18, 19, 23, 40, 45, 46, 50, 52, 53, 54, 55, 57, 58, 59, 60, 62, 65, 68, 72, 73, 80, 85, 86, 88	5[a], 38, 39, 44, 47 48, 61	
Both	14/14	8/8	22/22
	9, 13, 20, 21, 22, 25, 31, 34, 51, 63, 71, 82, 83, 84	24, 27, 28, 29, 30, 33, 74, 89	
Total	45/46	16/16	61/62

Note: In each cell the numerator of the fraction is the number of studies supporting goal setting theory. The denominator is the total number of studies fitting the cell. The list of numbers identifies the supporting studies.
[a]Correlational-survey studies.
[b]The nonsupporting study is 66.

Table 6–3
Soft and Hard Criteria

	Lab	Field	Total
Hard	43[a]/44	14/14	57/58
	2, 8, 9, 10, 13, 15, 17, 18, 19, 20, 21, 22, 23, 24, 25, 37, 40, 42, 43, 45, 46, 50, 51, 52, 53, 54, 55, 57, 58, 59, 60, 62, 63, 67, 68, 71, 72, 73, 80, 82, 85, 86, 88	4, 11[b], 27, 28, 33, 34, 38, 39, 44, 47, 48, 61, 74, 76	
Soft	0/0	4/4	4/4
		5[b], 41, 49[b], 69	
Both	4/4	3/3	7/7
	31, 65, 83, 84	29, 30, 89[b]	
Total	47/48	21/21	68/69

Note: In each cell the numerator of the fraction is the number of studies supporting goal setting theory. The denominator is the total number of studies fitting the cell. The list of numbers identifies the supporting studies.
[a]The nonsupporting study is 66.
[b]Correlational-survey designs.

Table 6-4
The Individual or Group as the Unit of Analysis

	Lab	Field	Total
Individual	45[a]/46	17/17	62/63
	2, 8, 9, 10, 13, 15, 17, 18, 19, 20, 21, 22, 23, 25, 31, 37, 40, 42, 43, 45, 46, 50, 51, 52, 53, 54, 55, 57, 58, 59, 60, 62, 63, 65, 67, 68, 71, 72, 73, 80, 82, 83, 84, 85, 88	5[b], 11[b], 27, 28, 29, 30, 33, 34, 38, 41, 44, 48, 61, 69, 74, 76, 89[b]	
Group	1/1	4/4	5/5
	86	4, 39, 47, 49[b]	
Total	46/47	21/21	67/68

Note: In each cell, the numerator of the fraction is the number of studies supporting goal setting theory. The denominator is the total number of studies fitting each cell. The list of numbers identifies supporting studies.
[a]The nonsupporting study is 66.
[b]Correlational-survey designs.

Table 6-4 lists those studies that had either the individual or the group as the unit of analysis. For individuals, the data are again overwhelming in terms of the positive effects of goal setting in both laboratory and field settings. Only one laboratory study used the group as the unit of analysis. However, four field studies replicated the conclusion that goal setting improves the performance of the group as well as of the individual.

Table 6-5 lists those studies that compared the effect of participatively versus nonparticipatively (such as assigned) set goals on performance. (See also chapter

Table 6-5
Participatively versus Nonparticipatively Set Goals

	Lab	Field
Participation leads to higher task or job performance than assigned goals, self-set goals, or a control group ("other")	43 ($n = 1$)	41, 47[a] ($n = 2$)
Assigned goals or a control group ("other") lead to higher task or job performance than participation	46 ($n = 1$)	($n = 0$)
No difference between participatively and nonparticipatively set goals	42, 44, 45, 46 ($n = 4$)	27, 28, 40, 48, 51[a], 89[b] ($n = 6$)

Note: The numbers in each cell identify the supporting studies.
[a]Only one of two groups within this study was supportive. The other group was not supportive.
[b]Correlational-survey study.

8.) Thirteen articles (allowing fourteen comparisons) were located. Four laboratory and six field studies reported no difference between the effects of participatively versus nonparticipatively set goals on performance. One laboratory and two field studies reported the superiority of participatively set versus nonparticipatively set goals on performance. However, this was because participation resulted in the setting of harder goals than was the case when the goals were assigned. One lab study showed assigned goals to be superior. There is little evidence that participation per se yields an increase in performance. This finding reinforces Meyer, Kay, and French (1965). It is the setting of a goal that is important rather than the method by which it is set.

Discussion

In examining the results of this study, three issues emerge. First, why is goal setting effective? Second, why do the results for goal setting generalize so readily from the laboratory to the field? Third, what is the value of these two research settings for studying goal setting?

The answer to the first question can be found in the clinical psychology literature, specifically social learning theory (Bandura, 1977). A goal is symbolic in that it enables a person to engage in foresightful action. Goal specificity is important because it enables an individual to attend to a specific aspect of performance. A departure from a goal triggers self-regulatory behavior to bring the behavior either in line with the goal or to raise the goal if it is easily being exceeded. However, such self-adjustive responses occur only to the extent that the behavior is valued by the person. Empirical studies in both laboratory (Simon, 1979) and field settings (Bandura & Simon, 1977) show that a person may value a goal or activity regardless of whether it was assigned. It is the goal, not the method by which it is set, that makes one's responses and their consequences salient. Making self-rewarding reactions contingent upon attaining a specific target creates self-inducement to persist in one's efforts until performance matches the goal. Thus specific goals are effective because they provide the basis for regulating one's efforts and evaluating how one is doing.

It should be noted that both the organizational and the clinical psychology literature have been concerned almost exclusively with proximal rather than the distal goals (for example, a five-year plan) that usually are of interest in the field of business policy. Proximal goals, like distal goals, serve a directive function, but more importantly, they determine the immediate choice of activities and how hard the person will work at their attainment. Distal goals may be too far removed in time to serve as an effective incentive or guide for present action. By focusing on the distant future, it is too easy to put off today what can be done tomorrow. The issue of proximal versus distal goals has implications for the frequency with which goals are set for formal performance appraisals in industry.

Why do laboratory studies of goal setting generalize so readily to field studies of the same subject matter? A key to the answer may be the simplicity of goal setting techniques. As Dunnette noted in 1976, our science is still so imprecise that very simple concepts, methods, and techniques are likely to be more fruitful than those that are unduly complicated. It was for this reason that he cited goal setting as one of eight milestones in organizational psychology.

Pinder (1984) has echoed this sentiment. Because the theory is comparatively simple, it requires testing procedures that are accordingly simple, and less subject to many of the methodological difficulties that have hindered the refinement of other motivation theories. In addition, he offers another hypothesis that piggybacks on the first. He points out that a relatively small number of researchers have studied goal setting in contrast to equity and expectancy theories. The result has been the development of a set of research techniques and experimental paradigms that have proven to be effective and relatively sound from a scientific point of view.

We would offer at least one more reason that is also tied to the previous two. When things are simple, transfer of learning, specifically transfer of principles, occurs for the researcher (Bass & Vaughn, 1966). The theory of transfer of training through principles, as we are using it here, implies that researchers need not be concerned with the process of specific identical elements in laboratory and field situations, but that positive transfer results when they apply those principles learned in one situation to another. The beauty of this explanation is that it places a much lighter burden on the location of a study. If carried to its logical end, it considerably changes the problem of generalizability. The primary focus now becomes the creation of circumstances that best help the researcher help subjects apply goal setting techniques. Laboratory versus field experiment is no longer a central issue.

A primary value of using both research settings is that each facilitates interpretation of the data collected in the other arena. Moreover, laboratory results on goal setting increase the probability that the time of subjects in subsequent field experiments will be well used. Field experiments in turn raise questions that can be answered expeditiously in the laboratory. The issue of whether a study is conducted in a laboratory or in the field becomes secondary to what it is we are interested in discovering, and how best that interest can be explored.

For example, the early laboratory experiments by Locke defined goal setting constructs and their interrelationships. The early field experiments by Latham shifted the question from asking "Does goal setting work?" to "Where does it work?" and "How can we improve it?" Boundary conditions and limits to goal setting later became salient issues worth exploring in both laboratory and field settings. The importance of participation relative to setting goals illustrates this point.

Field experiments (Latham & Yukl, 1975; Latham et al., 1978) suggested the value of participation in goal setting. But laboratory experiments showed that the issue crucial to goal setting effectiveness was goal difficulty (Latham & Saari, 1979a). This finding was replicated in the laboratory and then applied in the field (Dossett et al., 1979).

There has been considerable debate on the role of goal setting versus feedback (for example, Komaki, 1981; Locke, 1980). Laboratory experiments showed that feedback affected behavior only to the extent that it led to the setting of specific, hard goals (Locke, Cartledge, & Koeppel, 1968). A field experiment confirmed this finding. People received explicit feedback during a performance appraisal. No goals were set. The people were told to anticipate either praise, public recognition, or a monetary bonus for demonstrating specific behavior. They were even informed that six other groups were formally setting specific hard goals. Nevertheless, there was no increase in their performance relative to that of a control group (Latham et al., 1978).

A laboratory experiment (Erez, 1977) showed that goal setting in the absence of feedback does not affect behavior. A field experiment showed that feedback in the absence of goal setting has no effect on behavior even when the person is maximally participating in it, that is, self-monitoring (Bandura & Simon, 1977). A laboratory experiment (Simon, 1979) explains why. Neither the goal nor the feedback is sufficient in itself to bring about a behavior change. The task for which the goal is set and the feedback that is given must be valued by the person. Employee participation in decision making is not the only way to get people to value a course of action.

As a result of systematically studying goal setting in both laboratory and field settings, few people in the scientific community question whether goal setting works. Boundary conditions of goal setting continue to be examined (Austin & Bobko, 1984). For example, what are the theoretical and empirical connections between it and theories of job design, task interdependence, communication patterns, and Pfeffer's (1981) ideas on symbolic management? Under what conditions do goals become distal rather than proximal? It would be unfortunate if in answering these questions an underlying issue continues to be whether the laboratory is a fit place to examine these concerns.

It is imperative to the advancement of knowledge in our field that this issue be put to rest. As Bernstein, Hakel, and Harlan (1975) stated a decade ago, "The time has come to set aside prejudices regarding the use of student samples (whether they be pro or con)" (p. 268). Similarly, Runkel and McGrath (1972) have argued cogently that neither the laboratory nor the field experiment has any natural or scientific claim to greater respect from researchers—each serves the other. We must guard against our colleagues admiring us for using one strategy rather than the other. From the point of view of the grand strategy of science, each method compliments the other (Runkel & McGrath, 1972).

The publication of this book is a healthy sign in that it signifies that many researchers are willing to examine generalizability empirically in diversified research settings rather than endorse the use of one setting over another as the place to conduct research.

References

Adam, E.E. (1975) Behavior modification in quality control. *Academy of Management Journal, 18*, 662–679.

Austin, J.T., & Bobko, P. (1984) The application of goal setting: Some boundary conditions and future research. *Academy of Management Proceedings '84*, 197–201.

Bandura, A. (1977) *Social learning theory.* Englewood Cliffs, N.J.: Prentice-Hall.

Bandura, A., & Simon, K.M. (1977) The role of proximal intentions in self regulation of refractory behavior. *Cognitive Therapy and Research, 1*, 177–193.

Bass, B.M., & Vaughn, J.A. (1966) *Training in industry: The management of learning.* Belmont, Calif.: Wadsworth.

Bavelas, J.B. (1978) System analysis of dyadic interaction: Prediction from individual parameters. *Behavioral Science, 23*, 177–186.

Berkowitz, L., & Donnerstein, E. (1982) External validity is more than skin deep. *American Psychologist, 37*, 245–257.

Bernstein, V., Hakel, M.D., & Harlan, A. (1975) The college student as interviewer: A threat to generalizability? *Journal of Applied Psychology, 60*, 266–268.

Campbell, D.J., & Ilgen, D.R. (1976) Additive effects of task difficulty and goal setting in subsequent task performance. *Journal of Applied Psychology, 61*, 319–324.

Campbell, J.P., Dunnette, M.D., Lawler, E.E., & Weick, K.E. (1970) *Managerial behavior, performance and effectiveness.* New York: McGraw-Hill.

Chidester, T.R., & Grigsby, W.C. (1984) A meta-analysis of the goal setting-performance literature. In J.A. Pearce, II, & R.B. Robinson, Jr. (Eds.), *Academy of Management Proceedings '84*, 202–206.

Dipboye, R.L., & Flanagan, M.F. (1979) Research settings in industrial and organizational psychology. Are findings in the field more generalizable than in the laboratory? *American Psychologist, 34*, 141–150.

Dossett, D.L., Latham, G.P., & Mitchell, T.R. (1979) The effects of assigned versus participatively set goals, KR, and individual differences when goal difficulty is held constant. *Journal of Applied Psychology, 64*, 291–298.

Dossett, D.L., Latham, G.P., & Saari, L.M. (1980) The impact of goal setting on survey returns. *Academy of Management Journal, 23*, 561–567.

Dunnette, M.D. (1976) Mishmash, mush, and milestones in organizational psychology: 1974. In H. Meltzer and F.R. Wickert (Eds.), *Humanizing organizational behavior.* Springfield, Ill.: Charles C. Thomas.

Erez, M. (1977) Feedback: A necessary condition for the goal setting—performance relationship. *Journal of Applied Psychology, 62*, 624–627.

Guion, R.M. (1983) Editorial comments from the new editor. *Journal of Applied Psychology, 68*, 547–551.

Heneman, H.G., III, & Schwab, D.P. (1972) Evaluation of research on expectancy theory prediction of employee performance. *Psychological Bulletin, 78*, 1–9.

Henshel, R.L. (1980) The purpose of laboratory experimentation and the virtues of deliberate artificiality. *Journal of Experimental Social Psychology, 16*, 466–478.

Ivancevich, J.M. (1977) Different goal setting treatments and their effects on performance and job satisfaction. *Academy of Management Journal, 20*, 406–419.

Komaki, J. (1981) A behavioral view of paradigm debates: Let the data speak. *Journal of Applied Psychology, 66,* 111–112.

Landy, F.J., & Bates, F. (1973) Another look at contrast effects in the employment interview. *Journal of Applied Psychology, 58,* 141–144.

Latham, G.P., & Baldes, J.J. (1975) The "practical significance" of Locke's theory of goal setting. *Journal of Applied Psychology, 60,* 122–124.

Latham, G.P., & Kinne, S.B., III (1974) Improving job performance through training in goal setting. *Journal of Applied Psychology, 59,* 187–191.

Latham, G.P., & Locke, E.A. (1975) Increasing productivity with decreasing time limits: A field replication of Parkinson's law. *Journal of Applied Psychology, 60,* 524–526.

Latham, G.P., & Marshall, H.A. (1982) The effects of self set, participatively set and assigned goals on the performance of government employees. *Personnel Psychology, 35,* 399–404.

Latham, G.P., Mitchell, T.R., & Dossett, D.L. (1978) Importance of participative goal setting and anticipated rewards on goal difficulty and job performance. *Journal of Applied Psychology, 63,* 163–171.

Latham, G.P., & Saari, L.M. (1979a) The effects of holding goal difficulty constant on assigned and participatively set goals. *Academy of Management Journal, 22,* 163–168.

Latham, G.P., & Saari, L.M. (1979b) Importance of supportive relationships in goal setting. *Journal of Applied Psychology, 64,* 151–156.

Latham, G.P., & Saari, L.M. (1982) The importance of union acceptance for productivity improvement through goal setting. *Personnel Psychology, 35,* 781–787.

Latham, G.P., & Steele, T.P. (1983) The motivational effects of participation versus goal setting on performance. *Academy of Management Journal, 26,* 406–417.

Latham, G.P., Steele, T.P., & Saari, L.M. (1982) The effects of participation and goal difficulty on performance. *Personnel Psychology, 35,* 677–685.

Latham, G.P., & Yukl, G.A. (1975) Assigned versus participative goal setting with educated and uneducated wood workers. *Journal of Applied Psychology, 60,* 299–302.

Locke, E.A. (1968) Toward a theory of task motivation and incentives. *Organizational Behavior and Human Performance, 4,* 35–42.

Locke, E.A. (1975) Personnel attitudes and motivation. *Annual Review of Psychology, 26,* 457–480.

Locke, E.A. (1980) Latham versus Komaki: A tale of two paradigms. *Journal of Applied Psychology, 65,* 16–23.

Locke, E.A., & Bryan, J.F. (1969) The directing formation of goals in task performance. *Organizational Behavior and Human Performance, 4,* 35–42.

Locke, E.A., Cartledge, N., & Koeppel, J. (1968) Motivational effects of knowledge of results: A goal setting phenomenon? *Psychological Bulletin, 70,* 474–485.

Locke, E.A., & Latham, G.P. (1984) *Goal setting: A motivational technique that works.* Englewood Cliffs, N.J.: Prentice-Hall.

Locke, E.A., Shaw, K.N., Saari, L.M., & Latham, G.P. (1981) Goal setting and task performance: 1969–1980. *Psychological Bulletin, 90,* 125–252.

Mento, A.J., Cartledge, N.D., & Locke, E.A. (1980) Maryland vs. Michigan vs. Minnesota: Another look at the relationship of expectancy and goal difficulty to task performance. *Organizational Behavior and Human Performance, 25,* 419–440.

Meyer, H.H., Kay, E., & French, J. (1965) Split roles in performance appraisal. *Harvard Business Review, 43,* 123–129.

Pfeffer, J. (1981) Management as symbolic action: The creation and maintenance of organizational paradigms. In L.L. Cummings & B.M. Staw (Eds.), *Research in Organizational Behavior* (Vol. 3). Greenwich, Conn.: JAI Press, 1–52.

Pinder, C.C. (1977) Concerning the application of human motivation theories in organizational settings. *Academy of Management Review, 2,* 384–397.

Pinder, C.C. (1984) *Work motivation.* Glenview, Ill.: Scott, Foresman.

Runkel, P.J., & McGrath, J.E. (1972) *Research on human behavior: A systematic guide to method.* New York: Holt, Rinehart & Winston.

Simon, K.M. (1979) Self-evaluative reactions: The role of personal valuation of the activity. *Cognitive Therapy and Research, 3,* 111–116.

Weick, K.E. (1965) Laboratory experimentation with organizations. In J.G. March (Ed.), *Handbook of organizations.* Chicago: Rand McNally, 194–260.

Wexley, K.N., & Nemeroff, W.F. (1975) Effectiveness of positive reinforcement and goal setting as methods of management development. *Journal of Applied Psychology, 60,* 446–450.

References Cited in Tables

1. Adam, E.E. (1975) Behavior modification in quality control. *Academy of Management Journal, 18,* 662–679.

2. Bandura, A., & Cervone, D. (1983) Self-evaluative and self-efficacy mechanisms governing the motivational effects of goal systems. *Journal of Personality and Social Psychology, 45,* 1017–1028.

3. Bandura, A., & Simon, K.M. (1977) The role of proximal intentions in self-regulation of refractory behavior. *Cognitive Therapy and Research,* 1977, *1* 177–193.

4. Becker, L.J. (1978) Joint effect of feedback and goal setting on performance: A field study of residential energy conservation. *Journal of Applied Psychology, 63,* 428–433.

5. Blumenfeld, W.S., & Leidy, T.R. (1969) Effectiveness of goal setting as a management device: Research note. *Psychological Reports, 24,* 752.

6. Brass, D.J., & Oldham, G.R. (1976) Validating an in-basket test using an alternative set of leadership scoring dimensions. *Journal of Applied Psychology, 61,* 652–657.

7. Burke, R.J., & Wilcox, D.S. (1969) Characteristics of effective employee performance review and development interviews. *Personnel Psychology, 22,* 291–305.

8. Campbell, D.J. (1984) The effects of goal contingent payment on the performance of a complex task. *Personnel Psychology, 37,* 23–40.

9. Campbell, D.J., & Ilgen, D.R. (1976) Additive effects of task difficulty and goal setting on subsequent task performance. *Journal of Applied Psychology, 61,* 319–324.

10. Campion, M.A., & Lord, R.G. (1982) A control systems conceptualization of the goal setting process. *Organizational Behavior and Human Performance, 30* (2), 265–287.

11. Carroll, S.J., Jr., & Tosi, H.L. (1970) Goal characteristics and personality factors in a management-by-objectives program. *Administrative Science Quarterly, 15,* 295–305.

12. Chung, K.H., & Vickery, W.D. (1976) Relative effectiveness and joint effects of three selected reinforcements in a repetitive task situation. *Organizational Behavior and Human Performance, 16,* 114–142.

13. Das, B. (1982) Effects of production feedback and standards on worker productivity in a repetitive production task. *IIE Transactions,* March.

14. Dockstader, S.L. (1977) *Performance standards and implicit goal setting: Field testing Locke's assumption.* Paper presented at the meeting of the American Psychological Association, San Francisco.

15. Dossett, D.L., Latham, G.P., & Mitchell, T.R. (1979) The effects of assigned versus participatively set goals, KR, and individual differences when goal difficulty is held constant. *Journal of Applied Psychology, 64,* 291–298.

16. Dossett, D.L., Latham, G.P., & Saari, L.M. (1980) The impact of goal setting on survey returns. *Academy of Management Journal, 23,* 561–567.

17. Erez, M. (1977) Feedback: A necessary condition for the goal setting-performance relationship. *Journal of Applied Psychology, 62,* 624–627.

18. Erez, M., & Zidon, I. (1984) Effect of goal acceptance on the relationship of goal difficulty to performance. *Journal of Applied Psychology, 69,* 69–78.

19. Frost, P.J., & Mahoney, T.A. (1976) Goal setting and the task process: I. An interactive influence on individual performance. *Organizational Behavior and Human Performance, 17,* 328–350.

20. Garland, H. (1982) Goal levels and task performance: A compelling replication of some compelling results. *Journal of Applied Psychology, 67,* 245–248.

21. Garland, H. (1983) The influence of ability, assigned goals, and normative information on personal goals and performance: A challenge to the goal attainability assumption. *Journal of Applied Psychology, 68,* 20–30.

22. Garland, H. (1984) Relation of effort-performance expectancy to performance in goal setting experiments. *Journal of Applied Psychology, 69,* 79–84.

23. Hamner, W.C., & Harnett, D.L. (1974) Goal-setting, performance and satisfaction in an interdependent task. *Organizational Behavior and Human Performance, 12,* 217–230.

24. Hannan, R.L. (1975) *The effects of participation in goal setting on goal acceptance and performance: A laboratory experiment.* Unpublished doctoral dissertation, University of Maryland, College Park.

25. Huber, V.L. (1984) *The motivational effects of task difficulty and goal setting on performance and task satisfaction.* Unpublished manuscript, Cornell University.

26. Ivancevich, J.M. (1974) Changes in performance in a management by objectives program. *Administrative Science Quarterly, 19,* 563–574.

27. Ivancevich, J.M. (1976) Effects of goal setting on performance and job satisfaction. *Journal of Applied Psychology, 61,* 605–612.

28. Ivancevich, J.M. (1977) Different goal setting treatments and their effects on performance and job satisfaction. *Academy of Management Journal, 20,* 406–419.

29. Ivancevich, J.M., & McMahon, J.T. (1982) The effects of goal setting, external feedback and self generated feedback on outcome variables: A field experiment. *Academy of Management Journal, 25,* 359–372.

30. Ivancevich, J.M., & Smith, S.V. (1981) Goal setting interview skills training: Simulated on-the-job analysis. *Journal of Applied Psychology, 66,* 697–705.

31. Jackson, S.E., & Zedeck, S. (1982) Explaining performance variability: Contributions of goal setting, task characteristics, and evaluative contexts. *Journal of Applied Psychology, 67,* 759–768.

32. Kaplan, R., & Rothkopf, E.Z. (1974) Instructional objectives as directions to learners: Effect of passage length and amount of objective-relevant content. *Journal of Educational Psychology, 66,* 448–456.

33. Kim, J.S. (1984) Effect of behavior plus outcome goal setting and feedback on employee satisfaction and performance. *Academy of Management Journal, 27,* 139–149.

34. Kim, J.S., & Hammer, W.C. (197) Effect of performance feedback and goal setting on productivity and satisfaction in an organizational setting. *Journal of Applied Psychology, 61,* 48–57.

35. Kolb, D.A., & Boyatzis, R.E. (1970) Goal-setting and self-directed behavior change. *Human Relations, 23,* 439–457.

36. Komaki, J., Barwick, K.D., & Scott, L.R. (1978) A behavioral approach to occupational safety: Pinpointing and reinforcing safe performance in a food manufacturing plant. *Journal of Applied Psychology, 64,* 434–445.

37. LaPorte, R.E., & Nath, R. (1976) Role of performance goals in prose learning. *Journal of Educational Psychology, 68,* 260–264.

38. Latham, G.P., & Baldes, J.J. (1975) The "practical significance" of Locke's theory of goal setting. *Journal of Applied Psychology, 60,* 122–124.

39. Latham, G.P., & Kinne, S.B. III. (1974) Improving job performance through training in goal setting. *Journal of Applied Psychology, 59,* 187–191.

40. Latham, G.P., & Marshall, H.A. (1982) The effects of self set, participatively set and assigned goals on the performance of government employees. *Personnel Psychology, 35* 399–404.

41. Latham, G.P., Mitchell, T.R., & Dossett, D.L. (1978) Importance of participative goal setting and anticipated rewards on goal difficulty and job performance. *Journal of Applied Psychology, 63,* 163–171.

42. Latham, G.P., & Saari, L.M. (1979a) The effects of holding goal difficulty constant on assigned and participatively set goals. *Academy of Management Journal, 22,* 163–168.

43. Latham, G.P., & Saari, L.M. (1979b) Importance of supportive relationships in goal setting. *Journal of Applied Psychology, 64,* 151–156.

44. Latham, G.P., & Saari, L.M. (1982) The importance of union acceptance for productivity improvement through goal setting. *Personnel Psychology, 35,* 781–787.

45. Latham, G.P., & Steele, T.P. (1983) The motivational effects of participation versus goal setting on performance. *Academy of Management Journal, 26,* 406–417.

46. Latham, G.P., Steele, T.P, & Saari, L.M. (1982) The effects of participation and goal difficulty on performance. *Personnel Psychology, 35,* 677–685.

47. Latham, G.P., & Yukl, G.A. (1975) Assigned versus participative goal setting with educated and uneducated woods workers. *Journal of Applied Psychology, 60,* 299–302.

48. Latham, G.P., & Yukl, G.A. (1976) Effects of assigned and participative goal setting on performance and job satisfaction. *Journal of Applied Psychology, 61,* 166–171.

49. Lee, C., & Niedzweidz, E. *The effects of goal setting under different levels of task interdependence.* Unpublished manuscript, University of Maryland, College Park.

50. Locke, E.A. (1982) Relation of goal level to performance with a short work period and multiple goal levels. *Journal of Applied Psychology, 67,* 512–514.

51. Locke, E.A., & Bryan, J.F. (1969a) The directing function of goals in task performance. *Organizational Behavior and Human Performance, 4,* 35–42.

52. Locke, E.A., & Bryan, J.F. (1969b) Knowledge of score and goal level as determinants of work rate. *Journal of Applied Psychology, 53,* 59–65.

53. Locke, E.A., Bryan, J.F., & Kendall, L.M. (1968) Goals and intentions as mediators of the effects of monetary incentives on behavior. *Journal of Applied Psychology, 52,* 104–121.

54. Locke, E.A., Cartledge, N., & Knerr, C.S. (1970) Studies of the relationship between satisfaction, goal setting, and performance. *Organizational Behavior and Human Performance, 5,* 135–158.

55. Locke, E.A., Frederick, E., Lee, C., & Bobko, P. (1984) Effect of self-efficacy, goals, and task strategies on task performance. *Journal of Applied Psychology, 69,* 241–251.

56. Locke, E.A., Mento, A.J., & Katcher, B.L. (1978) The interaction of ability and motivation in performance: An exploration of the meaning of moderators. *Personnel Psychology, 31,* 269–280.

57. Locke, E.A., Zubritzky, E., Cousins, E., & Bobko, P. (1984) Effect of previously assigned goals on self-set goals and performance. *Journal of Applied Psychology, 69,* 694–699.

58. London, M., & Oldham, G.R. (1976) Effects of varying goal types and incentive systems on performance and satisfaction. *Academy of Management Journal, 19,* 537–546.

59. Matsui, T., Okada, A., & Inoshita, O. (1983) Mechanism of feedback affecting task performance. *Organizational Behavior and Human Performance, 31,* 114–122.

60. Matsui, T., Okada, A., & Kakuyama, T. (1982) Influence of achievement need on goal setting, performance, and feedback effectiveness. *Journal of Applied Psychology, 67,* 645–648.

61. McCaul, K.D., & Kapp, J.T. (1982) Effects of goal setting and commitment on increasing metal recycling. *Journal of Applied Psychology, 67,* 377–379.

62. Mento, A.J., Cartledge, N.D., & Locke, E.A. (1980) Maryland vs. Michigan vs. Minnesota: Another look at the relationship of expectancy and goal difficulty to task performance. *Organizational Behavior and Human Performance, 25,* 419–440.

63. Meyer, J.P., & Schacht, B. (1984) *An examination of the cognitive mechanisms by which assigned goals affect task performance.* Paper presented at the annual convention of the Canadian Psychological Association, Ottawa, Ontario.

64. Migliore, R.H. (1977) *MBO: Blue collar to top executive.* Washington, D.C.: Bureau of National Affairs.

65. Mossholder, K.W. (1980) Effects of externally mediated goal setting on intrinsic motivation: A laboratory experiment. *Journal of Applied Psychology, 65,* 202–210.

66. Motowidlo, S., Loehr, V., & Dunnette, M.D. (1978) A laboratory study of the effects of goal specificity on the relationship between probability of success and performance. *Journal of Applied Psychology, 63,* 172–179.

67. Mowen, J.C., Middlemist, R.D., & Luther, D. (1981) Joint effects of assigned goal level and incentive structure on task performance: A laboratory study. *Journal of Applied Psychology, 66,* 598–603.

68. Mueller, M. (1983) *The effects of goal setting and competition on performance: A laboratory study.* Unpublished master's thesis, University of Minnesota, Department of Psychology.

69. Nemeroff, W.F., & Cosentino, J. (1979) Utilizing feedback and goal setting to increase performance appraisal interviewer skills of managers. *Academy of Management Journal, 22,* 566–576.

70. Oldham, G.R. (1976) The motivational strategies used by supervisors: Relationships to effectiveness indicators. *Organizational Behavior and Human Performance, 15,* 66–86.

71. Organ, D.W. (1977) Intentional vs. arousal effects of goal-setting. *Organizational Behavior and Human Performance, 18,* 378–389.

72. Pritchard, R.D., & Curtis, M.I. (1973) The influence of goal setting and financial incentives on task performance. *Organizational Behavior and Human Performance, 10,* 175–183.

73. Rakestaw, T.L., & Weiss, H.M. (1981) The interaction of social influences and task experiences and goals, performance, and performance satisfaction. *Organizational Behavior and Human Performance, 27,* 326–344.

74. Reber, R.A., & Wallin, J.A. (1984) The effects of training, goal setting, and knowledge of results on safe behavior: A component analysis. *Academy of Management Journal, 27*, 544–560.

75. Reynolds, R.E., Standford, S.N., & Anderson, R.C. (1979) Distribution of reading time when questions are asked about a restricted category of text information. *Journal of Educational Psychology, 71*, 183–190.

76. Ronan, W.W., Latham, G.P., & Kinne, S.B., III. (1973) Effects of goal setting and supervision on worker behavior in an industrial situation. *Journal of Applied Psychology, 58*, 302–307.

77. Rosswork, S.G. (1977) Goal setting: The effects on an academic task with varying magnitudes of incentive. *Journal of Educational Psychology, 69*, 710–715.

78. Rothkopf, E.Z., & Billington, M.J. (1975) A two-factor model of the effect of goal-descriptive directions on learning from text. *Journal of Educational Psychology, 67*, 692–704.

79. Rothkopf, E.Z., & Kaplan, R. (1972) Exploration of the effect of density and specificity of instructional objectives on learning from text. *Journal of Educational Psychology, 63*, 295–302.

80. Silver, H.C., & Greenhaus, H.J. *The impact of goal, task, and personal characteristics on goal setting behavior.* Unpublished manuscript, Stevens Institute of Technology, Hoboken, N.J.

81. Steers, R.M. (1975) Task-goal attributes, in achievement, and supervisory performance. *Organizational Behavior and Human Performance, 13*, 392–403.

82. Strang, H.R., Lawrence, E.C., & Fowler, P.C. (1978) Effects of assigned goal level and knowledge of results on arithmetic computation: A laboratory study. *Journal of Applied Psychology, 63*, 446–450.

83. Terborg, J.R. (1976) The motivational components of goal setting. *Journal of Applied Psychology, 61*, 613–621.

84. Terborg, J.R., & Miller, H.E. (1978) Motivation, behavior, and performance: A closer examination of goal setting and monetary incentives. *Journal of Applied Psychology, 63*, 29–39.

85. Umstot, D.D., Bell, C.H., Jr., & Mitchell, T.R. (1976) Effects of job enrichment and task goals on satisfaction and productivity: Implications for job design. *Journal of Applied Psychology, 61*, 379–394.

86. Watson, C. (1983) *Motivational effects of feedback and goal setting on group performance.* Paper presented at the meeting of the American Psychological Association, Anaheim, Calif.

87. Wexley, K.N., & Nemeroff, W.F. (1975) Effectiveness of positive reinforcement and goal setting as methods of management development. *Journal of Applied Psychology, 60*, 446–450.

88. White, S.E., Mitchell, T.R., & Bell, C.H., Jr. (1977) Goal setting, evaluation apprehension, and social cues as determinants of job performance and job satisfaction in a simulated organization. *Journal of Applied Psychology, 62*, 665–673.

89. Yukl, G.A., & Latham, G.P. (1978) Interrelationships among employee participation, individual differences, goal difficulty, goal acceptance, goal instrumentality, and performance. *Personnel Psychology, 31*, 305–323.

7
Objective Feedback

Richard E. Kopelman

For decades researchers have debated the extent to which findings from laboratory experiments can be generalized to field settings. On one side of the debate are those who point out that laboratory experiments typically entail the observation of college students performing contrived tasks, in an artificial setting, for a very brief period of time, for trivial or no rewards. The conclusion: laboratory experiments lack ecological validity (Brunswik, 1955); hence, results cannot safely be generalized to the "real world." In this vein, Gibbs (1979, p. 138) has noted that, "It is commonplace to observe the rarified and aimless trivia that dominate the pages of experimental journals." As a consequence, states Gibbs (1979, p. 127), "The most popular reformist plea in contemporary psychological research is the call for ecologically oriented inquiry." Cognitive psychologists, for example, increasingly have been enjoined "to replace tachistoscopic flashes, nonsense syllables, and arbitrary sequences of words with significant task situations." In short, the argument is that excessive concern for experimental control and scientific rigor may lead to useless research (and rigor mortis).

On the other side of the debate, it is pointed out that college students are people, and that human mental and motor processes are situationally indifferent (see Berkowitz & Donnerstein, 1982; Littman, 1961). Whether in a laboratory or a field setting, people will tell you that the number 5 is greater than the number 3. Moreover, it is often argued that what matters is experimental realism (the extent to which the intended essence of theoretical variables is captured) rather than mundane realism (the resemblance of experimental setting and procedure to the real world) (Carlsmith, Ellsworth, & Aronson, 1976). As Berkowitz and Donnerstein have put it, "The meaning subjects assign to the situation they are in and the behavior they are carrying out plays a greater part in determining the generalizability of an experiment's outcome than does the sample's demographic representativeness or the setting's surface realism" (p. 249).

The author gratefully acknowledges the help of Edwin A. Locke and Lynn S. Mullins in locating copies of many of the articles describing laboratory experiments. The field experimental data reported here as tables 7–2 and 7–3 will also appear in Richard Kopelman's forthcoming book, *Managing productivity in organizations: A practical, people-oriented perspective* (New York: McGraw-Hill, 1986).

Yet for many areas of research the debate continues. There are no definitive answers to the question of generalizability; the jury is still out. The primary reason for this inconclusive state of affairs is simple: there has been an abundance of logical, deductive argumentation, but very little inductive, empirical evidence gathering. Investigators have generally ignored the sage advice of Jack Webb: too few have been in search of the facts, just the facts.

With such a need in mind, this paper examines and compares the results of laboratory and field experiments performed in connection with a particular topic area: the effects of objective feedback on task performance. The purpose of this enterprise is to answer a number of questions: What has been the direction of effect? How consistent or reliable is this finding? What has been the average magnitude of impact? How often does the experimental treatment produce a sizable effect? What is the impact of time on effect size?

Objective feedback is defined as information about work behavior or job performance that is relatively factual and incontrovertible. Of course, objectivity is a matter of degree; judgment cannot entirely be eliminated from any human measurement. But it does seem meaningful to distinguish relatively objective indicators (such as absences, percent defective, and output per hour) from the vast collection of relatively subjective criteria that are widely researched (for example, satisfaction scores, stress reactions, attributions, perceptions, performance ratings, and attitudes). (A review of the entire contents of the *Academy of Management Journal* for the years 1979–1983 indicates that only 10 percent of all published articles contained one or more objective criteria.)

In general terms, the research question explored is: Does the provision of objective feedback have a similar impact on task performance in laboratory experiments as compared to field experiments?

Method

A literature review was conducted subject to two delimitations. Studies were included only if they: (1) involved normal, adult humans and (2) dealt with cognitive or motor work activities. Accordingly, studies of the effects of objective feedback on such activities as dieting, home energy conservation, and heart rate (bio-feedback) were excluded. In the present review only summary feedback was examined; studies providing epistemic or learning feedback were excluded.

A total of thirty laboratory and forty-two field studies were located. Field experiments were distinguished from laboratory experiments based on the purpose and context of the work activity. In field experiments subjects actually produced goods or provided services for others; in laboratory experiments the primary purpose of the work activity was to generate data or knowledge. It should be noted, though, that a liberal definition was employed in connection with what constitutes an experiment. A number of field interventions consisted of single group before-

and-after case studies, what Campbell and Stanley (1963) would call "pre-experiments." Others employed comparison groups without random assignment ("quasi-experiments").

Results were analyzed in terms of the percentage change in the criterion variable. For example, a decrease in an undesired verbal behavior (such as interrupting a client) from 20 percent of conversations to 5 percent would be treated as an improvement of 75 percent. Further, where possible, comparisons were made between the baseline level and the average level of the criterion throughout the intervention period. This minimized the possible (upward) bias that might result if (1) researchers ended their study on a high note, and (2) comparisons were made between baseline and final criterion scores.

Field studies were subdivided into two categories: those that focused on input processes or intermediate criteria (work behavior), and those that related to various measures of goal attainment (job performance indicators). Also examined was a subset of the second category, those studies that reflected the amount of goods produced or services rendered (output). The rationale for this classification scheme was that these measures represent different stages of the causal process. Work behaviors should influence goal accomplishment, which in turn should be reflective of outputs (Campbell, Dunnette, Lawler, & Weick, 1970). Of course, judgment was involved in classifying field studies, but in most cases the appropriate classification was fairly obvious. Examples of work behaviors include handwashing by kitchen workers, smiling by fast-food servers, interruptions by telephone reservation clerks, the frequency of safe work practices, punctuality, and absenteeism. Besides outputs such as units produced and productivity, a number of other indicators were also classified as performance criteria, for example, cost performance, percentage defective (quality), amount of backlog, and timeliness of task performance.

Results

The laboratory experiments are summarized in table 7–1. In twenty-three of the thirty studies (77 percent), subjects were college students, graduate students, or military cadets. In this regard, the studies reviewed are representative of those published in three prominent journals, *Journal of Applied Psychology, Organizational Behavior and Human Performance,* and *Personnel Psychology.* A survey of the entire contents of the 1966, 1970, and 1974 volumes of these journals found that students were the subjects in 75 percent of all laboratory studies reported (Dipboye & Flanagan, 1979). In ten of the thirty studies (33 percent) the treatment coupled explicit goal setting with objective feedback. The most common task, solving some form of arithmetic problem, appeared in 33 percent of the studies; next most common was a button or switch depression task designed to measure response latency (27 percent).

Table 7-1
Effects of Objective Feedback on Task Performance: Laboratory Experiments

Study	Sample/ Tasks[a]	Type of Feedback[b]	Other Interventions[c]	Impact on Task Performance	Comments
Wright 1906	9 S; carriage depression task	Pvt. I.	GS	21.1% more work performed over approximately 3 to 15 hours	Performance increased in 17 out of 18 observations
Arps 1920	3 S; finger lifting exercise	Pvt. I.		18% greater work rate with feedback—over 40 hours	Experimental data collected over a period of roughly 1 year
Book and Norvell 1922	124 CS; 4 different tasks	Pvt. I.	GS	25.2% greater improvement in average task performance —over roughly 2 hours	Feedback confounded with GS
Johanson 1922	3 S; auditory reaction time	Pvt. I.	PP	6% faster reaction time over approximately 10 to 15 minutes	
Crawley 1926	5 MS; weight lifting tasks	Pvt. I.	GS	Task performance increased by 14.7% over approximately 36 hours	Feedback confounded with GS
Ross 1927	59 CS; tallying by lines	Pvt. I. Pub. G.		8% greater performance of correct work, 4.4% greater performance in total work performed over 10 minutes	Comparing full feedback with no feedback
Manzer 1935	68 MCS, 60 FCS; hand dynamometer contraction	Pvt. I.		7.4% greater force with feedback among males; 11.6% greater force with feedback among females—over 15 minutes	

Study	Task	Sector	Code	Results	Comments
Mace 1935	Visual accuracy task	Pvt. I.		18% improvement in performance (reduction in inaccuracy)	
Elwell and Grindley 1938	20 FCS; target tracking task	Pvt. I.		Discontinuance of feedback resulted in a decline in performance of approximately 40% in experiment 1 (over 2 hours) and a decline of approximately 20% in experiment 2 (over 48 minutes)	Feedback made task more "interesting" and "more enjoyable"
Mackworth 1950	80 MS; vigilance and weight pull tasks	Pvt. I.	GS, P (pull task only)	18.6% improvement in visual vigilance over 2 hours; 49.4% improvement in auditory vigilance over 2 hours; 58.6% more work performed in pull task over 4 hours	
Gibbs and Brown 1955	12 S; copying documents with copying machine	Pub. I.		Work performed increased by 31.2% over 32 hours	In another experiment with 4 MS, feedback yielded 117.4% greater output
Payne and Hauty 1955	144 MS; target tracking task	Pvt. I.	GS	Approximately 30% improvement in task proficiency (% of time on target) over 4 hours	Explicit (but incorrectly low) feedback vs. vague feedback
McCormack 1959	10 FS; visual vigilance task	Pvt. I.		11.5% faster reaction time over 50 minutes	
McCormack, Binding, and Chylinksi 1962	44 CS; switch depression task	Pvt. I.		4.4% faster reaction time over 35 minutes	
McCormack, Binding, and McElheran 1965	100 MS; switch depression task	Pvt. I.		3.3% faster reaction time over 40 minutes	Several feedback groups vs. no feedback

Table 7-1 continued

Study	Sample/Tasks[a]	Type of Feedback[b]	Other Interventions[c]	Impact on Task Performance	Comments
Adams and Humes 1963	45 MCS; visual monitoring task	Pvt. I.		Approximately 14.5% faster reaction speed in group with feedback over 6 hours	Improved performance persisted after feedback ended; vague feedback had no effect on performance
Chapanis 1964	16 MCS; punching digits on paper tape	Pvt. I.		No significant effect (assume 0%) over 24 hours	Mean scores not reported
Montague and Webber 1965	40 MCS; visual monitoring task	Pvt. I.		3.3% improvement in latency of response; 12% more errors of omission—over 6 hours	Only nonspecific feedback was provided (e.g., "superior," "adequate"), not actual data
Church and Camp 1965	40 CS; button pressing task	Pvt. I.		7.9% faster reaction time (with fixed warning signal) over 2½ hours	Subjects without feedback "seemed far more bored than those with" feedback
Locke and Bryan 1966	70 CS; complex computation task	Pvt. I.		20.1% more problems solved correctly over 1½ hours	
Locke 1967	36 CS; arithmetic problems	Pvt. I.	GS	Approximately 1.5% increase in number of problems completed correctly over 1 hour	Feedback had slightly greater effect with hard goal vs. "do best" goal
Locke and Bryan 1968	61 CS; complex computational task	Pvt. I.		Approximately 9.5% more problems solved correctly over 1½ hours	

Study	Description	Setting		Results	Comments
Locke 1968	50 S; switch depression task	Pvt. I.		Approximately 12.5% faster reaction time over roughly 45 minutes	4 types of feedback vs. no feedback
Locke and Bryan 1969	40 CS; simple arithmetic task	Pvt. I.		Approximately 0.5% fewer problems attempted over roughly 2 hours	
Chung and Vickery 1976	80 CS; coding task	Pvt. I.		16.6% better overall performance (quantity and quality) with feedback—over 2 hours	
Erez 1977	86 CS; number checking task	Pvt. I.		13.4% more problems solved correctly over 10 minutes	Feedback seen as necessary condition for success of GS
Strang, Lawrence, and Fowler 1978	100 FCS; arithmetic problems	Pvt. I.	GS	3.4% faster problem solving speed; 12.5% reduction in error rate—over approximately 20 minutes	
Dossett, Latham, and Mitchell 1979	60 F clerical workers; arithmetic problems	Pvt. I.	GS	6.4% fewer problems attempted over 6 minutes	
Shaw, Locke, Bobko, and Beitzell 1981	94 CS; arithmetic problems	Pvt. I.	GS	10.6% increased in adjusted (for ability) number of problems attempted over 30 minutes (study 2)	
Matsui, Okada, and Inoshita 1983	87 FCS, 103 MCS; arithmetic problems	Pvt. I.	GS	5% increase in number of problems attempted (FCS), 6.6% increase in number of problems attempted (MCS), over 5 minutes	

[a]CS = college student; F = female; M = male; S = subject.
[b]Pvt. I. = private individual; Pub. I. = public individual; Pub. G. = public group.
[c]GS = goal setting; PP = physical punishment; P = praise.

Table 7-2
Effects of Objective Feedback on Work Behavior: Field Experiments

Study	Sample	Type of Feedback[a]	Other Interventions[b]	Impact on Work Behavior	Comments
Allen 1976	30 telephone reservation clerks for Aer Lingus	Pvt. I. Pub. G.	GS	66.5% reduction in undesired verbal behaviors; 84.4% increase in desired verbal behaviors; over-all effect was a 77.9% improvement after 3 months	Clerks had a positive reaction to the program
Quilitch 1978	80 employees in a mental health organization	Pub. I. (posting of replies to suggestions offered)		222.7% increase in the number of suggestions offered over 32 weeks	98% of employees said the program should be continued
Shook, Johnson, and Uhlman 1978	6 therapists at a health service center	Pvt. I. Pub. G.	T, P, R, GS	429% increase in the percentage of graphs of client behavior completed over 8½ weeks	Pvt. I. was superior in impact to Pub. G.; Pvt. I. + Pub. G. was superior to Pvt. I.
Sulzer-Azaroff 1978	Supervisors and staff at 30 university laboratories	Pvt. G. (sent to supervisor)	P	45.4% reduction in observed frequency of hazards over 7 to 14 months	Feedback was adopted as a permanent part of a new safety system
Komaki, Barwick, and Scott 1978	28 employees in 2 departments of a food manufacturing plant	Pub. G.	T, GS, R	32.5% increased in the proportion of observed work incidents performed safely over 11 weeks	Lost time accidents in the plant declined by 80% after 1 year
Collins, Komaki, and Temlock 1979	All salespersons in 5 departments of a department store	Pub. G.	T, R	95% increase in the percentage of customers approached by salespeople; service behavior score rose by 4% over 5 to 11 weeks	
McNees, Gilliam, Schnelle, and Risley 1979	All workers in a fast-food snack bar	Pub. G.		94% reduction in employee theft over 1 to 4 weeks	

Authors	Participants/Setting	Setting[a]	Technique[b]	Results	Comments
Komaki, Heinzmann, and Lawson 1980	55 employees in a city's vehicle maintenance department	Pub. G.	T, GS	41.4% improvement in behavioral safety scores over 34 to 36 weeks	83% decrease in the number of lost-time accidents; employees had a favorable reaction to the program
Komaki, Blood, and Holder 1980	11 front-line employees in a fast-food restaurant	Pvt. I.	T, P, R	58% increase in friendliness behavior (smiling) over 1½ to 10 weeks	
Geller, Eason, Phillips, and Pierson 1980	9 kitchen workers in a large university cafeteria	Pvt. I.	T	203.7% increase in the frequency of handwashing over 3 weeks	In comparison, training alone increased the frequency of handwashing by only 21.7%
Silva, Duncan, and Doudna 1981	20 clerical employees in the home office of a large insurance company	Pub. I. Pub. G.	P	9% reduction in absenteeism over 3 months (previously feedback alone without P resulted in a 50% decrease in absenteeism over 6 weeks)	The department manager failed to praise as required; apparently the use of P was quite alien
Frederiksen, Richter, Johnson, and Solomon 1981–82	21 clinical therapists at a psychological services center	Pub. I.	T	21% average reduction in 4 types of charting errors over 29 weeks	Feedback affected only the specific behaviors targeted
Haynes, Pine, and Fitch 1982	100 transit operators (bus drivers) at a regional transportation authority (325 operators in control group)	Pub. I. Pub. G.	TR, team competition	24.9% reduction in accident rate (compared to control group) over 18 weeks; over last 10 weeks the improvement was 35.2%	Annualized savings totaled $9,400; if extended to all drivers it would have been $30,500
Newby and Robinson 1983	15 part-time cashiers in a retail drugstore	Pub. G. Pub. I.	TR + GS	21.7% improvement in punctuality; 20.7% increase in the percentage of required checkout behaviors performed; 24% reduction in cashiered money discrepancies—over 38 days	Pub. I. and Pub. I + TR (and GS) were both far more effective than Pub. G.

[a]Pvt. I. = private individual; Pub. I. = public individual; Pvt. G. = private group; Pub. G. = public group.

[b]GS = goal setting; T = training; P = praise; R = public recognition; TR = token reinforcers.

Table 7-3
Effects of Objective Feedback on Job Performance: Field Experiments

Study	Sample	Type of Feedback[a]	Other Interventions[b]	Impact on Outputs and/or Other Objective Job Performance Criteria	Comments
Hundal 1969	18 metal workers in India	Pub. I		11.8% increase in output over one week (explicit feedback vs. no feedback)	3.3% increase in output in group with vague feedback
Panyan, Boozer, and Morris 1970	25 staff employees in 3 units of a residential child-treatment facility	Pub. I. Pub. G.		76% increase in the proportion of possible training sessions actually conducted over 21 to 24 weeks	Performance improved in the absence of direct, daily supervision
Organizational Dynamics 1974	Sales and shipping employees at Emery Air Freight	Pvt. I. Pub. G.	GS, P, R	150% increase in frequency of time meeting customer service standard; 110% increase in frequency of full use of containers over 4 years	Annualized savings of roughly $1 million
Pommer and Streedback 1974	9 staff employees in a residential child-treatment facility	Pvt. I.	T and public notice of individual job assignments	105% increase in the percentage of new jobs and procedures performed within 1 week of assignment over 3 months	The combination of feedback and T was more effective than either component alone
Adam 1975	43 die-casting operators	Pvt. I. Pub. G.	P, E	6.1% increase in production over 36 weeks	Annualized savings of $77,000
Quilitch 1975	17 mental health technicians in 4 residential child-treatment units	Pub. I	T, GS, and an instructional memo (in 2 units)	357% increase in the proportion of patients participating in planned activities over 2 to 8 weeks	Prior training and an instructional memo had no effect
Kim and Hamner 1976	4 groups of 113 blue collar, unionized service workers	Pvt. I.	GS, P	7.9% improvement in cost performance; 11.6% increase in service—over 3 months (also 13.6% improvement in safety)	Best results were obtained in the group which used all interventions

Study	Subjects	Setting	Feedback	Results	Additional Results
Kreitner, Reif, and Morris 1977	8 mental health technicians	Pub. I.		120% increase in group therapy sessions; 150% increase in one-on-one therapy sessions; 70% increase in daily routine duties over 4 to 8 weeks	Decrease in staff conflict and in patient complaints
Kirby 1977	Production employees in 3 plants	Pub. G.	GS	18.8% average increase in productivity over 2 years (excluding effects in one plant due to other factors)	75% decline in grievance rate; increase in employee suggestions for improving performance
Runnion, Johnson, and McWhorter 1978	58 plant managers and 92 truck drivers	Pvt. I. to both plant managers and truck drivers	TR	12% increase in total shipping productivity; 43.9% decrease in truck turnaround time over 29 weeks	
Emmert 1978	32 nonunionized industrial workers at PPG Industries	Pvt. I. Pub. G.	P, E	8.7% increase in productivity over 4 months	Productivity was higher with both forms of feedback than with Pub. G. alone
McCarthy 1978	Doffers in a textile yarn mill	Pvt. I. Pub. G.	GS, P	74.6% reduction in the incidence of high bobbins (causing tangles in thread)—over 8 weeks	When feedback was discontinued the incidence of high bobbins increased by 64%
Lamal and Benfield 1978	1 draftsman in an engineering firm	Pvt. I.		72.7% increase in time spent working over 4 weeks (sustained during follow-up after 11 weeks)	Marked improvement in punctuality
Dick 1978	4 textile machine operators at PPG Industries	Pvt. I.	GS, P	7.8% increase in output over an average study period of 32 weeks	Annualized savings of $3500; improved relationships between operators and the foreman
Runnion, Watson, and McWhorter 1978	195 truck drivers for textile company	Pvt. I. Pub. I. Pub. G.	R, TR	5.1% increase in miles per gallon; 56.7% increase in use of company-owned fuel terminals over 2 years	Dollar savings from increased fuel efficiency described as "very substantial"

Table 7-3 continued

Study	Sample	Type of Feedback[a]	Other Interventions[b]	Impact on Outputs and/or Other Objective Job Performance Criteria	Comments
Eldridge, Lemasters, and Szypot 1978	23 inspectors at Eastman Kodak	Pvt. I. Pub. G.	GS, P	30% increase in productivity over 40 weeks	Annualized savings of $105,000; increased contact between workers and supervisor; job seen as more interesting
Stoerzinger, Johnston, Pisor, and Monroe 1978	6 repair shop workers	Pub. G.	GS	20% increase in productivity over 22 weeks	Annualized savings of $57,200
Koch 1979	Approximately 150 sewing machine operators in a garment factory	Pub. G.	GS	62% reduction in defective garments ("seconds") over 12 months	Pay satisfaction declined
Schneier and Pernick 1979	Approximately 12 workers in a personnel department of a federal agency	Pvt. I.	GS, P, PWA, TO, CL	69.7% average improvement in 11 output measures over 7 months	9 of 11 performance indicators improved; 1 showed a decline
Kopelman 1979	Clerical employees in the payroll office of a large city personnel department	Pvt. I. Pub. G.		37.6% decrease in average backlog of work over 8 weeks	Backlogs decreased in 17 out of 18 categories; 1 was unchanged
Rhodes 1980	3 sales correspondents in an industrial products company	Pvt. I.	More complete sales information from salesmen	67% reduction in price quotation turnaround time over 3 years	Contributed to a 45% increase in sales and a 78% increase in profits

Milne and Doyle 1980	Back-office employees in the trust department of the Marine Midland Bank	Pvt. I. Pub. G.	P, R, and group problem solving	71.9% reduction in outstanding daily accounts receivable (increasing cash flow) over 1 year	Annualized savings of $440,350 (assuming a 15% cost of money)
Prue, Krapfl, Noah, Cannon, and Maley 1980	All employees in 16 departments of a large state hospital	Pvt. G. Pub. G.		83% increase in staff treatment programs, staff treatment hours, and client participation hours with private group feedback over 15–23 weeks; 178% increase in the same three criteria with public group feedback over 38 weeks	Work-related conversations increased among employees at all levels
Nadler, Cammann, and Mirvis 1980	Tellers and financial consultants in 10 branches of a Midwestern bank (and 10 comparison branches)	Pvt. G.	Group problem solving in some units	15.2% increase in work efficiency; 46.5% increase in work quality (compared to comparison branches) over 1 year	Feedback included objective and subjective components; intervention was not implemented in some branches and was only marginally adopted in others
Frost, Hopkins, and Conrad 1981	6 employees on a machine-paced manufacturing operation at Cramer Products, Inc.	Pub. G.	P	26% increase in productivity over 1 week	2100% return on investment
Rowe 1981	Independent appraisal firm that reported to the branch claim department of a casualty insurance company	Pvt. I. Pub. G.	GS	482% increase in the proportion of timely automobile accident reports filed over 18 months	Job performance improved among employees working for another company (who received the reports)

Table 7–3 continued

Study	Sample	Type of Feedback[a]	Other Interventions[b]	Impact on Outputs and/or Other Objective Job Performance Criteria	Comments
Ivancevich and McMahon 1982	209 engineers in five locations	Pvt. I. from 3 sources (supervisors, coworkers, and self)	GS, R	5.4% increase in 3 objective indicators in the feedback-only groups; 5.5% increase in the feedback + GS groups over 9 months	Self-generated feedback was superior to externally generated feedback
Kim 1984	93 salespeople in 4 branches of a large retail organization	Pvt. I. Pvt. G.	GS	12.2% increase in mean sales performance in the 3 experimental groups over 10 weeks; 0% change in the control group	Behavioral + outcome feedback was superior to either component alone

[a]Pvt. I. = private individual; Pub. I. = public individual; Pvt. G. = private group; Pub. G. = public group.
[b]CL = commendation letters; E = encouragement; GS = goal setting; P = praise; R = public recognition; TR = token reinforcement; PWA = preferred work assignments; T = training; TO = training opportunities.

Table 7–2 presents data on field studies where objective feedback was used to influence work behavior. In thirteen out of fourteen experiments (93 percent), subjects were full-time employees; in one case (7 percent) subjects were part-time employees. In five of the studies (36 percent), explicit goal setting was combined with objective feedback. The most common criterion, safety behavior, was used in 29 percent of the studies.

Data on field studies where objective feedback was used to influence job performance are presented in table 7–3. In all twenty-eight interventions, subjects were full-time employees; thirteen of the studies provided data pertinent to outputs. In thirteen interventions (46 percent), explicit goal setting was also employed.

Table 7–4 presents summary data pertinent to the direction of the effect of objective feedback in laboratory and field experiments (based on the average result per study). In twenty-six out of thirty laboratory experiments effects were positive; in forty-two out of forty-two field experiments objective feedback improved work behavior or job performance. The relatively small difference in success rates (87 percent versus 100 percent) might actually have been smaller had exact output data been reported in one laboratory experiment (Chapanis, 1964). Chapanis merely reported a nonsignificant effect for objective feedback, and it was assumed to be zero for the purpose of this analysis. Also, one laboratory experiment reported a positive result in terms of response latency, but a negative result for accuracy, the average result being negative (Montague & Webber, 1965). A slightly higher success rate for laboratory experiments would have been found had data been analyzed based on the total number of results reported (rather than average result per study)—34 out of 38 results were positive, or 89 percent.

Median effect sizes are reported in table 7–5. Based on the average result per study, median effects were as follows: field experiments using behavioral criteria, 47.5 percent; field experiments using performance criteria, 34.3 percent; field experiments using outputs only, 15.2 percent; and laboratory experiments, 11.1 percent. Examining results in terms of the proportion of sizable positive effects (an increase in the criterion of at least 10 percent), the pattern of results paralleled that obtained for effect size: field experiments, work behavior, 100 percent; field

Table 7–4
Direction of Effect of Objective Feedback on Performance Criteria: Frequency of Positive and Nonpositive Average Results in Laboratory and Field Experiments

Direction of Effect	Laboratory Experiments	Field Experiments Behavioral Criteria	Field Experiments Performance Criteria
Positive results	26	14	28
Nonpositive results (zero or negative)	4	0	0

Note: Table 7–4 is based on studies reported in tables 7–1, 7–2, and 7–3.

Table 7–5
A Comparison of Laboratory and Field Studies of Feedback:
Summary Analysis

Research Dimensions	Laboratory Experiments	Field Experiments		
		Behavioral Criteria	*Performance Criteria*	*Outputs Only*[a]
Research base				
Number of results	38	19	37	13
Number of studies	30	14	28	13
Magnitude of impact				
Median effect all results	11.6%	43.4%	46.5%	15.2%
Median effect per study	11.1%	47.5%	34.3%	15.2%
Reliability of impact[b]				
Proportion positive effect (> 0%)	87%	100%	100%	100%
Proportion sizable positive effect (> 10%)	50%	100%	82%	77%
Effects of time[b]				
Median experimental period	70 minutes	10¼ weeks	29½ weeks	29 weeks
Effect size by duration of study				
Above median duration	16.6%	41.4%	46.4%	17.0%[c]
Below median duration	7.1%	49.5%	32.8%	16.1%[c]

[a]A subset of performance criteria studies.
[b]Based on average result per study.
[c]Comparison of the six longest versus six shortest duration experiments.

experiments, all performance criteria, 82 percent; field experiments, outputs, 77 percent; and laboratory experiments, 50 percent.

With respect to the effects of time, there was some evidence of a positive relationship between the duration of the experiment and effect size as shown in table 7–5. Specifically, median effects in long and short duration field experiments using performance indicators were 46.4 percent and 32.8 percent, respectively. Even more pronounced was the effect of time in laboratory experiments. In long-duration laboratory experiments, the median effect of objective feedback was more than twice as great compared to the impact in short-duration experiments (16.6 percent versus 7.1 percent).

As noted previously, explicit goal setting was combined with objective feedback in many experiments. In general, however, effect sizes were similar in those experiments that incorporated goal setting compared to those that did not do so explicitly. Median effects, respectively, were: field experiments, behavioral criteria, 49.5 percent versus 45.4 percent; field experiments, all performance indicators, 30.0 percent versus 37.6 percent; field experiments, outputs, 19.4 percent versus 12.0 percent; and laboratory experiments, 12.7 percent versus 11.5 percent.[1] One possible explanation for the similarity of results with and without explicit goal setting is that subjects provided their own self-set goals in the absence of externally established ones. Consistent with this explanation, in one experiment 70 percent of the subjects receiving feedback only reported (in a post-experiment questionnaire) that they set their own goals (Bandura & Cervone, 1983).

Discussion

Because laboratory experiments typically entail the performance of simple tasks that take little time (for example, button pushing), it could be reasoned that the effects of objective feedback in the laboratory would most resemble field experiments that focus on simple work behaviors (such as smiling, interrupting, and handwashing). Yet the results suggest that in laboratory experiments, objective feedback typically produces a far smaller median impact than is the case in field experiments that focus on work behavior (11.1 percent versus 47.5 percent).

Why have the effects of objective feedback generally been greater in field experiments compared to laboratory experiments? Perhaps the best way to answer this question is by reviewing explanations for why objective feedback affects task performance.[2]

One major reason why objective feedback works is because it can improve role clarity and, hence, task-specific ability: it can instruct (or remind) people as to the specific behaviors that should, or should not, be performed, and/or the specific outcomes that should, or should not, be produced. French and Caplan (1973) found that more than 60 percent of the employees in a government agency were uncertain as to what was expected of them. Logically, objective feedback reduces role ambiguity and prompts appropriate behaviors and/or outputs.

Pertinent to the instructional capability of objective feedback, evidence has repeatedly shown that the effects are limited to the specific focal behaviors (or outputs) for which feedback is provided. For example, after workers in a snack bar were given feedback about the disappearance of potato chips, the theft rate for potato chips dropped dramatically, but there was no change in the theft rates for ice cream, milk, or sandwiches (McNees, Gilliam, Schnelle, & Risley, 1979). Similarly, feedback to mental health technicians about the frequency of group therapy sessions increased the frequency of such sessions but did not affect the frequency of one-on-one therapy sessions or other assigned tasks (Kreitner, Reif, & Morris, 1977).

Accordingly, it is not surprising that the more specific the objective feedback, the greater the effects (Annett, 1961). For example, Locke (1968) provided subjects with four different types of feedback. In one group, individuals were provided raw scores after each trial; in the other three treatment groups individuals were informed as to whether their most recent performance was better than their best, worst, or immediately prior performance. Subjects receiving raw data showed a 21½ percent faster response time than the control group; those receiving one of the three types of comparative feedback showed a response time that was 9½ percent faster than the controls. Similarly, in the visual monitoring laboratory experiment by Montague and Webber (1965), nonspecific feedback (whereby performance was categorized as superior, adequate, or poor) had only a minimal effect on task performance.

The development of task-specific ability may take a good deal of time in many jobs, depending, of course, on the task and the person. Perhaps one reason why the effects of feedback have been greater in field experiments than in laboratory experiments is because the former have generally been conducted over far longer time periods. Median work periods in field experiments have been 10¼ weeks for behavioral criteria and 29 to 29½ weeks for performance criteria; in contrast, the median work period for laboratory experiments has been 90 minutes. However, for some tasks, skill acquisition may take more than 90 minutes. Consistent with this premise, median performance improvements for long- and short-duration laboratory experiments were 16.6 percent and 7.1 percent, respectively.

Another ability-related factor that may have limited the effects of objective feedback in laboratory experiments is the relatively greater incidence of response latency studies. How quickly a person can respond to a stimulus is in large measure a function of innate factors. Further, because response latency is scored as a reduction in time required, the absolute maximum improvement is 100 percent; but improvements in rate of working can exceed 100 percent. Not surprisingly, therefore, the effects of objective feedback on response latency have been rather modest, the median result being an improvement of 6.95 percent. When these studies are put aside, the median effect of objective feedback in laboratory experiments was 14.1 percent; and for long-duration, nonresponse latency laboratory experiments, the median effect was an improvement of 16.6 percent.

A second major reason why objective feedback improves task performance is because it can enhance motivation. This can happen if objective feedback causes internal, social, or external consequences (Kopelman, 1982–83).

It has been argued elsewhere that information per se is not inherently motivating (Locke, Cartledge, & Koeppel, 1968). (Indeed, when, for example, a college professor hands out additional articles for students to read, the extra information may be viewed by the recipients as a punisher, rather than a reinforcer.)

While information in general may not be a reinforcer, information about one's own task performance often is. According to Hackman and Oldham (1976), this will be the case if (1) the person experiences the task to be meaningful, *and* (2) the person feels responsible for how well the task is performed. Under these conditions, and especially if the person has a strong need for personal growth and achievement, the provision of feedback will influence internal work motivation. That is, the person will experience feelings of increased self-approval and heightened self-regard upon performing well, and the opposite feelings upon performing poorly.

Because meaningfulness, responsibility, and knowledge of results are seen as combining multiplicatively, a very low score on any one will cause internal work motivation to be low (Hackman & Oldham, 1980). It follows, therefore, that to the extent that tasks are seen as insignificant or trivial, the effects of objective feedback on internal work motivation should be minimal. Stated in other terms, the absence of any one of the three necessary conditions should result in low ego involvement.

Hence, the relatively smaller effects of objective feedback in laboratory experiments (compared to field experiments) may in part be explained by the perceived insignificance of the tasks themselves. Tasks that have no clear bearing on the lives of other people and which do not result in the production of valued goods or services will likely be experienced as lacking in meaningfulness. In brief, the effects of objective feedback may be minimal due to a lack of internal, psychological consequences.

Consistent with this explanation, objective feedback generated strong positive effects in Mackworth's series of laboratory experiments pertinent to vigilance tasks. The experiments were conducted during the 1940s using Royal Air Force cadets. Subjects performed a number of tasks that "were actuated by the emergence during the second world war of a number of acute practical problems . . . problems relating to men fighting a war" (Mackworth, 1950, pp. 3, 7).

In another laboratory experiment where objective feedback produced strong positive effects (Gibbs & Brown, 1955), the task consisted of using a copying machine to copy documents (a task that exists in the real world). However, in a so-called replication experiment by Chapanis (1964) the task consisted of punching random digits in a paper tape. Whereas Gibbs and Brown reported an increase in output of 31.2 percent, Chapanis found no significant effects on output resulting from objective feedback, although exact output results were not reported.

Another explanation for how objective feedback can increase internal work motivation is provided by White's notion of the need for mastery or competence. Effectance motivation resides in the innate satisfaction associated with successful performance. Clearly, the provision of objective feedback can enable the individual "to find out how the environment can be changed" (White, 1959, p. 329), and thereby can sustain a sense of competence.

Another explanation for how objective feedback causes internal consequences is provided by theorizing and research on goal setting. Objective feedback permits individuals to establish specific goals; and there is abundant evidence that specific (and difficult) goals affect performance by directing attention, mobilizing effort, and increasing persistence (Locke, Shaw, Saari, and Latham, 1981). Still another explanation relates to control theory. According to this view, feedback influences behavior by a process that resembles a servomechanism: goal setting, measurement, evaluation, and discrepancy reduction (Taylor, Fisher, and Ilgen, 1984).

Further, a number of individual difference variables have been theorized to moderate the effects of objective feedback on task performance. Research suggests that objective feedback should be most promotive of internal work motivation among individuals with an internal locus of control, a high degree of self-esteem, a high need for achievement, and a high degree of perceived self-efficacy (Bandura

& Cervone, 1983; Ilgen, Fisher, & Taylor, 1979; Taylor et al., 1984). Among such individuals, performance improvement is seen, presumably, as both important and possible.

Objective feedback can also increase motivation to the extent that it creates social consequences. When performance feedback is made public, not only does the individual know how well he or she has performed, but so do other people. Public feedback may create competition among people, as they vie for respect and recognition; and many people will strive to avoid the possible embarrassment that may accompany poor performance. In one field experiment, truck drivers received objective feedback concerning fuel efficiency, and those who achieved six miles per gallon had their names posted on a bulletin board recognizing their achievement. The result was a significant reduction in energy consumption over two years (Runnion, Watson, & McWhorter, 1978). Five field studies have reported the use of public individual feedback by itself, yielding a median improvement in the criterion of 113 percent; in contrast, nine field studies have reported on the use of private individual feedback by itself, the median effect being an improvement in the criterion of 67 percent. Only one laboratory experiment (Gibbs & Brown, 1955) used public individual feedback, and, as noted previously, the result was an improvement in performance of 31.2 percent.

Individual difference factors have also been theorized to exert a moderating influence in connection with the social consequences of feedback. Objective feedback with social consequences should be most promotive of task motivation among individuals with an external locus of control and a high need for affiliation (Ilgen et al., 1979).

A third reason why objective feedback motivates improved task performance is because it can lead to the anticipation of gaining (or losing) external rewards. In expectancy theory terms, objective feedback can help establish, maintain, or strengthen various perceived effort-reward contingencies (see Ilgen et al., 1979). More specifically, it can influence perceived behavior-performance beliefs (expectancies) and performance-reward relationships (instrumentalities). In short, objective feedback serves to notify individuals directly or by implication of the new or now to be enforced contingencies operating in the organization (Prue & Fairbank, 1981).

In broad terms, the idea that objective feedback highlights potential external consequences is related to the notion of evaluation apprehension: namely, the desire to look good or make a good impression on the experimenter/intervener in order to obtain possible rewards, and the desire to avoid looking bad to avoid possible penalties. In laboratory experiments, evaluation apprehension is considered a threat to internal validity (Berkowitz & Donnerstein, 1982); hence efforts are often made to downplay perceptions of possible experimenter-controlled rewards or penalties (Fromkin & Streufert, 1976). However, such apprehension may actually increase external validity. In field experiments, objective feedback naturally serves to raise evaluation apprehension. Its provision alerts people to the many possible bases of comparison: against prior levels of accomplishment; against the accomplishments of others; against some standard level of accomplishment (explicit goal); or against some combination of these bases for comparison. Further, it signals the possibility of rewards or punishers.

In the field experiment involving a draftsman who was required to monitor the time he spent working, objective feedback led to a 72 percent increase in the proportion of time actually spent working. The researchers wrote: "The fact that the subject's behavior changed so dramatically with the onset of self-monitoring lends plausibility to the interpretation that the behavior changes were the result of perceived aversive consequences for failing to meet acceptable levels of performance" (Lamal & Benfield, 1978, p. 147).

Along these lines, in the laboratory experiment by Gibbs and Brown (1955) where objective feedback raised output by 31.2 percent, there were two reasons to suspect the influence of evaluation apprehension. First, subjects were paid an hourly wage and they worked four hours a day; therefore, the experiment more closely resembled a real job than many other lab experiments (and the subjects likely thought that job performance might affect chances for continued employment, or employment in other experiments). Second, there was a constant and obvious monitoring of performance via a photograph of the copy machine counter (a measure of output) that was taken every ten minutes. In contrast, in the replication experiment by Chapanis, the experimenter deliberately attempted to create the impression that she cared little about performance on the task, saying that accuracy was "not imperative" and that she was "not at all interested in individual performances" (Chapanis, 1964, pp. 264–65). Further, there was no obvious monitoring of performance. Chapanis concluded that "Gibbs and Brown did not really succeed in isolating the incentive aspect of knowledge of performance" (p. 267). This is probably true. Restated somewhat, Gibbs and Brown found a sizable positive effect because their experimental procedure possessed a high degree of mundane realism; it elevated evaluation apprehension.

As Donald Law, a management consultant with Arthur Young & Company, has observed, the absence of performance measurement implies that management finds any level of performance to be acceptable (Law, 1975). However, upon institution of performance measurement and objective feedback, the implicit message seems to be that management is interested, possibly vitally interested, in the proficiency of each individual and/or work group. There is the accompanying implicit threat that ineffective workers will be treated less favorably than others; and conceivably, individuals whose contributions are the greatest will be recognized and rewarded. Importantly, the institution of objective feedback communicates these messages by actions, not merely by words.

Conclusions

Evidence from thirty laboratory and forty-two field experiments indicates that objective feedback: (1) consistently has a positive effect in both the laboratory and the field; (2) has a stronger average effect in the field; and (3) more often has a sizable positive effect in the field.

Four primary explanations for these findings were advanced, each representing what Locke (see chapter 1) would call an "essential element." First, on the average, work periods have been substantially longer in field experiments, presumably allowing greater time for skill acquisition. Second, because tasks and performance in field settings generally are seen as more significant, the internal work motivation of subjects is more greatly affected by the provision of objective feedback. Third, part of the difference in effects can be attributed to the greater use of public feedback in field settings. Public feedback adds social consequences to task performance. And fourth, in field settings the provision of objective feedback strongly implies that external consequences may result from task performance, otherwise why bother. In laboratory experiments, however, researchers typically have striven to eliminate the possibly confounding effects of evaluation apprehension. While the effects of objective feedback have been stronger in field experiments compared to laboratory experiments, in both settings results have consistently been positive. Those differences in results that do exist can be explained in terms of four essential elements (ability-related and motivational variables)—differences that make a difference.

Ironically, although laboratory experiments are often seen as overestimating the effects of various interventions, the opposite has been the case with respect to objective feedback. Presumably, this is because laboratory experiments typically control for or minimize the effects of four essential factors. Yet laboratory experiments could, and should, be designed that will isolate and examine the effects of these factors.

Notes

1. Results for laboratory experiments with and without explicit goal setting include separate treatments for the one Mackworth (1950) experiment that did include goal setting and the two that did not.

2. Although objective feedback performs multiple functions that in practice cannot be isolated (Ilgen, et al., 1979), they are separated in this paper for expository purposes.

References

Adam, E.E., Jr. (1975) Behavior modification in quality control. *Academy of Management Journal, 18*, 662–679.

Adams, J.A., & Humes, J.M. (1963) Monitoring of complex displays: IV. Training for vigilance. *Human Factors, 5*, 147–153.

Allen, S.A. (1976) *Aer Lingus—Irish (B).* Boston: Intercollegiate Case Clearinghouse, case ♀ 9-477-640, 1–20.

Annett, J. (1961) *The role of knowledge of results in learning: A survey* (United States Naval Training Device Center Report 342-3). Arlington, Va.: Armed Services Technical Information Agency.

Arps, G.F. (1920) Work with knowledge of results versus work without knowledge of results. *Psychological Review Monograph Supplement, 28* (3, Whole No. 125), 1–41.

Bandura, A., & Cervone, D. (1983) Self-evaluative and self-efficacy mechanisms governing the motivational effects of goal systems. *Journal of Personality and Social Psychology, 45,* 1017–1028.

Berkowitz, L., & Donnerstein, E. (1982) External validity is more than skin deep: Some answers to criticisms of laboratory experiments. *American Psychologist, 37,* 245–257.

Book, W.F., & Norvell, L. (1922) The will to learn: An experimental study of incentives in learning. *Pedagogical Seminary, 29,* 305–362.

Brunswik, E. (1955) Representative design and probabilistic theory in a functional psychology. *Psychological Review, 62,* 193–217.

Campbell, D.T., & Stanley, J.C. (1963) *Experimental and quasi-experimental designs for research.* Chicago: Rand McNally.

Campbell, J.P., Dunnette, M.D., Lawler, E.E., III, & Weick, K.E., Jr. (1970) *Managerial behavior, performance, and effectiveness.* New York: McGraw-Hill.

Carlsmith, J.M., Ellsworth, P.C., & Aronson, E. (1976) *Methods of research in social psychology.* Reading, Mass.: Addison-Wesley.

Chapanis, A. (1964) Knowledge of performance as an incentive in repetitive, monotonous tasks. *Journal of Applied Psychology, 48,* 263–267.

Chung, K.H., & Vickery, W.D. (1976) Relative effectiveness and joint effects of three selected reinforcements in a repetitive task situation. *Organizational Behavior and Human Performance, 16,* 114–142.

Church, R.M., & Camp, D.S. (1965) Change in reaction-time as a function of knowledge of results. *American Journal of Psychology, 78,* 102–106.

Collins, R.L., Komaki, J., & Temlock, S. (1978) *Behavioral definition and improvement of customer service in retail merchandising.* Paper presented at the American Psychological Association meeting, New York.

Crawley, S.L. (1926) An experimental investigation of recovery from work. *Archives of Psychology, 13* (85), 1–66.

Dick, H.W. (1978) Increasing the productivity of the day relief textile machine operator. *Journal of Organizational Behavior Management, 2,* 45–57.

Dipboye, R.L., & Flanagan, M.F. (1979) Research settings in industrial and organizational psychology: Are findings in the field more generalizable than in the laboratory? *American Psychologist, 34,* 141–150.

Dossett, D.L., Latham, G.P., & Mitchell, T.R. (1979) Effects of assigned versus participatively set goals, knowledge of results, and individual differences on employee behavior when goal difficulty is held constant. *Journal of Applied Psychology, 64,* 291–298.

Eldridge, L., Lemasters, S., & Szypot, B. (1978) A performance feedback intervention to reduce waste: Performance data and participant responses. *Journal of Organizational Behavior Management, 1,* 268–280.

Elwell, J.L., & Grindley, G.C. (1938) The effect of knowledge of results on learning and performance. *British Journal of Psychology, 29,* 39–54.

Emmert, G.D. (1978) Measuring the impact of group performance feedback versus individual performance feedback in an industrial setting. *Journal of Organizational Behavior Management, 1,* 134–141.

Erez, M. (1977) Feedback: A necessary condition for the goal setting-performance relationship. *Journal of Applied Psychology, 62,* 624–627.

Frederiksen, L.W., Richter, W.T., Jr., Johnson, R.P., & Solomon, L.J. (1981–82). Specificity of performance feedback in a professional service delivery setting. *Journal of Organizational Behavior Management, 3*(3), 1–53.

French, J.R.P., Jr., & Caplan, R.D. (1973) Organizational stress and individual strain. In A.J. Morrow (Ed.), *The failure of succcess* (pp. 30–65). New York: Amacom.

Fromkin, H.L., & Streufert, S. (1976) Laboratory experimentation. In M.D. Dunnette (Ed.), *Handbook of industrial and organizational psychology* (pp. 415–465). Chicago: Rand McNally.

Frost, J.M., Hopkins, B.L., & Conrad, R.J. (1981) An analysis of the effects of feedback and reinforcement on machine-paced production. *Journal of Organizational Behavior Management, 3*(2), 5–17.

Geller, E.S., Eason, S.L., Phillips, J.A., & Pierson, M.D. (1980) Interventions to improve sanitation during food preparation. *Journal of Organizational Behavior Management, 2,* 229–240.

Gibbs, C.B., & Brown, I.D. (1955) *Increased production from the information incentive in a repetitive task* (Report No. 230). Cambridge, Great Britain: Medical Research Council, Applied Psychology Unit.

Gibbs, J.C., (1979) The meaning of ecologically oriented inquiry in contemporary psychology. *American Psychologist, 34,* 127–140.

Hackman, J.R., & Oldham, G.R. (1976) Motivation through the design of work: Test of a theory. *Organizational Behavior and Human Performance, 16,* 250–279.

Hackman, J.R,. & Oldham, G.R. (1980) *Work redesign.* Reading, Mass.: Addison-Wesley.

Haynes, R.S., Pine, R.C., & Fitch, H.G. (1982) Reducing accident rates with organizational behavior modification. *Academy of Management Journal, 25,* 407–416.

Hundal, P.S. (1969) Knowledge of performance as an incentive in repetitive industrial work. *Journal of Applied Psychology, 53,* 224–226.

Ilgen, D.R., Fisher, C.D., & Taylor, M.S. (1979) Consequences of individual feedback on behavior in organizations. *Journal of Applied Psychology, 64,* 349–371.

Ivancevich, J.M., & McMahon, J.T. (1982) The effects of goal setting, external feedback, and self-generated feedback on outcome variables: A field experiment. *Academy of Management Journal, 25,* 359–372.

Johanson, A.N. (1922) Influence of incentive and punishment on reaction time. *Archives of Psychology, 8* (54), 1–53.

Kim, J.S. (1984) Effect of behavior plus outcome goal setting and feedback on employee satisfaction and performance. *Academy of Management Journal, 27,* 139–149.

Kim, J.S., & Hamner, W.C. (1976) Effect of performance feedback and goal setting on productivity and satisfaction in an organizational setting. *Journal of Applied Psychology, 61,* 48–57.

Kirby, P.G. (1977) Productivity increases through feedback systems. *Personnel Journal, 56*(10), 512–515.

Koch, J.L. (1979) Effects of goal specificity and performance feedback to work groups on peer leadership, performance, and attitudes. *Human Relations, 32,* 819–840.

Komaki, J., Barwick, K.D., & Scott, L.R. (1978) A behavioral approach to occupational safety: Pinpointing and reinforcing safe performance in a food manufacturing plant. *Journal of Applied Psychology, 63,* 434–445.

Komaki, J., Blood, M.R., & Holder, D. (1980) Fostering friendliness in a fast food franchise. *Journal of Organizational Behavior Management, 2*, 151–164.

Komaki, J., Heinzmann, A.T., & Lawson, L. (1980) Effect of training and feedback: Component analysis of a behavioral safety program. *Journal of Applied Psychology, 65*, 261–270.

Kopelman, R.E. (1979) [Effect of objective feedback on work backlogs in the personnel department of a municipal government]. Unpublished raw data.

Kopelman, R.E. (1982–83) Improving productivity through objective feedback: A review of the evidence. *National Productivity Review, 2*, 43–55.

Kreitner, R., Reif, W.E., & Morris, M. (1977) Measuring the impact of feedback on the performance of mental health technicians. *Journal of Organizational Behavior Management, 1*, 105–109.

Lamal, P.A., & Benfield, A. (1978) The effect of self-monitoring on job tardiness and percentage of time spent working. *Journal of Organizational Behavior Management, 1*, 142–149.

Law, D.E. (1975) Managing for productivity. *The Arthur Young Journal*, Summer/Autumn, 2–13.

Littman, R.A. (1961) Psychology: The socially indifferent science. *American Psychologist, 16*, 232–236.

Locke, E.A. (1967) The motivational effects of knowledge of results: Knowledge or goal setting? *Journal of Applied Psychology, 51*, 324–329.

Locke, E.A. (1968) Effects of knowledge of results, feedback in relation to standards, and goals on reaction-time performance. *American Journal of Psychology, 81*, 556–574.

Locke, E.A., & Bryan, J.F. (1966) The effects of goal-setting, rule-learning, and knowledge of score on performance. *American Journal of Psychology, 79*, 451–457.

Locke, E.A., & Bryan, J.F. (1968) Goal-setting as a determinant of the effect of knowledge of score on performance. *American Journal of Psychology, 81*, 398–406.

Locke, E.A., & Bryan, J.F. (1969) Knowledge of score and goal level as determinants of work rate. *Journal of Applied Psychology, 53*, 59–65.

Locke, E.A., Cartledge, N., & Koeppel, J. (1968) Motivational effects of knowledge of results: A goal-setting phenomenon? *Psychological Bulletin, 70*, 474–485.

Locke, E.A., Shaw, K.N., Saari, L.M., & Latham, G.P. (1981) Goal setting and task performance: 1969–1980. *Psychological Bulletin, 90*, 125–152.

Mace, C.A. (1935) *Incentives: Some experimental studies* (Report No. 72). Great Britain: Industrial Health Research Board.

Macworth, N.H. (1950) *Researches on the measurement of human performance.* (Special Report No. 268, pp. 1–157). London: Medical Research Council.

Manzer, C.W. (1935) The effect of knowledge of output on muscular work. *Journal of Experimental Psychology, 18*, 80–90.

Matsui, T., Okada, A., & Inoshita, O. (1983) Mechanism of feedback affecting task performance. *Organizational Behavior and Human Performance, 31*, 114–122.

McCarthy, M. (1978) Decreasing the incidence of "high bobbins" in a textile spinning department through a group feedback procedure. *Journal of Organizatioal Behavior Management, 1*, 150–154.

McCormack, P.D. (1959) Performance in a vigilance task with and witout knowledge of results. *Canadian Journal of Psychology, 13*, 68–71.

McCormack, P.D., Binding, F.R.S., & Chylinski, J. (1962) Effects on reaction-time of knowledge of results of performance. *Perceptual and Motor Skills, 14*, 367–372.

McCormack, P.D., Binding, F.R.S., & McElheran, W.G. (1963) Effects on reaction time of partial knowledge of results of performance. *Perceptual and Motor Skills, 17,* 279–281.

McNees, P., Gilliam, S.W., Schnelle, J.F., & Risley, T. (1979) Controlling employee theft through time and product identification. *Journal of Organizational Behavior Management, 2,* 113–119.

Milne, J.K., & Doyle, S.X. (1980) Rx for ailing bank trust departments. *The Bankers Magaine, 163*(1), 54–57.

Montague, W.E & Webber, C.E. (1965) Effects of knowledge of results and differential monetary reward on six uninterrupted hours of monitoring. *Human Factors, 7,* 173–180.

Nadler, D.A., Cammann, C., & Mirvis, P.H. (1980) Developing a feedback system for work units: A field experiment in structural change. *The Journal of Applied Behavioral Science, 16,* 41–59.

Newby, T.J., & Robinson, P.W. (1973) Effects of grouped and individual feedback and reinforcement on retail employee performances. *Journal of Organizational Behavior Management, 5*(2), 51–68.

Organization Dynamics (1974) At Emergy Air Freight: Positive reinforcement boosts performance. *1*(3), 41–50.

Panyan, M., Boozer, H., & Morris, N. (1970) Feedback to attendants as a reinforcer for applying operant techniques. *Journal of Applied Behavior Analysis, 3,* 1–4.

Payne, R.B., & Hauty, G.T. (1955) Effect of psychological feedback upon work decrement. *Journal of Experimental Psychology, 50,* 343–351.

Pommer, D.A., & Streedback, D. (1974) Motivating staff performance in an operant learning program for children. *Journal of Applied Behavior Analysis, 7,* 217–221.

Prue, D.M., & Fairbank, J.A. (1981) Performance feedback in organizational behavior management: A review. *Journal of Organizational Behavior Management, 3*(1), 1–16.

Prue, D.M., Krapfl, J.E., Noah, J.C., Cannon, S., & Maley, R.F. (1980) Managing treatment activities of state hospital staff. *Journal of Organizational Behavior Management, 2,* 165–181.

Quilitch, H.R. (1975) A comparison of three staff-management procedures. *Journal of Applied Behavior Analysis, 8,* 59–66.

Quilitch, H.R. (1978) Using a simple feedback procedure to reinforce the submission of written suggestions by mental health employees. *Journal of Organizational Behavior Management, 1,* 155–163.

Rhodes, L. (1980) It pays to be on time. *Inc.,* June, 59–64.

Ross, C.C. (1927) An experiment in motivation. *Journal of Educational Psychology, 18,* 337–346.

Rowe, B.J. (1981) Use of feedback and reinforcement to increase the telephone reporting of independent automobile appraisers. *Journal of Organizational Behavior Management, 3*(2), 35–40.

Runnion, A., Johnson, T., and McWhorter, J. (1978) The effects of feedback and reinforcement on truck turnaround time in materials transportation. *Journal of Organizational Behavior Management, 1,* 110–117.

Runnion, A., Watson, J.O., & McWhorter, J. (1978) Energy savings in interstate transportation through feedback and reinforcement. *Journal of Organizational Behavior Management, 1,* 180–191.

Schneier, C.E., & Pernick, R. (1979) *Increasing public sector productivity through organizational behavior modification: A successful application.* Paper presented at the National meeting of the Academy of Management, Atlanta.

Shaw, K.N., Locke, E.A., Bobko, P., & Beitzell, B. (1981) *The interaction of goal difficulty/specificity and feedback on task performance* (Technical Report No. GS-10). Arlington, Va.: Office of Naval Research, Organizational Effectiveness Research Program.

Shook, G.L., Johnson, C.M., & Uhlman, W.F. (1978) The effect of response effort reduction, instructions, group and individual feedback, and reinforcement on staff performance, *Journal of Organizational Behavior Management, 1,* 206–215.

Silva, D.B., Duncan, P.K., & Doudna, D. (1981) The effects of attendance-contingent feedback and praise on attendance and work efficiency. *Journal of Organizational Behavior Management, 3*(2), 59–69.

Stoerzinger, A., Johnston, J.M., Pisor, K., & Monroe, C. (1978) Implementation and evaluation of a feedback system for employees in a salvage operation. *Journal of Organizational Behavior Management, 1,* 268–280.

Strang, H.R., Lawrence, E.C., & Fowler, P.C. (1978) Effects of assigned goal level and knowledge of results on arithmetic computation: A laboratory study. *Journal of Applied Psychology, 63,* 446–450.

Sulzer-Azaroff, B. (1978) Behavioral ecology and accident prevention. *Journal of Organizational Behavior Management, 2,* 11–44.

Taylor, M.S., Fisher, C.D., & Ilgen, D.R. (1984) Individuals' reactions to performance feedback in organizations: A control theory perspective. In K. Rowland & J. Ferris (Eds.), *Research in personnel and human resources management* (Vol. 2, pp. 81–124). Greenwich, Conn.: JAI Press.

White, R.W. (1959) Motivation reconsidered. *Psychological Review, 66,* 297–333.

Wright, W.R. (1906) Some effects of incentives on work and fatigue. *Psychological Review, 13,* 23–34.

8
Participation in Decision Making

David M. Schweiger
Carrie R. Leana

F ew topics in the field of organizational behavior have held the attention of researchers with as much persistence as the issue of subordinate participation in decision making (PDM). For over fifty years, numerous researchers have investigated PDM in settings ranging from controlled laboratory conditions to a wide variety of organizational contexts. Yet our ability to make accurate predictions regarding the overall effects of PDM remains rather negligible.

Reviews of the PDM literature (for example, Lowin, 1968; Locke & Schweiger, 1979; Bass, 1981; Yukl, 1981) seem unanimous in their conclusions that decades of research have primarily served to underscore what we do *not* know about the efficacy of PDM rather than to provide us with immediate answers concerning its effective implementation. Locke and Schweiger, for example, have noted that the primary area of agreement among PDM studies lies with a collective failure to show any clear trend concerning either the superiority or the inferiority of PDM. Similarly, Bass concludes that "about every possible alternative emerges" from a search for universal prescriptions regarding PDM (p. 323).

There are several potential reasons for this lack of consistency in results. Primary among these are the lack of consistency in how researchers have defined the concept of PDM, and the diversity of approaches taken by researchers in operationalizing participation in their studies. PDM can vary in scope, content, and degree, whether it is formal or informal, and whether it is forced or voluntary (Locke & Schweiger, 1979). Moreover, it can take many different forms ranging from group decision making among subordinates to superior-subordinate joint decision making to participation through subordinate representation (Bass, 1981). While this diversity in approach accurately reflects the real variety of procedures used by managers to include subordinates in decision making, it also suggests little agreement among researchers on both the conceptual and the operational definition of PDM. Indeed, Dachler (1978) has noted that "the major problem underlying participation research is that it is nearly impossible to determine what participation entails" (p. 17).

A second potential reason for the lack of consistency in PDM results concerns factors that might moderate the relationship between PDM and commonly investigated outcomes such as subordinate satisfaction and performance. Many different moderating factors have been suggested in the PDM research. Leader characteristics such as skills (Maier & Sashkin, 1971) and personality (McCurdy & Eber, 1963), for example, have been found to influence the effectiveness of PDM. Subordinate knowledge (Vroom & Yetton, 1973) and personality characteristics (Vroom, 1960) have also been found to be significant moderating factors. Other potential influences on the effectiveness of PDM include situational, environmental, or contextual factors such as task attributes (Shaw & Blum, 1966), hierarchical level (Lowin, 1968), and environmental uncertainty (Burns & Stalker, 1961).

One potential contextual factor that has not been adequately addressed in previous reviews of the PDM literature concerns the research environment in which participation has been examined. Just as PDM may be effective for some subordinates and not for others, consistent findings concerning the effects of PDM may depend, at least in part, on the research setting in which PDM is being investigated. Potential differences between two types of research environments, laboratory settings and field settings, are the subject of this review. Before presenting a comparison of research results obtained in the laboratory and the field, however, it is useful to first offer a framework for examining the variety of operational definitions that have been applied to PDM.

Most researchers agree that participation is a process of sharing in some activity between and/or among superiors and subordinates (Bass, 1981). While this definition may be sufficiently broad to encompass most of the PDM research, it is not sufficiently precise to identify sources of variation among the PDM studies. More specifically, what are not included in this definition are differences among the PDM studies in: (1) the *content* of the activities of interest (such as decision making, goal setting, and job changes), (2) the *number of people involved* in the activity (for example, one subordinate or a group of subordinates), and (3) the *degree of involvement* of the participants in the activity (for example, no involvement, consultation, or equal involvement between superior and subordinates).

In compiling our review of potential differences in PDM results that may be attributable to research settings, we have attempted to categorize the laboratory and field studies according to these three factors. What emerges from this categorization are: (1) many studies with a moderate degree of comparability on these factors, and (2) relatively few studies with a strong degree of comparability. The first group consists of studies conducted by numerous researchers in a variety of disciplines (for example, psychology, sociology, and organizational behavior) using many different research approaches. In general, these studies do not appear to be part of a consistent research stream. Nor do they follow similar definitions or operationalizations of PDM and, for that matter, non-PDM. All of the studies, however, operationalize PDM as a process of sharing among individuals in an activity and are thus classified as "broad-based PDM studies."

Within the second group of studies there are two distinct research streams with comparable laboratory and field research. These are: (1) studies examining participation in goal setting, and (2) studies testing the Vroom and Yetton leadership model.

Due to the inherent differences among these categories, the three groups of studies are independently analyzed in the following review for potential differences between laboratory and field results. Before presenting a discussion of our methods of analysis, however, a caveat is in order. The review to be presented here does not attempt a comprehensive analysis of fifty years of PDM literature. Instead, we have provided a representative sample of broad-based PDM research and comprehensive coverage of more recent investigations of PDM that have used a common conceptual framework (for example, research on participation in goal setting and the Vroom and Yetton leadership studies). We have, therefore, concentrated much of our analysis on those areas within the PDM research where: (1) variables are operationalized in relatively equivalent manners, and (2) there are both laboratory and field examinations using these similar operationalizations. While this approach necessitates the elimination of many PDM studies from our review, it does provide at least two groups of meaningful laboratory-field comparisons that are relatively unconfounded by the myriad of other differences among the PDM studies. Our somewhat narrow focus, then, is a deliberate one where precise and meaningful comparisons are emphasized at the expense of a more comprehensive yet largely uninterpretable analysis of the PDM literature in its entirety.

Method

For each of the three analyses conducted (broad-based, goal setting, and the Vroom and Yetton research), a basis of comparison between laboratory and field studies had to be selected. Common dependent variables being investigated in each area of analysis were used as this basis. For the broad-based PDM studies, performance and satisfaction were key dependent variables. For the studies examining participation in goal setting, the most commonly reported dependent variables were performance, goal acceptance, and goal difficulty. Finally, research on the Vroom and Yetton model used two broad sets of dependent variables, the degree of agreement in predicting the use of PDM and the degree of effectiveness associated with agreement with the normative aspects of the model.

A method for cumulating, analyzing, and comparing the results from laboratory and field studies also had to be selected. Recently, Hunter, Schmidt and Jackson (1982) have criticized commonly used methods such as percentages, chi-square analyses, and qualitative judgment calls. They have argued that these methods fail to account for sampling error, measurement error, range variations, and computational error and, for these reasons, distort the conclusions that can be drawn from them. As an alternative, they propose the use of a quantitative procedure, meta-analysis. This method attempts to correct for several of these errors, and provides a more realistic assessment of cumulated results in the form of average correlation and effect size.

For each of the three analyses, the applicability and practicality of applying these various methods were evaluated.

To conduct a meta-analysis, means, correlations, and standard deviations for each study must be obtained. Unfortunately, there has been little consistency in the reporting of these statistics (especially means and standard deviations) among PDM studies. Moreover, many of the PDM studies that were used in the analyses were published so long ago that the data and statistics associated with them had been discarded by the researchers. Thus, if meta-analysis were undertaken, many if not most of the participation studies would have to be eliminated due to a lack of reported statistics. For this reason, meta-analysis was not chosen.

As a second alternative, chi-square analysis was considered. The sample sizes and expected frequencies of the cells used in the classification scheme (to be discussed later) were insufficient to justify the use of this statistic. It was therefore decided that for both the broad-based participation studies and participation in goal setting studies, the research results in each group would be cumulated using frequencies and percentages, and then judgmentally evaluated. For the analysis of the Vroom and Yetton studies, qualitative judgment was used. Due to the nature of the research and paucity of studies, the use of frequency and percentage data would not have been meaningful.

Comparative Analyses of Participation Studies

Broad-Based PDM Studies

The studies included in this section were taken from the review of the PDM research by Locke and Schweiger (1979) and an updating of that review. Due to the sheer volume of published studies, we do not claim that our review is complete. We did not, for example, include multivariate studies where causality was unclear (for example, Coch & French, 1948). Our selection of studies, however, was unbiased and representative, and the general conclusions that can be drawn from an examination of these studies are similar to those found in other reviews of PDM research such as Yukl (1981).

Many PDM studies have taken a normative focus in assessing the relative effect of some form of PDM on subordinate performance and satisfaction. Due to this consistency in normative focus, a large number of studies could be meaningfully classified according to whether PDM was found to be superior or inferior to non-PDM, or demonstrated no differences or differences only in subgroupings of study participants.

Table 8–1 shows those studies that compared the effects of PDM on measures of performance. As indicated in the table, the results are similar in laboratory and field settings. In neither the laboratory nor the field is there evidence to suggest that PDM is consistently superior or inferior to non-PDM. In fact, the percentages of "superior" and "inferior" findings within each research setting are iden-

Table 8–1
Participation in Decision Making (PDM): Performance

	PDM Superior	PDM Inferior	No Differences	Subgroup Differences
Laboratory	4 (31%) [39, 58, 59, 60]	4 (31%) [14, 37, 53, 76]	3 (23%) [38, 62, 63]	2 (15%) [10, 77]
Field correlations	4 (27%) [3, 36, 68, 69]	3 (20%) [57, 78, 85]	6 (40%) [1, 8, 35, 62, 78, 82]	2 (13%) [3, 80]
Field experiments	1 (14%) [12]	2 (29%) [65, 75]	4 (57%) [11, 18, 21, 70]	0 (0%)
Field total	5 (23%)	5 (23%)	10 (45%)	2 (9%)
Total	9	9	13	4

Note: Numbers in brackets are studies contained in references.

tical. In addition, a number of studies in both settings found no differences or subgroup differences.

Table 8–2 shows those studies that compared the effects of PDM on subordinate satisfaction. Like the performance data, the results found in the laboratory are consistent with those found in the field research. In a large percentage of laboratory and field studies, PDM was found to be superior to non-PDM. Several of the field studies reported subgroup differences, however, whereas none of the laboratory studies reported these differences.

Participation in Goal Setting Studies

The research on participation in goal setting (PGS) provides a better opportunity to compare results obtained in the laboratory with those in the field. Unlike the

Table 8–2
Participation in Decision Making (PDM): Satisfaction

	PDM Superior	PDM Inferior	No Differences	Subgroup Differences
Laboratory	5 (71%) [20, 37, 53, 63, 74]	2 (29%) [14, 23]	0 (0%)	0 (0%)
Field correlations	13 (62%) [2, 7, 16, 49, 50, 51, 64, 67, 71, 73, 74, 79, 85]	1 (5%) [8]	2 (10%) [68, 72]	5 (23%) [19, 49, 71, 73, 83]
Field experiments	5 (83%) [12, 21, 48, 65, 75]	0 (0%)	1 (17%) [52]	0 (0%)
Field total	18 (67%)	1 (3%)	3 (11%)	5 (19%)
Total	23	3	3	5

Note: Numbers in brackets are studies contained in references.

broad-based PDM research, all of the PGS studies are guided by a common conceptual framework and use similar definitions and operationalizations of PGS, (that is, superior-subordinate participative goal setting is always compared with superior-assigned goal setting). All available nonmultivariate PGS studies where causality could be inferred were included in this analysis.

Three dependent variables (performance, goal acceptance, and goal difficulty) are consistently reported in PGS studies and thus provide the bases of comparison between the laboratory and field. Similar to our classification of the broad-based PDM studies, we classified the PGS studies according to whether participatively set goals were found to be superior or inferior to assigned goals, or demonstrated no differences or differences only in subgroups of study participants.

Table 8–3 shows those studies that compared the effects of participatively set versus assigned goals on performance. In the majority of cases there was no difference in either setting. Field studies by French, Kay, and Meyer (1966) and Latham and Yukl (1975) found only partial support for the superiority of PGS, whereas only one laboratory study (Latham & Saari, 1979a) clearly supported PGS. In the French et al. and Latham and Yukl (1975) studies, several factors moderated the relationship between PGS and performance. One field study (Dossett, Latham, & Mitchell, 1979) supported the superiority of assigned goal setting, whereas none of the laboratory studies did. None of the remaining field studies (Carroll & Tosi, 1973; Ivancevich, 1976, 1977; Latham & Yukl, 1976; Latham, Mitchell, & Dossett, 1978; Dossett et al., 1979; Latham & Saari, 1979b; Latham & Marshall, 1982) or laboratory studies (Hannan, 1975; Latham, Steele, & Saari, 1982; Latham & Steele, 1983) found significant performance differences between participatively set and assigned goals. In the Ivancevich studies there were some significant performance differences between participatively set and assigned goals six months after the goals were set although these differences were not significant after one year. For this reason, these two studies were classified as indicating no significant differences attributed to the goal setting approach used.

Table 8–3
Participation in Goal Setting (PGS): Performance

	PGS Superior	PGS Inferior	No Differences	Subgroup Differences
Laboratory	1 (25%) [41]	0 (0%)	3 (75%) [24, 44, 45]	0 (0%)
Field	0 (0%)	1 (9%) [15]	8 (73%) [11[a], 15, 26, 27, 40, 41, 43, 47]	2 (18%) [22, 46]
Total	1	1	11	2

Note: Numbers in brackets are studies contained in references.

[a]All PGS field studies reported in this table are experiments with the exception of no. 11, which is a correlational study.

It is argued by Locke, Shaw, Saari, and Latham (1981) that PGS may not directly motivate subjects to increase their effort or performance. Instead, goal setting theory would predict PGS to enhance performance only if it leads to the setting of and/or acceptance of more difficult goals. For this reason, the effects of PDM on goal acceptance and goal difficulty were also examined.

Table 8–4 shows those studies that investigated goal acceptance. Similar to the performance results, the largest percentage of laboratory and field studies found no differences between participatively set and assigned goals. In one field study (Latham & Yukl, 1975), participatively set goals led to greater goal acceptance than assigned goals. In the Latham and Yukl study, however, this was the case for only one of two subgroups (uneducated logging crews). In the second subgroup examined (educated logging crews) there was no difference. Two studies were reported by Dossett et al. (1979). In the first study, there was no significant difference in acceptance between participatively set and assigned goals, whereas in the second study, participatively set goals showed significantly lower acceptance. One laboratory study (Hannan, 1975) found greater acceptance under PGS than under assigned goal setting. In a number of both field (Latham et al., 1978; Latham & Marshall, 1982) and laboratory (Latham & Saari, 1979a, b; Latham et al., 1982; Latham & Steele, 1983) studies, no differences in goal acceptance were found.

Table 8–5 shows those studies investigating goal difficulty. Unfortunately, there were few PGS studies investigating this variable. Many of the PGS studies have controlled goal difficulty rather than investigate its effects directly. The field study by Latham et al. (1978) found that participatively set goals led to greater objective goal difficulty than did assigned goals. No differences were found in one field study (Latham & Yukl, 1976) and two laboratory studies (Latham & Saari, 1979; Latham et al., 1982). In the Latham and Yukl (1975) study, subgroup differences were found. For the uneducated logging crews, participatively set goals led to greater goal difficulty than assigned goals. There were no significant differences between goal setting conditions for the educated crews.

Table 8–4
Participation in Goal Setting (PGS): Goal Acceptance

	PGS Superior	PGS Inferior	No Differences	Subgroup Differences
Laboratory	1 (20%) [24,]	0 (0%)	4 (80%) [42, 43, 44, 45]	0 (0%)
Field	0 (0%)	1 (17%) [15]	4 (66%) [15, 22a, 40, 41]	1(17%) [41]
Total	1	1	8	1

Note: Numbers in brackets are studies contained in references.

[a]All PGS field studies reported in this table are experiments with the exception of no. 22, which is a correlational study.

Table 8–5
Participation in Goal Setting (PGS): Goal Difficulty

	PDM Superior	PDM Inferior	No Differences	Subgroup Differences
Laboratory	0 (0%)	0 (0%)	2 (100%) [43, 45]	0 (0%)
Field	1 (33%) [42]	0 (0%)	1 (33%) [47]	1 (33%) [46]
Total	1	0	3	1

Note: Numbers in brackets are studies contained in references.

Overall, the research on PGS suggests that the results for the laboratory and field studies are relatively similar. Caution, however, should be exercised in interpreting these results. Comparisons of the nonsignificant findings regarding goal acceptance are particularly problematic. Essentially, the laboratory and field research findings are similar only inasmuch as they both support the null hypothesis; that is, no differences between PGS and assigned goal setting. The lack of significance in acceptance, in particular, may be attributed to invalid measures of goal acceptance or ceiling effects (Locke et al., 1981).

Studies of the Vroom and Yetton Leadership Model

More recent research on PDM has shifted from an emphasis on simple (yet varied) conceptualizations and operationalizations of PDM and toward more complex (yet uniform) theories of the participative process. Instead of examining the differences between bipolar extremes (as was the case with the broad-based PDM studies), more recent models of PDM have encompassed different gradations of subordinate participation. In addition, there has been a much greater emphasis on situational and contextual factors that might affect both the use and the effectiveness of PDM. This shift toward including these factors in the PDM research has made potential distinctions between laboratory and field settings particularly important. When the focus variables become aspects of the environment itself (that is, situational factors), potential differences in results between laboratory and field investigations become critical concerns.

Perhaps the best example of systematic research focusing on situational predictors of PDM is the work conducted on the Vroom and Yetton leadership model (Vroom & Yetton, 1973). This model identifies five decision-making styles which are gradations in the level of subordinate participation in decision making. These styles range from autocratic decision making to consultative processes to joint decision making between superior and subordinate. Seven situational factors (decision rules) are also specified which determine the conditions under which each of the five styles may be effectively employed by managers. Using a decision tree, the model specifies the appropriate set of styles (feasible set) based on the rules. (Vroom and Yetton provide a more complete discussion of the decision-making styles and the decision rules underlying their use.)

Since the development of the model, Vroom and his colleagues have conducted a number of descriptive and normative studies examining both predictors and outcomes of the decision making styles. In general, two different methods of study have been employed in this research. The first involves descriptions of decisions and their disposition (that is, degree of PDM) as recalled by managers from actual job experiences. Aspects of the decision situation are then classified posthoc from the managers' descriptions. This retrospective methodology can be classified as field research since data are collected from actual work settings and are provided by practicing decision makers.

The second method commonly used in the Vroom and Yetton research requires managers to respond to decision scenarios which are constructed by the researcher(s) and contain different combinations of situational attributes (that is, decision rules). Respondents are asked to indicate how participative they would be in the prescribed situations. Thus, this scenario method entails artificial construction of the decision environment by the researcher(s) and can be properly classified as laboratory research. With the retrospective methodology (that is, manager-recalled problems), however, respondents provide the decision environment. The distinction here is not the research setting in which the data are gathered since for both methods data are typically collected during management training programs. Rather, the distinction concerns the setting from which the data are provided. One is constructed and reported by the participating manager about his/her work setting (retrospective field methodology) while the other is constructed entirely by the researcher (scenario laboratory methodology).

Six field studies using the retrospective methodology and five laboratory studies using the scenario methodology have been reported. In addition, Jago and Vroom (1978) used a combination of the two methods, and two laboratory studies (Field, 1982; Jago & Ettling, 1982) used experiential manipulations of the predictors of PDM rather than the scenario manipulations. Finally, Margerison and Glube (1979) used a combination of laboratory and field research environments. Margerison and Glube used the scenario methodology to determine managers' mean levels of participation but assessed dependent measures of performance and subordinate satisfaction from actual work settings. All the available studies are reported in table 8–6.

Descriptive Research. The results of the descriptive studies conducted in the laboratory and the field are relatively similar. Vroom and Yetton (1973), for example, found that 69 percent of managers' recalled dispositions of problems (that is, retrospective field methodology) were classified as falling within the set of situational conditions specified by the Vroom and Yetton model. In their laboratory in-

Table 8-6
Vroom and Yetton Model

Study	Independent Variables	Samples/Task	Dependent Variables	Results	Research Environment
Descriptive studies					
Vroom & Yetton 1973	Problem attributes: decision quality requirement, leader information, problem structure, importance of acceptance, probability of acceptance, goal congruence, conflict	Managers/recalled problems	Degree of PDM	Over 65% agreement with Vroom-Yetton rules	Field
Vroom & Jago 1974	Problem attributes	Managers/standardized scenarios	Degree of PDM	Over 65% agreement with Vroom-Yetton rules	Lab
Jago & Vroom 1975	Information source	Managers and subordinates/standardized scenarios	Agreement between manager and subordinate reports of degree of PDM	Little agreement	Lab
Jago & Vroom 1978	Research methodology	Managers/standardized scenarios and recalled problems	Agreement between recalled and scenario behavior	Scenario behavior and recalled behavior matched only for successful problems	Lab and Field
Jago 1978	Hierarchical level, problem attributes	Managers/standardized scenarios varying hierarchical level	Degree of PDM	Variance explained by attributes less when hierarchical level controlled	Lab
Jago 1981	(1) Problem attributes hierarchical level (2) Quality requirement hierarchical level	Managers/standardized scenarios	Degree of PDM	More PDM at lower hierarchical level Higher PDM when both quality requirement and hierarchical level are low	Lab

Study	Independent variables	Sample/task	Dependent measures	Findings	Setting
Jago & Vroom 1977	Hierarchical level	Managers and subordinates/standardized scenarios	Degree of PDM	More PDM at higher hierarchical level	Field
Vroom & Jago 1974	Problem attributes: decision quality requirement, leader information, problem structure, importance of acceptance, probability of acceptance, goal congruence, subordinate information	Managers/standardized scenarios	Degree of PDM (includes delegation)	Importance of acceptance, goal congruence, subordinate information positively related to PDM; quality, leader information, problem structure negatively related to PDM	Field
Normative studies					
Field 1982	Degree of PDM	Students/group problems	Ratings of decision quality, acceptance, overall effectiveness	Partial support for rules governing the Vroom-Yetton model	Lab
Jago & Ettling 1982	Degree of PDM	Students/desert survival problem	Ratings of decision quality, acceptance	Support for conflict rule of Vroom-Yetton model	Lab
Margerison & Glube 1979	Degree of PDM	Dry cleaning franchise managers and subordinates/standardized scenarios	Unit performance, subordinate satisfaction with supervisor	Higher productivity, subordinate satisfaction when agreement with Vroom-Yetton model	Field
Vroom & Jago 1978	Degree of PDM	Managers/successful and unsuccessful recalled problems	Ratings of decision quality, acceptance, overall effectiveness	68% of successful and 22% of unsuccessful decisions in agreement with Vroom-Yetton model; main effect for PDM on quality and acceptance; goal congruence and conflict rules not supported	Field
Jago & Vroom 1980	Degree of PDM	Managers/successful and unsuccessful recalled problems	Ratings of decision quality, acceptance, overall effectiveness	Support for Vroom-Yetton model	Field

vestigation, where situational conditions were manipulated through scenarios, Vroom and Jago (1974) found 68 percent of responses to be in the feasible set. In a later study, however, Jago and Vroom (1978) compared results obtained using both the scenario and retrospective methodologies and found only partial agreement between the two approaches.

One situational factor that has received individual attention in the Vroom and Yetton descriptive research is the effect of organizational hierarchical level on managers' choices of decision making styles. For the laboratory research (see Jago, 1978, 1981), hierarchical level was manipulated within the scenario descriptions. In the one field study (Jago & Vroom, 1977), hiearchical level was measured based on the job classifications of the respondents completing the problem set. For both the measured (Jago & Vroom, 1977) and manipulated (Jago, 1978, 1981) assessments of hiearchical level, respondents completed the scenario problem sets.

The findings from these studies were different. Jago and Vroom (1977) found that managers who actually occupied higher hierarchical positions in organizations were more participative when responding to the problem set. Conversely, Jago's (1981) laboratory investigation found that respondents were more participative when the scenarios described them as being at a lower hierarchical level. This hierarchical level effect was moderated, however, by the importance (quality requirement) of the decision being made. Thus, the laboratory and field results were not entirely comparable when hierarchical level was the predictor of PDM.

Normative Research. Vroom and his colleagues have also used the retrospective and scenario methodologies to examine the association between various decision making styles and overall decision effectiveness, decision quality, and decision acceptance. As indicated in table 8–6, the laboratory and field research findings were largely in agreement. Using the retrospective methodology, Vroom and Jago (1978) found that 68 percent of problems described by managers as successful were in agreement with the normative predictions, while only 22 percent of the "unsuccessful" problems were in agreement. Similarly, Margerison and Glube (1979) found that managers of dry cleaning stores whose responses to scenarios agreed with the normative predictions showed significantly higher productivity rates and satisfaction with supervision among subordinates than did managers whose responses did not agree with the predictions.

With regard to the specific rules governing the model's prescriptions, Vroom and Jago (1978) found support for all but two ("goal congruence" and "conflict") of the seven rules. That is, contrary to the model's predictions, the use of participation did not attenuate subordinate acceptance of decisions under conditions of low leader-subordinate goal congruence and did not significantly enhance decision effectiveness under conditions of conflict. The differences regarding conflict were in the predicted direction, but failed to reach statistical significance due to the small sample of problems available to test the conflict rule. Field's (1982) laboratory study found similar results regarding the effects of goal congruence on acceptance. Jago and Ettling's (1982) laboratory study of the conflict rule also showed participation to be more effective under conflict conditions. This investigation, however, only included two types of decision styles and was therefore more limited in its scope.

The research findings for both the descriptive and normative aspects of the Vroom and Yetton model generally show agreement between results found in the laboratory and those in the field, although some inconsistencies such as hierarchical level effects have been found between research environments. To date, however, there have been relatively few studies conducted, making it premature to interpret the laboratory and field methodologies as relatively interchangeable.

Summary and Conclusions

As the results suggest, a reasonable degree of generalizability from the laboratory to the field has been demonstrated in the PDM research. Specifically, the broad-based PDM studies show moderate agreement between laboratory and field findings. The goal setting research suggests a high degree of agreement between the laboratory and the field. Although the number of studies examining the Vroom and Yetton model is relatively small, this research also suggests that the laboratory results are relatively similar to those obtained in the field.

To what can these differences in generalizability be attributed? In the case of the broad-based PDM studies, both the laboratory and field research point to the importance of contextual variables in moderating the relationship between PDM and performance. Essentially, no single approach, whether autocratic, consultative, or totally participative, can be effectively employed with all subordinates for all types of activities. The arguments presented by Locke and Schweiger (1979) and Yukl (1981) as well as the empirical evidence provided by the Vroom and Yetton research tend to confirm this. With regard to the broad-based PDM studies, the research conducted in laboratory settings has been particularly flawed by a failure to encompass this complexity.

Many of the broad-based laboratory studies tended to investigate PDM using very simple manipulations while showing little consideration of important contextual variables such as employee knowledge and nature of the decision. These contextual factors, however, may well have influenced the outcomes of the studies, regardless of whether they were measured or ignored. In table 8–1, for example, 54 percent of the field investigations of PDM reported either no difference in performance or differences only in subgroups of study participants, whereas for the laboratory research, this figure was 38 percent. These discrepancies between laboratory and field findings may be partially due to the context-free environment often created by laboratory researchers.

The similarity of the laboratory and field research on PGS appears to be largely a function of both the equivalence and the simplicity of the operationalizations of the variables examined in both research environments. Moreover, both the laboratory and field studies were conducted as part of a common research stream using the same theoretical framework. Similarity on these dimensions has helped to ensure that researchers have examined the same phenomenon, regardless of the research environment.

This similarity, however, is not due to laboratory researchers incorporating the complexity of real work settings into their research designs. Instead, much of the field research on PGS has focused on a controlled, experimental approach. In this regard, both the laboratory and the field research have examined only one very specific application of participation under highly similar conditions and with very similar manipulations. Similarity in results obtained between research environments, then, is attributable more to a shared simplicity than to a shared complexity in both the scope undertaken and the methods used in the laboratory as well as in the field.

It is also important to recognize that the similarity in results between the PGS studies conducted in the laboratory and the field rests with a lack of significant differences in variables such as goal acceptance and performance. This lack of significance in the findings may be attributable to either invalid measures, ceiling effects, or the legitimate absence of significant differences between participatively set and assigned goal setting with respect to the variables being investigated. If invalid measures were used, for example, then the conclusions reached here concerning generalizability may not be accurate. Only if *significant* findings are reported in future laboratory and field studies will interpretation of the sources of generalizability become less equivocal.

The relatively high degree of agreement between laboratory and field research examining the Vroom and Yetton model may be attributable to several factors. First, in all but two of the Vroom and Yetton studies (Field, 1982; Jago & Ettling, 1982), actual managers were used as subjects. Although in the laboratory scenario studies the situations were artificially structured by the researchers, the respondents were presumably faced with decisions similar to those that they might face in their jobs and, for this reason, may have been easily assimilated into the scenario situations. The scenarios were in fact developed on the basis of managers' descriptions of actual decisions (Vroom & Yetton, 1973; Vroom & Jago, 1974). Second, similar to the PGS studies, a common theoretical framework coupled with similar definitions and operationalizations of variables has guided both laboratory and field research. Again, it appears that this equivalence has enhanced generalizability. This equivalence, however, has taken the form of a shared complexity rather than a shared simplicity regarding both the scope and the design of studies conducted in both the laboratory and field.

Unlike most of the broad-based PDM research, laboratory studies examining the Vroom and Yetton model have attempted to encompass the complexity inherent in field settings. The Vroom and Yetton scenario methodology, while obviously contrived and inherently artificial, does encompass many important contextual factors (such as locus of information and decision importance) that are commonly associated with actual managerial decision making situations. Other laboratory research on the Vroom and Yetton model that has manipulated these contextual variables through experiential means rather than scenario descriptions (for example, Field, 1982; Jago and Ettling, 1982) has produced largely convergent results both with the research using the scenario methodology (such as Vroom and Jago, 1978) and, more importantly, with investigations conducted in the field (such as Margerison and Glube, 1979).

A further distinction between the Vroom and Yetton research and the broad-based PDM studies is that the Vroom and Yetton model recognizes PDM as a continuum of decision-making styles rather than as a simple "all or none" dichotomy. The broad-based laboratory and field investigations of PDM tended to focus exclusively on comparisons between some type of subordinate involvement in decision making (which was labeled "participation") and some type of autocratic or nonparticipative approach. This simplicity in how PDM was conceptualized, coupled with a lack of consistency in how PDM was operationally defined in the laboratory and the field, has no doubt contributed to the equivocal findings among broad-based PDM studies, regardless of the research environment.

Conversely, both laboratory and field investigations of the Vroom and Yetton model have relied on a common five-point continuum of subordinate involvement in decision making which distinguishes between, for example, subordinate consultation and superior-subordinate joint decision making. In fact, consultation and joint decision making, although not always differentiated in the broad-based PDM studies, are not used interchangeably and differ in both their incidence and their effects in the Vroom and Yetton model. In this regard, the Vroom and Yetton laboratory investigations are better able to capture the complexity of the work environment influencing the choice of styles used by managers to involve subordinates in decision making. Moreover, since the theoretical framework underlying these investigations has specified a variety of participative methods, laboratory as well as field research has been better able to capture these distinctions in a systematic manner that permits comparability across studies.

In conclusion, our analyses suggest that the research results obtained in the laboratory generally agree with those obtained in the field. Although the findings are not identical, they are similar enough to conclude that the laboratory is capable of producing findings that are generalizable to the field. It is essential to realize, however, that generalizability is not to be assumed. As we have noted throughout our discussion, the conceptual and operational similarity of variables studied in both the laboratory and field are of paramount importance in enhancing this generalizability. As we have seen from the Vroom and Yetton research, however, complexity in variable specification need not be sacrificed to achieve this similarity. From a developmental perspective, then, it appears that PDM researchers have placed more emphasis on laboratory-field comparability and, as it has been incorporated into their research streams, generalizability has become a less critical issue for the PDM literature as a whole.

References

1. Adams, S. (1952) Effects of equalitarian atmospheres upon the performance of bomber crews. *American Psychologist, 7,* 398.

2. Alutto, J.A., & Acito, F. (1974) Decisional participation and sources of job satisfaction: A study of manufacturing personnel. *Academy of Management Journal, 17,* 160–167.

3. Argyle, M., Gardner, G., & Cioffi, F. (1958) Supervisory methods related to productivity, absenteeism and labour turnover. *Human Relations, 11,* 23–40.

4. Bass, B.M. (1981) *Stogdill's handbook of leadership: A survey of theory and research.* New York: Macmillan.

5. Bass, B.M., Valenzi, E., Farrow, D.L., & Solomon, R.J. (1975) Management styles associated with organizational, task, personal and interpersonal contingencies. *Journal of Applied Psychology, 60,* 720–729.

6. Baumgartel, H. (1956) Leadership, motivations, and attitudes in research laboratories. *Journal of Social Issues, 12,* 24–31.

7. Baumgartel, H. (1957) Leadership style as a variable in research administration. *Administrative Science Quarterly, 2,* 344–360.

8. Berkowitz, L. (1953) Sharing leadership in small, decision-making groups. *Journal of Abnormal and Social Psychology, 48,* 231–238.

9. Burns, T., & Stalker, G.M. (1961) *The management of innovation.* Chicago: Quadrangle Books.

10. Calvin, A.D., Hoffmann, F.K., & Harden, E.L. (1957) The effect of intelligence and social atmosphere on group problem solving behavior. *Journal of Social Psychology, 45,* 61–74.

11. Carroll, S.J., & Tosi, H.L. (1973) *Management by objectives: Applications and research.* New York: Macmillan.

12. Coch, L., & French, J.R.P. (1948) Overcoming resistance to change. *Human Relations, 1,* 512–532.

13. Dachler, H.P. (1978) The problem nature of participation in organizations: A conceptual evaluation. In B. King, S. Sweufert, & F.E. Fiedler (Eds.), *Managerial control and organization democracy* (pp. 17–29). New York: John Wiley & Sons.

14. Dill, W., Hoffman, W., Leavitt, H.J., & O'Mara, T. (1961) Experiences with a complex management game. *California Management Review, 3,* 38–51.

15. Dossett, D.L., Latham, G.P., & Mitchell, T.R. (1979) The effects of assigned versus participatively set goals, KR, and individual differences when goal difficulty is held constant. *Journal of Applied Psychology, 64,* 291–298.

16. Falcione, R.L. (1974) Credibility: Qualifier of subordinate participation. *Journal of Business Communication, 11,* 43–54.

17. Field, R.H.G. (1982) A test of the Vroom-Yetton normative model of leadership. *Journal of Applied Psychology, 67,* 523–532.

18. Fleishman, E.A. (1965) Attitude versus skill factors in work group productivity. *Personnel Psychology, 18,* 253–266.

19. Foa, U.G. (1957) Relation of workers expectation to satisfaction with supervisor. *Personnel Psychology, 10,* 161–168.

20. Fox, W.M. (1957) Group reaction to two types of conference leadership. *Human Relations, 10,* 279–289.

21. French, J.R.P., Israel, J., & As, D. (1960) An experiment in a Norwegian factory: Interpersonal dimensions in decision-making. *Human Relations, 13,* 3–9.

22. French, J.R.P., Kay, E., & Meyer, H.H. (1966) Participation and the appraisal system. *Human Relations, 19,* 3–20.

23. Gibb, C.A. (1951) An experimental approach to the study of leadership. *Occupational Psychology, 25,* 233–248.

24. Hannan, R.L. (1975) *The effects of participation in goal setting on goal acceptance and performance: A laboratory experiment.* Unpublished Ph.D. dissertation, University of Maryland, College Park.

25. Hunter, J.E., Schmidt, F.L., & Jackson, G.B. (1982) *Meta-analysis: Cumulating research findings across studies.* Beverly Hills: Sage.

26. Ivancevich, J.M. (1976) Effects of goal setting on performance and job satisfaction. *Journal of Applied Psychology, 61,* 605–612.

27. Ivancevich, J.M. (1976) Different goal setting treatments and their effects on performance and job satisfaction. *Academy of Management Journal, 20,* 406–419.

28. Jago, A.G. (1978) A test of spuriousness in descriptive models of leader behavior. *Journal of Applied Psychology, 63,* 383–387.

29. Jago, A.G. An assessment of the deemed appropriateness of participative decision making for high and low hierarchical levels. *Human Relations, 34,* 379–396.

30. Jago, A.G, & Ettling, J.T. (1982) *Participation under conditions of conflict: More on the validity of the Vroom-Yetton model.* Paper presented at the conference of the American Institute for Decision Sciences, San Francisco.

31. Jago, A.G., & Vroom, V.H. (1975) Perceptions of leadership style: Superior and subordinate descriptions of decision making behavior. In J.G. Hunt & L.L. Larson (Eds.), *Leadership Frontiers.* Kent, OH: Kent State University Press.

32. Jago, A.G., & Vroom, V.H. (1977) Hierarchical level and leadership style. *Organizational Behavior and Human Performance, 18,* 131–145.

33. Jago, A.G., & Vroom, V.H. (1978) Predicting leader behavior from a measure of behavioral intent. *Academy of Management Journal, 21,* 715–721.

34. Jago, A.G., & Vroom, V.H. (1980) An evaluation of two alternatives to the Vroom-Yetton normative model. *Academy of Management Journal, 23,* 347–355.

35. Katz, D., Maccoby, N., Gurin, G., & Floor, L.G. (1951) *Productivity, supervision and morale among railroad workers.* University of Michigan, Institute for Social Research, Survey Research Center, Ann Arbor.

36. Katz, D., Maccoby, N., & Morse, N. (1950) *Productivity, supervision and morale in an office situation,* Part I. University of Michigan, Institute for Social Research, Survey Research Center.

37. Katzell, R.A., Miller, C.E., Rotter, N.G., & Venet, T.G. (1970) Effects of leadership and other inputs on group processes and outputs. *Journal of Social Psychology, 80,* 157–169.

38. Kidd, J.S., & Christy, R.T. (1961) Supervisory procedures and work-team productivity. *Journal of Applied Psychology, 45,* 388–392.

39. Lanzetta, J.T., & Roby, T.B. (1960) The relationship between certain group process variables and group problem-solving efficiency. *Journal of Social Psychology, 52,* 135–148.

40. Latham, G.P., & Marshall, H.A. (1982) The effects of self-set, participatively set and assigned goals on the performance of government employees. *Personnel Psychology, 35,* 399–404.

41. Latham, G.P., Mitchell, T.R., & Dossett, D.L. (1978) Importance of participative goal setting and anticipated rewards on goal difficulty and job performance. *Journal of Applied Psychology, 63,* 163–171.

42. Latham, G.P., & Saari, L.M. (1979a) Importance of supportive relationships in goal setting. *Journal of Applied Psychology, 64,* 151–156.

43. Latham, G.P., & Saari, L.M. (1979b) The effects of holding goal difficulty constant on assigned and participatively set goals. *Academy of Management Journal, 22,* 163–168.

44. Latham, G.P., & Steele, T.P. (1983) The motivational effects of participation versus goal setting on performance. *Academy of Management Journal, 26,* 406–417.

45. Latham, G.P., Steele, T.P., & Saari, L.M. (1982) The effects of participation and goal difficulty on performance. *Personnel Psychology, 35,* 677–686.

46. Latham, G.P., & Yukl, G.A. (1975) Assigned versus participative goal setting with educated and uneducated woods workers. *Journal of Applied Psychology, 60,* 299–302.

47. Latham, G.P., & Yukl, G.A. (1976) Effects of assigned and participative goal setting on performance and job satisfaction. *Journal of Applied Psychology, 61,* 166–171.

48. Lawler, E.E., & Hackman, J.R. (1969) Impact of employee participation in the development of pay incentive plans: A field experiment. *Journal of Applied Psychology, 53,* 467–471.

49. Lee, C., & Shuler, R.S. (1982) A constructive replication and extension of a role and expectancy perception model of participation in decision making. *Journal of Occupational Psychology, 55,* 109–118.

50. Ley, R. (1966) Labor turnover as a function of worker differences, work environment, and authoritarianism of foremen. *Journal of Applied Psychology, 50,* 497–500.

51. Lischeron, J., & Wall, T.D. (1974) Attitudes towards participation among local authority employees. *Human Relations, 28,* 499–517.

52. Lischeron, J., & Wall, T.D. (1975) Employee participation: An experimental field study. *Human Relations, 28,* 863–884.

53. Litwin, G.H., & Stringer, R.A. (1968) *Motivation and organizational climate.* Harvard University, Graduate School of Business Administration, Division of Research, Boston.

54. Locke, E.A., & Schweiger, D.M. (1979) Participation in decision making: One more look. In B. Staw (Ed.), *Research in organizational behavior* (Vol. 1). Greenwich, Conn.: JAI Press, 265–339.

55. Locke, E.A., Shaw, K.N., Saari, L.M., & Latham, G.P. (1981) Goal setting and task performance: 1969–1980. *Psychological Bulletin, 90,* 125–152.

56. Lowin, A. (1968) Participative decision making: A model, literature, critique, and prescriptions for research. *Organizational Behavior and Human Performance, 3,* 68–106.

57. Mahoney, T.A., (1967) Managerial perceptions of organizational effectiveness. *Management Science, 14,* 76–91.

58. Maier, N.R.F. (1950) The quality of group decision as influenced by the discussion leader. *Human Relations, 3,* 155–174.

59. Maier, N.R.F. (1953) An experimental test of the effect of training on discussion leadership. *Human Relations, 6,* 161–173.

60. Maier, N.R.F., & Sashkin, M. (1971) Specific leadership behaviors that promote problem solving. *Personnel Psychology, 24,* 35–44.

61. Margerison, C., & Glube, R. (1979) Leadership decision-making: An empirical examination of the Vroom and Yetton model. *Journal of Management Studies, 16,* 45–55.

62. McCurdy, H.G., & Eber, H.W. (1953) Democratic versus authoritarianism: A further investigation of group problem-solving. *Journal of Personality, 22,* 258–269.

63. McCurdy, H.G., & Lambert, W.E. (1952) The efficiency of small human groups in the solution of problems requiring genuine co-operation. *Journal of Personality, 20,* 478–494.

64. Miles, R.E., & Ritchie, J.B. (1971) Participative management: Quality vs. Quantity. *California Management Review, 13,* 48–56.

65. Morse, C., & Reimer, E. (1956) The experimental change of a major organizational variable. *Journal of Abnormal and Social Psychology, 52,* 120–129.

66. Mulder, M. (1959) Power and satisfaction in task-oriented groups. *Acta Psychologica, 16,* 178–225.

67. Mullen, J.H. (1965) Differential leadership modes and productivity in a large organization. *Academy of Management Journal, 8,* 107–126.

68. Patchen, M. (1964) Participation in decision-making and motivation: What is the relation? *Personnel Administration, 27,* 24–31.

69. Pelz, D.C. (1956) Some social factors related to performance in a research organization. *Administrative Science Quarterly, 1,* 310–325.

70. Powell, R.M., & Schlacter, J.L. (1971) Participative management: A panacea? *Academy of Management Journal, 14,* 165–173.

71. Runyon, K.E., (1973) Some interactions between personality variables and management styles. *Journal of Applied Psychology, 57,* 288–294.

72. Sadler, P.J. (1970) Leadership style, confidence in management, and job satisfaction. *Journal of Applied Behavioral Science, 6,* 3–19.

73. Schuler, R.S. (1977) Role perceptions, satisfaction and performance moderated by organizational level and participation in decision making. *Academy of Management Journal, 20,* 165–169.

74. Schuler, R.S. (1980) A role and expectancy perception model of participation in decision making. *Academy of Management Journal, 23,* 331–340.

75. Seeborg, I.S. (1978) The influence of employee participation in job redesign. *Journal of Applied Behavioral Science, 14,* 87–98.

76. Shaw, M.E. (1955) A comparison of two types of leadership in various communication nets. *Journal of Abnormal and Social Psychology, 50,* 127–134.

77. Shaw, M.E., & Blum, J.M. (1966) Effects of leadership style upon group performance as a function of task structure. *Journal of Personality and Social Psychology, 3,* 238–242.

78. Stagner, R. (1969) Corporate decision making: An empirical study. *Journal of Applied Psychology, 53,* 1–13.

79. Tosi, H. (1970) A reexamination of personality as a determinant of the effects of participation. *Personnel Psychology, 23,* 91–99.

80. Vroom, V. (1960) *Some personality determinants of the effects of participation,* Englewood Cliffs, N.J.: Prentice-Hall.

81. Vroom, V.H., & Jago, A.G. (1974) Decision making as a social process: Normative and descriptive models of leader behavior. *Decision Sciences, 5,* 743–769.

82. Vroom, V.H., & Jago, A.G. (1978) On the validity of the Vroom/Yetton model. *Journal of Applied Psychology, 63,* 151–162.

83. Vroom, V.H., & Mann, F. (1960) Leader authoritarianism and employee attitudes. *Personnel Psychology, 13,* 125–140.

84. Vroom, V.H., & Yetton, P. (1973) *Leadership and decision making.* Pittsburgh: University of Pittsburgh Press.

85. Weschler, I.R., Kahane, M., & Tannenbaum, R. (1952) Job satisfaction, productivity and morale: A case study. *Occupational Psychology, 26,* 1–14.

86. Yukl, G.A. (1981) *Leadership in organizations.* Englewood Cliffs, N.J.: Prentice-Hall.

9
Financial Incentives

G. Douglas Jenkins, Jr.

Compensation is a central element in the vast majority of our work organizations. In fact, it is so central that a special term, *volunteer organizations,* is needed to describe those work organizations where compensation is *not* relevant. Given the centrality of compensation in organizations, I was surprised at how sparse our scientific information is in its regard. The sparseness is particularly notable with respect to the aspect of compensation that constitutes the focus of this chapter, the impact of financial incentives on performance. The little empirical evidence that does exist is integrated here to draw some conclusions about the generalizability of laboratory findings about financial incentives to real world settings.

The Role of Financial Incentives

Ask a person on the street—a researcher, a practitioner, a manager, a worker, a student, a young child, whomever—if giving financial rewards for performance will lead to higher performance, and the answer will be yes, or at least a qualified yes. As Locke, Bryan, and Kendall (1968) note, "Incentive programs are based on the implicit assumption that incentives will affect behavior more or less automatically" (pp. 120–121). That the effects of financial incentives on performance seem so self-evident may partly account for the dearth of solid empirical investigations. The evidence that has been generated tends to focus on the effects of *variations* in incentive conditions, and not on whether performance-based pay per se raises performance levels. Only one of the studies reviewed here (Toppen, 1965) focused exclusively on the simple difference between an incentive condition (piece-rate pay) and a nonincentive condition (hourly pay), and in this study, hourly pay was the experimental, not the control, condition! This says something striking about the frequency of our scientific investigation of the basic effect of financial incentives.

It is no wonder that two decades ago, Opsahl and Dunnette (1966) and Grinyer and Kessler (1967) bemoaned the sorry state of experimental data on the role of money in improving performance. Opsahl and Dunnette went so far as to urge more laboratory investigations of the issue. It is surprising that the situation has still not improved much (Yetton, 1979). In some ways, it is amazing that we can be discussing the generalizability of laboratory findings to field settings, given that there are so few findings to generalize from or to.

As in most cases, the situation is not as bleak as it first appears to be. First, there are various theoretical formulations that explicate the role of financial incentives. Second, case reports, anecdotes, cross-sectional field studies, and other works shed some empirical light on the matter. Third, some studies do investigate the effects of various levels of incentives, and from these studies some knowledge can also be gleaned.

Before discussing the empirical work, it is well to ask why performance-based pay *should* raise performance. The first formal statement can probably be traced to Taylor (1911) and his "thrifty Dutchman." Since then, various theoretical approaches have attempted to explain the incentive or reinforcing value of money. Money has been seen as an acquired drive, a secondary reinforcer, a conditioned incentive, or a mechanism for obtaining valued outcomes. Lawler (1971) reviewed these perspectives, and they will not be repeated here. It is, however, perhaps safe to argue that expectancy theory (for example, Porter & Lawler, 1968) elucidated the effects of financial incentives on performance most fully. In the language of this theory, when financial rewards are tied to performance, then, other things being equal, extrinsic motivation to expend effort in the service of performance is increased. Given the prevalence of money as a central factor in most work organizations, it is probably unnecessary to argue that money is a valued outcome for workers at large. Thus, people are motivated to try and behave in ways that would allow them to obtain this valued outcome.

These and other elaborate formulations can probably be boiled down to a simple statement about the role of money: people exhibit behaviors they believe will be rewarded; money is a reward; if money is linked to performance, people will try to perform well (Jenkins & Gupta, 1982). This seems to capture the role of money as a performance motivator.

Parameters of the Empirical Evidence

To address the empirical evidence on the role of financial incentives, the major academic journals generally used by researchers in organizational behavior, industrial-organizational psychology, and personnel/human resources management were reviewed. Certain decision rules were used to hone the focus of the review.

First, published articles for only the last twenty-five years (1960–1985) were included. This decision came about for a variety of reasons. The classic research of Georgopoulos, Mahoney, and Jones (1957) stimulated a renewed interest in linking behaviors and outcomes, and research on the role of financial incentive saw some increase after this time. Also, Marriott's (1957) review of incentive systems concluded about the same time that previous studies generally lacked the scientific rigor necessary for strong conclusions to be possible. These two factors, combined with the need to retain feasibility in the present review, led to the decision to confine the search to articles published since 1959.

Second, the present review specifically excluded practitioner reports and journals. These reports tend to be anecdotal accounts or case studies that generally suffer from the same lack of rigor that characterized the studies reviewed by Marriott (1957). The interested reader is referred to Jenkins and Gupta (1982) for a discussion of some of these reports.

Third, the research had to have been experimental to fall within the purview of this chapter. Field studies that were cross-sectional or correlational in nature were excluded from consideration. Comparable laboratory investigations using this research design are unavailable, making moot the issue of generalizability of correlational findings from one setting to the other. Furthermore, the issue of interest here is basically causal—does performance-based monetary reward enhance performance? This issue cannot be addressed unambiguously in a cross-sectional, correlational framework.

Fourth, only studies using "hard" performance measures as the relevant outcome were included in the review. Studies linking other work behaviors such as absenteeism (Lawler & Hackman, 1969) and suggestions to financial rewards were excluded. Again, the rationale was to retain comparability between laboratory and field investigations. The performance outcome was defined to include quality of performance, quantity of performance, or some combination of the two.

Fifth, the review included only those studies using individually based financial incentives. Research focusing on group bonuses and organizational level incentives, such as Scanlon plans and gain-sharing plans, was excluded because of the lack of comparable laboratory investigations. A notable exception is the London and Oldham (1977) report, which examined both individual and group incentives in a laboratory setting.

Sixth, the scope of the review was limited to those studies that explicitly manipulated the performance contingency of financial incentives at the individual level. In addition, for a study to be included, it had to have either a premeasure or a control group where financial rewards were not contingent on performance (for example, straight hourly pay). Thus, this review does not cover studies where various amounts of the reward were compared (such as Mento, Cartledge, & Locke, 1980) or where the extent to which performance-contingent rewards were linked to performance (that is, the degree of positive contingency) was manipulated, as in many tests of expectancy theory. In this way, the effects of having/not having performance-based financial rewards could be examined directly.

Seventh, investigations where performance was linked to nonmonetary outcomes such as lottery tickets, records, days off, and discounts, were excluded (see Neider, 1980; 1977), as were investigations using token economies (such as

Mowen, Middlemist, & Luther, 1981). Again, this decision rule was developed to retain comparability between laboratory and field settings. The single exception to the rule was the research reported by Pritchard, DeLeo, and Von Bergen (1976), which used chits that could be used exactly like money.

Eighth, all the studies within the scope of the review involved normal adult populations (if undergraduates can be so classified) in "work" settings. For laboratory investigations, this meant that the authors intended to generalize their findings to work settings and outcomes (for example, Deci, 1971), or constructed their tasks to be "genotypically similar" (Weick, 1965) to those in work settings. For field investigations, this meant that studies were excluded if they failed to involve employees (for example, Ayllon & Azrin, 1965) or to focus on work outcomes (such as seat belt use or driving behavior, Foxx & Schaeffer, 1981).

Using these eight, perhaps overly restrictive criteria, twenty-eight studies were identified.[1] Of these, fifteen were laboratory experiments, five were experimental simulations, and the remaining eight were field experiments. Another early decision was to classify the five experimental simulations together with the laboratory experiments.

The logic of this decision may not be immediately apparent since there are arguments for combining experimental simulations with field experiments, as Locke, Feren, McCaleb, Shaw, and Denny (1980) did. As a class of research strategies, experimental simulations share similarities with both laboratory and field experiments (Runkel & McGrath, 1972). The decision to classify them with laboratory experiments reflects the fact that, in both lab experiments and experimental simulations, the research setting is created by the researcher. In other words, with both strategies the setting exists solely for the purpose of the research study and has no prior existence, history, or culture. Following Runkel and McGrath, one can argue that actors are in the setting primarily to participate in the study. This is somewhat different from why employees are in ongoing work organizations. The subjects in laboratory experiments and experimental simulations on the one hand and those in field experiments on the other, therefore, have different relationships to the setting. Lawler (1981) argued that compensation systems are inextricably bound in the culture and history of an organization and that there must be consistency among these elements for effective functioning. If this argument is valid, it seems more appropriate to group experimental simulations with the laboratory experiments on the grounds that both lack the characteristics of history and organizational culture. The ramifications of this decision will be examined later in this chapter.

Commonalities between Laboratory and Field Investigations

Given the twenty-eight studies relevant to this review, what does the evidence say? What are the similarities in results between studies in laboratory and field settings? What are the differences? What accounts for these similarities and differences?

To answer these questions, the first task was to classify the studies according to whether or not performance in contingent-pay conditions was better than in noncontingent-pay conditions. Performance improvement was considered to have occurred if there was: (1) a significant pre-post difference in single group studies, (2) a significant difference between the posttest performances of treatment and control groups in multigroup studies, (3) a significant difference in pretest-posttest change in the performance of treatment and control groups in multigroup studies, or (4) a significant difference between groups or conditions after controlling for other variables. Studies showing negative results (for example, performance decrements) were classified with those showing no differences, as were studies reporting mixed results.

Two other aspects of the classification are relevant. The first concerns the outcome variables of interest. Several studies reported effects in terms of both performance quality and performance quantity. Others reported performance (presumably quantity) controlling for quality, or performance as a composite measure where quality is essential for quantity (such as number of spindled cards where spindling is possible only if quality of performance is perfect). Still other studies used only measures of performance quantity. Studies were classified as mixed for the initial tabulation if both quality and quantity measures were used, but showed different results. The effects are disentangled in later analyses.

The second relevant aspect is that of statistical significance. When authors reported significance levels (a value of $p < .05$ was taken as the cutoff), their reports were taken at face value. In several studies, however, financial incentives were not the sole focus or constituted only part of the treatment condition (for example, no pay, hourly pay, piece-rate pay). For these studies, the significance of any increments in performance had to be recalculated for the present review, using reported cell means and variances. In a few cases, cell means were presented only graphically. It was necessary in these cases to derive estimates of cell values and compute appropriate contrasts using the overall error term in the denominator.

Table 9-1 shows the results of this initial performance improvement/no performance improvement comparison between laboratory and field experiments. The

Table 9–1
Effect of Financial Incentives on Performance Quantity and/or Quality

	Laboratory Experiments	*Field Experiments*
Performance increase[a]	10 (50%) [2, 6, 13, 22, 32, 35, 36, 43, 44, 51]	6 (75%) [14, 15, 23, 30, 39, 49]
No performance increase or performance decrease, mixed results	10 (50%) [3, 7^1, 7^2, 11, 20^1, 20^2, 34, 41, 42, 47]	2 (25%) [37, 50]

Note: Numbers in brackets are studies contained in list of references. When multiple studies are reported in a single article, the studies are treated separately. The number of the study within the report is noted with a superscript number.

[a]Z for differences in percentages = 1.276, n.s.

tabulation indicated that ten of the twenty combined laboratory experiments and experimental simulations showed positive effects of financial incentives; six of the eight field experiments showed similar results. This reflects a success rate of 50 percent among laboratory experiments and 75 percent among field experiments. Surprisingly, then, a larger proportion of potentially "contaminated" field experiments than of the "cleaner" laboratory experiments is supportive of the proposition that performance-based pay improves performance.

Before taking these results at face value, however, certain elements of the studies under review must be considered. As noted above, quality and quantity of performance outcomes were considered together for the initial analysis. When quality measures alone are compared, the results change somewhat. Four laboratory investigations (Chung & Vickery, 1976; Terborg, 1976; Terborg & Miller, 1978; Wimperis & Farr, 1979) reported the effects of financial incentives on performance quality separately. All four showed no significant positive effects. The one field experiment reporting separately on quality (Pritchard, DeLeo, & Von Bergen, 1976) also found no effects of financial incentives. With respect to performance quality, then, laboratory and field experiments alike appear to be unanimous: financial incentives do not improve performance quality. This conclusion must be moderated, however, in view of the fact that only five studies addressed performance quality and, more important, in view of the fact that in not one of the five studies was pay contingent on performance quality (financial rewards were contingent on quantity instead). In essence, the null results confirm the obvious, that for rewards to improve a particular behavior, the rewards must be contingent on that behavior specifically. Quantity-contingent pay does not as a consequence improve quality.

Table 9–2 compares laboratory and field effects of financial incentives on the quantity of performance. Studies using distinct quantity measures, as well as those using composite measures, were of concern in this table. The picture that emerges when studies are arrayed on the basis of quantity is a little different from that in table 9–1. As table 9–2 shows, fourteen, or 70 percent, of the twenty laboratory investigations and seven, or 87.5 percent, of the eight field investigations found

Table 9–2
Effect of Financial Incentives on Quantity of Performance

	Laboratory Experiments	Field Experiments
Performance increase[a]	14 (70%) [2, 3, 6, 13, 22, 32, 35, 36, 41, 42, 43, 44, 47, 51]	7 (87.5%) [14, 15, 23, 30, 37, 39, 49]
No performance increase or performance decrease	6 (30%) [7[1], 7[2], 11, 20[1], 20[2], 34]	1 (12.5%) [50]

Note: Numbers in brackets are studies contained in list of references. When multiple studies are reported in a single article, the studies are treated separately. The number of the study within the report is noted with a superscript number.

[a]Z for differences in percentages = 1.023, n.s.

enhancements of performance quantity in the contingent-pay conditions. The proportions of confirmation in laboratory versus field investigations are not significantly different ($Z = 1.023$, n.s.). Thus, laboratory and field investigations seem to agree on the effects of financial incentives on performance quantity, although not with the same degree of unanimity.

In all, the results thus far show that both laboratory and field experiments support the positive effects of financial incentives on performance quantity, but not on performance quality. Furthermore, field experiments generally provided more supportive results for the effect on quantity than did laboratory investigations.

In this context, an issue of interest is the role of experimental simulations in the results when grouped with laboratory experiments. What if this classification is inappropriate? It was argued earlier that subjects in experimental simulations were in the setting for reasons different from those of workers in real organizations. What if this were false? An examination of the five experimental simulations included here (Berger, Cummings, & Heneman, 1975; Jorgenson, Dunnette, & Pritchard, 1973; Pritchard & DeLeo, 1973; Terborg, 1976; Yukl, Wexley, & Seymore, 1972) revealed that, in each, subjects were recruited for short-term, part-time "jobs." In other words, they may well have been in the setting for precisely the same reasons that workers are in work organizations. In this case, it may be more appropriate to classify experimental simulations the way Locke et al. (1980) did, that is, with field experiments.

The role of experimental simulations in the issue at hand was examined in two ways using the performance quantity comparison only. First, experimental simulations were reclassified with the field experiments. Since all five experimental simulations found significant performance improvements, the revised results showed 60 percent of the laboratory investigations and 92 percent of the field investigations with positive effects ($Z = 1.977$, $p < .05$). Thus, when experimental simulations are classified with laboratory experiments, differences between the laboratory and the field are nonsignificant. When they are classified with field experiments, however, the field provides significantly more positive effects than does the laboratory.

The second way to explore the role of experimental simulations was to exclude them from consideration altogether as being neither fish nor fowl. Using performance quantity as the outcome again, nine of the fifteen laboratory experiments (60 percent) and seven of the eight field experiments (87.5 percent) confirmed performance increments due to financial incentives ($Z = 1.428$, n.s.).

In all, since the five experimental simulations showed positive effects, their inclusion with the laboratory studies increases supportive results in the laboratory, and their inclusion with the field increases supportive results in the field. Perhaps the cleanest comparison, where experimental simulations are excluded altogether, shows nonsignificant differences in the direction of the findings between laboratory and field investigations.

Taken together, what does the review show about the effects of financial incentives? It shows that:

1. The studies in the laboratory and the field are in agreement that there are no effects on performance quality.

2. The studies in both the laboratory and, to a greater extent, the field show greater support for positive effects than for negative or no effects on performance quantity.

3. The most consistent support is obtained in experimental simulations, with field experiments a close second, and the least consistent support in laboratory experiments.

Issues and Concerns

The literature review seemed to substantiate overall that positive incentive effects on performance can be found in the laboratory, in the field, and in experimental simulations. But beyond this simple conclusion, several aspects of the studies reviewed and of the review itself are worthy of note and can shed light on the generalizability concern.

First, the proportions of studies with positive effects in different settings did not show striking significant differences, but were nonetheless different. The lack of strong statistical significance can in part be attributed to small sample sizes (fifteen laboratory studies, five experimental simulations, and eight field studies). But beyond the issue of statistical significance, looking only at the raw numbers, the differences seem noteworthy. For instance, using the performance quantity outcome, only 60 percent of the laboratory experiments, but all of the simulations and almost all (87.5 percent) of the field experiments reported incentive effects. Somewhat different dynamics may be operating in the different settings, dynamics that are not captured by the significance tests.

It may be well to wonder why support for the effect is most consistent in simulations and least consistent in laboratory studies, with the field investigations in between. A reasonable hypothesis would be that experimental simulations combine the best of both worlds: they incorporate the control possible in the laboratory with the realism of the field. This would suggest that financial incentives do affect performance, but only when real world conditions are closely captured in the setting. Although laboratory studies may allow control, the artificiality of the situation may mask real effects. In this context, it should be noted that the one disconfirming field experiment (Yukl, Latham, & Pursell, 1976) showed performance increments that, while classified as nonsignificant, approached statistical significance ($p < .06$). Overall, then, this review suggests that, at least with respect to financial incentives, laboratory studies provide, at best, a conservative estimate of the real world effects on performance.

I also wondered what characteristics distinguished confirming from disconfirming laboratory experiments. There were no substantial mean differences in the sample sizes of the groups. There was, however, a clear distinction between the two in terms of the tasks subjects were performing. Among those laboratory studies that showed a positive incentive effect, four (Farr, 1976; Pinder, 1976; Terborg & Miller, 1978; Wimperis & Farr, 1979) used construction tasks such as tinker toy assembly or erector set connections; four (Chung & Vickery, 1976; London & Oldham, 1977; Pritchard & Curtis, 1973; Turnage & Muchinsky, 1976) used clerical tasks such as sorting computer cards or scoring grade sheets; and one (Toppen, 1965) used a physical task (pulley pulls). Of the nonsupportive laboratory experiments, only two (Hamner & Foster, 1975, Locke et al., 1968[2]) used clerical or construction tasks (in both, while the differences were nonsignificant, performance was higher in the contingent pay condition). The remaining four used problem-solving tasks such as thinking up uses for an object (Locke et al., 1968[1]), and solving Soma puzzles (Farr, Vance, & McIntyre, 1977[1,2]) or chess problems (Pritchard, Campbell, & Campbell, 1977).

In the field experiments, on the other hand, the tasks were varied, but were not heavily cognitive in nature. They included tasks such as beaver trapping, tree planting, and quality checking. The tasks in the experimental simulations tended to be clerical in nature. Exceptions were a field experiment (Pritchard et al., 1976) and an experimental simulation (Terborg, 1976), both of which used programmed learning tasks.

Despite minor variations, then, it seems safe to conclude that regardless of setting, performance effects of financial incentives are more likely to emerge when physical or clerical tasks are involved. Thus, laboratory experiments may yield the same results as studies in field settings when the tasks involved are structurally similar. In the laboratory, shifting to cognitive tasks such as solving puzzles may produce a radical difference in the tasks, not only with respect to the surface resemblance to tasks studied in ongoing organizations, but in structural and situational characteristics as well.

Furthermore, these results may argue that the effects of financial incentives on performance are limited to physical and construction tasks. It may well be that highly cognitive tasks possess properties that obey different laws with respect to the impact of financial incentives than do "production" tasks (Zelditch & Evan, 1962). Deci and Ryan (1980) have argued that with cognitively challenging tasks, motivation is already high due to intrinsic rewards and that increasing motivation further with extrinsic rewards may have detrimental effects. Similarly, McGraw (1978) reviewed a series of laboratory studies (primarily using nonadult subjects) on the effect of extrinsic rewards (not always involving money) on cognitive tasks (such as learning and perceptual recognition) and tasks requiring insight and creativity. He concluded that when the task was inherently attractive or required cognitive coding and mediation (that is, successful performance requires the use of heuristics), rewards are detrimental to performance. It should be noted that none of the relevant field experiments focuses on the effects of financial incentives in jobs that have a heavy cognitive, problem-solving, heuristic quality (for example, upper-level management jobs), so whether Deci and Ryan's and McGraw's conclusions are supported in field settings is yet to be determined.

Turning to a different issue, the fact that an effect is present, significant, and in the right direction does not necessarily mean much. The size of the improvements and whether these improvements are meaningful is perhaps the more critical issue. Are larger improvements obtained in the field? Apparently not. The average percentage difference (either a pre-post increase or a treatment-control group difference) was 28.4 percent for the laboratory experiments that showed positive significant effects. (One study, Toppen [1965] was excluded from this computation as an extreme outlier, since the increase was 225 percent!) In field experiments, the comparable increase was 33.2 percent, whereas in experimental simulations it was 27.6 percent. These percentage increases seem to argue that, when the settings and tasks are structured similarly, comparable gains can be obtained. The gains found in the present review are also similar to those reported by Lawler (1968) and Locke et al. (1980) in their reviews of the impact of financial incentives. In general, then, it is reasonable to conclude that linking pay to performance will lead to about a 30 percent increase in performance. Whether this increase is offset by the costs of implementation and administration is, of course, a situational question.

A persistent handicap during this review process was the small number of field experiments. It is difficult to discuss common elements between laboratory and field experiments when so few field experiments are conducted. Why are there so few well-conducted field experiments? A variety of possible reasons come to mind. It may be that, as noted above, the proposition—linking financial incentives to performance improves performance—seems self-evident. Managers may view proposing to study it as another case of academics wasting money confirming the obvious. Second, it may be that pay is so sensitive and central an issue in most organizations that managers are hesitant to tamper, much less experiment with it. Third, labor unions are generally opposed to piece-rate pay, the simplest and most widely-recognized incentive system (Lawler, 1971). Organizations may fear labor troubles—either in disputes or grievances, in future contract negotiations in unionized settings, or in organizing attempts in nonunionized settings—if they institute such incentive systems. Fourth, incentive systems can be expensive in terms of both total wage bill and administrative costs, whereas their payoffs are not always obvious. Fifth, managers may fear restriction of output and similar phenomena described by Dalton (Whyte, 1955) and the Hawthorne studies. And last but not least, field experiments are costly and time consuming. With dwindling research funding and increasing pressure to publish for promotions, tenure, and pay raises (financial incentives in the academic setting), researchers may be tempted to take the easy way and choose research arenas that yield quick and easy results and publication. Whatever the reason for their infrequency, more field experiments on the role of financial incentives are desperately needed if we are to confirm what we generally hold to be true about their impact on individual performance.

In summary, then, what did this literature review tell us? First, it told us that there are too few studies for strong conclusions to be possible. Any inferences about generalizability from the laboratory to the field are thus necessarily tentative. Second, the review suggests that generalizations may be possible under certain conditions. When experiments are structured so that people participate for the same reasons that people do in work organizations, when laboratory tasks are carefully chosen to reflect structural and situational similarity to real world tasks, and when conditions in general approximate those of real organizations, laboratory results are likely to parallel those of the field. Third, the review highlights that the ideal combination includes both control and realism, hence the consistency in results of the experimental simulations. To the extent that field experiments can isolate and eliminate extraneous effects, and to the extent that laboratory experiments can build in realism in their settings and tasks, results from either research arena will be more useful. Fourth, the review highlights the importance of studying the *relevant* outcome. If financial incentives are linked to performance quantity, it is fruitless to use performance quality as the criterion variable. Furthermore, it is important to design an uncontaminated measure of performance quantity for the effects of financial incentives to be clearly disentangled. Finally, the literature review shows that our knowledge of the effects of financial incentives seems to be confined to clerical and production type tasks. Clearly, researchers, especially field experimenters, must broaden their scope to include other types of jobs as well.

Overall, we can conclude that, given limited evidence, there is reason to believe that laboratory findings about financial incentives do generalize to field settings, but only when certain specified conditions are met.

Note

1. When multiple studies are reported in a single article, the studies are treated separately. The number of the study within the report is noted with a superscript number.

References

1. Ayllon, T., & Azrin, N.H. (1965) The measurement and reinforcement of behavior of psychotics. *Journal of Experimental Analysis of Behavior, 8,* 357–383.

2. Berger, C.J., Cummings, L.L., & Heneman, H.G., III (1975) Expectancy theory and operant conditioning predictions of performance under variable ratio and continuous schedules of reinforcement. *Organizational Behavior and Human Performance, 14,* 227–243.

3. Chung, K.H., & Vickery, W.D. (1976) Relative effectiveness and joint effects of three selected reinforcements in a repetitive task situation. *Organizational Behavior and Human Performance, 16,* 114–142.

4. Deci, E.L. (1971) Effects of externally mediated rewards on intrinsic motivation. *Journal of Personality and Social Psychology, 18,* 105–115.

5. Deci, E.L., & Ryan, R.M. (1980) The empirical exploration of intrinsic motivational processes. *Advances in Experimental Social Psychology, 13,* 39–80.

6. Farr, J.L. (1976) Task characteristics, reward contingency, and intrinsic motivation. *Organizational Behavior and Human Performance, 16,* 294–307.

7. Farr, J.L., Vance, R.J., & McIntyre, R.M. (1977) Further examinations of the relationship between reward contingency and intrinsic motivation. *Organizational Behavior and Human Performance, 20,* 31–53.

8. Foxx, R.M., & Schaeffer, M.H. (1981) A company-based lottery to reduce the personal driving of employees. *Journal of Applied Behavior Analysis, 14,* 273–285.

9. Georgopoulos, B.S., Mahoney, G.M., & Jones, N.W. (1957) A path-goal approach to productivity. *Journal of Applied Psychology, 41,* 345–353.

10. Grinyer, P.H., & Kessler, S. (1967) The systematic evaluation of methods of wage payment. *Journal of Management Studies, 4,* 309–321.

11. Hamner, W.C., & Foster, L.W. (1975) Are intrinsic and extrinsic rewards additive: A test of Deci's cognitive evaluation theory of task motivation. *Organizational Behavior and Human Performance, 14,* 398–415.

12. Jenkins, G.D., Jr., & Gupta, N. (1982) Financial incentives and productivity improvement. *Journal of Contemporary Business, 11*(2), 43–56.

13. Jorgenson, D.O., Dunnette, M.D., & Pritchard, R.D. (1973) Effects of the manipulation of a performance-reward contingency on behavior in a simulated work setting. *Journal of Applied Psychology, 57,* 271–280.

14. Komaki, J., Waddell, W.M., & Pearce, M.G. (1977) The applied behavior analysis approach and individual employees: Improving performance in two small businesses. *Organizational Behavior and Human Performance, 19,* 337–352.

15. Latham, G.P., & Dossett, D.L. (1978) Designing incentive plans for unionized employees: A comparison of continuous and variable ratio reinforcement schedules. *Personnel Psychology, 31,* 47–61.

16. Lawler, E.E. (1968) Equity theory as a predictor of productivity and work quality. *Psychological Bulletin, 70,* 596–610.

17. Lawler, E.E., III (1971) *Pay and organizational effectiveness: A psychological view.* New York: McGraw-Hill.

18. Lawler, E.E., III (1981) *Pay and organizational development.* Reading, Mass.: Addison-Wesley.

19. Lawler, E.E., III, & Hackman, J.R. (1969) The impact of employee participation in the development of pay incentive plans: A field experiment. *Journal of Applied Psychology, 53,* 467–471.

20. Locke, E.A., Bryan, J.F., & Kendall, L.M. (1968) Goals and intentions as mediators of the effects of monetary incentives on behavior. *Journal of Applied Psychology, 52,* 104–121.

21. Locke, E.A., Feren, D.B., McCaleb, V.M., Shaw, K.N., & Denny, A.T. (1980) The relative effectiveness of four methods of motivating employee performance. In K.D. Duncan, M.M. Gruneberg, & D. Wallis (Eds.), *Changes in working life* (pp. 363–388). London: John Wiley & Sons, Ltd.

22. London, M., & Oldham, G.R. (1977) A comparison of group and individual incentive plans. *Academy of Management Journal, 20,* 34–41.

23. Luthans, F., Paul, R., & Baker, D. (1981) An experimental analysis of the impact of contingent reinforcement on salespersons' performance behavior. *Journal of Applied Psychology, 66,* 314–323.

24. Marriott, R. (1957) *Incentive payment systems: A review of research and opinion.* London: Staples.

25. McGraw, K.O. (1978) The detrimental effects of reward on performance: A literature review and a predictive model. In M.R. Lepper & D. Greene (Eds.), *The hidden costs of reward* (pp. 33–60). Hillsdale, N.J.: Lawrence Erlbaum.

26. Mento, A.J., Cartledge, N.D., & Locke, E.A. (1980) Maryland vs Michigan vs Minnesota: Another look at the relationship of expectancy and goal difficulty to task performance. *Organizational Behavior and Human Performance, 25*, 419–440.

27. Mowen, J.C., Middlemist, R.D., & Luther, D. (1981) Joint effects of assigned goal level and incentive structure on task performance: A laboratory study. *Journal of Applied Psychology, 66*, 598–603.

28. Neider, L.L. (1980) An experimental field investigation utilizing an expectancy theory view of participation. *Organizational Behavior and Human Performance, 26*, 425–442.

29. Opsahl, R.L., & Dunnette, M.D. (1966) The role of financial compensation in industrial motivation. *Psychological Bulletin, 66*, 94–118.

30. Orpen, C. (1982) The effects of contingent and noncontingent rewards on employee satisfaction and performance. *The Journal of Psychology, 110*, 145–150.

31. Peters, L.H. (1977) Cognitive models of motivation, expectancy theory and effort: An analysis and empirical test. *Organizational Behavior and Human Performance, 20*, 129–148.

32. Pinder, C.C. (1976) Additivity versus nonadditivity of intrinsic and extrinsic incentives: Implications for work motivation, performance, and attitudes. *Journal of Applied Psychology, 61*, 693–700.

33. Porter, L.W., & Lawler, E.E., III (1968) *Managerial attitudes and performance.* Homewood, Ill.: Irwin-Dorsey.

34. Pritchard, R.D., Campbell, K.M., and Campbell, D.J. (1977) Effects of extrinsic financial rewards on intrinsic motivation. *Journal of Applied Psychology, 62*, 9–15.

35. Pritchard, R.D., & Curtis, M.I. (1973) The influence of goal setting and financial incentives on task performance. *Organizational Behavior and Human Performance, 10*, 175–183.

36. Pritchard, R.D., & DeLeo, P.J. (1973) Experimental test of the valence-instrumentality relationship in job performance. *Journal of Applied Psychology, 57*, 264–270.

37. Pritchard, R.D., DeLeo, P.J., & Von Bergen, C.W., Jr. (1976) A field test of expectancy-valence incentive motivation techniques. *Organizational Behavior and Human Performance, 15*, 355–406.

38. Runkel, P.J., & McGrath, J.E. (1972) *Research on human behavior: A systematic guide to method.* New York: Holt, Rinehart, & Winston.

39. Saari, L.M., & Latham, G.P. (1982) Employee reactions to continuous and variable ratio reinforcement schedules involving a monetary incentive. *Journal of Applied Psychology, 67*, 506–508.

40. Taylor, F.W. (1911) *The principles of scientific management.* New York: Harper.

41. Terborg, J.R. (1976) The motivational components of goal setting. *Journal of Applied Psychology, 61*, 613–621.

42. Terborg, J.R., & Miller, H.E. (1978) Motivation, behavior and performance: A closer examination of goal setting and monetary incentives. *Journal of Applied Psychology, 63*, 29–39.

43. Toppen, J.T. (1965) Money reinforcement and human operant (work) behavior: III. Piecework-payment and time-payment comparisons. *Perceptual and Motor Skills, 21*, 907–913.

44. Turnage, J.J., & Muchinsky, P.M. (1976) The effects of reward contingency and participative decision making on intrinsically and extrinsically motivating tasks. *Academy of Management Journal, 19,* 482–489.

45. Weick, K.E. (1965) Laboratory experimentation with organizations. In J.G. March (Ed.), *Handbook of organizations* (pp. 194–260). Chicago: Rand McNally.

46. Whyte, W.F. (1955) *Money and motivation.* New York: Harper.

47. Wimperis, B.R., & Farr, J.L. (1979) The effects of task content and reward contingency upon task performance and satisfaction. *Journal of Applied Social Psychology, 9,* 229–249.

48. Yetton, P. (1979) Efficiency of a piecework incentive payment system. *Journal of Management Studies, 16,* 253–269.

49. Yukl, G.A., & Latham, G.P. (1975) Consequences of reinforcement schedules and incentive magnitudes for employee performance: Problems encountered in an industrial setting. *Journal of Applied Psychology, 60,* 294–298.

50. Yukl, G.A., Latham, G.P., & Pursell, E.D. (1976) The effectiveness of performance incentives under continuous and variable ratio schedules of reinforcement. *Personnel Psychology, 29,* 221–231.

51. Yukl, G.A., Wexley, K.N., & Seymore, J.D. (1972) Effectiveness of pay incentives under variable ratio and continuous reinforcement schedules. *Journal of Applied Psychology, 56,* 19–23.

52. Zelditch, M., & Evan, W.M. (1962) Simulated bureaucracies: A methodological analysis. In H. Guetzkow (Ed.), *Simulation in social science: Readings* (pp. 48–60). Englewood Cliffs, N.J.: Prentice-Hall.

10
Reinforcement Schedule Stretching Effects

Thomas C. Mawhinney

Operant schedules of reinforcement as independent variables which account for performance variations have captured the attention of industrial-organizational (I-O) psychologists and organizational behaviorists (OB). Excitement about schedule effects is no doubt due to a counterintuitive effect of one schedule procedure upon performance rates (Yukl, Wexley, & Seymore, 1972). By slowly increasing the number of responses (N) required to obtain a reinforcer on a variable-ratio (VR-N) schedule, operant researchers have been able to obtain higher performance rates in pigeons with fewer and fewer reinforcers (Ferster & Skinner, 1957). Human subjects working for bonus pay on a VR-2 schedule performed at a higher rate than subjects working on a continuous schedule in a lab study performed by I-O psychologists (Yukl et al., 1972). The implications of these results for efficiency in the work force should be apparent.

Attempts to replicate the lab results in field settings were, however, frought with difficulties. The problems associated with implementing schedules in field settings discouraged some researchers in the I-O tradition. The current position among these researchers is captured in the following conclusion: "It can be difficult, if not impossible, to predict when [a reinforcement schedule] will work, or even that it will work under certain circumstances" (Saari & Latham, 1982, p. 506). This conclusion suggests that effects of reinforcement schedules observed in the lab do not generalize to field settings. The validity of this argument depends, of course, upon whether the conditions required to test for schedule effects in the lab have been established in field settings.

The purpose of this chapter is to trace the origins of I-O and OB researchers' interests in operant reinforcement schedules (Ferster & Skinner, 1957) and determine whether a particular schedule effect ("stretching") observed in lab studies has been replicated in (generalized to) field settings. This is accomplished in the following steps: (1) a review of important operant terms, concepts, and research findings, (2) evidence of animal research results replicated in humans (children), (3) specification of requirements for considering I-O and OB studies as valid tests of generalization from the operant to the I-O or OB lab work-simulation and field experiment, (4) a review of I-O and OB research which qualifies to address the schedule effect issue, and (5) a discussion of the evidence presented and some conclusions regarding the schedule effect issue.

The Operant Perspective on Reinforcement: A Review

The operant paradigm can be considered a scientific method and technology for exploring the law of effect. The law of effect is assumed to govern the interaction between an organism and its environment. Skinner (1969) asserts that "by using rate of responding as a dependent variable, it is possible to formulate the interaction between an organism and its environment more adequately" (p. 7). *Reinforcers* are response consequences which increase response rate when they follow an operant response. An operant response is a response upon which a reinforcer is contingent, "to suggest the action on the environment [operant response] followed by reinforcement" (Skinner, p. 7). *Schedules of reinforcement* specify how reinforcers follow an operant independent of any effect of the schedule upon response rate (Ferster & Skinner, 1957). Skinner has asserted, however, that "each schedule, with given values of the parameters, generates a characteristic performance" (p. 24). And this assertion coupled with evidence for it (Ferster & Skinner) is responsible for I-O and OB researchers giving schedules the status of a powerful independent variable.

I-O and OB researchers are most familiar with continuous and intermittent schedules which relate response rate and reinforcement rate directly as in the case of fixed and variable ratio schedules. Interval schedules have attracted virtually no attention by these researchers. The interest in ratio schedules is likely due to the counterintuitive evidence concerning ratio schedule effects in animal research results. These counterintuitive results have been replicated in some human studies.

Schedule Stretching in Basic Operant Research

Ferster and Skinner (1957) noted that the rate of operant responding in pigeons could be increased even as the number of responses required for each reinforcement received was increased. Their procedure involved training the bird to respond at a moderately high rate on a ratio schedule and then systematically increasing the ratio size. Variable-ratio schedules were found to be particularly effective in maintaining high rates of responding for relatively few reinforcers. The procedure is now called *ratio schedule stretching* or *stretching the ratio* (Mawhinney, 1975).

Evidence supporting replication of stretching would be a constant or an increased response rate as ratio schedule requirements are increased. Thus, evidence against stretching is a decline in response rate as the ratio schedule requirements are increased.

Schedule stretching effects observed in pigeons (Ferster & Skinner, 1957) have been replicated in children. Children pressed a telegraph key or pulled a Lindsley manipulandum and received trinkets, pennies, and projected thirty-five-millimeter Kodachrome transparencies as reinforcers in twenty-five-minute sessions (Long, Hammack, May, & Campbell, 1958). Reinforcers were scheduled on fixed and variable-ratio schedules with values of the ratio ranging from fifteen to 150. The importance of this study concerns the fact that in almost every respect (such as the operant response characteristics, absence of delay in response reinforcement relationship, and reinforcement schedule programming) the animal experimental arrangements were replicated in the human study. The replication extended to response rate effects as well. Equal or higher response rates were evident even as the ratio requirement for reinforcement was systematically increased from small (for example, *VR-15*) to larger and larger values of the parameter (such as *VR-30* and eventually *VR-60*). The experiment serves to demonstrate that lab conditions which almost perfectly replicate animal study results can be achieved with human subjects.

Operant research in the pure operant tradition is clearly lab research with the most rigorous experimental controls. Research in the I-O and OB traditions typically concerns the practical implications of pure operant research. And the distinction between lab and field research in these traditions is less clear. Thus, the criteria which serve to distinguish between the two research contexts are described before considering the research evidence in the applied sciences.

The I-O and OB Lab-Field Research Distinction

The lab and field settings for research probably represent a continuum. But for present purposes a dichotomy is required. The dichotomy is based upon the characteristics of subjects and the organization which employed them when an experiment took place. To qualify as a field experiment, the subjects must have been employed by an organization which utilized their output directly or indirectly to produce its product. Thus, working in an organization constructed for purposes of research data gathering (for example, learning from training manuals) (Pritchard, Hollenback, & DeLeo, 1980; Pritchard, Leonard, Von Bergen, & Kirk, 1976) would not qualify as a field setting since neither the material learned nor the tests completed would ultimately be a product or part of a product. Tree planters, on the other hand, would serve in the earliest production phases of some wood-based product such as lumber or paper (for example, Yukl & Latham, 1975). Further, to qualify as a field experiment, the subjects must have been hired to perform a job which would have been performed whether or not the field experiment was conducted. Thus, organizations set up solely for purposes of hiding the experimental nature of the work situation would not satisfy this criterion for a field experimental setting. These criteria define the situations in which an experimental manipulation of a monetary reinforcement schedule can be considered a field experiment. Any experiment not qualifying as a field experiment is considered a lab experiment.

I-O and OB Lab Work-Simulation Studies

Schedule stretching effects require a within-subjects research design and treatment orders involving a change from a smaller to a larger ratio schedule requirement (Mawhinney, 1975). I-O and OB researchers have, however, attempted to evaluate the stretching effect with between-subjects designs. Within-subjects stretching holding constant monetary reinforcer magnitude is practically impossible in most work settings. Thus, between-subjects evaluations are a pragmatic approach to schedule effect studies. They fail immediately, however, as evidence concerning the generalization of stretching effects from the operant lab to the I-O or OB lab work-simulation situation. Limiting schedule stretching studies to those which are within-subjects and include a change of the ratio requirement from a smaller to a larger value eliminates all but one study (Mawhinney, 1976). In this study a change from continuous reinforcement to a *VR-2* schedule and a reversal of the treatment order produced no significant differences in response rates due to ratio requirement increases.

If between group schedule comparisons are considered, the studies which qualify increase the study count by two (Berger, Cummings, & Heneman, 1975; Yukl et al., 1972). In one study response rate on a *VR-2* was significantly higher than on a continuous schedule, with reinforcer magnitudes held constant across schedules (Yukl et al., 1972). In the other study (Berger et al.) the same schedule contrasts yielded no significant difference between response rates on the two schedules.

A conservative evaluation of the generalization issue would suggest we admit only one study in support of the generalizability of stretching from the operant lab to the I-O or OB lab work-simulation situation. A more liberal approach would permit inclusion of two more studies in support of this generalization question.

I-O and OB Field Studies

None of four I-O field experiments involving reinforcement schedules can be considered valid evaluations of the schedule stretching question (Latham & Dossett, 1978; Saari & Latham, 1982; Yukl & Latham, 1975; Yukl, Latham, & Pursell, 1976). In no case was reinforcement magnitude held constant across schedules with differing ratio requirements, whether in a within-subjects or between-subjects design.

Discussion and Conclusions

The question of whether reinforcement schedule stretching generalizes from lab to field settings was considered in three comparisons. First, results of operant animal studies were compared with a rigorously controlled operant lab replication of the animal studies using children as subjects. In this case the generalization from animal to human lab was evident. Next, results of the operant animal and human studies were compared with results of lab work-simulation studies by I-O and OB researchers. Again, one solid replication was evident. And, by admitting between-subjects comparisons of schedule effects (a liberal approach), two more studies could be considered support for generalization from the operant to I-O and OB lab settings. Finally, none of four I-O field experiments aimed at the schedule stretching issue satisfied the minimum requirements for addressing the generalization question.

Based upon this review it is reasonable to conclude that the phenomenon of reinforcement schedule stretching has been replicated at two levels. One, the generalization from animals to humans in the highly controlled operant lab has been accomplished. The second level of generalization is from the operant human lab to the I-O and OB lab work-simulation setting.

A pessimistic conclusion concerning the probability of generalization from the work-simulation setting to the field seems in order with respect to monetary reinforcement schedule stretching. It is unlikely to be established with monetary reinforcers simply because managers and union officials are unlikely to permit implementation of the process in a real work environment. We have seen the phenomenon, however, in indirect nonexperimental evidence. An example is the give-backs in pay by unions to the auto companies. Thus, while one cannot conclude that stretching of monetary reinforcement schedules has been generalized from the lab to the field, the reason is simply that no adequate tests have been conducted at this time. Until such testing has occurred, it is reasonable to withhold any judgment regarding the eventual outcome of future research into this question. Absence of generalization from the lab to the field in this case is due to constraints upon the conduct of research in the field. It is not because the phenomenon is unlikely to generalize. Only additional carefully conducted field experimental research will answer the schedule stretching generalization question.

References

Berger, C.J., Cummings, L.L., & Heneman, H.G. III (1975) Expectancy theory and operant conditioning predictions of performance under variable ratio and continuous schedules of reinforcement. *Operational Behavior and Human Performance, 14,* 227–243.

Ferster, C.B., & Skinner, B.F. (1957) *Schedules of reinforcement.* New York: Appleton-Century-Crofts.

Latham, G.P., & Dossett, D.L. (1978) Designing incentive plans for unionized employees: A comparison of continuous and variable ratio reinforcement schedules. *Personnel Psychology, 31,* 47–61.

Long, E.R., Hammack, J.T., May, R., & Campbell, B.J. (1958) Intermittent reinforcement of operant behavior in children. *Journal of the Experimental Analysis of Behavior, 1,* 315–339.

Mawhinney, T.C. (1975) Operant terms and concepts in the description of individual work behavior: Some problems of interpretion, application, and evaluation. *Journal of Applied Psychology, 60,* 704–712.

Mawhinney, T.C. (1976) *An experimental analysis of differing predictions of individual work behavior from operant and expectancy models.* Paper presented at the meeting of the Academy of Management, Kansas City, Mo.

Pritchard, R.D., Hollenback, J., & DeLeo, P.J. (1980) The effects of continuous and partial schedules of reinforcement on effort, performance, and satisfaction. *Organizational Behavior and Human Performance, 25,* 336–353.

Pritchard, R.D., Leonard, D.W., Von Bergen, C.W., Jr., & Kirk, R.J. (1976) The effects of varying schedules of reinforcement on human task performance. *Organizational Behavior and Human Performance, 16,* 205–230.

Saari, L.M., & Latham, G.P. (1982) Employee reactions to continuous and variable ratio reinforcement schedules involving a monetary incentive. *Journal of Applied Psychology, 67,* 506–508.

Skinner, B.F. (1969) *Contingencies of reinforcement.* Englewood Cliffs, N.J.: Prentice-Hall.

Yukl, G.A., & Latham, G.P. (1975) Consequences of reinforcement schedules and incentive magnitudes for employee performance: Problems encountered in an industrial setting. *Journal of Applied Psychology, 60,* 294–298.

Yukl, G.A., Latham, G.P., & Pursell, E.D. (1976) The effectiveness of performance incentives under continuous and variable ratio schedules of reinforcement. *Personnel Psychology, 29,* 221–231.

Yukl, G., Wexley, K.N., & Seymore, J.D. (1972) Effectiveness of pay incentives under variable ratio and continuous reinforcement schedules. *Journal of Applied Psychology, 56,* 19–23.

IV
Attitudes

This part reports on studies of the relationships between job attributes, job attitudes, and job performance.

Eugene Stone summarizes the results of studies relating job scope to job satisfaction. Twenty-six out of twenty-seven field studies and five out of five laboratory studies found a significant relationship ($p < .10$ or better) between job scope and job satisfaction. The laboratory and field results were also similar for the job scope-overall job satisfaction relationship. Furthermore, the effect sizes were also similar. For the job scope-job satisfaction relationship the mean r was .88 in the field and .93 in the lab. No conclusions could be drawn regarding job scope-job performance relationships because the number of studies was far too small.

Philip Podsakoff and Larry Williams summarize studies on a topic which has intrigued researchers for decades: the relationship between job satisfaction and job performance. In an extremely thorough review, they find that the results for laboratory and field settings are much the same regardless of whether performance is correlated with work, pay, or overall job satisfaction. About half the studies in both cases show positive correlations, while the other half do not. In all cases the overall mean correlations are uniformly low, typically below .20.

A unique aspect of Podsakoff and Williams's review was the subdivision of the studies based on whether a performance-reward contingency was present or absent. In both lab and field settings, the presence of a contingency led to higher, more positive correlations. Virtually the only difference between lab and field results occurred where only studies in which the reward contingency was not present or unknown were compared. However, these results, as the authors state, are inconclusive because in most of the field studies the contingencies, since they were unknown, could actually have been present.

Once again the similarity of laboratory and field results is startling not only with respect to consistency of results but with respect to effect size. One ironic aspect of Podsakoff and Williams's results is that the conclusions reached and even the effect size (mean r) are much the same as those obtained by Vroom (1964) some twenty years ago with a much smaller number of studies.

Now that the futility of expecting job satisfaction to correlate with job performance (except where a contingency is present) seems established beyond doubt, we can begin to consider alternative ways of conceptualizing the whole issue. For example, we know that satisfaction can affect performance, even if it does not do so consistently. Fisher (1980) has suggested that overall satisfaction might correlate with (and causally affect) a composite measure of job performance, one which includes numerous and varied types of actions such as productivity, cooperation, lateness, grievances, absenteeism, griping, and drug use. Similarly, Henne and Locke (in press) have argued that job attitudes can be expressed in action in many different ways (or even not at all) and that we need a theory that will predict and explain how people choose among these alternative courses of action.

References

Fisher, C.D. (1980) On the dubious wisdom of expecting job satisfaction to correlate with job performance. *Academy of Management Review, 5,* 607–612.

Henne, D., and Locke, E.A. (in press) Job dissatisfaction: What are the consequences? *Internatinal Journal of Psychology.*

Vroom, V. (1964). *Work and motivation.* New York: Wiley.

11
Job Scope-Job Satisfaction and Job Scope-Job Performance Relationships

Eugene F. Stone

Relationships between job scope (that is, the degree to which a job is enriched) and various types of criteria (for example, job performance and affective reactions of job incumbents) have been the focus of a considerable number of empiricalstudies in the behavioral sciences. Most such research has been of the nonexperimental, field study variety (for example, Hackman & Lawler, 1971; Hackman & Oldham, 1976; Stone, 1975, 1976; Stone & Porter, 1975). Although greatly limited in number, studies dealing with job design have also been performed using such empirical research strategies as field experimentation (such as Bishop & Hill, 1971; Lawler, Hackman, & Kaufman, 1973; Orpen, 1979) and laboratory experimentation/simulation (for example, Farh & Scott, 1983; Ganster, 1980; Umstot, Bell, & Mitchell, 1976).[1]

The existence of evidence on job scope-job outcome relationships from both laboratory- and field-based research provides an opportunity to assess the convergence of findings from these two settings or contexts. To the degree that such findings converge, we have strengthened our confidence in the legitimacy of given relationships, such as job scope-job satisfaction and job scope-job performance. The reason for this is that each specific empirical research strategy (for example, field study, field experiment, and laboratory experiment) that one employs in studying a phenomenon has associated with it a set of relative strengths and weaknesses that may influence the internal validity, external validity, construct validity, and statistical conclusion validity of research findings (see Cook & Campbell, 1979; Stone, 1978). For example, the laboratory experiment, while often viewed as being low on the dimension of mundane realism, affords a level of control over extraneous (confounding) variables that is not possible with either nonexperimental or experimental field-based research.

I thank Edwin Locke for reading a version of this chapter and providing numerous helpful comments. In addition, I thank Keith Fabes for his assistance in assembling a substantial proportion of the reference materials used in the preparation of this chapter.

In spite of the existence of evidence on job scope-job outcome relationships from a large number of empirical studies, to date there has been no comprehensive, quantitative review dealing with this evidence. The major purpose of this chapter, therefore, is to quantitatively assess (see Rosenthal, 1978; Rosenthal & Rosnow, 1984) the degree of convergence between the findings of laboratory- and field-based research on job scope-job outcome relationships. As is noted elsewhere (for example, Rosenthal, 1978) quantitatively oriented literature reviews are generally superior to "traditional" (nonquantitative) literature reviews or summaries.

Some Issues Raised in Previous, Nonquantitative Reviews

The literature on job design has been nonquantitatively reviewed several times in recent years (for example, Roberts & Glick, 1981). The research connected with this literature has been severely criticized by such analysts as Roberts and Glick (1981) and Salancik and Pfeffer (1977). For example, on the basis of a review of more than sixty empirical studies dealing with the job characteristics model (Hackman & Lawler, 1971; Hackman & Oldham, 1976), Roberts and Glick concluded that common methods variance may seriously threaten our ability to validly interpret the results of field-based studies dealing with relationships between measures of job characteristics and affective reactions to jobs. In a similarly critical vein, Salancik and Pfeffer argued that field-based research findings of relationships between job characteristics and affective responses to jobs may represent nothing more than the manifestation of priming and consistency-based artifacts. For example, having reported that a job is low on the dimension of autonomy, the respondent feels compelled to report that it is not very satisfying. Interestingly, while many organizational researchers have deemed as noteworthy the potential biasing effects of such artifacts in job design research, a number of independently conducted empirical studies have failed to provide support for the existence of the same artifacts (for example, Brief & Aldag, 1977; Spector & Michaels, 1983; Stone & Gueutal, 1984; Stone & Hollenbeck, 1982). Moreover, the validity of the empirical evidence used by Salancik and Pfeffer (1977) to buttress their arguments has been questioned (see Stone, 1984).

It deserves noting that the findings of field-based studies have been the focus of virtually all of the criticisms that have been raised about empirical research on job scope-job satisfaction and job scope-job performance relationships (for example, criticisms concerning common methods variance, priming artifacts, and consistency artifacts). Consequently, one method of assessing the validity of such criticisms is to compare the findings of field-based and laboratory-based studies. As noted previously, the present paper details the results of a quantitative comparison of such findings.

The Job Scope Construct

For the purposes of this chapter, job scope is viewed as being conceptually equivalent to job enrichment (see Hackman & Oldham, 1976; Stone, 1975, 1976). Jobs of large scope (that is, enriched jobs) are those that result in job incumbents experiencing their work as meaningful, perceiving that they are responsible for the outcomes of the work, and receiving appropriate feedback about their job-related performance (Hackman & Oldham, 1976, pp. 255–258). Of vital importance to the concept of job scope is the notion of autonomy (that is, the extent to which the job incumbent is free to determine such things as the methods used in performing job-related tasks, the sequencing of such tasks, and the time spent on the tasks). It deserves noting that job enrichment does not result through such strategies as simply increasing the variety of tasks performed by a worker (that is, job enlargement) or the level of his or her task goals (that is, job difficulty changes).

Method

In order to allow for the comparison of field- and laboratory-based findings, a quantitatively oriented review of the literature on job scope-job satisfaction and job scope-job performance relationships was conducted using methods recommended by Rosenthal (1978) and Rosenthal and Rosnow (1984).

Scope of Literature Reviewed

The periodical literature in psychology for the period of January 1967 to February 1984 was searched for all references having to do with job design (job enrichment or job analysis) and job outcome (job satisfaction or job performance) relationships. This resulted in 219 references that were candidates for consideration by the present review. Of these references, however, 166 proved to be unworthy or inappropriate for further consideration because of one or more of the following issues: (1) the paper was not a report of empirical research (for example, a literature review); (2) the publication reported its findings in nonquantitative terms (for example, results of case studies); (3) the report failed to provide information vital to the determination of an effect size (for example, author failed to report a correlation coefficient, a t value, an F value, or an *eta* value; Maher, 1971, is an example); (4) the study's independent variable was not job scope or a reasonable surrogate of job scope (for example, the job difficulty variable in the Ivancevich & Smith, 1982, study was not a reasonable surrogate of job scope); (5) the research employed data analytic techniques that are known to be faulty (such as the use of cross-lagged correlations by Ivancevich, 1978); (6) statistical test results were only partially reported (for example, an effect size was reported, but no information was given about degrees of freedom or statistical significance); and (7) the study's dependent variable was not a measure of affect or performance (for example, self-reports of internal work motivation).

In some cases, the results of a study were partially considered by the present review. This was done when authors adequately reported the results of some analyses, but failed to do so in the case of other analyses. For example, in the report by Farh and Scott (1983), statistical data were reported for the impact of task autonomy on quantity of task performance, but no such data were reported for either the relationship between task autonomy and performance quality or the relationship between task autonomy and task satisfaction.

In addition to considering and using research reported in the periodical literature, this review also considered and selectively used relevant research results from other types of works. Two examples illustrate this. First, the results of a number of job design/redesign experiments reported in Maher (1971) were considered for possible inclusion in the quantitative summary reported here. However, for one or more of the reasons listed above, these experiments were deemed to be unworthy of further consideration. Second, the data reported in an unpublished but comprehensive technical report by Oldham, Hackman, and Stepina (1978) were considered and used since they dealt with quantitative evidence on job scope-job outcome relationships for a sample of 6,930 subjects working in 876 different jobs.

Combinatorial Procedures

In order to quantitatively combine the results of the empirical studies considered by this review, procedures recommended by Rosenthal (Rosenthal, 1978; Rosenthal & Rosnow, 1984) were employed. More particularly, in this review an estimate of the combined, sample size-weighted effect size of all studies dealing with a particular predictor-criterion relationship was determined using the weighted effect size combinatorial procedure outlined in Rosenthal and Rosnow (1984, pp. 377–379) and Rosenthal (1978, pp. 188–189). Weighted effect size estimates were determined for the following combinations of study setting and predictor-criterion pairs: (1) field studies/experiments concerned with job scope-job satisfaction relationships (within the criterion categories of overall satisfaction and satisfaction with the work itself, growth, and intrinsic aspects of the job); (2) laboratory experiments dealing with job scope-job satisfaction relationships (within the criterion categories of overall satisfaction and satisfaction with the work itself, growth, and intrinsic aspects of the job); (3) field studies/experiments concerned with task variety-job satisfaction and task autonomy-job satisfaction relationships (within the criterion categories of overall satisfaction and satisfaction with the work itself, growth, and intrinsic aspects of the job). This group of studies was included because task autonomy and task variety represent two important components of job scope. Thus, these characteristics may serve as useful surrogates of job scope; (4) field studies/experiments concerned with job scope-job performance (within the criterion categories of self-ratings, objective/hard criteria, overall supervisory ratings, supervisor ratings of quality of performance, supervisor ratings of quantity of performance, and measures of absenteeism); and (5) laboratory experiments dealing with job scope-job performance relationships (within the criterion categories of self-ratings, objectively measured quality of performance, and objectively measured quantity of performance).

In the case of all studies included in the meta-analysis, the correlation coefficient (r) was used as the effect size estimate. In cases where a study did not report r values for job scope-job outcome relationships, t, F, eta, or other statistical data were used to determine r equivalent values (cf. Rosenthal & Rosnow, 1984). Since the r distribution is not normal, r values were converted to their Fisher's Z equivalents for the purpose of computing weighted effect size estimates. The resulting weighted Z values were then converted to r equivalents.

It deserves adding that the method of combining weighted Zs (cf. Rosenthal, 1978) was chosen over a number of alternative strategies for synthesizing the results of multiple, independent studies. One specific alternative that was rejected was the method of counting the number of studies that showed positive effects, no effects, and negative effects. This counting method has a number of problems that make it less useful or informative than the method of combining weighted Zs (cf. Hedges & Olkin, 1980; Rosenthal, 1978). (For additional arguments against the use of tables showing counts of supportive, inconclusive, or nonsupportive findings, see Green & Hall, 1984.) In view of this, the tables presented in this review show effect size estimates for studies rather than counts of studies that demonstrated or failed to demonstrate support for a particular relationship.

Results

Information associated with individual studies included in this chapter is presented in tables 11–1 through 11–5. Results of combining the effect size estimates for the relevant studies are separately considered for the criterion categories of satisfaction and performance.

Satisfaction Criteria

Field study- and field experiment-based research dealing with job scope-job satisfaction relationships is summarized in table 11–1. For the criterion of overall (general) job satisfaction, the combined r value ($N = 13,637$) is .627. For the work itself (intrinsic, growth, or task) criterion, the combined r value ($N = 17,209$) is .880. It is clear that job scope relates more strongly to the narrower criterion of satisfaction with the work itself than it does to the broader, overall satisfaction criterion.

Table 11-1
Sample Sizes and Effect Size Estimates for Field-Based Research
Dealing with Job Scope-Job Satisfaction Relationships

| | Relationship between Job Scope and | | | |
| | Overall Satisfaction | | Satisfaction with Work | |
Study	N	Z	N	Z
Abdel-Halim (1979)			87	.648[e]
Arnold & House (1980)	90	.460[e]	90	.709[e]
Baird (1976)			214	.332[e]
Bishop & Hill (1971)			48	343[b]
Champoux (1981)				
R&D Sample A			1,152	.867[e]
R&D Sample B			1,193	.775[e]
Federal Agency A			66	.758[e]
Federal Agency B			160	.919[e]
Cherrington & England (1980)	3,050	.324[e]	3,050	.514[e]
Dunham (1976)			84	.485[e]
Griffin (1982)	100	.118	100	.549[e]
Hackman & Oldham (1975)	658	.536[e]	658	.741[e]
Hall et al. (1978)			153	.523[e]
Helphingstine et al. (1981)			24	.633[e]
Humphrys (1981)			90	.793[e]
Johns (1978)	208	.299[e]		
King et al. (1982)	1,524	.277[e]		
Lawler et al. (1973)	57	.040	52	.010
London & Klimoski (1973)			153	.253[d]
Oldham et al. (1978)	6,930	.497[e]	6,930	.678[e]
Oldham & Miller (1979)			625	.811[e]
O'Reilly (1977)	307	.017	307	.105[a]

Table 11–1 continued

| | Relationship between Job Scope and | | | |
| | Overall Satisfaction | | Satisfaction with Work | |
Study	N	Z	N	Z
Orpen (1979)			72	.348[d]
Pokorney et al. (1980)			102	.536[e]
Pritchard & Peters (1974)	576	.497[e]	576	.536[e]
Sarata & Jepsen (1977)	137	.354[e]		
Schneider et al. (1982)			140	.343[e]
Stone (1975)			149	.549[e]
Stone (1976)			594	.460[e]
Stone et al. (1977)			340	.400[e]
Total sample size	13,637		17,209	
Weighted effect size (Z)	.728		1.38	
r equivalent of weighted Z	.627[e]		.880[e]	

Note: All one-tailed tests.
[a]$p < .10$.
[b]$p < .05$.
[c]$p < .02$.
[d]$p < .01$.
[e]$p < .001$.

Laboratory-based research dealing with job scope-job satisfaction relationships is considered by table 11–2. As can be seen in the same table, the combined r estimates are .528 ($N = 150$) and .927 ($N = 422$), respectively for the criteria of overall satisfaction and satisfaction with the work itself. Note that these r values are very similar to those connected with field-based research dealing with job scope-job satisfaction relationships.

Table 11–3 summarizes the results of field research concerned with task variety-job satisfaction and task autonomy-job satisfaction relationships. For the task autonomy predictor, the combined r values are .564 ($N = 12,285$) and .665 ($N = 10,523$), respectively, for the criteria of general satisfaction and satisfaction with the work itself. For the task variety predictor, the corresponding r values are .487 ($N = 12,285$) and .639 ($N = 10,461$). These results indicate that while the scope components of task variety and task autonomy are about as effective as job scope in predicting overall satisfaction, they are not as effective as job scope in predicting satisfaction with the work itself.

Table 11–2
Sample Sizes and Effect Size Estimates for Laboratory-Based Research Dealing with Job Scope-Job Satisfaction Relationships

| | Relationship between Job Scope and | | | |
| | Overall Satisfaction | | Satisfaction with Work | |
Study	N	Z	N	Z
Ganster (1980)			190	.996[e]
Kim (1980)			96	1.256[e]
O'Reilly & Caldwell (1979)	42	.500[e]	42	.424[d]
Robey (1974)	60	.121		
Terborg & Davis (1982)	48	.485[d]		
Trow (1957)			44	.343[b]
Umstot et al. (1976)			50	.576[d]
Total sample size	150		422	
Weighted effect size (Z)	.589		1.637	
r equivalent of weighted Z	.528[e]		.927[e]	

Note: All one-tailed tests.
[a]$p < .10$.
[b]$p < .05$.
[c]$p < .02$.
[d]$p < .01$.
[e]$p < .001$.

Unfortunately, there is no laboratory study counterpart to table 11–3. The reason for this is that authors who studied job scope-job satisfaction relationships in laboratory contexts failed to provide information on relationships of scope components with indices of job satisfaction.

Performance Criteria

Table 11–4 summarizes the results of field-based research dealing with job scope-job performance relationships. Combined r values for the specific criteria considered by the analyses equal .492 ($N = 393$) for self-rated performance, .357 ($N = 317$) for hard/objective criteria, .301 ($N = 5,513$) for supervisor ratings of overall performance, .140 ($N = 355$) for supervisor ratings of performance quality, .130 ($N = 355$) for supervisor ratings of performance quantity, and $-.330$ ($N = 866$)

Table 11–3
Sample Sizes and Effect Size Estimates for Field-Based Research Dealing with Job Scope Component-Job Satisfaction Relationships

	Relationship between Task							
	Variety and Satisfaction				Autonomy and Satisfaction			
	Overall		Work		Overall		Work	
Study	N	Z	N	Z	N	Z	N	Z
Abdel-Halim (1983)			229	.436[e]				
Brief & Aldag (1975)	104	.321[d]	104	.338[e]	104	.563[e]	104	.563[e]
Brief & Aldag (1976)			77	.436[e]			77	.436[e]
Dunham (1976)			784	.388[e]			784	.377[e]
Hackman & Oldham (1975)	658	.448[e]	658	.576[e]	658	.460[e]	658	.662[e]
Katz (1978)	3,058	.234[e]			3,058	.288[e]		
Kiggundu (1983)	138	.648[e]	138	.693[e]	138	.709[e]	138	.693[e]
Lawler & Hall (1970)							291	.424[e]
Martin (1981)	133	.377[e]			133	.388[e]		
O'Brien & Humphrys (1982)	396	.510[e]	396	.448[e]	396	.400[e]	396	.245[e]
Oldham et al. (1978)	6,930	.343[e]	6,930	.523[e]	6,930	.436[e]	6,930	.604[e]
Pokorney et al. (1980)			102	.388[e]			102	.775[e]
Rousseau (1977)	201	.662[e]			201	.523[e]		
Sarata & Jepsen (1977)			137	.213[c]			137	−.05
Schneider et al. (1982)			140	.536[e]			140	.497[e]
Sims & Szilagyi (1976)			766	.604[e]			766	.266[e]
Walsh et al. (1980)								
Shop	486	.332[e]			486	.321[e]		
Office	96	.121			96	.245[c]		
Managerial	58	.203			58	.400[d]		
Total sample size	12,285		10,461		12,285		10,523	

Table 11–3 continued

	Relationship between Task							
	Variety and Satisfaction				Autonomy and Satisfaction			
	Overall		Work		Overall		Work	
Study	N	Z	N	Z	N	Z	N	Z
Weighted effect size (Z)		.534		.758		.639		.802
r equivalent of weighted Z		.487[e]		.639[e]		.564[e]		.665[e]

Note: All one-tailed tests.
[a]$p < .10$.
[b]$p < .05$.
[c]$p < .02$.
[d]$p < .01$.
[e]$p < .001$.

for absenteeism. In general, these results indicate that job scope is only moderately related to the performance of job incumbents.

Laboratory-based research dealing with job scope-job performance relationships is summarized in table 11–5. Combined r values equal .281 ($N = 48$) and $-.258$ ($N = 99$), respectively, for the objectively measured criteria of performance quality and performance quantity.

The laboratory-based estimate of r for the performance quality criterion is similar to the field-based estimates of r for the objective/hard criterion category. However, the laboratory-based estimate of r for the quantity criterion ($-.258$) is quite discrepant from the field-based estimates of r for both the objective/hard criterion (.357) and the supervisor-rated performance quantity criterion (.130). It deserves noting, however, that the laboratory-based estimate is dominated by the findings of one study, Farh and Scott, 1983. Thus, the laboratory-based estimate of the job scope-performance quantity relationship may be less trustworthy than the field-based estimates of job scope-objective performance and job scope-rated quantity of performance relationships.

Discussion

The quantitative data presented show that the results of field-based and laboratory-based research indicate a high degree of convergence concerning the strength of (1) the job scope-overall satisfaction relationship and (2) the job scope-satisfaction with the work itself relationship. In addition, the field-based estimates of the task variety-overall satisfaction and task autonomy-overall satisfaction relationships are reasonably similar in magnitude to both the laboratory-based and the field-based

Table 11-4
Sample Sizes and Effect Size Estimates for Field-Based Research Dealing with Job Scope–Job Performance Relationships

	Relationship between Job Scope and the Criterion Type												
	Self-Ratings		Objective Criteria		Overall		Supervisor Rating				Absenteeism	
							Quality		Quantity			
Study[a]	N	Z	N	Z	N	Z	N	Z	N	Z	N	Z
2					229	.182[d]						
3	87	.365[e]			87	.080						
5			16	−.662[d]								
8					77	−.090						
10					2,844	.180[e]						
16			100	.497[e]								
18					658	.245[e]					658	−.255[e]
19	153	.412[e]										
23											208	−.332[e]
24	153	.203[c]			85	.266[c]						
30			201	.224[d]	153	.266[d]						
34					201	.161[b]						
36							355	.141[d]	355	.131[b]		
37					298	.049						
48					766	.151[d]						
49					115	.110						
Total sample size (N)	393		317		5,513		355		355		866	
Weighted effect size (Z)	.540		.374		.312		.141		.131		−.343	
r equivalent of Z	.492[e]		.357[e]		.301[e]		.140[d]		.130[b]		−.330[e]	

Note: All one-tailed tests.

[a]Numbers in column labeled "Study" correspond to the numbering of entries in the list of references.

[b]$p < .05.$

[c]$p < .02.$

[d]$p < .01.$

[e]$p < .001.$

Table 11–5

Sample Sizes and Effect Size Estimates for Laboratory-Based Research Dealing with Job Scope-Job Performance Relationships

| | Relationship between Job Scope and the Criterion Type | | | |
| | Actual Quality of Performance | | Actual Quantity of Performance | |
Study	N	Z	N	Z
Farh & Scott (1983)			80	$-.412^c$
Terborg & Davis (1982)	48	$.288^a$		
Umstot et al. (1976)				
Group 1			10	.472
Group 3			9	$.758^a$
Total sample size	48		99	
Weighted effect size (Z)	.288		$-.264$	
r equivalent of weighted Z	$.281^a$		$-.258^b$	

Note: All one-tailed tests.
[a] $p < .10$.
[b] $p < .02$.
[c] $p < .001$.

estimates of the job scope-overall satisfaction relationship. However, both the laboratory- and field-based estimates of the job scope-satisfaction with the work itself relationship are much stronger than the field-based estimate of the task autonomy-satisfaction with the work itself relationship. In spite of these latter differences, the overall pattern of results is highly consistent. Job scope is a strong predictor of individuals' affective responses to both the work that they perform and their job in general.

In contrast to the generally high degree of consistency found for the various estimates of the job scope-job satisfaction relationship is the generally low degree of convergence between laboratory- and field-based estimates of job scope-job performance relationships. Five issues concerning the latter set of relationships appear especially worthy of note:

1. Job scope-job performance relationships are generally of only modest magnitude. Several explanations can be offered for this, one of which is that the job scope-job performance relationship may be less determined by the presumed effect of job scope on intrinsic motivation than some analysts have speculated (for example, Hackman & Oldham, 1976). This is not to say that intrinsic motivation is an unimportant determinant of job performance.

Rather, its role in determining performance may simply be less potent than some have assumed it to be. Taken together, other factors such as ability differences, incentive systems, and group production norms may be more influential in determining performance than is internal work motivation. Another plausible explanation of the generally low degree of association between job scope and job performance is that the various operational indicants of performance may have large degrees of contamination (that is, bias and error/unreliability).

2. Also worthy of note concerning the job scope-job performance findings is that job scope is more strongly related to self-rated performance than it is to other types of criteria. One seemingly plausible explanation for this finding is that incumbents in high scope jobs tend to be more intelligent and have higher levels of chronic self-esteem than incumbents in low scope jobs. Consequently, incumbents in high scope jobs may generally perceive themselves to be better performers than incumbents in low scope jobs. This tendency may serve to make the estimate of the job scope-self-rated performance relationship greater than that found between job scope and any externally assessed criterion such as supervisor ratings.

3. There is no consistency between the laboratory-based estimate of the job scope-performance quantity relationship and the field-based estimate of the job scope-performance quantity (supervisor ratings) relationship. In the cases of both these estimates, however, data were available from only a limited number of studies. Only one field study dealt with this relationship, while, although two laboratory investigations considered a performance quantity criterion, their findings were highly discrepant. Moreover, the sample sizes of both the field- and laboratory-based investigations are relatively low. Consequently, even tentatively stated conclusions about the job scope-performance quantity relationship seem imprudent.

4. Unfortunately, there are only a few published reports of laboratory-based research dealing with job scope-job performance relationships. Unless and until more such findings become available, firm conclusions about the correspondence between laboratory- and field-based studies of the job scope-job performance relationship cannot be offered.

5. Even if there were greater numbers of laboratory- and field-based studies dealing with job scope-job performance relationships, and such studies were to employ highly similar criterion measures, their results might not show high convergence. One reason for this is that when jobs are enriched in field settings, it is often the case that not only do job characteristics change, but there are also changes in other job-related variables such as the level of workers' pay and the degree to which they are supervised. On the other hand, laboratory-based comparisons of unenriched and enriched jobs generally have the capacity to hold these other variables constant.

A Final Word

Several factors precluded the possibility of preparing a more comprehensive, quantitative summary of research findings related to job scope-job outcome relationships. Among these were that research reports frequently failed to provide adequate amounts of information about sample sizes, effect sizes, degrees of freedom for statistical tests, reliability estimates for predictor and criterion variables, and other relevant factors. Such information should be routinely provided by the authors of published and unpublished reports of empirical research. Moreover, in instances where authors fail to initially provide complete reports of such information, editors of journals should insist that it be part of any published study. Only when the results of empirical research are more fully and consistently reported will it be possible to perform thorough, quantitative summaries of research.

Note

1. In the case of certain studies, controversy might arise over the issue of study setting (laboratory versus field). This is especially true for the research by Umstot et al. (1976). While I classified this as a laboratory study because it took place in a simulated organization, it could have just as easily been assigned to the field study category because the setting of the research was not as artificial as it is in such laboratory research as that of Ganster (1980) and Robey (1974). In view of the way in which I classified the study by Umstot et al., a legitimate question that might be raised is whether the conclusions of this research synthesis would have differed if the Umstot et al. study had been regarded as a field experiment rather than a laboratory experiment/simulation. In the case of the relationship between job scope and job satisfaction, the conclusion of similarity between laboratory- and field-based findings would remain unaltered. In the case of the job scope-job performance relationship, shifting the Umstot et al. results from the laboratory to the field setting category would have increased the apparent between-setting discrepancy. However, in view of (1) the extremely small number of laboratory studies that have reported data on job scope-job performance relationships, and (2) the tremendous heterogeneity of criterion measures considered by both laboratory and field studies, definitive performance-related conclusions would be as unwarranted under the revised as the original classification.

References

1. Adbel-Halim, A.A. (1979) Individual and interpersonal moderators of employee reactions to job characteristics: A reexamination. *Personnel Psychology, 32*, 121–137.

2. Abdel-Halim, A.A. (1983) Effects of task and personality characteristics on subordinate responses to participative decision making. *Academy of Management Journal, 26*, 477–484.

3. Arnold, H.J., & House, R.J. (1980) Methodological and substantive extensions to the job characteristics model of motivation. *Organizational Behavior and Human Performance, 25*, 161–183.

4. Baird, L.S. (1976) Relationship of performance to satisfaction in stimulating and non-stimulating jobs. *Journal of Applied Psychology, 61,* 721–727.

5. Bishop, R.C., & Hill, J.W. (1971) Effects of job enlargement and job change on contiguous but nonmanipulated jobs as a function of workers' status. *Journal of Applied Psychology, 55,* 175–181.

6. Brief, A.P., & Aldag, R.J. (1975) Employee reactions to job characteristics: A constructive replication. *Journal of Applied Psychology, 60,* 182–186.

7. Brief, A.P., & Aldag, R.J. (1977) Order effects and organizational research. Paper presented at the Academy of Management.

8. Brief, A.P., & Aldag, R.J. (1976) Correlates of role indices. *Journal of Applied Psychology, 61,* 468–472.

9. Champoux, J.E. (1981) The moderating effect of work context satisfactions on the curvilinear relationship between job scope and affective responses. *Human Relations, 34,* 503–515.

10. Cherrington, D.J., & England, J.L. (1980) The desire for an enriched job as a moderator of the enrichment-satisfaction relationship. *Organizational Behavior and Human Performance, 25,* 139–159.

11. Cook T.D., & Campbell, D.T. (1979) *Quasi-experimentation: Design and analysis issues for field settings.* Chicago: Rand McNally.

12. Dunham, R.B. (1976) The measurement and dimensionality of job characteristics. *Journal of Applied Psychology, 61,* 404–409.

13. Farh, J., & Scott, W.E. (1983) The experimental effects of "autonomy" on performance and self-reports of satisfaction. *Organizational Behavior and Human Performance, 31,* 203–222.

14. Ganster, D.C. (1980) Individual differences and task design: A laboratory experiment. *Organizational Behavior and Human Performance, 26,* 131–148.

15. Green, B.F., & Hall, J.A. (1984) Quantitative methods for literature reviews. In M.R. Rosenzweig & L.W. Porter (Eds.), *Annual Review of Psychology, 35,* 37–53.

16. Griffin, R.W. (1982) Perceived task characteristics and employee productivity and satisfaction. *Human Relations, 35,* 927–938.

17. Hackman, J.R., & Oldham, G.R. (1975) Development of the job diagnostic survey. *Journal of Applied Psychology, 60,* 159–170.

18. Hackman, J.R., & Oldham, G.R. (1976) Motivation through the design of work: Test of a theory. *Organizational Behavior and Human Performance, 16,* 250–279.

19. Hall, D.T., Goodale, J.G., Rabinowitz, S., & Morgan, M.A. (1978) Effects of top-down departmental and job change upon perceived employee behavior and attitudes: A natural field experiment. *Journal of Applied Psychology, 63,* 62–72.

20. Hedges, L.V., & Olkin, I. (1980) Vote counting methods in research synthesis. *Psychological Bulletin, 88,* 359–369.

21. Helphingstine, S.R., Head, T.C., & Sorensen, P.F. (1981) Job characteristics, job satisfaction, motivation and satisfaction with growth: A study of industrial engineers. *Psychological Reports, 49,* 381–382.

22. Humphrys, P. (1981) The effect of importance upon the relationship between perceived job attributes, desired job attributes, and job satisfaction. *Australian Journal of Psychology, 33,* 121–133.

23. Johns, G. (1978) Attitudinal and nonattitudinal predictors of two forms of absence from work. *Organizational Behavior and Human Performance, 22,* 431–444.

24. Katz, R. (1978) The influence of longevity on employee reactions to task characteristics. *Human Relations, 31,* 703–725.

25. Kiggundu, M.N. (1983) Task interdependence and job design: Test of a theory. *Organizational Behavior and Human Performance, 31,* 145–172.

26. Kim, J.S. (1980) Relationships of personality to perceptual and behavioral responses in stimulating and nonstimulating jobs. *Academy of Management Journal, 23,* 307–319.

27. King, M., Murray, M.A., & Atkinson, T. (1982) Background, personality, job characteristics, and satisfaction in a national sample. *Human Relations, 35,* 119–133.

28. Lawler, E.E., Hackman, J.R., & Kaufman, S. (1973) Effects of job redesign: A field experiment. *Journal of Applied Social Psychology, 3,* 49–62.

29. Lawler, E.E., & Hall, D.T. (1970) Relationship of job characteristics to job involvement, satisfaction, and intrinsic motivation. *Journal of Applied Psychology, 54,* 305–312.

30. London, M., & Klimoski, R.J. (1973) Self-esteem and job complexity as moderators of attitudes toward work and effectiveness as seen by self, supervisors, and peers. *Proceedings of the 81st Annual Convention of the American Psychological Association,* pp. 597–598.

31. Martin, T.N. (1981) A path analytic model of human capital and organizational job characteristics on female job satisfaction. *Human Relations, 34,* 975–988.

32. O'Brien, G.E., & Humphrys, P. (1982) The effects of congruency between work values and perceived job attitudes upon the job satisfaction of pharmacists. *Australian Journal of Psychology, 34,* 91–101.

33. Oldham, G.R. (1976) Job characteristics and internal motivation: The moderating effect of interpersonal and individual variables. *Human Relations, 29,* 559–569.

34. Oldham, G.R., Hackman, J.R., & Pearce, J.L. (1976) Conditions under which employees respond positively to enriched work. *Journal of Applied Psychology, 61,* 395–403.

35. Oldham, G.R., Hackman, J.R., & Stepina, L.P. (1978) *Norms for the job diagnostic survey* (Technical Report No. 16). New Haven, Conn.: Yale University, School of Organization and Management.

36. Oldham, G.R., & Miller, H.E. (1979) The effect of significant other's job complexity on employee reactions to work. *Human Relations, 32,* 247–260.

37. O'Reilly, C.A. (1977) Personality-job fit: Implications for individual attitudes and performance. *Organizational Behavior and Human Performance, 18,* 36–46.

38. O'Reilly, C.A., & Caldwell, D.F. (1979) Informational influence as a determinant of perceived task characteristics and job satisfaction. *Journal of Applied Psychology, 64,* 157–165.

39. Orpen, C. (1979) The effects of job enrichment on employee satisfaction, motivation, involvement, and performance: A field experiment. *Human Relations, 32,* 189–217.

40. Pokorney, J.J., Gilmore, D.C., & Beehr, T.A. (1980) Job Diagnostic Survey dimensions: Moderating effect of growth needs and correspondence with dimensions of job rating form. *Organizational Behavior and Human Performance, 26,* 222–237.

41. Pritchard, R.D., & Peters, L.H. (1974) Job duties and job interests as predictors of intrinsic and extrinsic satisfaction. *Organizational Behavior and Human Performance, 12,* 315–330.

42. Roberts, K.H., & Glick, W. (1981) The job characteristics approach to task design: A critical review. *Journal of Applied Psychology, 66,* 193–217.

43. Robey, D. (1974) Task design, work values, and worker response: An experimental test. *Organizational Behavior and Human Performance, 12,* 264–273.

44. Rosenthal, R. (1978) Combining results of independent studies. *Psychological Bulletin, 85,* 185–193.

45. Rosenthal, R., & Rosnow, R.L. (1984) *Essentials of behavioral research: Methods and data analysis.* New York: McGraw-Hill.

46. Rousseau, D.M. (1977) Technological differences in job characteristics, employee satisfaction, and motivation: A synthesis of job design research and sociotechnical systems theory. *Organizational Behavior and Human Performance, 19,* 18–42.

47. Salancik, G.R., & Pfeffer, J. (1977) An examination of need-satisfaction models of job attitudes. *Administrative Science Quarterly, 22,* 427–456.

48. Sarata, B.P.V., & Jepsen, J.C. (1977) Job design and staff satisfaction in human service settings. *American Journal of Community Psychology, 5,* 229–236.

49. Schneider, B., Reichers, A.E., & Mitchell, T.M. (1982) A note on some relationships between the aptitude requirements and reward attributes of tasks. *Academy of Management Journal, 25,* 567–574.

50. Sims, H.P., & Szilagyi, A.D. (1976) Job characteristic relationships: Individual and structural moderators. *Organizational Behavior and Human Performance, 17,* 211–230.

51. Spector, P.E., & Michaels, C.E. (1983) A note on item order as an artifact in organizational surveys. *Journal of Occupational Psychology, 56,* 35–36.

52. Steers, R.M., & Spencer, D.G. (1977) The role of achievement motivation in job design. *Journal of Applied Psychology, 62,* 472–479.

53. Stone, E.F. (1975) Job scope, job satisfaction, and the Protestant ethic: A study of enlisted men in the U.S. Navy. *Journal of Vocational Behavior, 7,* 215–224.

54. Stone, E.F. (1976) The moderating effect of work-related values on the job scope-job satisfaction relationship. *Organizational Behavior and Human Performance, 15,* 147–167.

55. Stone, E.F. (1978) *Research methods in organizational behavior.* Glenview, Ill.: Scott, Foresman.

56. Stone, E.F. (1984) Misrepresenting and/or misperceiving the facts: A reply to Salancik. *Journal of Management, 10,* 255–258.

57. Stone, E.F., & Gueutal, H.G. (1984) On the premature death of need satisfaction models: An investigation of Salancik and Pfeffer's views on priming and consistency artifacts. *Journal of Management, 10,* 237–258.

58. Stone, E.F., & Hollenbeck, J.R. (1982) An experimental investigation of priming and consistency artifacts in studies of need satisfaction models. *25th Annual Conference, Midwest Academy of Management,* 301–312.

59. Stone, E.F., Mowday, R.T., & Porter, L.W. (1977) Higher order need strengths as moderators of the job scope-job satisfaction relationship. *Journal of Applied Psychology, 62,* 466–471.

60. Stone, E.F., & Porter, L.W. (1975) Job characteristics and job attitudes: A multivariate study. *Journal of Applied Psychology, 60,* 57–64.

61. Terborg, J.R., & Davis, G.A. (1982) Evaluation of a new method for assessing change to planned job redesign as applied to Hackman and Oldham's characteristics model. *Organizational Behavior and Human Performance, 29,* 112–128.

62. Trow, D.B. (1957) Autonomy and job satisfaction in task-oriented groups. *Journal of Abnormal and Social Psychology, 54,* 204–209.

63. Umstot, D.D., Bell, C.H., & Mitchell, T.,R. (1976) Effects of job enrichment and task goals on satisfaction and productivity: Implications for job design. *Journal of Applied Psychology, 61,* 379–394.

64. Walsh, J.T., Taber, T.D., & Beehr, T.A. (1980) An integrated model of perceived job characteristics. *Organizational Behavior and Human Performance, 25,* 252–267.

12

The Relationship between Job Performance and Job Satisfaction

Philip M. Podsakoff
Larry J. Williams

A considerable amount of debate has occurred over the past few decades regarding the relative strengths and weaknesses of laboratory and field methodologies (cf. Berkowitz & Donnerstein, 1982; Bickman & Henchy, 1972; Borgatta & Bohrnstedt, 1974; Calder, Phillips, & Tybout, 1981, 1982, 1983; Campbell & Stanley, 1966; Dipboye & Flanagan, 1979; Fromkin & Streufert, 1976; Henshel, 1980; Lynch, 1982, 1983; McGrath & Brinberg, 1983; Mook, 1983; Orne, 1969; Silverman, 1977; Warneryd, 1968). Much of this debate centers on the external validity or generalizability of laboratory findings. Proponents of field research have enumerated several problems that are encountered in conducting research in laboratory settings which presumably make the findings obtained in these settings less generalizable. Included among these criticisms are that laboratory studies: (1) are susceptible to experimental artifacts (Rosenthal, 1976; Rosenthal & Rosnow, 1969) and demand characteristics (Orne), (2) utilize artificial environments which may have no real-life equivalents (Borgatta & Bohrnstedt; Tajfel, 1972), and (3) frequently employ undergraduate students who are probably not representative of the types of people who work in actual organizational settings (Albert, 1967; Rosenthal & Rosnow). Of course, given the fact that laboratory research has served such a prominent role in the accumulation of knowledge regarding the behavior of human organisms in the recent past, it is not too surprising to find that many of these criticisms have been responded to by those who conduct research in such settings (cf. Fromkin & Streufert; Henshel; Khera & Benson, 1970; Oakes, 1972).

What is surprising, however, given the amount of debate, is that there have been so few attempts to assess whether the results obtained from laboratory settings truly differ from those that are reported in field settings. It would appear logical that one way to determine whether the results from laboratory research are

We wish to thank W.E. Scott, Jr., Donald Harnett, John Ivancevich, and Jiing-Lih Farh for providing additional details on some of the studies reported in this review. We also would like to thank Mary Post and David Pioch for their help in compiling the tables presented in the chapter.

similar to those obtained from field studies would be to compare the findings directly. Yet, with few exceptions, reviews of this nature are not to be found.

One possible reason for the lack of attention to the comparability of laboratory and field research findings is that those behavioral scientists involved in field research do not often conduct laboratory research and vice versa. Laboratory research employs different methods and procedures from those which are utilized in field studies, and while it is true that the skills needed to conduct research in the laboratory are not mutually exclusive of those skills required to conduct research in field settings, it is relatively rare to find a researcher who feels equally adept at conducting research in both domains. Related to this is the fact that research conducted in the laboratory appears to be designed for different purposes than research conducted in field settings. Several behavioral scientists, for example, have noted that while most field research is designed to examine the covariation between variables, the majority of laboratory research is designed to establish cause and effect relationships.

Within the context of these issues, the purpose of this chapter is to compare the findings from laboratory and field studies on the relationship between employee performance and satisfaction. A comparative analysis of research on the relationship between these two variables appears particularly worthwhile for two reasons. First, despite the amount of empirical evidence which has accumulated in this area, there is still a considerable amount of theoretical and conceptual disagreement regarding the relationship between employee performance and satisfaction (cf. Cherrington, Reitz, & Scott, 1971; Fisher, 1980; Greene, 1972; Greene & Craft, 1977; Locke, 1970, 1976; Lorenzi, 1978; Organ, 1977, 1978; Porter & Lawler, 1968; Schwab & Cummings, 1970). Second, and more important to the issue at hand, even though several reviews of the literature on the relationship between employee performance and satisfaction have been conducted in the past (cf. Brayfield & Crockett, 1955; Greene & Craft, 1977; Herzberg, Mausner, Peterson, & Capwell, 1957; Schwab & Cummings, 1970; Vroom, 1964), in general, these reviews (1) are somewhat dated and therefore only include a subset of the studies which have been conducted,[1] and (2) make no attempt to analyze the differential effects, if any, of the results obtained from laboratory and field settings. In the first part of this chapter, particular attention is focused on the similarities and differences in the results obtained from the laboratory and field studies. Following this is a discussion of the findings obtained in these two research domains.

Review Methodology

Our goal while searching through the literature was to identify published, empirical laboratory and field studies on the relationship between performance and satisfaction. To this end, several methods of searching for relevant literature were used. First, an attempt was made to obtain information regarding all of the studies cited in earlier reviews of the relationship between performance and satisfaction (such as Brayfield and Crockett, 1955; Greene, 1972; Greene & Craft, 1977; Herzberg et al., 1957; Schwab & Cummings, 1970; Vroom, 1964). Next, all sources reported in the *Social Sciences Citations Index* (1966–1984) which cited Brayfield and Crockett's review were examined. Finally, another manual search was conducted of all of the issues of the *Academy of Management Journal, Journal of Applied Psychology, Journal of Vocational Behavior, Organizational Behavior and Human Performance,* and *Personnel Psychology* from 1963 to 1984.[2] In order to be as comprehensive as possible, any article found that reported a correlation between performance and satisfaction was included, even if the analysis of this relationship was not central to the focus of the research.

Once the relevant articles were identified, they were read and categorized as either theoretical or empirical in nature. Because the purpose of this chapter is to focus on the actual relationships obtained in laboratory and field settings (rather than on theoretical propositions), the empirical studies of the relationship between performance and satisfaction were then summarized.

Results of the Empirical Findings

We now turn our attention to the analysis of the empirical relationships between performance and satisfaction. Consistent with our intent, we have divided this discussion into two major parts. The first part reports the results of the field studies of the performance-satisfaction relationship. This is the most prevalent type of study in this line of research. Because of their comparability to the cross-sectional findings, also included in this section of the chapter are the results of the static correlations between employee performance and satisfaction obtained in longitudinal field studies. The second part of the chapter reports the results of laboratory studies which have examined these relationships.

Results of Field Studies

Tables 12–1 through 12–6 present the results of the cross-sectional field studies which have reported on the relationships between employee performance and the six facets of satisfaction which have been studied the most in the empirical literature: work satisfaction, supervisory satisfaction, coworker satisfaction, pay satisfaction, advancement satisfaction, and general satisfaction. While these tables are generally self-explanatory, a few points need elaboration.

The first point has to do with the column labeled *Reward Contingency*. This column indicates whether a contingency between performance and organizational rewards was present in the sample being examined. This information is included because, as noted later in the chapter, several studies have indicated the potential importance of such contingencies to the relationship obtained between performance and satisfaction. A Y in this column indicates that on the basis of the investigator's description of the sample, a reward contingency was present.[3] An N in this column indicates that a reward contingency was not present in the sample analyzed. Finally, a *?* in this column indicates that it was not possible to tell whether such a contingency did or did not exist in the particular sample under consideration.

The second point has to do with the data reported in the column labeled *Satisfaction Measure*. This column reports the nature of the measures utilized to assess satisfaction in each of the studies. As indicated in this column, while the job descriptive index (Smith, Kendall, & Hulin, 1969) is the most widely employed measure of satisfaction in the field studies reported to date, a variety of different scales have actually been employed in this domain. In an attempt to condense this information, scales which were said to measure the same dimension of satisfaction (for example, supervisory satisfaction) were labeled similarly. While this practice may obscure some differences in the findings obtained from the different measures of the facets of satisfaction, it was considered necessary to increase the interpretability of the results.

The final point regarding the tables has to do with the column labeled *r-Value*. This column indicates the size and direction of the correlation coefficient reported by the investigators of the study being summarized. Coefficients listed under the $+$ sign were positive and significant, while those listed under the $-$ sign were negative and significant. Those coefficients listed under the zero were reported to be nonsignificant. Significance levels were calculated for those studies in which this information was not provided by using the conversion tables of Fisher and Yates (1953).

The Employee Performance-Work Satisfaction Relationship. As indicated in table 12–1, the relationship between work satisfaction and employee performance has been examined in thirty-one different samples ($N = 4,185$). The findings of this research were about equally divided between sixteen positive and fourteen nonsignificant relationships. The mean correlation coefficient across all thirty-one samples was .18. Of the thirty-one samples, only two (Kesselman et al., 1974; Kirchner, 1965) had a contingency between performance and rewards. Thus, even though the correlation between performance and work satisfaction in both of these samples was greater than the overall r-value, little can be concluded from this data.

The Employee Performance-Supervisory Satisfaction Relationship. Table 12–2 summarizes the relationships between supervisory satisfaction and employee performance that have been obtained in field research. This table indicates that of the twenty-seven samples ($N = 4,203$) that have been used to examine this performance-satisfaction relationship, fourteen samples have reported positive relationships, ten samples have reported nonsignificant relationships, and three samples have reported negative relationships. The mean (overall) r-value

Table 12-1
Summary of Relationships between Work Satisfaction and Employee Performance in Field Studies

Study	Sample	Satisfaction Measure	Performance Measure	Reward Contingency	N	r Value +	r Value 0	r Value −
Kirchner (1965)	Outdoor advertising salesmen	Author-developed scale[a]	Objective measures	Y	72	.26[b]		
Gavin & Ewen (1974)	Caucasian airline employees	11-item scale[c]	Supervisor ratings	?	390	.23[d]		
Gavin & Ewen (1974)	Black airline employees	11-item scale[c]	Supervisor ratings	?	81	.37[d]		
Kesselman, Wood, & Hagen (1974)	Draftswomen	JDI[e]	Supervisor ratings	Y	37	.58		
Kesselman, Wood, & Hagen (1974)	Toll operators	JDI	Supervisor ratings	N	39	.53		
Baird (1976)	State employees (high job stimulation)	JDI	Supervisor ratings	?	116		.01	
Baird (1976)	State employees (low job stimulation)	JDI	Supervisor ratings	?	51	.35		
Brief & Aldag (1976)	Nursing aides	JDI	Supervisor ratings	?	77			−.18
Jacobs & Solomon (1977)	Salesmen and managers	JDI	Supervisor ratings	?	251		.08	
Bhagat & Chassie (1978)	Students	JDI	Student GPA	?	137		.14	
Hall, Goodale, Rabinowitz, & Morgan (1978)	Transportation workers	JDI	Self ratings	?	153	.22		
Kerr Inkson (1978)	Meat processors	JDI	Supervisor ratings	?	93		.19	
Dipboye, Zultowski, Dewhirst, & Arvey (1979)	Scientists and engineers (high self-esteem)	1-item scale	Self-ratings	?	114	.26		
Dipboye et al. (1979)	Scientists and engineers (low self-esteem)	1-item scale	Self ratings	?	108		.13	

Table 12-1 continued

Study	Sample	Satisfaction Measure	Performance Measure	Reward Contingency	N	r Value +	r Value 0	r Value −
Dipboye et al. (1979)	Homemakers (high self-esteem)	1-item scale	Self ratings	?	58		.11	
Dipboye et al. (1979)	Homemakers (low self-esteem)	1-item scale	Self ratings	?	55	.31		
Dipboye et al. (1979)	Firefighters (high self-esteem)	1-item scale	Supervisor ratings	?	35	.30		
Dipboye et al. (1979)	Firefighters (low self-esteem)	1-item scale	Supervisor ratings	?	38		.16	
Dipboye et al. (1979)	Clerical workers (high self-esteem)	1-item scale	Supervisor ratings	?	139	.18		
Dipboye et al. (1979)	Clerical workers (low self-esteem)	1-item scale	Supervisor ratings	?	114	.28		
O'Reilly & Roberts (1978)	Naval personnel	JDI	Supervisor ratings	?	301			−.19
Abdel-Halim (1980)	Retail drug employees	JDI	Supervisor ratings	?	123	.21		
Griffin (1980)	Hourly manufacturing employees	Alderfer's (1972) scale	Objective ratings	?	88		−.04	
Penley & Hawkins (1980)	Financial employees	JDI	Supervisor ratings	?	240		.04	
Wexley, Alexander, Greenawalt, & Couch (1980)	Part-time employed college students	JDI	Supervisor ratings	?	194		.01[f]	
Breaugh (1981)	Research scientists	JDS[g]	Supervisor ratings	?	112	.19[h]		
Stumpf & Rabinowitz (1981)	University faculty	JDI	Objective measures, peer and student ratings	?	102		.12[h]	
Lopez (1982)	MBA students	JDI	Supervisor ratings	?	579	.52		

Study	Sample	Satisfaction measure	Performance measure	Number of items	N	r
Podsakoff, Todor, & Skov (1982)	Supervisors and administrators	JDI	Supervisor ratings	?	72	.39
Green, Blank, & Liden (1983)	Bank employees	JDI	Supervisor ratings	?	100	−.01
Norris & Niebuhr (1984)	Technical employees	JDI	Supervisor ratings	?	116	−.02
Totals					4,185	16	14	1

Overall $x_r = .18$

[a] The number of items used in this scale was not provided by the author.
[b] The *r* value reported represents the average correlation between satisfaction and two objective measures of performance.
[c] As described by Gavin & Ewen (1974), the eleven items on this scale measure job and company satisfaction.
[d] The *r* value reported represents the correlation between satisfaction and a composite measure comprised of ten performance dimensions.
[e] Job descriptive index (Smith, Kendall, & Hulin, 1969).
[f] Average *r* value across five performance dimensions.
[g] Job diagnostic survey (Hackman & Oldham, 1975).
[h] Averge *r* value across four performance dimensions.

Table 12-2
Summary of Relationships between Supervisory Satisfaction and Employee Performance Reported in Field Studies

Study	Sample	Satisfaction Measure	Performance Measure	Reward Contingency	N	r Value +	r Value 0	r Value −
Kirchner (1965)	Outdoor advertising salesmen	Author developed scale[a]	Objective measures	Y	72	.31[b]		
Gavin & Ewen (1974)	Caucasian airline employees	13-item scale	Supervisor ratings	?	390	.32[c]		
Gavin & Ewen (1974)	Black airline employees	13-item scale	Supervisor ratings	?	81	.30[c]		
Kesselman, Wood, & Hagen (1974)	Draftswomen	JDI[d]	Supervisor ratings	Y	37		.21	
Kesselman, Wood, & Hagen (1974)	Toll operators	JDI	Supervisor ratings	N	39	.49		
London & Klimoski (1975)	Registered nurses (high complexity)	JDI	Supervisor ratings	?	34		−.21	
London & Klimoski (1975)	Registered nurses (optimal complexity)	JDI	Supervisor ratings	?	79		.10	
London & Klimoski (1975)	Registered nurses (low complexity)	JDI	Supervisor ratings	?	40			−.40
Baird (1976)	State employees (high job stimulation)	JDI	Supervisor ratings	?	116	.26		
Baird (1976)	State employees (low job stimulation)	JDI	Supervisor ratings	?	51		.21	
Brief & Aldag (1976)	Nursing aides	JDI	Supervisor ratings	?	77		.17	
Oldham, Hackman, & Pearce (1976)	Clerical bank employees	JDS[e]	Supervisor ratings	?	201			−.17
Jacobs & Solomon (1977)	Salesmen and managers	JDI	Supervisor ratings	?	251	.19		
Kerr Inkson (1978)	Meat processors	JDI	Supervisor ratings	?	93	.32		
O'Reilly & Roberts (1978)	Naval personnel	JDI	Supervisor ratings	?	301		−.11	
Abdel-Halim (1980)	Retail drug employees	JDI	Supervisor ratings	?	123	.22		

Study	Sample	Satisfaction measure	Performance measure	Number of items	N	r	r	r
Griffin (1980)	Hourly manufacturing employees	Alderfer's (1972) scale	Objective measures	?	88			−.26
Penley & Hawkins (1980)	Financial employees	JDI	Supervisor ratings	?	240		.07	
Schriesheim (1980)	Low/middle-level managers and clerical workers	JDI	Self ratings	?	308	.15		
Wexley, Alexander, Greenawalt, & Couch (1980)	Part-time employed college students	JDI	Supervisor ratings	?	194	.21[f]		
Breaugh (1981)	Research scientists	JDS	Supervisor ratings	?	112		.01[g]	
Fulk & Wendler (1982)	Clerical personnel and managers	JDI	Self ratings	?	308	.15		
Lopez (1982)	MBA students	JDI	Supervisor ratings	?	579	.45		
Podsakoff, Todor, & Skov (1982)	Supervisors and administrators	JDI	Supervisor ratings	?	72	.28		
Green, Blank, & Liden (1983)	Bank employees	JDI	Supervisor ratings	?	100		.06	
Norris & Niebuhr (1984)	Technical employees	JDI	Supervisor ratings	?	116		−.02	
Seers & Graen (1984)	Federal employees	JDS, ROI[h]	Supervisor ratings	?	101	.30[i]		
Totals					4,203	14	10	3

Overall x_r = .17

[a] The number of items used in this scale was not provided by the author.

[b] The r value reported represents the average correlation between satisfaction and two objective measures of performance.

[c] The r value reported represents the correlation between satisfaction and a composite measure comprised of ten performance dimensions.

[d] Job descriptive index (Smith, Kendall, & Hulin, 1969).

[e] Job diagnostic survey (Hackman & Oldham, 1975).

[f] Average r value across five performance dimensions.

[g] Average r value across four performance dimensions.

[h] Role orientation index (Graen, Dansereau, & Minami, 1972).

[i] Average r value across JDS and ROI scales.

obtained across these samples was .17. Two of the studies reported in this domain included reward contingencies in their design (Kesselman et al., 1974; Kirchner, 1965). Kirchner reported a positive relationship between performance and supervisory satisfaction for a sample of salespeople who were paid on the basis of their performance. Kesselman et al., however, reported evidence which runs contrary to the proposition (see Cherrington et al., 1971; Porter & Lawler, 1968) that the relationship between performance and satisfaction will be more positive when rewards are linked to performance than when rewards and performance are not linked. More specifically, Kesselman et al. reported a positive relationship between supervisory satisfaction and employee performance for toll operators (who were paid on the basis of seniority), but no relationship between performance and satisfaction for draftswomen (who were paid on the basis of their performance).

The Employee Performance-Coworker Satisfaction Relationship. The relationship between coworker satisfaction and employee performance has been examined in sixteen samples ($N = 2,462$). As indicated in table 12-3, only three of these samples reported a significant (positive) relationship. Of the remaining thirteen samples, twelve reported no significant relationship between employee performance and satisfaction, while one reported a negative relationship. The overall (mean) r-value reported across the sixteen studies was .11. Again, only the studies conducted by Kesselman et al. (1974) and by Kirchner (1965) included samples in which rewards were tied to performance. Consistent with their findings reported for supervisory satisfaction, Kesselman et al. reported the relationship between performance and peer satisfaction was positive for toll operators but not significant for draftswomen. Kirchner found no significant relationship between performance and coworker satisfaction in his sample of advertising salesmen.

The Employee Performance-Pay Satisfaction Relationship. Table 12–4 summarizes the relationships between employee performance and pay satisfaction that have been reported in twenty-eight different samples ($N = 4,456$). An analysis of this table indicates (1) that seven of the relationships reported have been positive, two have been negative, and the remaining nineteen have been nonsignificant, and (2) the mean correlation obtained across the studies was .07. Only four of the reported studies permitted an analysis of the effects of reward contingencies. Schneider and Olson (1970) found a positive relationship between performance and satisfaction only for those registered nurses who were paid on the basis of their effort. However, Kesselman et al. (1974) found a significant positive relationship between performance and pay satisfaction for both those paid on a contingent basis (draftswomen) and those paid on the basis of seniority (toll operators), and both Kirchner (1965) and Motowidlo (1982) found no relationship between performance and this facet of satisfaction for sales personnel paid on the basis of their performance.

The Employee Performance-Advancement Satisfaction Relationship.
Table 12–5 reports the relationships between employee performance and advancement satisfaction that have been obtained in seventeen different samples ($N = 2,823$). As indicated in this table, positive relationships have been reported in five samples, no significant relationships have been reported in twelve samples, and the mean (overall) r-value obtained across the seventeen samples was .14. Consistent with what would be expected if contingent rewards increase the relationship between performance and satisfaction, there was a positive relationship between performance and advancement satisfaction for those subjects in the Kesselman et al. (1974) study whose pay was tied to performance (draftswomen), but no relationship for respondents whose pay was not tied to performance (toll operators). Kirchner (1965), however, found no relationship between performance and advancement satisfaction in his sample of salesmen (whose pay was linked to performance).

The Employee Performance-General Satisfaction Relationship. A summary of the relationships obtained between employee performance and general satisfaction is reported in table 12–6. As indicated in this table, of the ninety-seven different samples ($N = 13,703$) which have examined this relationship, forty-nine samples have reported positive relationships and the remaining forty-eight have obtained nonsignificant relationships between performance and general satisfaction. None of the studies conducted to date has reported a significant negative relationship. The mean (overall) correlation coefficient obtained across all samples was .18. The results were found to be different, however, for those samples in which a reward contingency was present. In the sixteen samples, ($N = 2,521$) in which a contingency between performance and rewards was present, all but three of the relationships between performance and general satisfaction were positive and significant, and the r-value in these sixteen samples ($r = .27$) was found to be significantly higher ($Z = 4.77$, $p < .01$) than in the eighty-one samples in which the contingency was absent or unknown ($r = .17$).

Results of Laboratory Studies

Tables 12–7 through 12–9 report the results of the laboratory studies which have examined the relationships between performance and satisfaction with work, satisfaction with pay, and general satisfaction, respectively. While additional dimensions of satisfaction have been examined in some of the laboratory studies conducted to date, the majority of these other dimensions were (1) used only once or infrequently in laboratory research, or (2) had no equivalent in the field studies reported earlier, and were therefore not included.

A perusal of tables 12–7 through 12–9 indicates two major differences between the laboratory studies and the field studies reported in the preceding section. First, many fewer laboratory than field studies have been conducted to examine the performance-satisfaction relationship. Second, while the majority of the

Table 12-3
Summary of Relationships between Coworker Satisfaction and Employee Performance in Field Studies

Study	Sample	Satisfaction Measure	Performance Measure	Reward Contingency	N	r Value +	r Value 0	r Value −
Kirchner (1965)	Outdoor advertising salesmen	Author developed scale[a]	Objective measures	Y	72		.20[b]	
Gavin & Ewen (1974)	Caucasian airline employees	5-item scale[c]	Supervisor ratings	?	390			−.10[d]
Gavin & Ewen (1974)	Black airline employees	5-item scale[c]	Supervisor ratings	?	81		.18[d]	
Kesselman, Wood, & Hagen (1974)	Draftswomen	JDI[e]	Supervisor ratings	Y	37		.27	
Kesselman, Wood, & Hagen (1974)	Toll operators	JDI	Supervisor ratings	N	39	.44		
Baird (1976)	State employees (high job stimulation)	JDI	Supervisor ratings	?	116		.11	
Baird (1976)	State employees (low job stimulation)	JDI	Supervisor ratings	?	51		.07	
Jacobs & Solomon (1977)	Salesmen and managers	JDI	Supervisor ratings	?	251		−.04	
Kerr Inkson (1978)	Meat processors	JDI	Supervisor ratings	?	93		.11	
Abdel-Halim (1980)	Retail drug employees	JDI	Supervisor ratings	?	123	.23		
Penley & Hawkins (1980)	Financial employees	JDI	Supervisor ratings	?	240		.04	
Stumpf & Rabinowitz (1981)	University faculty	JDI	Objective measures, peer and student ratings	?	102		.03[f]	
Lopez (1982)	MBA students	JDI	Supervisor ratings	?	579	.35		
Podsakoff, Todor, & Skov (1982)	Supervisors and administrators	JDI	Supervisor ratings	?	72		−.11	

Study	Sample	Satisfaction measure[e]	Performance measure		N	Items	r
Green, Blank, & Liden (1983)	Bank employees	JDI	Supervisor ratings	?	100	.05	1
Norris & Niebuhr (1984)	Technical employees	JDI	Supervisor ratings	?	116	.03	12
Totals					2,462	3	

Overall x_r = .11

[a]The number of items in this scale was not provided by the author.

[b]The r value represents the average correlation between satisfaction and two objective measures of performance.

[c]As described by Gavin & Ewen (1974), the five items on this scale measure cooperation among coworkers and supervisors.

[d]The r value reported represents the correlation between satisfaction and a composite measure comprised of ten performance dimensions.

[e]Job descriptive index (Smith, Kendall, & Hulin, 1969).

[f]Average r value across four performance dimensions.

Table 12-4
Summary of Relationships between Pay Satisfaction and Employee Performance Reported in Field Studies

Study	Sample	Satisfaction Measure	Performance Measure	Reward Contingency	N	r Value +	r Value 0	r Value —
Kirchner (1965)	Outdoor advertising salesmen	Author developed scale[a]	Objective measures	Y	72		.14[b]	
Schneider & Olson (1970)	Registered nurses (effort pay)	1-item scale	Supervisor ratings	Y	73	.24		
Schneider & Olson (1970)	Registered nurses (time pay)	1-item scale	Supervisor ratings	N	73		-.03	
Landy (1971)	Engineers	Elbert's (1966) scale	Coworker ratings	?	175*		.06[c]	
Gavin & Ewen (1974)	Caucasian airline employees	6-item scale[d]	Supervisor ratings	?	390	.12[e]		
Gavin & Ewen (1974)	Black airline employees	6-item scale[d]	Supervisor ratings	?	81		-.09[e]	
Kesselman, Wood, & Hagen (1974)	Draftswomen	JDI[f]	Supervisor ratings	Y	37	.39		
Kesselman, Wood, & Hagen (1974)	Toll operators	JDI	Supervisors ratings	N	39	.51		
Ivancevich & Donnelly (1975)	Trade salespeople ("tall" organization)	4-item scale	Objective measures	?	118		.16[g]	
Ivancevich & Donnelly (1975)	Trade salespeople ("medium" organization)	4-item scale	Objective measures	?	100		.11[g]	
Ivancevich & Donnelly (1975)	Trade salespeople ("flat" organization)	4-item scale	Objective measures	?	77		.16[g]	
Baird (1976)	State employees (high job stimulation)	JDI	Supervisor ratings	?	116	.24		
Baird (1976)	State employees (low job stimulation)	JDI	Supervisor ratings	?	51	.28		
Dyer & Theriault (1976)	U.S. managers	JDI	Self ratings	?	180			-.28
Dyer & Theriault (1976)	French-Canadian managers	JDI	Self ratings	?	133		-.01	
Dyer & Theriault (1976)	English-Canadian managers	JDI	Self ratings	?	79			-.36
Oldham, Hackman, & Pearce (1976)	Clerical bank employees	JDS[h]	Supervisor ratings	?	201		-.07	

Study	Sample	Scale	Performance measure		N		r
Jacobs & Solomon (1977)	Salesmen and managers	JDI	Supervisor ratings	?	251		.04
Kerr Inkson (1978)	Meat processors	JDI	Supervisor ratings	?	93		.08
Abdel-Halim (1980)	Retail drug employees	JDI	Supervisor ratings	?	123		.11
Penley & Hawkins (1980)	Financial employees	JDI	Supervisor ratings	?	240		-.01
Dreher (1981)	Managerial, professional, and technical employees	JDI	Supervisor ratings	?	692		
Stumpf & Rabinowitz (1981)	University faculty	JDI	Objective measures, peer and student ratings	?	102	.20	.10
Lopez (1982)	MBA students	JDI	Supervisor ratings	?	579		.08
Motowidlo (1982)	Sales representatives	7-item scale	Objective measures, supervisor and self ratings	Y	92		.17
Podsakoff, Todor, & Skov (1982)	Supervisors and administrators	JDI	Supervisor ratings	?	72		-.08
Norris & Niebuhr (1984)	Technical employees	JDI	Supervisor ratings	?	116		-.13
Seers & Graen (1984)	Federal employees	JDS, ROI[i]	Supervisor ratings	?	101		-.07[k]
Totals				7	4,456	19	2
Overall $x_r = .07$							

[a] The number of items used in this scale was not provided by the author.

[b] The r value reported represents the average correlation between satisfaction and two objective measures of performance.

[c] Average r value across six performance dimensions.

[d] As described by Gavin & Ewen (1974), the six items on this scale measure pay and working conditions.

[e] The r value reported represents the correlation between satisfaction and a composite measure comprised of ten performance dimensions.

[f] Job descriptive index (Smith, Kendall, & Hulin, 1969).

[g] Average r value between two objective performance measures and five facets of satisfaction.

[h] Job diagnostic survey (Hackman & Oldham, 1975).

[i] Average r value across four performance dimensions.

[j] Role orientation index (Graen, Dansereau, & Minami, 1972).

[k] Average r value across JDS and ROI scales.

Table 12-5
Summary of Relationships between Advancement Satisfaction and Employee Performance Reported in Field Studies

Study	Sample	Satisfaction Measure	Performance Measure	Reward Contingency	N	r Value +	r Value 0	r Value −
Kirchner (1965)	Outdoor advertising salesmen	Author developed scale[a]	Objective measures	Y	72		.17[b]	
Landy (1971)	Engineers	Elbert's (1966) scale	Coworker ratings	?	175		−.02[c]	
Gavin & Ewen (1974)	Caucasian airline employees	9-item scale	Supervisor ratings	?	390	.27[d]		
Gavin & Ewen (1974)	Black airline employees	9-item scale	Supervisor ratings	?	81		.15[d]	
Kesselman, Wood, & Hagen (1974)	Draftswomen	JDI[e]	Supervisor ratings	Y	37	.44		
Kasselman, Wood, & Hagen (1974)	Toll operators	JDI	Supervisor ratings	N	39		.26	
Baird (1976)	State employees (high job stimulation)	JDI	Supervisor ratings	?	116	.22		
Baird (1976)	State employees (low job stimulation)	JDI	Supervisor ratings	?	51		−.15	
Jacobs & Solomon (1977)	Salesmen and managers	JDI	Supervisor ratings	?	251	.17		
O'Reilly & Roberts (1978)	Naval personnel	JDI	Supervisor ratings	?	301		−.02	
Kerr Inkson (1978)	Meat processors	JDI	Supervisor ratings	?	93		.15	
Abdel-Halim (1980)	Retail drug employees	JDI	Supervisor ratings	?	123		.00	

Study	Sample	Scale	Performance measure	Items	N			r
Penley & Hawkins (1980)	Financial employees	JDI	Supervisor ratings	?	240			−.05
Stumpf & Rabinowitz (1981)	University faculty	JDI	Objective measures, peer and student ratings	?	102			.07[f]
Lopez (1982)	MBA students	JDI	Supervisor ratings	?	579	.31		.13
Podsakoff, Todor, & Skov (1982)	Supervisors and administrators	JDI	Supervisor ratings	?	72			.13
Seers & Graen (1984)	Federal employees	ROI[g]	Supervisor ratings	?	101			.02
Totals					2,823	5	12	0

Overall $x_r = .14$

[a] The number of items used in this scale was not provided by the author.

[b] The r value reported represents the average correlation between satisfaction and two objective measures of performance.

[c] Average r value across six performance dimensions.

[d] The r value reported represents the correlation between satisfaction and a composite measure comprised of ten performance dimensions.

[e] Job descriptive index (Smith, Kendall, & Hulin, 1969).

[f] Average r value across four performance dimensions.

[g] Role orientation index (Graen, Dansereau, & Minami, 1972).

Table 12-6
Summary of Relationships between General Satisfaction and Employee Performance Reported in Field Studies

Study	Sample	Satisfaction Measure	Performance Measure	Reward Contingency	N	r Value +	r Value 0	r Value −
Brody (1945)	Production employees	Hoppock's (1935) scale	Objective measures	Y	40	.68		
Mossin (1949)	Female sales clerks	10-item scale	Ratings by customers	?	94		−.05[a]	
Bernberg (1952)	Hourly paid workers	4 measures	Supervisor ratings	?	890		.05	
Gadel & Kreidt (1952)	IBM operators	10-item scale	Supervisor ratings	?	193		.08	
Hamid ud-Din (1953)	Insurance agents	3-item scale	Objective measure	?	552	.22		
Heron (1954)	Bus drivers	10-item scale	Objective measure	?	144	.31		
Baxter, Taaffe, & Hughes (1955)	Insurance agents	32- to 43-item scale	Ratings and objective measure	Y	223	.24		
Bellows (1955)	Airforce control tower operators	Brayfield-Rothe (1951)	Proficiency ratings	?	109		.01	
Brayfield (1955)	Female office workers	Brayfield-Rothe (1951)	Supervisor ratings	?	231	.14		
Brayfield & Mangelsdorf (1955)	Plumbers' apprentices	Brayfield-Rothe (1951)	Supervisor ratings	?	55		.20	
Brayfield & Marsh (1955)	Farmers	Brayfield-Rothe (1951)	Ratings	?	50		.12	
Sirota (1958)	Employees in electronics firm	—[b]	Ratings	?	377		.11	
Sirota (1958)	Supervisors in electronics firm	—[b]	Ratings	?	145		.13	
Vroom (1960)	Supervisors in package delivery company	—[b]	Ratings	?	96	.21		

Study	Group	[b]	Ratings		N		
Lopez (1962)	Administrative and technical personnel	_[b]		?	124		.12
Kirchner (1965)	Outdoor advertising salesmen	Brayfield-Rothe (1951)	Objective measures	Y	72	.44[c]	
Strauss (1966)	Government engineers and scientists	Hoppock's (1935) scale	Self, peer & supervisor ratings	?	49		.19[d]
Lawler & Porter (1967)	Middle and lower level mgrs.	Porter's (1961) scale	Supervisor and peer ratings	?	148	.31	
Carlson (1969)	Blue collar workers	Hoppock's (1935) scale	Supervisor ratings	?	254		.15
Carlson (1969)	White collar workers	Hoppock's (1935) scale	Supervisor ratings	?	252		.19
Doll & Gunderson (1969)	Navy enlisted men	Attitude survey items	Supervisor and peer ratings	?	129		.04
Doll & Gunderson (1969)	Scientists	Attitude survey items	Supervisor and peer ratings	?	66	.33	
Ghiselli & Johnson (1970)	Managers ("flat" organizations)	Porter's (1961) scale	Objective measure	?	217	.22[e]	
Ghiselli & Johnson (1970)	Managers ("tall" organizations)	Porter's (1961) scale	Objective measure	?	196		.10[e]
Lichtman (1970)	Middle managers, supervisors, and technical employees in the IRS	17-item scale	Supervisor ratings	?	95		.21
Schneider & Olson (1970)	Registered nurses (effort pay)	Porter's (1961) scale	Supervisor ratings	Y	73	.23[e]	
Schneider & Olson (1970)	Registered nurses (time pay)	Porter's (1961) scale	Supervisor ratings	N	73		−.12[e]
Pruden & Peterson (1971)	Building material salesmen	4-item scale	Self ratings	?	91		−.03
Slocum (1971)	First-line managers	Porter's (1961) scale	Supervisor and peer ratings	?	87	.26	
Slocum (1971)	Top/middle managers	Porter's (1961) scale	Supervisor and peer ratings	?	123	.42	

Table 12–6 continued

Study	Sample	Satisfaction Measure	Performance Measure	Reward Contingency	N	r Value +	r Value 0	r Value −
Ghiselli & Wyatt (1972)	Japanese managers (authoritarian)	Porter's (1961) scale	Objective measure	?	73	.40[e]		
Ghiselli & Wyatt (1972)	Japanese managers (democratic)	(Porter's (1961) scale	Objective measure	?	72		.16[e]	
Dawis & Ace (1973)	High school dropouts and graduates	—[b]	Supervisor ratings	?	244		−.01[f]	
Ewen (1973)	Students	1-item scale	Expected grade	?	25	.48		
Ewen (1973)	Students	1-item scale	Expected grade	?	67		.05	
Greene (1973)	Manufacturing managers	Bullock's (1952) scale	Peer ratings	Y	62		.22[g]	
Nathanson & Becker (1973)	Clinic physicians	9-item scale	Supervisor and nurse ratings	?	57	.39[h]		
Gavin & Ewen (1974)	Caucasian airline employees	53-item scale	Supervisor ratings	?	390	.30[i]		
Gavin & Ewen (1974)	Black airline employees	53-item scale	Supervisor ratings	?	81	.28[i]		
Orpen (1974)	South African factory workers	Brayfield-Rothe (1951)	Error-free production	Y	75	.69		
Orpen (1974)	South African factory workers	Brayfield-Rothe (1951)	Error-free production	Y	75	.30		
Orpen (1974)	South African factory workers	Brayfield-Rothe (1951)	Error-free production	?	75		.02	
Wanous (1974)	Female telephone operators	JDI[j], MSQ[k], and 2-item scale	Supervisor and objective ratings	?	80		.12[g]	
Ivancevich & Donnelly (1975)	Trade salespeople ("tall" organization)	16-item scale[l]	Objective measures	?	118		.10[m]	
Ivancevich & Donnelly (1975)	Trade salespeople ("medium" organization)	16-item scale[l]	Objective measures	?	100		.12[m]	

Author (year)	Population	Satisfaction scale	Performance measure		N		
Ivancevich & Donnelly (1975)	Trade salespeople ("flat" organization)	16-item scale	Objective measures	?	77		.18
Sheridan & Slocum (1975)	Managers in steel firm	4 1-item measures	Supervisor ratings	?			.20[g]
Sheridan & Slocum (1975)	Machine operators in steel firm	4 1-item measures	Salary records	?	59		.06[g]
Steers (1975)	Female first-line supervisors	JDS[n]	Supervisor ratings	?	133	.26	
Beehr, Walsh, & Taber (1976)	White collar employees	2-item scale	Self ratings	?	143	.21	
Kopelman (1976)	Engineers (1969)	4-item scale	Supervisor ranking	Y	142	.24	
Kopelman (1976)	Engineers (1969)	4-item scale	Supervisor ranking	Y	138		−.03
Kopelman (1976)	Engineers (1969)	4-item scale	Supervisor ranking	Y	119	.46	
Kopelman (1976)	Engineers (1973)[o]	4-item scale	Supervisor ranking	Y	59		.13
Kopelman (1976)	Engineers (1973)[o]	4-item scale	Supervisor ranking	Y	56	.36	
Kopelman (1976)	Engineers (1973)[o]	4-item scale	Supervisor ranking	Y	95	.47	
Schreisheim & Murphy (1976)	Social service organization employees	MSQ	Supervisor ratings	?	54		−.09
Oldham, Hackman, & Pearce (1976)	Clerical bank employees	JDS	Supervisor ratings	?	201		−.11[p]
Arvey & Gross (1977)	Female homemakers and job holders	13-items of MSQ	Self ratings	?	116	.38	
Jacobs & Solomon (1977)	Salesmen and 1st-level mangers	Faces scale	Supervisor ratings	?	251	.19	
Bagozzi (1978; 1980[q])	Industrial sales people	8-item scale	Sales volume	Y	123	.30	

Table 12-6 continued

Study	Sample	Satisfaction Measure	Performance Measure	Reward Contingency	N	r Value +	r Value 0	r Value −
Ivancevich (1978)	Machinists	MSQ	Supervisor ratings and objective measure	?	108		.16[g]	
Ivancevich (1978)	Machine repair technicians	MSQ	Supervisor ratings and objective measure	?	62	.22[g]		
O'Reilly & Roberts (1978)	Naval personnel	Faces scale	Supervisor ratings	?	301		−.13	
Orpen (1978)	Western black employees	Brayfield-Rothe (1951)	Supervisor ratings	?	47	.45		
Orpen (1978)	Tribal black employees	Brayfield-Rothe (1951)	Supervisor ratings	?	54		.02	
Dipboye, Zultowski, Dewhirst, & Arvey (1979)	Scientists and engineers (high self-esteem)	Short-form MSQ	Self ratings	?	114		.08	
Dipboye, Zultowski, Dewhirst, & Arvey (1979)	Scientists and engineers (low self-esteem)	Short-form MSQ	Self ratings	?	108		−.04	
Dipboye, Zultowski, Dewhirst, & Arvey (1979)	Homemakers (high self-esteem)	13-items of MSQ	Self ratings	?	52	.44		
Dipboye, Zultowski, Dewhirst, & Arvey (1979)	Homemakers (low self-esteem)	13-items of MSQ	Self ratings	?	46	.52		
Dipboye, Zultowski, Dewhirst, & Arvey (1979)	Firefighters (high self-esteem)	MSQ	Supervisor ratings	?	33	.36		
Dipboye, Zultowski, Dewhirst, & Arvey (1979)	Firefighters (low self-esteem)	MSQ	Supervisor ratings	?	38		.19	
Dipboye, Zultowski, Dewhirst, & Avery (1979)	Clerical workers (high self-esteem)	MSQ	Supervisor ratings	?	131	.22		
Dipboye, Zultowski, Dewhirst, & Avery (1979)	Clerical workers (low self-esteem)	MSQ	Supervisor ratings	?	99	.48		

Study	Sample	Satisfaction measure	Performance measure	?	N	r	r
Gould (1979)	Public agency employees	Short-form JDI	Supervisor ratings	?	153	.40	
Ivancevich (1979)	Power plant construction engineers	MSQ	Supervisor ratings and objective measure	?	48		.19[g]
Ivancevich (1979)	Government contract engineers	MSQ	Supervisor ratings and objective measure	?	42		.21[g]
Griffin (1980)	Hourly manufacturing employees	Alderfer's (1972) scale	Objective measure	?	88		−.13
Ivancevich (1980)	Engineers	MSQ	Objective measures	?	249		.12[f]
Sundstrum, Burt, & Kamp (1980)	Hospital clerical workers	1-item scale	Self ratings	?	30		.12
Sundstrum, Burt, & Kamp (1980)	University mechanics, secretaries, and clerical employees	1-item scale	Supervisor ratings	?	67		.12
Wexley, Alexander, Greenawalt, & Couch (1980)	Part-time employed college students	JDI	Supervisor ratings	?	194		.11[s]
Breaugh (1981)	Research scientists	JDS	Supervisor ratings	?	112	.19	
James, Hater, & Jones (1981)	Aircraft maintenance personnel	6-item scale and MSQ	Supervisor ratings	?	363	.12	
Mossholder, Bedian, & Armenakis (1981)	Nursing employees	Taylor & Bowers (1972)	Supervisor ratings	?	161		.11
Spencer & Steers (1981)	Hospital employees	Hackman & Lawler (1971)	Supervisor ratings	?	295	.17	
Bhagat (1982)	Retail managers	JDS	Supervisor ratings	Y	104	.35	
Ivancevich & McMahon (1982)	Engineers	MSQ	Supervisor ratings and objective measure	?	209	.28[f]	
Lopez (1982)	MBA students	JDI	Supervisor ratings	?	579	.32	

Table 12-6 continued

Study	Sample	Satisfaction Measure	Performance Measure	Reward Contingency	N	r Value +	r Value 0	r Value —
Tharenou & Harker (1982; 1984[f])	Electrical apprentices	JDS	Supervisor ratings	?	166		.11	
Bateman & Organ (1983)	University employees	JDI	Supervisor ratings	?	77	.41[g]		
Porac, Ferris, & Fedor (1983)	Registered nurses	1-item scale	Supervisor ratings	?	81	.72		
Porac, Ferris, & Fedor (1983)	Manufacturing employees	1-item scale	Self ratings	?	57	.69		
Smith, Organ, & Near (1983)	Bank employees	Scott's (1967) scale[u]	Supervisor ratings	?	220	.26		
Matteson, Ivancevich, & Smith (1984)	Life insurance agents	Modified MSQ	Objective measure	Y	355	.17[r]		
Norris & Niebuhr (1984)	Technical employees	JDI	Supervisor ratings	?	116		-.07	
Seers & Green (1984)	Federal employees	JDS, Hoppock (1935)	Supervisor ratings	?	101	.24[v]		
Totals					13,703	49	48	0

Overall $x_r = .18$

Reward contingency present $x_r = .27$

Reward contingency absent or unknown $x_r = .17$

[a] Average r value between two rated dimensions of performance and composite job satisfaction.

[b] Information on scales not provided.

[c] The r value reported represents the average correlation between satisfaction and two objective measures of performance.

[d] Average r value across self, peer, and supervisor ratings.

[e]Average *r* value across all five of Porter's (1961) need satisfaction scales.

[f]Average *r* value across graduate and dropout groups and past and present satisfaction.

[g]*r* value reported represents average correlation between all performance and satisfaction items across each cross-sectional component of a longitudinal study.

[h]Nathanson and Becker (1973) only reported split-groups (not overall) performance-satisfaction correlations. Thus, the *r* value reported here is the average of all of the split-groups' correlations (weighted by appropriate sample sizes).

[i]The *r* value reported represents the correlation between satisfaction and a composite measure comprised of ten performance dimensions.

[j]Job descriptive index (Smith, Kendall, & Hulin, 1969).

[k]Minnesota Satisfaction Questionnaire (Weiss, Dawis, England, & Lofquist, 1967).

[l]The sixteen items measured by Ivancevich and Donnelly (1975) assessed five facets of satisfaction: self-actualization, autonomy, innovativeness, social interaction, and security.

[m]Average *r* value between two objective performance measures and five facets of satisfaction.

[n]Job diagnostic survey (Hackman & Oldham, 1975).

[o]Engineers studied in the 1973 samples were a subset of those studied in 1969. Because of the long time lag between the first and second part of this study, however, these samples were treated independently.

[p]The *r* value reported represents the correlation between performance and a composite of four facets of satisfaction: pay, security, supervisor, and social. The sample reported in 1980 was essentially the same as that reported in 1978. Thus, only the data from the 1978 study are included.

[q]The *r* value reported represents the average correlation between all performance indices and satisfaction.

[r]The *r* value reported represents the average correlation between all performance indices and five performance dimensions.

[s]Average *r* value between intrinsic, extrinsic, and general satisfaction and general performance.

[t]The sample reported in 1984 was a subset of that reported in 1982. Thus, only the data from the 1982 study are included.

[u]General affective tone was used as the measure of general satisfaction from Scott's (1967) scale.

[v]Average *r* value across JDS and Hoppock's (1935) scale.

Table 12-7
Summary of Relationships between Work Satisfaction and Performance Reported in Laboratory Studies

Study	Sample	Satisfaction Measure	Performance Measure	Reward Contingency	N	r Value +	r Value 0	r Value −
Locke (1965)	College students	JDI	Proportion of successes	Y	71	.43		
Locke (1965)	College students	JDI	Proportion of successes	Y	112	.41		
Cherrington, Reitz, & Scott (1971)	College students	Scott's (1967) scale[a]	Objective	Y	42	.27[b]		
Cherrington, Reitz, & Scott (1971	College students	Scott's (1967) scale[a]	Objective	N	42		−.12[b]	
Waters & Roach (1972)	College students	JDI	Objective	?	109	.36		
Greenhaus & Badin (1974)	College students (high self-esteem)	1-item task satisfaction scale	Objective	Y	37	35[c]		
Greenhaus & Badin (1974)	College students (low self-esteem)	1-item task satisfaction scale	Objective	Y	24		.27[c]	
Baird & Hamner (1979)	College students	2-item performance satisfaction scale	Experimenter evaluation	Y	54	.49		
Baird & Hamner (1979)	College students	2-item performance satisfaction scale	Experimenter evaluation	N	54		.14	
Wimperis & Farr (1979)	College students	JDI	Quantity and quality	?	48		−.03	
Peters, O'Connor, & Rudolph (1980)	College students (facilitating condition)	JDI	Quantity and quality	?	35		.27	
Peters, O'Connor, & Rudolph (1980)	College students (inhibiting condition)	JDI	Quantity and quality	?	35		−.16	
Farh & Scott (1983)	College students	Scott's (1967) scale[a]	Quantity and quality	N	60		.00	
Totals					723	6	7	0

Overall $x_r = .24$

Reward contingency present $x_r = .39$

Reward contingency absent or unknown $x_r = .12$

[a]Task attractiveness was used as the measure of work satisfaction from Scott's (1967) scale.

[b]Composite of the r values between satisfaction at the end of the first experimental session and performance in the second session, plus performance in the second session and satisfaction in the second session.

[c]Composite of the r values between performance and satisfaction in the first experimental session, plus satisfaction in the first session and performance in the second session.

Table 12-8
Summary of Relationships between Pay Satisfaction and Performance Reported in Laboratory Studies

Study	Sample	Satisfaction Measure	Performance Measure	Reward Contingency	N	r Value +	r Value 0	r Value -
Cherrington, Reitz, & Scott (1971)	College students	Scott's (1967) scale[a]	Objective	Y	42	.57		
Cherrington, Reitz, & Scott (1971)	College students	Scott's (1967) scale[a]	Objective	N	42			-.43
Pritchard (1973)	College students	MSQ[b], JDI[c]	Objective	Y	48	.29		
Pritchard (1973)	College students	MSQ, JDI	Objective	N	58		.14	
Pritchard (1973)	College students	MSQ, JDI	Objective	Y	30		-.28	
Pritchard (1973)	College students	MSQ, JDI	Objective	N	30		-.15	
Hamner & Harnett (1974)	College students	Scott's (1967) scale[a]	Objective	Y	80	.50		
Baird & Hamner (1979)	College students	1-item scale	Experimenter's evaluation	Y	36	.58		
Baird & Hamner (1979)	College students	1-item scale	Experimenter's evaluation	N	36			-.35
Totals					402	4	3	2

Overall $x_r = .16$

Reward contingency present $x_r = .38$

Reward contingency absent $x_r = -.16$

[a] Satisfaction with pay was used as the measure of satisfaction from Scott's (1967) scale.
[b] Minnesota Satisfaction Questionnaire (Weiss, Davis, England, & Lofquist, 1967).
[c] Job descriptive index (Smith, Kendall, & Hulin, 1969).

Table 12-9
Summary of Relationships between General Satisfaction and Performance Reported in Laboratory Studies

Study	Sample	Satisfaction Measure	Performance Measure	Reward Contingency	N	r Value +	r Value 0	r Value −
Cherrington, Reitz, & Scott (1971)	College students	Scott's (1967) scale[a]	Objective	Y	42	.56		
Cherrington, Reitz, & Scott (1971)	College students	Scott's (1967) scale[a]	Objective	N	42			−.42
Peters, O'Connor, & Rudolf (1980)	College students (facilitating condition)	JDS[b]	Quantity and quality	?	35	.57		
Peters, O'Connor, & Rudolf (1980)	College students (inhibiting condition)	JDS	Quantity and quality	?	35		.21	
Farh & Scott (1983)	College students	Scott's (1967) scale[a]	Quantity and quality	?	60		.03	
Totals					214	2	2	1

Overall x_r = .16

[a]General affective tone was used as the measure of general satisfaction from Scott's (1967) scale.
[b]Job diagnostic survey (Hackman & Oldham, 1975).

field studies have not examined the effects of reward contingencies on the relationship between performance and satisfaction, a substantial number of the laboratory studies have implicitly or explicitly included this variable in their design.

Relationships between Work Satisfaction and Performance. Table 12–7 summarizes the relationships between work satisfaction and performance that have been obtained in laboratory studies. As indicated in this table, of the thirteen samples ($N = 723$) which have been examined, six obtained positive relationships, while the remaining seven samples obtained nonsignificant results. The mean (overall) correlation obtained across these samples was .24. Because several of the studies conducted in this particular domain included a reward contingency in their design, these studies also permitted an analysis of the effects of such contingencies on the satisfaction-performance relationship. An examination of the data in table 12–7 indicates that of the six samples which had a reward contingency present, all but one reported positive and significant relationships between performance and satisfaction, and the mean correlation coefficient for these six samples was .39. Of the remaining seven samples in which the reward contingency was either absent or unknown, all but one (Waters & Roach, 1972) reported nonsignificant relationships between performance and work satisfaction, and the mean correlation was .12. Comparison of this r-value with that obtained when the contingency was present ($r = .39$) indicates that they were significantly different ($Z = 3.89$, $p < .01$), suggesting that the presence of the reward contingency significantly increased the number of positive relationships found between performance and work satisfaction in the laboratory studies.

Relationships between Pay Satisfaction and Performance. The relationship between pay satisfaction and performance has been examined in nine different samples ($N = 402$) in laboratory settings. A summary of the results of these studies is provided in table 12–8. As indicated in this table, positive relationships have been obtained in four of these samples, negative relationships in two samples, and nonsignificant relationships in the remaining three samples. The mean r-value obtained across all nine of these samples was .16. When those studies that have included a reward contingency were separated from those samples in which such contingencies were absent, however, the correlation coefficients were found to change rather dramatically. In fact, in those five samples that have included a reward contingency, the mean r-value was .38, whereas in those studies that have not included a reward contingency, the mean r-value was $-.16$. These correlation coefficients were significantly different ($Z = 5.51$, $p < .01$).

Relationships between General Satisfaction and Performance. Table 12–9 reports the results of those laboratory studies that have examined the relationship between performance and general satisfaction. An examination of this table indicates that of the five samples studied, two reported positive relationships, two reported no relationship, and one reported a negative relationship between general satisfaction and performance. The mean correlation coefficient across these five samples was .16. Only one of the studies (Cherrington et al., 1971) reported in table 12–9 was explicitly designed to examine the effects of the presence or absence of a reward contingency. The results of this study clearly indicate that a positive relationship between performance and general satisfaction was obtained in that sample in which a reward contingency was present, but a negative relationship was obtained in that sample in which the reward contingency was absent. As in the field studies described earlier in which only a few samples had a reward contingency present, however, the importance of the findings of this one study must be interpreted with some caution.

Tests of the Differences between Laboratory and Field Research

In order to provide a test of the potential differences between the results obtained in laboratory and field settings, chi-square analyses were conducted to compare the number of positive, zero, and negative relationships obtained from the field studies with the number obtained from the laboratory research. For the purposes of these analyses, only those dimensions of satisfaction which were measured in both field and laboratory settings were considered. These included satisfaction with work, satisfaction with pay, and general satisfaction. The results of these analyses are reported in tables 12–10, 12–11, and 12–12. Because of the small number of negative relationships reported in the studies summarized in these tables, these relationships were combined with the nonsignificant relationships for the purposes of analysis. However, separation of the results into those which were negative and nonsignificant was not found to modify any of the conclusions.

As indicated in tables 12–10 through 12–12, the chi-square values for work, pay, and general satisfaction were .11 (n.s.), 1.23 (n.s.), and .21 (n.s.), respectively. This suggests that the results obtained from field studies of the relationship between performance and satisfaction were generally congruent with those obtained in laboratory settings.

Table 12–10

Comparison of Laboratory and Field Research Findings of the Relationship between Performance and Work Satisfaction

	+	0 or −	Total
Field studies	16	15	31
Laboratory studies	6	7	13
Total	22	22	44

χ^2 (1 d.f.) = 0.11 (n.s.)

Table 12-11
Comparison of Laboratory and Field Research
Findings of the Relationships between
Performance and Pay Satisfaction

	+	0 or −	Total
Field studies	7	21	28
Laboratory studies	4	5	9
Total	11	26	37

χ^2 (1 d.f.) = 1.23 (n.s.)

On the Comparability of Laboratory and Field Studies of the Relationship between Performance and Satisfaction

Our chi-square tests of the number of positive, zero, and negative relationships obtained between performance and satisfaction in laboratory and field settings suggest that the results are really quite similar. Across three different dimensions of satisfaction (satisfaction with work, satisfaction with pay, and general satisfaction), no significant differences in the pattern of results were obtained between field and laboratory settings. These findings might lead some to conclude that our review of the literature on the relationship between performance and satisfaction does provide support for the generalizability of laboratory findings into field settings. Such a conclusion deserves some caution, however, for several reasons. First, our chi-square analyses are admittedly crude and ignore the effects that sample sizes have on significance of the correlation coefficients reported. Second, such a conclusion does not take into account any of the measurement or analytical problems inherent to many of the studies. Finally, a closer examination of the laboratory and field studies indicates that there are several inherent differences between these studies which make them difficult to compare directly. For example, a perusal of tables 12-1 through 12-9 indicates that there have been numerous differences in the

Table 12-12
Comparison of Laboratory and Field Research
Findings of the Relationship between
Performance and General Satisfaction

	+	0 or −	Total
Field studies	49	48	97
Laboratory studies	2	3	5
Total	51	51	102

χ^2 (1 d.f.) = 0.21 (n.s.)

operationalizations of performance and satisfaction in field and laboratory settings. In general, the performance measures used in the laboratory have been quantitative, objective measures of specific aspects of a subject's performance, whereas the majority of measures employed in field settings have been more subjective, global measures of performance assessed by an employee's supervisor (or in some cases, by the employees themselves). Similar problems exist for the measures of satisfaction because few researchers in laboratory settings have utilized those measures of satisfaction which have been employed in field settings, and little research has been conducted to determine the comparability of many of these measures.

Perhaps the major difference between the laboratory and field studies that may preclude their comparability, however, is the proportion of studies which have either implicitly or explicitly included reward contingencies in these two research domains. As noted earlier, relatively few field studies have been designed to explicitly examine the effects that performance-reward contingencies have on the relationship between employee performance and satisfaction. In contrast to this, many of the laboratory studies conducted to date have included such contingencies in their designs. Thus, even though the results obtained from the laboratory appear to be similar to those obtained from the field, the similarity may be more imagined than real. Since many of the laboratory studies included reward contingencies in their design and most of the field studies did not, the similarities found in the results reported from these two domains may be misleading. We may actually be comparing the results of research on "apples" and "oranges." In light of this problem, perhaps a more appropriate test of the similarities and differences between laboratory and field research would be achieved by comparing the relationships between performance and satisfaction under similar reward conditions in these two settings.

In an attempt to explore the possible effects of reward contingencies on the results obtained in both laboratory and field settings, two types of analyses were conducted. In the first analysis, the results of all of the field studies which had a reward contingency present were compared with the results of those field studies in which a reward contingency was absent or unknown. A similar comparison was also made for all of those laboratory studies which contained a reward contingency and those that did not. These analyses were conducted to determine whether the presence of reward contingencies affected the pattern of relationships between performance and satisfaction within a given research setting. In the second analysis, (1) the results of the field studies in which a reward contingency was present were compared with the results of laboratory studies in which a reward contingency was present, and (2) the results of the field studies in which a reward contingency was absent or unknown were compared with those laboratory studies under which similar conditions existed. This analysis was conducted to determine whether reward contingencies affected the pattern of relationships between performance and satisfaction differentially across research settings.

The results of the analysis of the effects of reward contingencies in field studies are reported in table 12–13. A comparable analysis for laboratory studies

Table 12-13

Comparison of the Results of Field Studies in Which a Reward Contingency Was Present with Studies in Which It Was Absent or Unknown

	+	0 or −	Total
Contingency present	19	9	28
Contingency absent or unknown	75	113	188
Total	94	122	216

χ^2 (1 d.f.) = 7.75

$p < .01$

is reported in table 12–14. An examination of both of these tables indicates that there was a significant difference in both field and laboratory settings in the pattern of findings reported from studies in which a reward contingency was present from those studies in which a reward contingency was absent or unknown. More specifically, the results obtained indicate that the relationship between performance and satisfaction is generally more positive and less negative when reward contingencies are present than when such contingencies are absent or unknown.

The results of our analysis of the effects of reward contingencies across laboratory and field settings are presented in table 12–15. No significant differences in the pattern of positive versus negative or nonsignificant relationships between satisfaction and performance were obtained in laboratory or field settings, and the mean correlation between performance and satisfaction from these studies was .30.

An analysis of the pattern of relationships obtained in those laboratory and field studies in which the reward contingency was absent or unknown is provided in table 12–16. Unlike the findings reported in table 12–15, the results reported in this table indicate that there was a significant difference in the number of positive

Table 12-14

Comparison of the Results of Laboratory Studies in Which a Reward Contingency Was Present with Studies in Which It Was Absent or Unknown

	+	0 or −	Total
Contingency present	10	2	12
Contingency absent or unknown	2	13	15
Total	12	15	27

χ^2 (1 d.f.) = 13.23

$p < .01$

Table 12–15
Comparison of the Results of Field and
Laboratory Studies in Which Reward
Contingencies Were Present

	+	*0 or* −	*Total*
Field studies	19	9	28
Laboratory studies	10	2	12
Total	29	11	40

χ^2 (1 d.f.) = 1.01 (n.s.)
Average r = .30

versus negative and nonsignificant relationships in the laboratory and field settings. More specifically, the results of our analysis indicate that there was a greater proportion of positive relationships reported between performance and satisfaction in the field studies than in the laboratory studies. In addition, the average correlation coefficient obtained from these studies was .14, which is significantly less (Z = 8.89, p < .01) than that obtained in the laboratory and field studies in which a reward contingency was present.

Taken together with the results reported in tables 12–13 and 12–14, the pattern of results reported in tables 12–15 and 12–16 suggests that (1) the presence of reward contingencies appears to enhance the relationship between performance and satisfaction in both laboratory and field settings, and (2) the effects of reward contingencies which are absent or unknown on the performance-satisfaction relationship appear to be less positive in laboratory studies than in field settings.

Table 12–16
Comparison of the Results of Field and
Laboratory Studies in Which Reward
Contingencies Were Absent or Unknown

	+	*0 or* −	*Total*
Field studies	75	113	188
Laboratory studies	2	13	15
Total	77	126	203

χ^2 (1 d.f.) = 4.16
p < .01
Average r = .14

Discussion

The purpose of this chapter was to examine the similarities and differences in the relationships between performance and satisfaction observed in laboratory and field settings. In general, the results of our review suggest that the pattern of findings obtained in the laboratory are relatively congruent with the pattern or findings obtained in field settings. Indeed, our review indicates that no significant differences were obtained in the pattern of relationships in laboratory or field settings between performance and work satisfaction, pay satisfaction, or general satisfaction.

However, our review of the empirical evidence also suggests that some caution is necessary in interpreting these findings too literally. It would be misguided, for example, to conclude from the data provided in this chapter that any inherent relationship exists between satisfaction and performance. Indeed, based on the results of our review, such a conclusion is questionable at best. Consistent with the propositions provided by several behavioral scientists (for example, Cherrington et al., 1971; Porter & Lawler, 1968), our analysis suggests that in both laboratory and field settings, reward contingencies play a critical role in the pattern of relationships obtained between performance and satisfaction. More specifically, our analysis indicates that (1) a significantly larger number of positive relationships are obtained between performance and satisfaction in both laboratory and field settings when reward contingencies are present than when such contingencies are absent or unknown, and (2) there are no significant differences across laboratory and field studies in the pattern of relationships obtained between performance and satisfaction when reward contingencies are present.

While there was less consistency in the conclusions regarding the pattern of relationships obtained across laboratory and field studies in which reward contingencies were absent or unknown, it bears noting that in the majority of the laboratory settings in which the reward contingency was not present, it was generally absent, as opposed to being unknown, whereas in the field studies in which the reward contingency was not present, it was generally unknown, rather than being absent. Thus, one potential reason that the relationships between performance and satisfaction were generally more positive in field as opposed to laboratory settings when reward contingencies were absent or unknown could be that some of the field studies in which reward contingencies were classified as unknown may have been studies in which reward contingencies were actually present.

We also believe it would be unwise to conclude from our review that the results from laboratory settings invariably generalize to field settings. Recently, Jung (1981) has noted that there are two types of errors that one can make when generalizing from laboratory to field settings. The first type of error results when the claim is made that laboratory and field research yield different results when, in fact, the results are similar. Such situations in which the null hypothesis is mistakenly rejected are called type I errors. The second type of error occurs when a researcher concludes that there are no differences in the results obtained from laboratory and field settings, when such differences actually do exist. This, of course, is known as a type II error. Jung further notes that while the possibility of avoiding a type I error is more serious when making statistical inferences, in the case of determining the generalizability of findings, making a type II error may be more serious because it may include the assumption that there are no differences in laboratory and field studies other than the setting. He concludes that the ideal way to avoid the danger of committing a type II error and to test for the generalizability from laboratory to field settings more directly is to include the factor of interest (in this case, the study setting) as an independent variable while holding as many of the other variables in the study as constant as possible.

Of course, such a conclusion has little merit if it is taken literally to mean that all variables except the situation be held constant across laboratory and field studies. Trying to identify all of the possible variables that would need to be included in the design of such a study would be monumental, and "the cost of time, effort, and resources necessary to conduct parallel laboratory-life comparisons would be overwhelming" (Jung, 1981, p. 44). Moreover, such studies may not prove very worthwhile. For, as noted by Locke in the introductory chapter of this book, the only generalization that could be made from such a research effort would be from one laboratory setting to an identical or very similar field setting.

We, however, do feel that Jung's (1981) conclusion does have some merit if it is interpreted to mean that those variables that are found to influence the phenomenon under investigation are included in the design of, or held constant across, both laboratory and field settings. Such an interpretation would suggest that additional attention be given to those variables found to be critical to the relationship between satisfaction and performance in both research domains. While several variables, including locus of control (Steers, 1975), pressure to perform (Bhagat, 1981; Triandis, 1959), need for achievement (Steers), higher-order need strength (Abdel-Halim, 1980), career stage (Gould & Hawkins, 1978), and self-esteem (Korman, 1968), have been hypothesized to serve as potential moderators of the performance-satisfaction relationship, our present review suggests that one variable of rather substantial significance is the contingency established between performance and rewards. More specifically, our review indicates that in both laboratory and field research settings the relationship between performance and satisfaction is generally more positive and less negative when reward contingencies are present than when such contingencies are absent or unknown. These findings, therefore, suggest that future researchers would be well advised to consider this variable in the design of their studies or, at the very least, to control for its effects.

Conclusions

The debate regarding the comparative merits of laboratory and field research has continued relatively unabated for over two decades. Despite the amount of discussion that has occurred, however, few attempts have been made to assess the similarities or differences in the findings obtained in the laboratory with those that have been obtained in field settings. In this chapter, the comparability of the results of the laboratory and field studies of the relationship between satisfaction and performance was examined. Our comparison provided evidence that the pattern of relationships obtained in the laboratory is generally consistent with those obtained in field research.[4] However, our analysis also provided evidence that the relationship between performance and satisfaction is moderated by reward contingencies.

Taken together, our findings are generally consistent with the propositions of several behavioral scientists (cf. Cherrington et al., 1971; Greene, 1972; Porter & Lawler, 1968) who have suggested that performance and satisfaction will be more strongly related when rewards are made contingent upon performance than when they are not. The findings of our review also suggest the need for additional attention in three areas of research. First, there is a need to focus more attention on the nature of the reward contingencies that are present in field studies. At a minimum, field researchers should provide more detailed information regarding the types of performance-reward contingencies that exist in the samples they study. The findings of the present review also suggest the need for additional laboratory studies designed to examine the relationship between performance and satisfaction. Given the explicit control over the reward contingencies that can be afforded in the laboratory, it is unfortunate that only a small number of the studies reported have been conducted in these settings. Finally, additional attention should also be given to the effects that other types of rewards have on the performance-satisfaction relationship. The majority of studies reported to date have only examined the effects of monetary rewards. Relatively little research has focused on the effects that other types of intrinsic or extrinsic rewards may have on the performance-satisfaction relationship.

Notes

1. Two exceptions to this are the recent reviews reported by Petty, McGee, and Cavender (1984), and by Iaffaldano and Muchinsky (1985). However, our review differs in several ways from that conducted by Petty et al. First, Petty et al. generally did not include those studies which incorporated moderators in their design. Second, when examining the relationships between performance and facets of employee satisfaction, Petty et al. only intended to include those studies which used the job descriptive index (JDI) to measure job

satisfaction (although they did report evidence from a study conducted by Ben-Porat (1981) which did not utilize this scale, and which employed satisfaction with achievement as a measure of performance). Finally, and most importantly, Petty et al. only reported results of field studies on the relationship between performance and satisfaction, and not any of the results of laboratory studies which have examined this relationship. While the review conducted by Iaffaldano and Muchinsky is considerably more complete than that of Petty et al., these authors made no attempt to look at the differences in the pattern of relationships across laboratory and field studies, or the effects that reward contingencies might have on performance-satisfaction relationships.

2. There were two exceptions to the years covered in this review. The first issue of *Organizational Behavior and Human Performance* was published in 1966. The first issue of *Journal of Vocational Behavior* was published in 1971. Therefore, the years covered in these two journals were 1966–1984 and 1971–1984, respectively.

3. Samples which were identified as having a reward contingency present were those in which (1) monetary rewards were tied to performance (such as Bagozzi, 1978; Baird & Hamner, 1979; Baxter, Taaffe, & Hughes, 1955; Bhagat, 1982; Brody, 1945; Cherrington, Reitz, & Scott, 1971; Hamner & Harnett, 1974; Kesselman, Wood, & Hagen, 1974; Kirchner, 1965; Kopelman, 1976; Matteson, Ivancevich, & Smith, 1984; Motowidlo, 1982; Pritchard, 1973; Schneider & Olson, 1970), (2) positive feedback was provided for high performance (for example, Baird & Hamner), or (3) task success was linked to task performance (Locke, 1965).

4. It is important to note that the focus of this chapter was on similarities and differences in the pattern of relationships across field and laboratory settings, not on differences in the size of the relationships between performance and satisfaction in these two settings. We make this distinction because (1) an examination of the average correlation coefficient for those laboratory studies in which the reward contingency was present ($r = .40$) was found to be significantly greater ($p < .01$) than for those field studies in which the reward contingency was present ($r = .27$), and (2) an examination of the average correlation coefficient for those field studies in which reward contingencies were absent or unknown ($r = .15$) was found to be significantly greater ($p < .01$) than for those laboratory studies ($r = .04$) that had absent or unknown reward contingencies. These results were, however, not unanticipated by the present authors for two reasons. First, as noted earlier, in those laboratory studies in which the reward contingencies were not present, they were generally absent, as opposed to being unknown, whereas in the field studies in which reward contingencies were not present, they were generally unknown, rather than being absent. Thus, one reason for the higher correlations reported in the field than reported in the laboratory when the reward contingencies were absent or unknown could be that some of the field studies in which the reward contingencies were classified as unknown actually had a contingency present, thereby increasing the correlation between performance and satisfaction. Second, in those laboratory studies in which the reward contingency was present, the contingency was generally made explicit by the researchers, whereas in some of the field studies in which the contingency was present, it was established in concert with the base salary (such as a pay system in which salary and commission was used). Thus, one reason for the lower correlations obtained in the field when the reward contingencies were present is that some of these studies used less "pure" contingencies than the studies conducted in the laboratory.

References

Abdel-Halim, A.A. (1980) Effects of higher order need strength on the job performance-job satisfaction relationship. *Personnel Psychology, 33*, 335–347.

Albert, B. (1967) Non-businessmen as surrogates for businessmen in behavioral experiments. *Journal of Business, 40*, 203–207.

Alderfer, C.P. (1972) *Existence, relatedness, and growth.* New York: Free Press.

Arvey, R.D., & Gross, R.H. (1977) Satisfaction levels and correlates of satisfaction in the homemaker job. *Journal of Vocational Behavior, 10*, 13–24.

Bagozzi, R.P. (1978) Salesforce performance and satisfaction as a function of individual difference, interpersonal, and situational factors. *Journal of Marketing Research, 15*, 517–531.

Bagozzi, R.P. (1980) Performance and satisfaction in an industrial sales force: An examination of their antecedents and their simultaneity. *Journal of Marketing, 44*, 65–77.

Baird, L.S. (1976) Relationship of performance to satisfaction in stimulating and nonstimulating jobs. *Journal of Applied Psychology, 61*, 721–727.

Baird, L.S., & Hamner, W.C. (1979) Individual versus systems rewards: Who's dissatisfied, why, and what is their likely response? *Academy of Management Journal, 22*, 783–792.

Bateman, T.S., & Organ, D.W. (1983) Job satisfaction and the good soldier: The relationship between affect and employee "citizenship." *Academy of Management Journal, 26*, 587–595.

Baxter, B., Taaffe, A.A., & Hughes, J.F. (1955) Unpublished study, cited in Brayfield & Crockett, 1955.

Beehr, T.A., Walsh, J.T., & Taber, T.D. (1976) Relationship of stress to individually and organizationally valued states: Higher order needs as a moderator. *Journal of Applied Psychology, 61*, 41–47.

Bellows, unpublished study, cited in Brayfield and Crockett, 1955.

Ben-Porat, A. (1981) Event or agent: Toward a structural theory of job satisfaction. *Personnel Psychology, 34*, 523–534.

Berkowitz, L., & Donnerstein, E. (1982) External validity is more than skin deep. *American Psychologist, 37*, 245–257.

Bernberg, R.E. (1952) Socio-psychological factors in industrial morale: I. The prediction of specific indicators. *Journal of Social Psychology, 36*, 73–82.

Bhagat, R.S. (1981) Determinants of performance in an innovative organizational setting: A longitudinal analysis. *Journal of Occupational Behavior, 2*, 125–138.

Bhagat, R.S. (1982) Conditions under which stronger job performance-job satisfaction relationships may be observed: A closer look at two situational contingencies. *Academy of Management Journal, 25*, 772–789.

Bhagat, R.S., & Chassie, M.B. (1978) The role of self-esteem and locus of control in the differential prediction of performance, program satisfaction, and life satisfaction in an educational organization. *Journal of Vocational Behavior, 13*, 317–326.

Bickman, L., & Henchy, T. (1972) *Beyond the laboratory: Field research in social psychology.* New York: McGraw-Hill.

Borgatta, E.E., & Bohrnstedt, G. (1974) Some limitations on generalizability from social psychological experiments. *Social Methods and Research, 3*, 111–120.

Brayfield, unpublished study, cited in Brayfield and Crockett, 1955.

Brayfield, A.H., & Crockett, W.H. (1955) Employee attitudes and employee performance. *Psychological Bulletin, 52,* 396–424.

Brayfield & Mangelsdorf, unpublished study, cited in Brayfield and Crockett, 1955.

Brayfield, A.H., & Marsh, M.M. (1957) Aptitudes, interests, and personality characteristics of farmers. *Journal of Applied Psychology, 41,* 98–103.

Brayfield, A.H., & Rothe, H.F. (1951) An index of job satisfaction. *Journal of Applied Psychology, 35,* 307–311.

Breaugh, J.A. (1981) Relationships between recruiting sources and employee performance and work attitudes. *Academy of Management Journal, 24,* 142–147.

Brief, A.P., & Aldag, R.J. (1976) Correlates of role indices. *Journal of Applied Psychology, 61,* 468–472.

Brody, M. (1945) The relationship between efficiency and job satisfaction. Unpublished M.A. thesis, New York University.

Bullock, R.P. (1952) *Social factors related to job satisfaction.* Columbus: Ohio State University, Bureau of Business Research.

Calder, B.J., Phillips, L.W., & Tybout, A.M. (1981) Designing research for application. *Journal of Consumer Research, 8,* 197–207.

Calder, B.J., Phillips, L.W., & Tybout, A.M. (1982) The concept of external validity. *Journal of Consumer Research, 9,* 240–244.

Calder, B.J., Phillips, L.W., & Tybout, A.M. (1983) Beyond external validity. *Journal of Consumer Research, 10,* 112–114.

Campbell, D.T., & Stanley, J.C. (1966) *Experimental and quasi-experimental designs for research.* Chicago: Rand McNally.

Carlson, R.E. (1969) Degree of job fit as a moderator of the relationship between job performance and job satisfaction. *Personnel Psychology, 22,* 159–170.

Cherrington, D.L., Reitz, H.J., & Scott, W.E., Jr. (1971) Effects of reward and contingent reinforcement on satisfaction and task performance. *Journal of Applied Psychology, 55,* 531–536.

Dawis, R.V., & Ace, M.E. (1973) Dimensions of threshold work experience for high school graduates and dropouts: A factor analysis. *Journal of Vocational Behavior, 3,* 221–231.

Dipboye, R.L., & Flanagan, M.F. (1979) Research settings in industrial and organizational psychology: Are findings in the field more generalizable than in the laboratory? *American Psychologist, 34,* 141–150.

Dipboye, R.L., Zultowski, W.H., Dewhirst, H.D., & Arvey, R.D. (1979) Self-esteem as a moderator of performance-satisfaction relationships. *Journal of Vocational Behavior, 15,* 193–206.

Doll, R.E., & Gunderson, E.K.E. (1969) Occupational group as a moderator of the job satisfaction-job performance relationship. *Journal of Applied Psychology, 53,* 359–361.

Dreher, G.F. (1981) Predicting the salary satisfaction of exempt employees. *Personnel Psychology, 34,* 579–589.

Dyer, L., & Theriault, R. (1976) The determinants of pay satisfaction. *Journal of Applied Psychology, 61,* 596–604.

Elbert, A.J. (1966) *Factor analysis of work relevant need statements in two populations.* Unpublished master's thesis, Bowling Green State University, Bowling Green, Ohio.

Ewen, R.B. (1973) Pressure for production, task difficulty, and the correlation between job satisfaction and job performance. *Journal of Applied Psychology, 58*, 378–380.

Farh, J.L., & Scott, W.E., Jr. (1983) The experimental effects of "autonomy" on performance and self-reports of satisfaction. *Organizational Behavior and Human Performance, 31*, 203–222.

Fisher, C. (1980) On the dubious wisdom of expecting satisfaction to correlate with performance. *Academy of Management Review, 5*, 605–612.

Fisher, R.A., & Yates, F. (1953) *Statistical tables for biological, agricultural, and medical research* (4th ed.). Edinburgh: Oliver & Boyd.

Fromkin, H.L., & Streufert, S. (1976) Laboratory experimentation. In M.D. Dunnette (Ed.), *Handbook of industrial and organizational psychology*. Chicago: Rand McNally, 415–466.

Fulk, J., & Wendler, E.R. (1982) Dimensionality of leader-subordinate interactions: A path-goal investigation. *Organizational Behavior and Human Performance, 30*, 241–264.

Gadel, M.S., & Kriedt, P.H. (1952) Relationships of aptitude, interest, performance, and job satisfaction of IBM operators. *Personnel Psychology, 5*, 207–212.

Gavin, J.F., & Ewen, R.B. (1974) Racial differences in job attitudes and performance: Some theoretical considerations and empirical findings. *Personnel Psychology, 27*, 455–464.

Ghiselli, E.E., & Johnson, D.A. (1970) Need satisfaction, managerial success, and organizational structure. *Personnel Psychology, 23*, 569–576.

Ghiselli, E.E., & Wyatt, T.A. (1972) Need satisfaction, managerial success, and attitudes toward leadership. *Personnel Psychology, 25*, 413–420.

Gould, S. (1979) Age, job complexity, satisfaction, and performance. *Journal of Vocational Behavior, 14*, 209–223.

Gould, S., & Hawkins, B.L. (1978) Organizational career stage as a moderator of the satisfaction-performance relationship. *Academy of Management Journal, 21*, 434–450.

Graen, G., Dansereau, F., & Minami, T. (1972) Dysfunctional leadership styles. *Organizational Behavior and Human Performance, 7*, 216–236.

Green, S.G., Blank, W., & Liden, R.C. (1983) Market and organizational influences on bank employees' work attitudes and behaviors. *Journal of Applied Psychology, 68*, 298–306.

Greene, C.N. (1972) The satisfaction-performance controversy. *Business Horizons, 15*, 31–41.

Greene, C.N. (1973) Causal connections among managers' merit pay, job satisfaction, and performance. *Journal of Applied Psychology, 58*, 95–100.

Greene, C.N., & Craft, R.E., Jr. (1977) The satisfaction-performance controversy—revisited. In K. Downey, J.W. Slocum, & D. Hellriegel (Eds.), *Readings in organizational behavior*. St. Paul: West.

Greenhaus, J.H., & Badin, I.J. (1974) Self-esteem, performance, and satisfaction: Some tests of a theory. *Journal of Applied Psychology, 59*, 722–726.

Griffin, R.W. (1980) Relationships among individual, task design, and leader behavior variables. *Academy of Management Journal, 23*, 665–683.

Hackman, J.R., & Lawler, E.E., III. (1971) Employee reactions to job characteristics. *Journal of Applied Psychology, 55*, 259–286.

Hackman, J.R., & Oldham, G.R. (1975) Development of the job diagnostic survey. *Journal of Applied Psychology, 50*, 159–170.

Hall, D.T., Goodale, J.G., Rabinowitz, S., & Morgan, M.A. (1978) Effects of top-down departmental and job change upon perceived employee behavior and attitudes: A natural field experiment. *Journal of Applied Psychology, 63*, 62–72.

Hamid ud-Din, M. (1953) The relationship between job performance and job satisfaction. *Dissertation Abstracts, 13*, 434–435.

Hamner, W.C., & Harnett, D.L. (1974) Goal setting, performance, and satisfaction in an interdependent task. *Organizational Behavior and Human Performance, 12*, 217–230.

Henshel, R.L. (1980) The purposes of laboratory experimentation and the virtues of deliberate artificiality. *Journal of Experimental Social Psychology, 16*, 466–478.

Heron, A. (1954) Satisfaction and satisfactoriness: Complementary aspects of occupational adjustment. *Occupational Psychology, 28*, 140–153.

Herzberg, F., Mausner, B., Peterson, R.O., & Capwell, D.F. (1957) *Job attitudes: Review of research and opinion.* Pittsburgh: Psychological Service of Pittsburgh.

Hoppock, R. (1935) *Job satisfaction.* New York: Harper.

Iaffaldano, M.T., & Muchinsky, P.M. (1985) Job satisfaction and job performance: A meta-analysis. *Psychological Bulletin, 97*, 251–273.

Ivancevich, J.M. (1978) The performance to satisfaction relationship: A causal analysis of stimulating and nonstimulating jobs. *Organizational Behavior and Human Performance, 22*, 350–365.

Ivancevich, J.M. (1979) High and low task stimulation jobs: A causal analysis of performance-satisfaction relationships. *Academy of Management Journal, 22*, 206–222.

Ivancevich, J.M. (1980) A longitudinal study of behavioral expectation scales: Attitudes and performance. *Journal of Applied Psychology, 65*, 139–146.

Ivancevich, J.M., & Donnelly, J.H. (1975) Relation of organizational structure to job satisfaction, anxiety-stress, and performance. *Administrative Science Quarterly, 20*, 272–280.

Ivancevich, J.M., & McMahon, J.T. (1982) The effects of goal setting, external feedback and self-generated feedback on outcome variables. *Academy of Management Journal, 25*, 359–372.

Jacobs, R., & Solomon, T. (1977) Strategies for enhancing the prediction of job performance from job satisfaction. *Journal of Applied Psychology, 62*, 417–421.

James, L.R., Hater, J.J., Jones, A. (1981) Perceptions of psychological influence: A cognitive information processing approach for explaining moderated relationships. *Personnel Psychology, 34*, 453–477.

Jung, J. (1981) Is it possible to measure generalizability from laboratory to life, and is it really that important? In I. Silverman (Ed.), *Generalizing from laboratory to life.* San Francisco: Jossey-Bass.

Kerr Inkson, J.H. (1978) Self-esteem as a moderator of the relationship between job performance and job satisfaction. *Journal of Applied Psychology, 63*, 243–247.

Kesselman, G.A., Wood, M.T., & Hagen, E.L. (1974) Relationships between performance and satisfaction under contingent and noncontingent reward systems. *Journal of Applied Psychology, 59*, 374–376.

Khera, I.P., & Benson, J.D. (1970) Are students really poor substitutes for businessmen in behavioral research? *Journal of Marketing Research, 7*, 529–532.

Kirchner, W.K. (1965) Relationships between general and specific attitudes toward work and objective job performance for outdoor advertising salesmen. *Journal of Applied Psychology, 49*, 455–457.

Kopelman, R.E. (1976) Organizational control system responsiveness, expectancy theory constructs, and work motivation: Some interrelations and causal connections. *Personnel Psychology, 29,* 205–220.

Korman, A.K. (1968) Task success, task popularity, and self-esteem as influences on task liking. *Journal of Applied Psychology, 52,* 484–490.

Landy, F.J. (1971) Motivational type and the satisfaction-performance relationship. *Journal of Applied Psychology, 55,* 406–413.

Lawler, E.E., III, & Porter, L.W. (1967) The effect of performance on job satisfaction. *Industrial Relations, 7,* 20–28.

Lichtman, C.M. (1970) Some intrapersonal response correlates of organizational rank. *Journal of Applied Psychology, 54,* 77–80.

Locke, E.A. (1965) The relationship of task success to task liking and satisfaction. *Journal of Applied Psychology, 49,* 379–385.

Locke, E.A. (1970) Job satisfaction and job performance: A theoretical analysis. *Organizational Behavior and Human Performance, 5,* 484–500.

Locke, E.A. (1976) The nature and causes of job satisfaction. In M. Dunnette (Ed.), *Handbook of Industrial and Organizational Psychology.* Chicago: Rand McNally, 1297–1349.

London, M., & Klimoski, R.J. (1975) Self-esteem and job complexity as moderators of performance and satisfaction. *Journal of Vocational Behavior, 6,* 293–304.

Lopez, E.M. (1982) A test of the self-consistency theory of the job performance-job satisfaction relationship. *Academy of Management Journal, 25,* 335–348.

Lopez, F.M. (1962) A psychological analysis of the relationship of role consensus and personality consensus to job satisfaction and job performance. Unpublished Doctoral dissertation, Columbia University.

Lorenzi, P. (1978) A comment on Organ's reappraisal of the satisfaction-causes-performance hypothesis. *Academy of Management Review, 3,* 380–382.

Lynch, J.G., Jr. (1982) On the external validity of experiments in consumer research. *Journal of Consumer Research, 9,* 225–239.

Lynch, J.G., Jr. (1983) The role of external validity in theoretical research. *Journal of Consumer Research, 10,* 109–111.

Matteson, M.T., Ivancevich, J.M., & Smith, S.V. (1984) Relation of type A behavior to performance and satisfaction among sales personnel. *Journal of Vocational Behavior, 25,* 203–214.

McGrath, J.E., & Brinberg, D. (1983) External validity and the research process: A comment on the Calder/Lynch dialogue. *Journal of Consumer Research, 10,* 115–124.

Mook, D.G. (1983) In defense of external validity. *American Psychologist, 38,* 379–387.

Mossholder, K.W., Bedian, A.G., & Armenakis, A.A. (1981) Role perceptions, satisfaction, performance: Moderating effects of self-esteem and organizational level. *Organizational Behavior and Human Performance, 28,* 224–234.

Mossin, A.C. (1949) *Selling performance and contentment in relation to school background.* New York: Columbia University, Teachers' College, Bureau of Publications.

Motowidlo, S.J. (1982) Relationship between self-rated performance and pay satisfaction among sales representatives. *Journal of Applied Psychology, 67,* 209–213.

Nathanson, C.A., & Becker, M.H. (1973) Job satisfaction and job performance: An empirical test of some theoretical propositions. *Organizational Behavior and Human Performance, 9,* 267–279.

Norris, D.R., & Niebuhr, R.E. (1984) Attributional influences on the job performance-job satisfaction relationship. *Academy of Management Journal, 27,* 424–431.

Oakes, W. (1972) External validity and the use of real people as subjects. *American Psychologist, 27,* 959–962.

Oldham, G.R., Hackman, J.R., & Pearce, J.L. (1976) Conditions under which employees respond positively to enriched work. *Journal of Applied Psychology, 61,* 395–403.

O'Reilly, C.A., & Roberts, K.H. (1978) Supervisor influence and subordinate mobility aspirations as moderators of consideration and initiating structure. *Journal of Applied Psychology, 63,* 96–102.

Organ, D.W. (1977) A reappraisal and reinterpretation of the satisfaction-causes-performance hypothesis. *Academy of Mangement Review, 2,* 46–53.

Organ, D.W. (1978) Some brief notes toward a functional analysis of reward behavior: A reply to Lorenzi. *Academy of Management Review, 3,* 383–384.

Orne, M.T. (1969) Demand characteristics and the concept of quasi-controls. In R. Rosenthal & R.L. Rosnow (Eds.), *Artifact in behavioral research.* New York: Academic Press.

Orpen, C. (1974) The effect of reward contingencies on the job satisfaction-task performance relationship: An industrial experiment. *Psychology, 11,* 9–14.

Orpen, C. (1978) Relationship between job satisfaction and job performance among western and tribal black employees. *Journal of Applied Psychology, 63,* 263–265.

Penley, L.E., & Hawkins, B.L. (1980) Organizational communication, performance, and job satisfaction as a function of ethnicity and sex. *Journal of Vocational Behavior, 16,* 368–384.

Peters, L.H., O'Connor, E.J., & Rudolf, C.J. (1980) The behavioral and affective consequences of performance-relevant situational variables. *Organizational Behavior and Human Performance, 25,* 79–96.

Petty, M.M., McGee, G.W., & Cavender, J.W. (1984) A meta-analysis of the relationships between individual job satisfaction and individual performance. *Academy of Management Journal, 9,* 712–721.

Podsakoff, P.M., Todor, W.D., & Skov, R. (1982) Effects of leader contingent and noncontingent reward and punishment behaviors on subordinate performance and satisfaction. *Academy of Management Journal, 25,* 810–821.

Porac, J.F., Ferris, G.R., & Fedor, D.B. (1983) Causal attributions, affect, and expectations for a day's work performance. *Academy of Management Journal, 26,* 285–296.

Porter, L.W. (1961) A study of perceived job satisfaction in bottom and middle management jobs. *Journal of Applied Psychology, 45,* 1–10.

Porter, L.W., & Lawler, E.E. (1968) *Managerial attitudes and performance.* Homewood, Ill.: Irwin.

Pritchard, R.D. (1973) Effects of varying performance-pay instrumentalities on the relationship between performance and satisfaction: A test of the Lawler and Porter model. *Journal of Applied Psychology, 58,* 122–125.

Pruden, H.O., & Peterson, R.A. (1971) Personality and performance-satisfaction of industrial salesmen. *Journal of Marketing Research, 8,* 501–504.

Rosenthal, R. (1976) *Experimenter effects in behavioral research.* New York: Irvington.

Rosenthal, R., & Rosnow, R.L. (Eds.). (1969) *Artifact in behavioral research.* New York: Academic Press.

Schneider, B., & Olson, L.K. (1970) Effort as a correlate of organizational reward system and individual values. *Personnel Psychology, 23,* 313–326.

Schriesheim, C.A., & Murphy, C.J. (1976) Relationships between leader behavior and subordinate satisfaction and performance: A test of some situational moderators. *Journal of Applied Psychology, 61,* 634–641.

Schriesheim, J.F. (1980) The social context of leader subordinate relations: An investigation of the effects of group cohesiveness. *Journal of Applied Psychology, 65,* 183–194.

Schwab, D.P., & Cummings, L.L. (1970) Theories of performance and satisfaction: A review. *Industrial Relations, 9,* 408–430.

Scott, W.E., Jr. (1967) The development of semantic differential scales as measures of "morale." *Personnel Psychology, 20,* 179–198.

Seers, A., & Graen, G.B. (1984) The dual attachment concept: A longitudinal investigation of the combination of task characteristics and leader-member exchange. *Organizational Behavior and Human Performance, 33,* 283–306.

Sheridan, J.E., & Slocum, J.W., Jr. (1975) The direction and causal relationship between job satisfaction and work performance. *Organizational Behavior and Human performance, 14,* 159–172.

Silverman, I. (1977) Why social psychology fails. *Canadian Psychological Review, 18,* 353–358.

Sirota, D. (1958) Job performance as related to attitudes, motivation and understanding. Unpublished research report, University of Michigan.

Slocum, J.W., Jr. (1971) Motivation in managerial levels: Relationship of need satisfaction to job performance. *Journal of Applied Psychology, 55,* 312–316.

Smith, C.A., Organ, D.W., & Near, J.P. (1983) Organizational citizenship behavior: Its nature and antecedents. *Journal of Applied Psychology, 68,* 653–663.

Smith, P.C., Kendall, L.M., & Hulin, C.L. (1969) *The measurement of satisfaction in work and retirement.* Chicago: Rand McNally.

Spencer, D.G., & Steers, R.M. (1981) Performance as a moderator of the job satisfaction-turnover relationship. *Journal of Applied Psychology, 66,* 511–514.

Steers, R.M. (1975) Effects of need for achievement on the job performance-job attitude relationship. *Journal of Applied Psychology, 60,* 678–682.

Strauss, P.S. (1966) Psychology of the scientist: XIX. Job satisfaction and productivity of engineers and scientists. *Perceptual and Motor Skills, 23,* 471–476.

Stumpf, S.A., & Rabinowitz, S. (1981) Career stage as a moderator of performance relationships with facets of job satisfaction and role perceptions. *Journal of Vocational Behavior, 18,* 202–218.

Sundstrom, E., Burt, R.E., & Kamp, D. (1980) Privacy at work: Architectural correlates of job satisfaction and job performance. *Academy of Management Journal, 23,* 101–117.

Tajfel, H. (1972) Experiments in a vacuum. In J. Israel & H. Tajfel (Eds.), *The context of social psychology: A critical assessment.* London: Academic Press.

Taylor, J., & Bowers, D. (1972) *Survey of organizations.* Ann Arbor: University of Michigan, Institute for Social Research.

Tharenou, P., & Harker, P. (1982) Organizational correlates of employee self-esteem. *Journal of Applied Psychology, 67,* 797–805.

Tharenou, P., & Harker, P. (1984) Moderating influence of self-esteem on relationships between job complexity, performance, and satisfaction. *Journal of Applied Psychology, 69,* 623–632.

Triandis, H.C. (1959) A critique and experimental design for the study of the relationship between productivity and job satisfaction. *Psychological Bulletin, 56,* 309–312.

Vroom, V.H. (1960) *Some personality determinants of the effects of participation.* Englewood Cliffs, N.J.: Prentice-Hall.

Vroom, V.H. (1964) *Work and motivation.* New York: Wiley.

Wanous, J.P. (1974) A causal-correlational analysis of the job satisfaction and performance relationship. *Journal of Applied Psychology, 59,* 139–144.

Warneryd, K. (1968) Can results from psychological experiments be generalized to situations outside the laboratory? In P. Lindblom (Ed.), *Theory and method in behavioral sciences.* Scandinavian University Books.

Waters, L.K., & Roach, D. (1972) Self-esteem as a moderator of the relationship between task-success and task-liking. *Psychological Reports, 31,* 69–70.

Weiss, D.J., Dawis, R.V., England, G.W., & Lofquist, L.H. (1967) *Manual for the Minnesota Satisfaction Questionnaire.* Minneapolis: University of Minnesota, Work Adjustment Project, Industrial Relations Center.

Wexley, K.N., Alexander, R.A., Greenawalt, J.P., & Couch, M.A. (1980) Attitudinal congruence and similarity as related to interpersonal evaluations in manager-subordinate dyads. *Academy of Mangement Journal, 23,* 320–330.

Wimperis, B.R., & Farr, J.L. (1979) The effects of task content and reward contingency upon task performance and satisfaction. *Journal of Applied Social Psychology, 9,* 229–249.

V
Overview

The two concluding chapters by Daniel Ilgen and John Campbell present general overviews of the lab-field issue.

Ilgen's theme is that one cannot claim superiority for one setting over the other independent of the total context. Laboratory research, according to Ilgen, is most suitable: when the goal is to use the lab to simulate field settings for training or other purposes; when the goal is to use the lab as a basis for field application; when constraints such as time, money, or risk preclude field research; and when the goal of the research is to show that a particular cause-effect relationship can be obtained.

The last chapter by Campbell is a hard-hitting one in which he critiques, directly or by implication, just about everyone. He argues that the defining characteristics of lab and field settings are not fully clear. (Perhaps we should use the simplest possible definition: a place designed for experimental investigation.) He also questions what is meant by generalization from one setting to the other. Actually I would agree with him that the key meaning of generalization pertains to whether the same basic conclusions (for example, "X works") would be drawn from studies in each setting. This is why I asked the authors to focus primarily on consistency of results (direction of effect) rather than on effect size.

Campbell asserts that the lab-field issue is a false issue which scientists should have put aside long ago. Here I would take issue with him. My view is that the dispute cannot be dealt with adequately at the deductive level. That is why I initiated this book: to examine the issue inductively (see chapter 1).

Campbell makes some excellent points about meta-analysis: that it is an excellent tool but that it cannot compensate for poorly designed studies. He also disputes the importance of the distinction between hard and soft criteria. I have serious reservations about this view. I have believed for years, for example, that the best solution to the problem of how to make good performance appraisals is not to focus on designing better rating scales but rather to figure out how to eliminate ratings (insofar as this is possible) and substitute meaningful hard criteria for them. Granted, hard criteria are never perfect, but at the same time people are not very good at retaining, processing, and weighing large amounts of information over a long time period. Thus ratings are usually even worse. But that is another book.

Finally, Campbell asserts that the lab-field distinction is not a very useful one and that the more fundamental issues are: What phenomenon do you want to study and what method (including setting) best maximizes the (construct) validity of the variables you want to measure? This is a provocative assertion. In one respect I agree strongly with Campbell: researchers should be primarily problem-centered rather than method-centered. The failure to accept this principle is the central epistemological fallacy of behaviorism: it lets method dictate content. In another respect, however, I think that focusing on construct validity only pushes the lab-field issue back a step further. You then have to decide what you mean by validity. For example, is a valid manipulation of an independent variable in the lab one which represents the variable as it operates in real life or just one that works?

Whether one agrees with all of Campbell's ideas or not, they are stimulating and thought-provoking and properly make the question of lab versus field a much broader one that is simply asking: Which is better?

13
Laboratory Research: A Question of When, Not If

Daniel R. Ilgen

Actors, behaviors, and contexts represent three mutually exclusive and exhaustive categories for all variables in behavioral science research (Runkel & McGrath, 1972). Laboratory research is usually undertaken to gain control over variables in one or more of the three classes—control at a level that typically is not available in research outside the laboratory. Yet, this control is purchased at a price. Laboratory experiments by their very nature cannot create designs that truly represent all, or even most, of the conditions present in naturally occurring settings populated by people who exist, interact, and behave in these settings over a long time period (Berkowitz & Donnerstein, 1982). As a result, many behavioral scientists decry the use of any laboratory research and dismiss results obtained from such as irrelevant or, worse yet, misleading for the understanding of naturally occurring human behavior. They seek instead data collected exclusively in natural settings, often accepting the validity of such data as blindly as they deny the validity of laboratory data. More than a few organizational psychologists and organizational behaviorists, obligated by the nature of their chosen profession to address problems that have some relevance to human behavior in organizational settings, adamantly hold to the position just described.

Such an extreme position is neither empirically nor logically justified. This book contains numerous examples of the empirical fallacy of the position. Time and again, results of research conducted in the laboratory were found to generalize to organizational settings. Logically, the position is also weak. It is well accepted that all research, regardless of the setting, requires trade-offs (Runkel & McGrath, 1972). These trade-offs involve the nature of the actors, behaviors, and contexts that are selected to be researched and, equally important, the ones that are selected to be ignored. Thus, all settings, whether laboratory, field, or some combination of the two, create contextual conditions that have both advantages and disadvantages for contributing to knowledge that generalizes to human behavior

The writing of this chapter was supported in part by a grant from the Office of Naval Research (N0014-83-0756). The ideas expressed herein are those of the author and are not necessarily endorsed by the supporting agency.

in ongoing organizations. For example, the naturalness of the field setting is purchased at the cost of control. Without some control, it is often impossible to disentangle the effects of many different covarying and confounded variables on the behaviors of interest. Is it better to obtain more realism by going to the field yet sacrificing control, or is it better to gain the control in the laboratory but lose some of the naturalness? The obvious answer is that it depends. It depends on the types of trade-offs the researcher needs to make given the nature of the research problem.

Excellent guidance exists for selecting actors, behaviors, and contexts in behavioral research (see, for example, Cook & Campbell, 1979; Fromkin & Streufert, 1976; McGrath, Martin, & Kulka, 1982; Runkel & McGrath, 1972). Fromkin and Streufert focused directly upon laboratory research conducted for the purpose of understanding human behavior in organizations. The key to their approach was the notion of *boundary conditions*. These were those conditions likely to influence the extent to which laboratory research generalized to the field. They devoted considerable effort to describing specific variables the presence or absence of which would likely affect the generalizability of laboratory research to field settings.

The remainder of this chapter falls within the purview of a boundary approach to laboratory research. Underlying the discussion is an acceptance of the position that laboratory research can contribute to the understanding of human behavior at work. At the same time, it is also accepted that certain conditions must be met in order to increase the likelihood that laboratory research will be valuable. In contrast to Fromkin and Streufert (1976), who outlined specific variables in the research setting that influence the value of specific laboratory research, the perspective taken here focuses on those conditions that make the laboratory the preferred setting for gathering data on organizationally relevant problems. Although this perspective leads to looking at the problem of when to use laboratory research somewhat differently than has been done by others, it is recognized that a boundary conditions perspective may lead to the same conclusions in many instances. Thus, the present perspective should be seen as complimenting Fromkin and Streufert rather than as taking an opposing position.

Four general sets of conditions for using laboratory research are discussed. These conditions exist when: (1) high fidelity between the laboratory and the field can be established, (2) laboratory conditions are to be recreated in the field, (3) field conditions limit the feasibility of field research, and (4) the hypothesis of interest is one demanding simply the demonstration of an effect rather than direct generalization of that effect to a particular setting.

High Fidelity

It is a well-accepted belief that the generalization of laboratory findings to field settings is greatest when there is a high degree of similarity between the laboratory and the field. In this case, research is analogous to training where transfer is greatest when both the stimulus conditions and the behavioral responses are similar in the training setting and on the job to which the training is to transfer (Blum & Naylor, 1968). (See chapter 5 on the issue of transfer of training.) For high positive transfer of training, the actors should be identical in both conditions, the settings should be extremely similar, and the behaviors to be displayed should be identical or at least extremely similar. When these conditions exist, the training is said to have high fidelity with the job to which it is to transfer.

Laboratory research settings can also be viewed in terms of their fidelity with field settings. Often laboratory researchers attempt to obtain such fidelity.[1] Perhaps the greatest success creating laboratory settings which were very similar to field conditions occurred in human factors research with aircraft design for pilots. Highly elaborate simulators were constructed that matched in most every respect the conditions that pilots would face in aircraft cockpits. Experimentally controlled manipulations of particular variables could then be examined to see the effects that manipulations would have on behavior (Thorpe, Varney, MacFadden, LeMaster, & Short, 1978).

The high fidelity training analogy breaks down somewhat with respect to actors. In training, the actors are the same in both settings; in research rarely are the subjects in the laboratory research the same as those to which the research findings are to be applied. In fact, one of the greatest criticisms of laboratory research by organizational psychologists is that the research is frequently conducted on college sophomores and then generalized to adult members of the workforce. In attempts to answer critics, some laboratory researchers have used business school students instead of those enrolled in psychology classes, arguing that business students are likely to be more similar to the population of persons to whom the research is to generalize. In rare cases, such cosmetic changes may help; in most they are not very convincing. A more reasonable approach to the selection of actors is to carefully consider the possible ramifications of research subjects that are or are not similar to the population to which the research is to generalize. If actor similarity is important, then simply using business school students instead of psychology majors is unlikely to matter. If it is unimportant, either group will do.

How similar is similar? An answer to this question within each of the three domains—actors, behaviors, and contexts—would be extremely useful to laboratory researchers. Unfortunately, few general answers exist. The result in the training area is to go to elaborate ends to create simulated conditions that match those in the natural setting. This often requires large financial outlays simply because of an absence of adequate guidelines as to the trade-offs between, for example, reducing similarity of conditions and maintaining the desired similarity of learned behaviors.

For laboratory research, several general perspectives have been offered for dealing with the fidelity problem. Berkowitz and Donnerstein (1982) argue that the critical issue is whether or not the subject in the laboratory setting attributes the same meaning to the variables of interest as the subject would in a field setting. This meaning may or may not be obtained the same way in the laboratory as in the field. So, for example, if one wants to study the effects of role overload on performance, subjects in the laboratory could be assigned multiple tasks that have little or nothing in common with tasks that would be experienced on the job as long as the laboratory subjects perceive the multiple tasks as demanding the accomplishment of many more things than time allows. This assumes that the perception of multiple task demands, all of which cannot easily be accomplished, accompanied by strong motivation to accomplish all of the tasks, is part of role overload in any setting. In the introductory chapter of this book, Locke advocates the identification of the essential conditions in laboratory settings to allow for transfer to the field. Although he provides few general essential conditions across all research, he advocates being guided by theoretical views about the phenomena under investigation and the generation of empirical research on the essential features of laboratory research for generalization.

Fromkin and Streufert (1976) offer the most explicit framework for addressing the fidelity problem. They suggest consideration of the extent to which variables in the laboratory disrupt, compete with, or enhance each of the critical variables of interest in the field. Thus, one would consider the major actor, behavior, and context variables for a particular problem of interest, and then ask the extent to which it is likely that the laboratory conditions will disrupt, compete with, or enhance the behaviors of interest in the field. Although there are presently no standards for such considerations, a knowledge of the theoretical constructs of interest and the empirical relationships desired should guide an analysis of laboratory research conditions. It is an empirical question as to the extent to which high fidelity on particular variables can be modified and still maintain good generalizability to field settings. Furthermore, the empirical question can only be answered once specific settings and issues are known.

Replication of the Laboratory in the Field

The preceding section assumed that the researcher's goal is to understand the important parameters of field settings in order to construct conditions in the laboratory that are as similar as possible to the important features of field settings. In some cases, the reverse is desirable; the goal may be to construct field settings that are as similar as possible to laboratory conditions. Engineering units supporting manufacturing operations frequently attempt to match the field to the laboratory. New equipment is designed and first tested as a prototype of the manufacturing process that eventually will be constructed using the new equipment. In this case, the laboratory setting is designed to be feasible in the field but not to match present field conditions.

Although designing laboratory research settings in order that they be replicated in the field is less common in behavioral research, it has been done. An example is research on teaching machines. Laboratory research first controlled

variables important for learning using programmed instruction (Nash, Muczyk, & Vettori, 1971). The stimuli presented to the participants were controlled in such a way as to learn about the impact of variables under study on the behavior of the participants in the research, but, in addition, the methods of control were designed to be implementable in field settings in ways similar to the laboratory, assuming that the hypotheses being tested were supported. When the research was supported, learning centers were constructed to match the conditions of the laboratory as closely as possible.

Future research on the human interface with industrial robots and office information systems might do well to use laboratory research in the manner just described. Conditions set up and tested as prototypes of production work spaces, shop floor control, or offices could be used to develop conditions that, in the laboratory, produce desired patterns of behavior. The laboratory conditions that proved successful could then be replicated in the field.

Field Constraints

For many reasons, it may be impractical to do research in field settings. At the same time, it may be very desirable to learn more about some particular issue. Under such conditions, laboratory settings often provide excellent substitutes for research in the field while still producing results that generalize to those field settings where it is impractical or impossible to do the research. But what are the conditions that are likely to make the laboratory an attractive substitute research setting?

Time

Laboratory research allows for time compression; events that may be spread out over long periods of time can be studied in the laboratory in much less time. Behavioral decision making research is an example of a use of time compression. Models of decision making are frequently applied to situations where individuals have at their disposal a finite number of cues (sets of information) which they use to make some judgment (Einhorn & Hogarth, 1981). For example, an interviewer may look at four or five characteristics of each applicant for a job and then make a decision about whether or not to hire each person. Or a medical doctor may assess a patient's temperature, pulse, blood pressure, skin color, and breathing rate, and then reach a decision about the presence or absence of some disease based upon an assessment of these symptoms. It could take weeks, months, or years to wait for the interviewer to review enough applicants or the doctor to see enough patients to discover how interviewers, doctors, and people in general weight and combine cues to make decisions. On the other hand, in the laboratory, presenting interviewers, medical doctors, and others with large numbers of cases in a short period of time can lead to useful information about how these groups of people make decisions. Decision making models can be constructed from the laboratory data and these models can then be tested in the field. Although the development of decision making models in the laboratory does not guarantee that similar decisions will be made in the same way in the field, models developed from the laboratory can be tested in the field to judge their generalizability. The total amount of time needed for the laboratory research and its validation in the field almost always is much less than if all the research were conducted in the field.

Cost

Good field research is expensive, often prohibitively so. Good laboratory research can also be expensive. However, the issue is relative cost rather than absolute cost. If the problem of concern is one that appears adaptable to investigation in the laboratory, it is usually less expensive to conduct the research in a laboratory setting than in the field. The choice of setting raises a utility question: Considering all investments in the research in each setting and the probable information yield, which of the two settings has the higher utility? The answer to this question may lead to a preference for laboratory research over field research in many instances. Yet, it should always be kept in mind that the cost should only be considered along with potential yield in information. It is never reasonable to choose one setting over another if the loss in potentially valuable information drops below a level acceptable to the researcher.

Ethics

There may be times when important research questions cannot be addressed in field settings because of ethical reasons. In the laboratory, the ethical issues may be resolved. As a case in point, I was once involved in a research project that addressed the effects of reward systems and the structure of tasks on work motivation. To study work motivation, we felt we needed to present some very different levels of various incentives which were likely to create large differences in the amount of pay people received on the same job. We also felt that the behavior of employees at their work stations needed to be filmed so that we could measure more precisely the actual behaviors of the people over time. It was our conclusion that these restrictions would create inequities among employees on a regular job and would invade their privacy; in sum, we felt that the manipulations necessary to learn what we wanted to learn violated the implicit contract that the employees had with the firm when they were hired and thus should not be conducted with full-time employees on regular jobs. Our solution was to hire people to work on a part-time job that lasted from two weeks to a month and to explain to all applicants that part of our concern was to try out some different work practices and that, to evaluate them, a camera would record their work. Knowing this before accepting the job allowed the applicants to choose whether or not they wanted to accept employment under these conditions and removed our ethical concerns about the research.

Threats to Health and Safety

On jobs involving physical work with hand tools and other forms of equipment, the temperature of the workplace affects performance and the number of accidents that occur (McCormick & Ilgen, 1985). As might be expected there are optimal temperature ranges above and below which performance decreases and the number of accidents increases. Obviously, when designing work spaces or deciding whether iron workers should continue to work on building a skyscraper under particular weather conditions, it is extremely important to know the effects of temperature on work behavior. However, it is hardly acceptable to conduct research in the field when conditions are such that the researcher suspects the health and safety of workers are at stake simply to gather data about conditions that may lead to accidents. Laboratory data may be particularly useful for investigating such relationships. Under conditions in the laboratory that did not threaten the health and safety of participants in the research, behavioral decrements could be observed which, in the field, might increase the probability of an accident.

Research Not Possible in the Field

The final constraint to be discussed is the case in which the variable or variables cannot be investigated directly in the field. Recent concerns for the accuracy of performance appraisal ratings provide an example of this condition. In field settings, there rarely is any direct measure of rater accuracy. From knowledge about the nature of common rater errors, some inferences can be made about accuracy, but recent research has shown that even the presence of the commonly accepted rating error, halo, may not be related to accuracy (Bernardin & Pence, 1980). Thus, although rater accuracy remains an extremely important concern when performance appraisals are used in organizations, accuracy can rarely, if ever, be assessed directly in the field. On the other hand, laboratory conditions can be constructed that establish performance conditions against which ratings can be compared and accuracy can be assessed.

When the measurement of variables important in natural settings is possible in the laboratory but not in the field, generalization from the former setting to the latter is less direct than in most of the cases discussed so far. In particular, it is not possible to replicate laboratory research in the field because the primary variable of interest cannot be measured in the field. As a result, the evaluation of generalization must be indirect. In the case of performance accuracy, when variables affecting accuracy in the laboratory are introduced in the field, the effects of these variables on observable consequences expected to covary with accuracy can be assessed, and inferences about their effects on accuracy can be made. For example, if laboratory research demonstrates that observational frequency impacts on rating accuracy, then observing that changes in field conditions affect observation frequency in ways similar to those observed in the laboratory implies that accuracy may also have been affected by the changes even though it was not possible to measure accuracy in the field.

The "Can It Happen?" Hypothesis

There are times when the research question of interest deals with the need to demonstrate that some event, condition, or process *can* occur in contrast to demonstrating that it does occur in the settings to which generalization is of interest. Laboratory research is particularly well suited for testing hypotheses of this nature because the demands for generalization are less stringent; it is not necessary to show that the effect does occur with a specified frequency in the field but only that it is possible for such an effect to occur there (Mook, 1983). Berkowitz and Donnerstein (1982) used television violence as an example of this condition. They pointed out that laboratory research showing that children respond to contrived stimuli more aggressively after watching television with high violence as compared to low violence lacks ecological validity for generalizing to teenage crime. But, on the other hand, it is good to know whether or not films presented on television can influence aggressive behavior.

Within the domain of organizational behavior, initial tests of the social influence hypothesis with respect to job satisfaction fit the "Can it happen?" model. Salancik and Pfeffer (1977) questioned the adequacy of need discrepancy theories for explaining the source of job satisfaction. They suggested that employees may derive their views about satisfaction with their jobs in part from listening to how others on the same job feel about the job. According to the social influence hypothesis, if the others are quite satisfied with their jobs, and express their satisfaction in such a way that the target employees can observe the level of satisfaction, the target employees may decide they too are satisfied with it. This point of view became known as the social influence view of job satisfaction and was quite novel at the time it was introduced. Thus, it was of interest to discover if the satisfaction of people with a particular situation could be affected by how others say they feel about that situation. Laboratory studies showed that peoples' satisfaction could indeed be influenced by what others say about their own feelings (O'Reilly & Caldwell, 1979; Weiss & Shaw, 1979; White & Mitchell, 1979). The laboratory research was very useful even though no one would have required that the laboratory research generalize directly to the field. The research simply demonstrated that peoples' attitudes can be influenced by their beliefs about the attitudes of people around them about the same attitude object. Knowing this is possible allowed for further exploration of the possible ramifications of such effects in natural settings.

A second example is Lowen and Craig's (1968) study of leader behaviors. Field research on leader behaviors had tended to imply that causal links go from leader behavior to group performance; that is, the behavior of the leader cause certain levels of group performance. Lowen and Craig suggested that the causal direction of leader behavior and group performance may be the reverse—group performance at a particular level causes leaders to behave in certain ways. Their laboratory research demonstrated that the causal direction can be reversed. The knowledge of this fact was very useful for modifying implications made from field data about leadership behavior and group performance.

Another way to look at the purpose of laboratory research from this perspective is to see it as testing generalizations rather than making them (Mook, 1983). Mook's night vision example is a good one. A theory of vision was developed which described specific types of receptors (rods and cones) and postulated how they worked. Knowledge about the lack of speed in adjustment to dark and the insensitivity of cones to shorter wavelengths of light led to the use of laboratory research to test generalizations about the way the eye functions in vision. Once the generalizations were known about the function of the eye, it was hardly necessary to test whether the function of the eye was the same in the field as it was in the laboratory.

Application of research knowledge in the "can it happen?" case is not attempting to generalize conditions from the laboratory to the field. Rather it is to use the knowledge generated in the laboratory for issues relevant to the field. Thus, the use of red lights to avoid dark adaptation problems of people working in the environments which require good night vision is an application of theory tested in the laboratory, not an application of the laboratory study to the field.

Conclusions

The laboratory is only one of a number of settings for conducting research on organizational behavior. Although I strongly disagree with the tendency among organizational behaviorists to underestimate the potential contributions of laboratory research to understanding behavior in organizations, it cannot be denied that there are often times when the laboratory setting is inappropriate. I would further agree that the relative ease of access to laboratory research settings in comparison to field ones tends to increase both the frequency with which laboratory research is conducted and the frequency of its inappropriate use. In spite of these reservations, when the researcher considers carefully the advantages and disadvantages of all types of settings in which to conduct research on a particular problem, often the conclusion is that laboratory research can be very valuable. If one or more of the conditions described in this chapter are present, more than likely, laboratory research is appropriate for studying behavior relevant in organizational settings. In fact, under such conditions the laboratory may not only be an acceptable setting; it may be the preferred one.

Notes

1. Carlsmith, Ellsworth, and Aronson (1976) labeled this condition "mundane realism," in which the researcher tries to match the laboratory conditions to the field. They contrasted this type of realism with "experimental realism," where the focus is on creating experimental conditions which capture the theoretical nature of the construct.

References

Berkowitz, L., & Donnerstein, E. (1982) External validity is more than skin deep: Some answers to criticisms of laboratory experiments. *American Psychologist, 37,* 245–257.

Bernadin, H.J., & Pence, E. (1980) Effects of rater training: Creating new response sets and decreasing accuracy. *Journal of Applied Psychology, 65,* 60–66.

Blum, M.L., & Naylor, J.C. (1968) *Industrial psychology: Its theoretical and social foundations.* New York: Harper.

Carlsmith, J.M., Ellsworth, P.C., & Aronson, E. (1976) *Methods of research in social psychology.* Reading, Mass.: Addison-Wesley.

Cook, T.D. & Campbell, D.T. (1979) *Quasi-experimentation: Design and analysis issues for field settings.* Boston: Houghton Mifflin.

Dipboye, R.L., & Flanagan, M.F. (1979) Research settings in industrial and organizational psychology: Are findings in the field more generalizable than in the laboratory? *American Psychologist, 34,* 141–150.

Einhorn, H.J., & Hogarth, R.M. (1981) Behavioral decision theory: Processes of judgment and choice. *Annual Review of Psychology, 32,* 53–88.

Fromkin, H.L., & Streufert, S. (1976) Laboratory experimentation. In M.D. Dunnette (Ed.), *Handbook of industrial and organizational psychology* (pp. 415–466). Chicago: Rand McNally.

Lowen, A., & Craig, J.R. (1968) The influence of level of performance on managerial style: An experimental object-lesson in the ambiguity of correlational data. *Organizational Behavior and Human Performance, 3,* 440–458.

McCormick, E.J., & Ilgen, D.R. (1985) *Industrial and organizational psychology* (8th ed.). Englewood Cliffs, N.J.: Prentice-Hall.

McGrath, J.E., Martin, J., & Kulka, R.A. (1982) *Judgment calls in research.* Beverly Hills: Sage.

Mook, D.G. (1983) In defense of external invalidity. *American Psychologist, 38,* 379–387.

Nash, A.N., Muczyk, J.P., & Vettori, F.L. (1971) The relative practical effectiveness of programmed instruction. *Personnel Psychology, 24,* 397–410.

O'Reilly, C.A., III, & Caldwell, D.F. (1979) Informational influence as a determinant of perceived task characteristics and job satisfaction. *Journal of Applied Psychology, 64,* 157–165.

Runkel, P.J., & McGrath, J.E. (1972) *Research on human behavior: A systematic guide to method.* New York: Holt, Rinehart, & Winston.

Salancik, G.R., & Pfeffer, J. (1977) An examination of need satisfaction models of job satisfaction. *Administrative Science Quarterly, 22,* 427–456.

Thorpe, J.A., Varney, N.C., MacFadden, R.W., LeMaster, W.D., & Short, L.H. (1978) Training effectiveness of three types of visual systems for KC-135 flight simulators (AFHRL Technical Report 78-16). Williams Air Force Base, Arizona.

Weiss, H.M., & Shaw, J.B. (1979) Social influences on judgments about tasks. *Organizational Behavior and Human Performance, 24,* 126–140.

White, S.E., & Mitchell, T.R. (1979) Job enrichment versus social cues: A comparison and competitive test. *Journal of Applied Psychology, 64,* 1–9.

14

Labs, Fields, and Straw Issues

John P. Campbell

The Basic Issue

The principal question addressed by the chapters in this book is whether experimental results obtained in the laboratory generalize to the field.

Right off there is a problem with correctly designating a study as laboratory or field. What's the difference? Which studies go in one column and which go in the other? Unfortunately, when most people speak of lab studies they usually invoke a stereotype of a university location with students as subjects. However, virtually no one would admit publicly to those being the defining characteristics of laboratory studies. At another extreme perhaps, a laboratory study could be defined to occur whenever the act of studying an ongoing organizational phenomenon runs a significant risk of changing it. There is a lot of room between these two extremes and I do not believe that there is any way of drawing a line between them that is not free of major ambiguity.

In chapter 10 Tom Mawhinney makes the most direct attempt to explicate the difference when he asserts that field studies involve having people do what they would do even if there were no study taking place, and that field studies use dependent variables that measure something an organization would value and probably pay for. This is a nice try but it still leaves lots of room for argument. For example, is it lab or field when a temporary organization is set up and people are hired to spend two weeks performing work that a real employer might indeed pay for? Is it lab or field when real managers are called out of their office to respond to a job satisfaction questionnaire handed to them by a graduate student from the university and the scores are related to independent ratings of the manager's job scope? Is it lab or field when a group of public administrators travels to the university to have their weekly policy meeting so that the group interaction can be more easily observed and recorded? Is it lab or field when individual differences in psychomotor ability are used to predict pilot performance in a full flight simulator?

A much clearer distinction is the one traditionally drawn between research that uses the experimental method and research that is correlational or differential in nature (Cronbach, 1975). Can the differential versus experimental distinction be completely crossed with lab versus field in a meaningful fourfold table or are they confounded? The differential versus experimental issue is not really discussed in this volume but it seems just as important to inquire whether correlational research finds the same answers as experimental research as it does to ask whether lab generalizes to field. These two factors are confounded in some of the research domains that are included in this volume. For example, when considering the job scope by job satisfaction relation, the lab studies tend to produce job scope differences experimentally while the field studies measure it differentially. Consequently, if both lab and field produce the same effect sizes but from different perspectives, do the results mean the same thing?

Another bit of complexity concerns the meaning given to the term *generalize*. That is, what does "to generalize results from the lab to the field" mean? Consider the following sentence completions for "Generalizing from lab to field means that . . .":

1. Empirical results obtained in the field are *identical* to those obtained in the laboratory.

2. The *direction* of empirical relationships found in the field are the same as those found in the laboratory.

3. The *conclusions* drawn about a specific question are the same for field studies as they are for laboratory studies.

4. The *existence* of a particular phenomenon can be demonstrated in the laboratory as well as in the field.

5. Data from the laboratory can be used to justify or support the *application* of a particular practice or program in an operational setting.

Which of these people mean when they speak about the lab versus field issue is not always easy to discern. Alternative number one is probably what many people have in mind. Alternative two seems to reflect what the editor of this book views as crucial.

Alternative three seems more central. That is, the fundamental consideration is whether the same substantive conclusion would result from investigating a particular question in the laboratory as from investigating it in the field. For example, can we conclude from both laboratory and field studies that assessing someone's expectancy for achieving a particular performance level and multiplying this value times the valence of performance at that level accounts for enough variance in choice behavior to warrant a conclusion that "cognitive/expectancy models of motivation are useful?"

For the users of organizational research, perhaps alternative five is even more central, as when a management wonders whether training supervisors in how to set more specific goals will significantly enhance performance among their subordinates.

Given considerations such as the above, it is the thesis of this chapter that the lab versus field controversy is a false issue and one that the scientists and professionals should have put aside long ago. It detracts from the real issues of whether the substantive research questions themselves are useful and whether the specific methods, not a generic category of methods, used to answer them can be expected to provide valid answers. The authors of the previous chapters seem to share this view at the same time that they recognize that some overkill is necessary if we are ever going to put the lab versus field controversy to rest, at least within our own ranks. That is, the justification for this book speaks more to the politics than to substantive issues, which is certainly justification enough.

In general, the chapters in this book respond to the call of the editor and successfully neutralize (in the CIA sense) the lab versus field issue, hopefully once and for all, with a useful combination of rational argument, review of previous research literature, and meta-analysis. They are concisely written, cover a good mix of topics, and are well reasoned. However, even decisive victories are never total. For example, not all of the substantive questions examined by the chapter authors provide enough previous literature to permit an empirical judgment about lab versus field. The extremes are represented by the goal setting literature reported by Latham and Lee and the schedule stretching effects examined by Mawhinney. The former presents a rather nice balance between lab and field and clear conclusions can be drawn. For the latter, there is virtually no research to consider.

The lack of either field or lab research on a particular question leads to something of a dilemma. If the goal is a box score, but one of the boxes contains very few observations, then the choice is either not to make the comparison, or to aggregate studies across different kinds of variables, or to aggregate across somewhat different substantive questions, so as to build up the frequency of studies in each column. The latter option was used in several of the chapters. The danger in this strategy is that comparison between the aggregated field studies and aggregated lab studies is difficult to interpret and may not correspond to the substantive questions that originally were of interest. The same issue occurs in any meta-analysis when the investigator must decide how to define the population of previous research.

Interestingly, at least one chapter (chapter 3 by Bernardin and Villanova) ignores lab versus field as a general question and chooses to focus on other more specific issues that influence the validity of specific research questions pertaining to performance appraisal. That is, the purpose for which performance ratings are to be used, the reinforcement contingencies operating on the rater, the degree to which the rater believes the ratee controls his or her own fate, and the degree of knowledge the rater has about the job are far more important issues than lab versus field. The authors are of the opinion that it would be very difficult to validly manipulate some of these parameters in a lab setting, but then promptly go on to suggest a specific case in which it should be feasible.

Again, the basic theme here is that the lab versus field distinction is relatively meaningless. The usefulness of the research questions and the validity of the specific procedures used to study it are paramount.

Another interesting feature of Bernardin and Villanova's chapter is their survey of users and their attempt to specify a modal performance appraisal situation. In so doing, they were focusing very much on the problem of application and the importance of studying questions that have high relevance for operational problems. A similar approach would be beneficial for any number of other areas. At the same time it is also legitimate to worry about more basic issues such as the accuracy of human judgment as an important component of appraisal, *when all other extraneous influences are controlled* (such as the purpose of the rating). Both applied questions and more basic questions can be studied stupidly or validly in the lab or in the field. It is the former parameter that is of interest, not the latter.

Having said all this, it is somewhat disheartening to note that a few of the authors in this book still use language that seems to imply a belief in the basic inferiority of laboratory studies. If, after all the conceptual arguments and all the empirical comparisons, such beliefs persist within our own ranks, it is no wonder that the issue presents such problems with research sponsors and research consumers.

Meta Issues

It is not an objective of the current chapter to comment on the specifics of each of the preceeding chapters. Consequently, there will be no critique of the appropriateness of the substantive issues that were included or not included, nor will there be a discussion of whether each individual investigator interpreted his or her data correctly. Instead, I would like to discuss three general issues that frequently arise when a body of previous literature is used to address a general issue or controversy in our field. After that I will come back to the specifics of the lab versus field argument for a final word.

Meta-Analysis

Meta-analysis (for example, Hunter, Schmidt, & Jackson, 1982) is new and popular. It provides a systematic way to examine the variability in study to study results on a particular question and to consider whether such variance represents statistical artifacts or real differences in outcomes. Meta-analysis is a genuine breakthrough in data aggregation techniques. It is now possible to interpret cumulative data in a much more useful way than before. Some people feel so strongly about the benefits of meta-analysis that doing literature reviews the old fashioned way is regarded as being of little scientific value and as practiced only by the methodologically weak and infirm.

Since meta-analysis is new, it somewhat has the status of a fad. That is, because it was initially applied by knowledgeable people to appropriate data sets with very informative results, the tendency is to apply it everywhere in hopes that it might uncover something. Many valuable innovations have run afoul of a research/application cycle which begins with the initial innovative work and which is followed by a rush to application by a large number of people, some knowledgeable and some not. Job redesign might be a good case in point (Hackman, 1975). We can only hope that meta-analysis avoids the typical cycle of the fad (Campbell, 1971) and continues to be a highly useful analytic tool. In service to that goal the following points are made.

Meta-analysis is designed to correct for statistical artifacts, not substantive flaws. If a particular experimental result is attenuated by unreliability or restriction of range, or small sample sizes produce considerable variation in results across studies, these are statistical difficulties that are amenable to correction. However, meta-analysis cannot correct for treatments that have no construct validity or studies that ask the wrong questions. For example, one could do ninety-one studies of whether ability or motivation accounts for more variance in performance and compute an average effect size; but the mean effect size would have very little meaning. Neither can meta-analysis make up for dependent variables that purport to measure one thing but in fact measure another, as when self-rated effort is used as a dependent measure in research on motivation issues. A questionnaire measure of self-rated effort will show higher correlations with a questionnaire measure of motivational antecedents than an independent measure of effort. However, there is no empirical support for the construct validity of self-ratings as a measure of effort. Including such a measure in a meta-analysis is very misleading. To slightly modify an old analogy, "substantive garbage in—substantive garbage out, no matter what the reliability or sample size." In our field, meta-analysis has been used most frequently in the contexts of personnel selection and the evaluation of personnel programs such as training. By nature, these are much more homogeneous populations of individual studies than those that might be accumulated within some general category of basic research in organizational behavior. The dependent variable is virtually always a measure of individual performance, and the question being asked is whether a particular kind of test or a particular kind of program accounts for significant variance in performance. Again, lumping together studies that are too disparate in nature may be counterproductive. For any set of previous studies it is always possible to compute a mean effect size and to account for some of the study to study variation by correcting for sampling error. However, we must become much more careful about interpreting such results.

A number of the authors seem to acknowledge these issues when they opt *not* to do a meta-analysis even while other authors in this book are arguing that a literature review without a meta-analysis is no literature review at all. The former are being prudent, not naive.

Finally, it is noteworthy that one of the principal benefits of meta-analysis is completely ignored in these chapters, and in this case it is a crucial consideration. That is, the empirical outcomes of lab versus field comparisons are very much a function of the relative restriction of range of the independent and dependent variables in the two settings. Obviously, if a wide range in levels of a variable are used in one setting but the range is restricted in the other setting, the potential is high for an artificial difference in results between the two settings. Campbell, Daft, and Hulin (1982) have commented that virtually all such comparative questions (for example, Is ability or motivation more important?) in industrial psychology and organizational behavior are highly susceptible to this same kind of artifact.

Hard Core and Soft Core

Besides the lab versus field question there is another straw issue that appears in several chapters. It is the distinction between hard and soft criteria or dependent variables. Within the conventional wisdom the intended meaning is clear: hard is good, soft is bad. One can easily imagine a volume of collected papers devoted to the issue of whether hard criteria generalize to soft criteria. The usual difficulties in interpretation would also arise. The term *hard* seems to refer to dependent variables that consist of countable outcomes. They are objective in the sense that they can be counted by an independent party. Sales volume, pieces produced, promotion rate, percent of capacity actually used, and number of articles published are all examples. *Soft* measures seem to refer to those which are based on human judgment or scaling considerations. That is, if an individual's behavior is scaled by expert judgment along some continuum of performance, it is a soft measure.

I wish to argue that just as with lab versus field, the relative worth of hard or soft criteria is a function of the construct validity of each particular measure. It takes only a very little experience in the real world to discover that so-called hard measures can be very misleading. They can be influenced by many more things than a particular individual's performance. Also, a lot of subjective judgment is frequently employed before an objective record appears. For example, quality control judgments about which units can be counted as finished production can vary tremendously depending on the pressure for production that exists at a particular time. Perhaps it is not too far from a truism to say that objective (hard) measures are really only subjective (soft) measures at least one step removed.

The moral here is that just as lab versus field is much too simplistic and misleading a comparison to make, so is the hard versus soft dichotomy. Run a sword through it and boil it in oil.

On Boundary Conditions

One frequent reaction to the oversimplifications implied by the lab versus field distinction, as well as other controversies of the same form, is to speak of moderator variables, boundary conditions, or other parameters that govern when one or the other setting is more appropriate. However, such a position runs up against at least two major difficulties.

First, as has already been mentioned, there is not a clear dichotomy between lab and field. If one sets up a temporary organization, hires people, imposes experimental treatments that appear to be part of the business operation, and assesses results unobtrusively, is it the lab or the field? If one persuades the management of an organization to experiment with different reinforcement schedules by manipulating the existing pay system and setting up systematic data recording procedures, is it laboratory or field research? So-called real world behavior may be more serverely constrained or altered in the latter case than in the former. How then can we set up boundary conditions for when to use lab versus field when the designation for which is which is so unclear?

Second, it seems extremely difficult to set up rules or boundary conditions for when to use the lab or the field in the absence of the specific question of substantive interest. It seems far more appropriate that, given a specific research question, we then ask what specific research method(s) incorporate the most construct validity for the independent and dependent variables. Viewed in this way, a good laboratory study may certainly produce more useful data than a bad field study. Perhaps much of the criticism directed at laboratory research is actually directed at bad research. That is, if a lab study uses a treatment that has little construct validity for the question being asked, it is not the laboratory method that is at fault, it is the skill of the experimenter. For example, one could have subjects judge the interpersonal skills of interviewers as portrayed in a written description or on video tape. If an objective is to determine if subjects can perceive individual differences in interviewer interpersonal skills, then the video tape should be more valid. Even here, however, there would still be a question of how validly the video tape portrayed individual differences in interpersonal skills.

In sum, the fundamental argument is that the substantive question must come before the method, and it is the validity of a specific method for answering a specific question that is the crucial issue. Appealing to boundary conditions does not seem to help all that much.

Now, What About Lab versus Field?

The above remarks, as well as much of the material in the other chapters, have repeatedly drawn the conclusion that the lab versus field distinction is not a very useful one. Research studies do not fit cleanly into these two categories and the distinction is often confounded with a number of other parameters. Confounds that have been discussed are the quality of the research, the experimental versus differential nature of the studies, general/theoretical versus specific/applied questions, students versus real people as subjects, and the degree to which the study obtrusively controls for extraneous variables. Each of these parameters could be correlated negatively or positively with the lab versus field distinction, but in the minds of the critics, laboratory research is of low quality, experimental in nature, theoretical and esoteric, and rigidly controlled to the point of sterility. Worst of all, it uses students as subjects.

On an intellectual/scientific/professional level, the negative stereotype of the laboratory study has been exterminated with both rational and empirical arguments. The previous statements by Weick (1965), Fromkin and Streufert (1976), Berkowitz and Donnerstein (1982), and Mook (1983) are an adequate defense of the laboratory method. However, reasonable standards seem not to apply with this issue.

If the intent of this book is to find an empirical sword to slay the dragon of negativism about laboratory research, then it certainly accomplishes its goal. In spite of the gaps in the research record mentioned earlier, the message is clear: the data do not support the belief that lab studies produce different results than field studies. Perhaps college students really are people. After all, probably the vast majority of them work, or have worked, at a job. Why their disguise fools many observers into thinking otherwise is not clear.

On rational grounds, it seems obvious that many of the characteristics that make up the negative stereotype of laboratory research can just as easily be found in field research. A lot of field research uses bad instrumentation (for example, measuring independent, dependent, and moderator variables with one unvalidated questionnaire), investigates esoteric theoretical questions, and removes individuals from their normal work routine. Although objective or "hard" in nature, the dependent variables are frequently so confounded with other factors that interpretation is difficult.

To continue being rational for a moment, if laboratory research is defined to mean research done at a university location with students as subjects and brief tasks as dependent variables, then we must ask what specific influences the experience of the subjects, the specific characteristics of the setting, and the content of stimulus materials could be expected to have on the phenomena under study. That is, for what substantive reasons would we expect these parameters to significantly affect the results of the research? Invoking the notions that students are not really people or that university settings are not the real world is no argument at all. It might even be called sophomoric.

To pursue the above point further, two crucial substantive questions might be whether the nature of the task or the specific work experiences of the subjects influence the phenomena being studied in such a way that they confound the results of the study. For example, when asked to choose which group or individual problem solving strategies, from among the Vroom and Yetton (1973) array of strategies, they would apply to a standard set of case problems, experienced managers may indeed choose different problem solving strategies than college sophomores. Also, both groups may choose different problem solving strategies when responding to written case problems than when trying to implement problem solving strategies behaviorally. While each of these questions is interesting in its own right, neither has anything directly to do with the question of whether the normative prescriptions made by the Vroom and Yetton model are the most effective strategies for solving problems. That question could be investigated profitably in several different varieties of lab and field settings. Relevant to this example is the long history of research on individual versus group problem solving in many different laboratory and field settings (Bouchard & Hare, 1970; Campbell, 1968; Dunnette, Campbell, & Jaastad, 1963; Taylor, Berry, & Block, 1958; Hill, 1982). The evidence is clear. Results are quite similar and the same conclusions can be drawn across the different settings. When students sit down as a group to generate a solution to a substantive problem of interest to them, the same kind of intra group phenomena and the same shortfall in group problem solving occur as when "real" groups in real organizations do it.

In general, trying to decide whether lab or field is best or even trying to describe the limiting conditions under which each is best seems to be asking the wrong question first. It puts the initial focus on the method rather than the substantive question of interest. Campbell et al. (1982) have complained about this before, in the context of research in industrial-organizational psychology, and their rantings need not be repeated here. However, the moral of the story as it translates into the lab versus field issue is the following. Articulating the question you want to study must be the first step. Once that is done, the research methods should be chosen so as to maximize the construct validity of the independent and dependent variables (or their relevant counterparts in a correlational study). That is, do the methods used to study the phenomenon give a valid portrayal of it? Construct validity (Cronbach & Meehl, 1955) is inferred from a variety of sources, and designating whether it is high or low is a judgment call (McGrath, Martin, & Kulka, 1982). Be that as it may, the sentence to be completed by the investigator is, "I believe that my research methods have construct validity for answering my research questions because . . . " Critics must then respond in kind. A statement to the effect that the research method is valid because it takes place in a real organization or that a method is invalid because it is used in a lab study is no argument at all and is unbecoming a scientist/scholar. Let us be done once and for all with lab versus field arguments.

Research Producers and Research Users

Having said all this, we must also remember that besides research producers there are research users. Sometimes they are the same people, as when we produce basic research results that are used by our fellow scientists to modify, enhance, or conform their own work. However, if application is a goal, then the user is often not a behavioral scientist or human resource specialist and the conventional wisdom among lay people is also most likely biased against laboratory research. At this point we must come back to the issue of what it means to ask whether lab results generalize to the field. For example, it is one thing to ask whether the effects of specific hard goals are the same in the lab as in the field. It is another thing to ask how that general finding might be used to promote long-term sustained enhancement of performance in a particular organization. The latter question may indeed require additional R&D work that takes into account the major contingencies that operate in an organization. That is, establishing that results are similar in lab versus field does not really address questions of application (Hakel, Sorcher, Beer, & Moses, 1982). These issues should probably be the subject of another volume. The current volume has really not addressed the questions of how to apply established research findings or how to persuade users that data produced in the laboratory can legitimately be used to support application.

Let me offer an inflammatory example. I will assert that the effects of reinforcement schedules on certain aspects of behavior seem so well established that if the effects are not found in the field, it calls into question the nature of the field study, not the validity of the laboratory findings. In fact, much could be learned by systematically investigating the reasons why the schedule effects were not found. Was the intended reinforcer not a reinforcer? Did the intended intermittent schedule really turn out to be a continuous schedule? Perhaps instead of asking whether lab generalizes to field, we should be asking what else we can learn by trying to apply well established findings in a variety of settings.

A Final Word

This chapter has tried to make the case that the lab versus field distinction is largely a straw issue, and a simplistic one at that. There are more important things to worry about. Hopefully the publication of this book will allow us to do that.

However, there is one feature of the controversy that is of some benefit to the field. That is, it seems undeniable that a lot of interesting research has in fact been stimulated in the name of answering the critics of laboratory research. For example, would the editor of this book and his colleagues have done so much field research on goal setting if they had not been goaded into it by carping critics? Also, one of the most famous studies in all of organizational behavioral science would never have been done if it had not been for the lab versus field argument. This was, of course, the Coch and French (1948) study of the effects of participation on productivity and resistance to change conducted at Harwood. According to one of the principal investigators (French, 1981), the study was designed in direct response to the question of whether or not the Lewin, Lippitt, and White (1939) results on the effects of democratic leadership in children's play groups would replicate in a real organization.

Perhaps we could burn this straw issue but still find some way to stimulate people to use multiple methods and to replicate research findings.

References

Berkowitz, L., & Donnerstein, E. (1982) External validity is more than skin deep. *American Psychologist, 37*, 245–257.

Bouchard, T.J., & Hare, M. (1970) Size, performance, and potential in brainstorming groups. *Journal of Applied Psychology, 54*, 51–55.

Campbell, J.P. (1968) Individual versus group problem solving in an industrial sample. *Journal of Applied Psychology, 52*, 205–210.

Campbell, J.P. (1971) Personnel training and development. In P.H. Mussen & M.R. Rosenzweig (Eds.), *Annual Review of Psychology*. 565–602.

Campbell, J.P., Daft, R.L., & Hulin, C.L. (1982) *What to study: Generating and developing research questions*. Beverly Hills: Sage.

Coch, L., & French, J.R.P. (1948) Overcoming resistance to change. *Human Relations, 1*, 512–532.

Cronbach, L.J. (1975) Beyond the two disciplines of scientific psychology. *American Psychologist, 30*, 116–127.

Cronbach, L.J., & Meehl, P.E. (1955) Construct validity in psychological tests. *Psychological Bulletin, 52*, 281–302.

Dunnette, M.D., Campbell, J., & Jaastad, K. (1963). The effect of group participation on brainstorming effectiveness for two industrial samples. *Journal of Applied Psychology, 47*, 30–37.

French, J.R.P. (1981) Personal communication.

Fromkin, H.L., & Streufert, S. (1976) Laboratory experimentation. In M. Dunnette (Ed.), *Handbook of industrial and organizational psychology*. Chicago: Rand McNally, 415–466.

Hackman, J.R. (1975) On the coming demise of job enrichment. In E. Cass & F. Zimmer (Eds.), *Man and work in society*. New York: Van Nostrand, Reinhold, 97–115.

Hakel, M.D., Sorcher, M., Beer, M., & Moses, J.L. (1982) *Making it happen: Designing research with implementation in mind*. Beverly Hills: Sage.

Hill, G.U. (1982) Group vs. individual performance: Are $N + 1$ heads better than one? *Psychological Bulletin, 11*, 517–539.

Hunter, J.E., Schmidt, F.L., & Jackson, G.B. (1982) *Meta analysis: Cumulating research findings across studies*. Beverly Hills: Sage.

Lewin, K., Lippitt, R., & White, R.K. (1939) Patterns of aggressive behavior in experimentally created social climates. *Journal of Social Psychology, 10*, 271–301.

McGrath, J.E., Martin, J., & Kulka, R.A. (1982) *Judgment calls in research*. Beverly Hills: Sage.

Mook, D.G. (1983) In defense of external invalidity. *American Psychologist, 38*, 379–387.

Taylor, D.W., Berry, P.C., & Block, C.H. (1958) Does group participation when using brainstorming facilitate or inhibit creative thinking? *Administrative Science Quarterly, 3*, 23–47.

Vroom, V.H., & Yetton, P.W. (1973) *Leadership and decision making*. Pittsburgh: University of Pittsburgh Press.

Weick, K.E. (1965) Laboratory experiments with organizations. In J. March (Ed.), *Handbook of organizations*. Chicago: Rand McNally, 194–260.

Epilogue

Summary Ratings of Laboratory and Field Results by Chapter

Chapter	Topic	Direction[a] of Effect	Size of[b] Effect
2	Staffing		
	Expectancy theory and job choice	5	NA
	All other	NA	NA
3	Performance appraisal (training)	5	NA
4	Attribution theory	NA	4
5	Training (transfer)	NA	NA
6	Goal setting	5	NA
7	Objective feedback	4	2
8	Participation		
	Job performance	4	NA
	Job satisfaction	4	NA
9	Financial incentives	4	5
10	Reinforcement schedules	NA	NA
11	Job scope-job satisfaction	5[c]	5
	Job scope-job performance	NA	NA
12	Job satisfaction-job performance	5	5(4)[d]

[a]Scale: 5 = virtually identical; 4 = highly similar; 3 = moderately similar; 2 = somewhat dissimilar; 1 ≐ totally dissimilar; NA ≐ not applicable, was not or could not be calculated.

[b]Scale: 5 = virtually no difference; 4 = small difference; 3 = moderate difference; 2 = fairly large difference; 1 = very large difference; NA = same as above.

[c]Job scope-job satisfaction relationship significant at $p < .10$ or better in 26 of 27 field studies and 5 of 5 lab studies. The Ns were too small to make similar calculations for other relationships.

[d]The rating of 5 is based on the mean rs between overall satisfaction and performance (.16 vs. .18 for lab and field, respectively). Note that the Schmidt-Hunter methodology was not used here, however, the rating of 4 is based on the fact that for the work and pay satisfaction the mean rs are slightly different. In addition, there are differences when contingencies are taken into account. However, as the authors state, this may be due to contingencies not being measured in field settings.

Index

About the Contributors

Allan G. Bateson received an M.A. in industrial-organizational psychology from the University of Akron, where he is currently a doctoral candidate. His areas of interest include cognitive processes for computer programming, attribution theory, and performance appraisal.

H. John Bernardin is the director of research for the College of Business and Public Administration at Florida Atlantic University. He is the author of a book and over fifty empirical studies on the subject of performance appraisal.

John P. Campbell received his Ph.D. from the University of Minnesota and an M.S. in psychology from Iowa State University. He was an assistant professor of psychology at the University of California at Berkeley and is now professor of psychology and industrial relations and director of the industrial-organizational psychology graduate program at the University of Minnesota. He is also principal scientist for the multiyear Selection and Classification Project sponsored by the Army Research Institute for the Behavioral Sciences. He has served as president of the Division of Industrial and Organizational Psychology of the American Psychological Association and as editor of the *Journal of Applied Psychology*. His most recent book is *What to Study: Generating and Developing Research Questions*, with Richard Daft and Charles Hulin. His current research interests are performance assessment, personnel classification, and decision making.

Christy L. De Vader received an M.A. in industrial-organizational psychology from the University of Akron, where she is currently a doctoral candidate. Her research focuses on gender and leadership perceptions, and attribution theory.

Irwin L. Goldstein is professor and chair of the Department of Psychology at the University of Maryland. His theoretical and empirical work has focused on topics related to training, including needs assessment and evaluation. His revised text on training will be published by Brooks/Cole in 1986.

Daniel R. Ilgen is the John A. Hannah Professor of Organizational Behavior at Michigan State University. He received his Ph.D. in organizational psychology from the University of Illinois at Urbana-Champaign. He has served on the faculties at the University of Illinois, Purdue University, the University of Washington, and the U.S. Military Academy. He is coauthor of two books, *Industrial and Organizational Psychology* (1985), with E.J. McCormick, and *A Theory of Behavior in Organizations* (1980), with J.C. Naylor and R.D. Pritchard. Currently he is associate editor of the *Journal of Organizational Behavior and Human Decision Processes*.

G. Douglas Jenkins, Jr. is an associate professor of management at the University of Arkansas. He has been studying the motivational consequences of pay for ten years. He is currently involved in a nationwide study of a pay-for-knowledge (skill-based) compensation system.

Richard E. Kopelman is professor of management at Baruch College, and co-director of the Baruch/Cornell Masters program in industrial and labor relations. His research, writing, and consulting have focused on productivity management, reward systems, and professional career development.

Gary Latham is an associate professor in the Business School and Department of Psychology at the University of Washington in Seattle. He serves on the editorial boards of the *Journal of Applied Psychology, Academy of Management Journal*, and *Journal of Organization Behavior Management*. He is the author or coauthor of more than one hundred scientific articles and technical reports. He was formerly manager of human resource research at Weyerhaeuser Company and staff psychologist of the American Pulpwood Association.

Carrie R. Leana is assistant professor of management at the University of Florida. Her current research includes studies of delegation, participative decision processes, and the bases of authority and influence in organizations.

Thomas W. Lee is an assistant professor of management and organization at the University of Washington. His recent research interests include employee attachment to the organization, job boredom, goal setting, and turnover rates.

Robert G. Lord is professor of psychology and chairman of the industrial-organizational psychology program at the University of Akron. He received his Ph.D. in organizational psychology from Carnegie-Mellon University. He has authored or coauthored numerous articles in scholarly journals. His research focuses on understanding leadership perceptions, social perceptions, and behavioral measures in terms of rater information processing.

Thomas C. Mawhinney received his Ph.D. from The Ohio State University and is associate professor of management in the College of Business Administration, Butler University, in Indianapolis. He is editor of the *Journal of Organizational Behavior Management*.

Gary R. Musicante is an instructor at the University of Maryland, where he is completing a doctoral dissertation in the area of comparable worth. His recent Master's thesis focused on contextual factors in teaching appraisal.

Judy D. Olian is assistant professor of human resources management and industrial relations at the College of Business and Management, University of Maryland. She does research on several human resource issues, including the employment matching process.

Philip M. Podsakoff is assistant professor of personnel and organizational behavior in the Indiana University Graduate School of Business. He received his doctoral degree from Indiana University and returned there after two years of teaching at The Ohio State University. He is the author of articles appearing in *Psychological Bulletin, Organizational Behavior and Human Performance, Academy of Management Journal*, and several other journals. His current research interests lie in the areas of employee performance and satisfaction, social power and influence processes, leadership effectiveness, and employee selection and evaluation procedures.

David M. Schweiger is assistant professor of management systems and strategy in the College of Business Administration, University of Houston, University Park. His research interests include participation in decision making, strategic decision making, and the effects of mergers and acquisitions on employees.

Eugene F. Stone is an associate professor of psychology at Virginia Polytechnic Institute and State University, where he teaches courses in industrial-organizational psychology, research design, and psychological measurement. His current research interests include job design, performance appraisal, and responses to performance-related feedback.

Peter Villanova is a Ph.D. candidate in the applied psychology program at Virginia Polytechnic Institute and State University. His interest areas include criterion development and evaluation, performance appraisal, and applied attribution theory.

Larry J. Williams is a doctoral candidate in organizational behavior at the Indiana University Graduate School of Business. His current research interests include turnover, leadership, and organizational structure. He received his B.S. and M.S. in psychology from the Purdue University School of Science at Indianapolis.

About the Editor

Edwin A. Locke is professor of business and management and of psychology at the University of Maryland. He is on the editorial boards of the *Journal of Applied Psychology* and *Organizational Behavior and Human Decision Processes*. The recipient of an Outstanding Teacher-Scholar Award at the University of Maryland, he has published over one hundred books and articles. He is the coauthor, with Gary Latham, of *Goal Setting: A Motivational Technique that Works*, published by Prentice-Hall in 1984.